D0521065

Mobile HTML5

Estelle Weyl

Beijing · Cambridge · Farnham · Köln · Sebastopol · Tokyo

Mobile HTML5

by Estelle Weyl

Printed in the United States of America.

Published by O'Reilly Media, Inc., 1005 Gravenstein Highway North, Sebastopol, CA 95472.

O'Reilly books may be purchased for educational, business, or sales promotional use. Online editions are also available for most titles (*http://my.safaribooksonline.com*). For more information, contact our corporate/institutional sales department: 800-998-9938 or *corporate@oreilly.com*.

Editors: Simon St. Laurent and Meghan Blanchette
Production Editor: Kristen Brown
Copyeditor: Kiel Van Horn
Proofreaders: Troy Mott and Jasmine Kwityn

Indexer: Lucie Haskins
Cover Designer: Randy Comer
Interior Designer: David Futato
Illustrator: Rebecca Demarest

November 2013:   First Edition

Revision History for the First Edition:

2013-11-12:   First release

See *http://oreilly.com/catalog/errata.csp?isbn=9781449311414* for release details.

ISBN: 978-1-449-31141-4

[LSI]

Table of Contents

Introduction

We're going to learn how to develop mobile web applications. Note the word "web." This book focuses on web application development for mobile devices like Android, iPod, iPhone, BlackBerry, and tablets. This book is not about native application development requiring the iOS or Android SDK. Nothing we will learn is operating system specific.

Mobile web applications are websites or web applications that leverage the markup of desktop web applications with the functionality of touch-enabled devices. Web applications, whether accessed via a phone, tablet, or laptop, are built with HTML, CSS, and JavaScript, optionally with image, video, and audio assets and server-side technologies.

By upgrading to using newer HTML5, CSS3, and JavaScript features, we can create web applications with the look and feel of native applications. Because mobile web apps are web based, they are compatible with desktops, smartphones, tablets, and any other device that has a modern browser. Because our web applications are web based, we can distribute them directly to our users, with no need to be listed in the Apple App Store or Google Play, with their sometimes complex, expensive, and lengthy approval processes.

This book will teach you what you need to know to create applications that work in a browser using CSS3, HTML5,[1] and JavaScript. This is about technologies you already know: technologies that are portable to most devices. Everything discussed is operating system agnostic.

In other words, what we learn will not only work on the iPhone, the iPad, and Android devices, but also on other mobile platforms, including Firefox OS and Windows Phone, and on modern desktop browsers and other devices that have a modern browser (such as gaming consoles like the Wii). Yes, this book is focusing on developing for mobile, but what you learn here is usable on a plethora of devices, big and small, as long as that device has a browser that adheres to modern web standards.

---

1. We will be using the term "HTML5" to mean what is also called "HTML: The Living Standard."

The abilities of applications on native platforms stayed rather consistent for over 10 years, but the past several years have seen the web platform increase its ability to handle web applications, with almost the same fidelity as native applications.

The iPhone added canvas, application cache, database, and SVG. Safari 4.0 included those features, adding video, audio, and web workers. Later in 2009, we saw the addition of geolocation and canvas—not just to the iPhone, but to Chrome, Opera, Firefox, Internet Explorer, and Android.

With web browsers, we've been able to take advantage of HTML, CSS, the DOM, SVG, and XHR for years. In this book, we expand our horizons to include HTML5 and CSS3: the skills needed to make web applications that are comparable to native applications, features that are already supported in modern mobile and desktop browsers.

Native Applications Versus Web Applications

Yes, you can sell native iPhone applications in the App Store, which sounds cool. You can sell native Android applications via Google Play, Amazon, or a plethora of other online venues. But with web-based applications, you can bypass the app stores with their approval[2] processes,[3] annual fees, and sales fees, and market directly to your consumer base via your website and through other marketing channels. Yes, you miss the very slim opportunity of having your application noticed among the hundreds of thousands of applications available through the app store, but the benefits of web application versus native application development greatly outweigh the costs.

With web applications, it is easier to build and iterate. You can make changes to your live web application whenever you want—multiple times a day if need be.

With a native iPhone app for example, you have the 3-week+ approval process. Once your application is approved and pushed to production, you have to wait for users to sync and update their application. With web applications built using CSS3 and HTML5, your changes are live basically immediately, but can also be accessible when the user is offline—just like native applications.

If you accidentally forget to include your boss or misspell your mother's name in the credits of your native application, those oopsies are going to haunt you not only until you are able to push the correction through the app store, but they'll stick around until the user syncs your app with an updated iTunes download. That could be a long time.

---

2. Apple actually censors applications. No risqué pictures. No adult violence. It appears that cute violence can get approval, so if you want to include violence, target children?

3. You have to pay Apple an annual "developer fee" to submit your native iPhone applications to the App Store, whether or not your application is successful or even approved.

I am skilled at becoming "obsolete." I never updated from the original versions of Bump, Twitterific, and Gowalla on my original iPhone. I assume I am not the only one who has "antique" iPhone applications. Don't assume that your native application users update their applications.

By using HTML5 to develop your web applications, your application can be available offline, just like a native application. Although the native application can take weeks to update, the web application can be forced to update itself the next time your application is used when connected to the Internet. We'll cover this when we discuss offline applications in Chapter 6.

HTML5 web application development takes advantage of the HTML and CSS skills you already know. We're building upon your existing skills rather than asking you to learn completely new ones. Not a different technology, not a different platform. Not a new language that only works on one platform!

Using browser markup of HTML5 and CSS3 gives you the potential to be cross-platform over time. Native iPhone applications work on the iPod touch and on ithe Phone, and most likely on the iPad, but not on Windows, BlackBerry, or Android (and they never will). Native Android applications work only on Android devices, not on iOS-based products. Native GoogleTV applications will never work on iOS either. Et cetera. Unlike native applications, your HTML5/CSS3 web applications can be made to work on all WebKit, IE10, Blink, Opera Mobile (not mini), and Firefox mobile browsers. And your web applications will work on other devices that have modern browsers that by default support features of HTML5 and CSS3.

Web applications built with HTML5 and CSS3, for the most part, already work in modern browsers. While not supported in Internet Explorer 8 or earlier versions, Internet Explorer 9 has support for some, but not all, of HTML5 and CSS3. Internet Explorer 10 has come a long, long way in supporting many features in the ever-evolving specifications.

Since the release of the iPhone SDK in 2008, most of the applications for the iPhone have been created as native apps. Before the release of the SDK, we only had web applications. People moved from web applications to native applications because HTML5 just wasn't ready. Now that mobile browsers support many HTML5 APIs, we are able to create fast, responsive, and visually appealing web applications.

One last reason: video! The iPhone, iPod, and iPad do not support Flash, and they never will. However, all iOS devices have the Safari WebKit browser that supports the HTML5 <video> element, which we'll discuss in Chapter 5.

Pep Talk (or Leaving Old Internet Explorer Behind)

With the proliferation of standards-compliant and forward-thinking browsers, which handheld devices have helped disseminate, we now have the opportunity to move the discipline of web development forward into the twenty-first century.

While learning the lessons of this book, I want you to forget about old versions of Internet Explorer. The Web is moving forward, and it's moving forward fast. Have you been holding back from learning and using CSS3 and HTML5 because of IE6, IE7, or even IE8? These old browsers are not found on mobile devices, and their popularity on desktop computers is dwindling. Stop holding yourself back.

Because of the continued omnipresence of legacy, non-standards-compliant browsers —most notably, Internet Explorer 6 through 8—web developers have been held back from developing kickass websites. Catering to the whims and quirks of IE6 and IE7 forced us to use archaic code; it prevented us from implementing, without some trepidation, advanced older standards as well as not-so-new proposed standards. In this book, we'll learn all about technologies that we can use because we don't have to cater to behind-the-times browsers.

As you work through this book, take HTML5 and CSS3 as far as you can. Don't think: "Oh, this may not work in browser X." Instead think: "This is awesome!" Learn the skills. Learn the syntax. You'll be ahead of the game when all browsers eventually support these newer features. And, in the meantime, you'll have learned some major skills and possibly created a kickass web application.

The Browser Landscape

Safari, Chrome, Firefox, Opera, and IE10 (in both their desktop and mobile versions) all support modern web standards, including HTML 4.01, XHTML, and parts of HTML5; almost all of CSS 2.1 and most of CSS3; JavaScript, including AJAX technologies; and DOM Level 2. Windows was a bit late to the game, but newer phones are supporting HTML5. Did you even know anyone with a Windows mobile phone in 2010? Not until February 2012 when I asked "Who here has a Windows phone?" in a conference hall did someone answer "me." Now Windows phones are becoming a little more popular. We're not catering to the old "Windows Mobile," but this book does cater to those buying the new Windows phone.

This book focuses on designing and developing websites for mobile browsers, providing us the opportunity to use the most cutting-edge web technologies. We've decided that we don't need to think about archaic browsers (you're with me on that one, right?). However, I like my websites and web applications to render correctly (though not necessarily identically) on all browsers. I assume you do, too. When relevant, we'll briefly discuss quirks, tips, and tricks to handle the feature at hand in other common, non-mobile browsers.

Web Applications Versus Native Applications: A Brief History

Within a week of the original iPhone launch in June 2007, the first iPhoneDevCamp was held in San Francisco, CA. When the iPhone was originally released, there was no SDK available. Therefore, all the original iPhone applications were web based.

When the iPhone first launched, the iPhone's OS was less powerful than the newer phones on the market today, and being on the EDGE network, downloads were painfully slow. With these limitations, a main focus in developing applications was ensuring less than 10 KB downloads, less than 10 KB of images, and less than 10 KB of JavaScript.

At the first iPhoneDevCamp, participants developed their own documentation, helping each other gain the skills to develop fun (all web-based) iPhone applications. Originally, there was no default onOrientationChange event. Instead, we added a timer to regularly check the phone's orientation, and switched CSS classes with JavaScript based on the returned value.

During that first weekend after the iPhone's launch, Joe Hewitt wrote iUI, the first Java-Script and CSS library for the iPhone and shared it with the developers present. He, Nicole Lazarro, and three others created Tilt, the first iPhone game that used iPhone's motion-sensing capacity. Dori Smith created iPhone Bingo, a purely JavaScript iPhone game. Richard Herrera, Ryan Christianson, Wai Seto, and I created Pickleview, a Twitter/Major League Baseball AJAX mash-up that allows users to virtually watch any baseball game and tweet about it. It was liberating: for the first time, I was using multiple background images, border images, CSS3 selectors, and opacity without having to worry about supporting a multitude of browsers, browser versions, and operating systems.

For the first nine months of the iPhone's life, there were only web applications and Apple-controlled native applications: there was no native iPhone app development in the wild. Because of bandwidth limitations and a dearth of Apple developer documentation, iPhone web applications didn't skyrocket. Because of the inability of the iPhone WebKit Safari browser to access native iPhone OS features, web application development for the iPhone did not take off. Application development for the iPhone finally skyrocketed with the release of the SDK.

Release of the SDK: Beginning of Third-Party Applications

The iPhone SDK was first released on March 6, 2008. The iPhone SDK allowed third-party (i.e., non-Apple) developers to make applications for the iPhone (and later the iPod touch and iPad), with availability in the App Store following in July of 2008. With the release of the SDK, and the opening of the App Store, not to mention the ability for developers to make money from selling their Apps in the App Store, the focus of iPhone development quickly and wholeheartedly switched to building native iPhone applications.

The fact that the focus of iPhone application development has been mostly on the development of native iPhone applications since the release of the SDK makes sense to a great extent—but we're going to change that! In 2008, the limitations of web-application over native-application development discouraged focusing on web apps, as the following lists show:

Cons for web apps in 2008

- 10 MB file-size limit in iPhone Safari

- Lack of storage for data via web apps, and very limited cache

- Lack of support for most CSS3 and HTML5 features in not only Safari for the iPhone, but all browsers

Pros for native apps in 2008

- Ease of development using XCode

- Ability to sell applications in the App Store

In 2013, however, the tables have turned. The arguments for developing web apps versus native apps has caught up, if not surpassed, the arguments against, as the following lists show:

Pros for web apps in 2013

- Easier to build and iterate (developers can push multiple times a day, providing for quick iteration)

- Uses existing skills in HTML and CSS (building upon skills rather than requiring developers to master completely different ones)

- Same technology, same platform

- Potential to be cross-platform

Cons for native iPhone apps in 2013

- 3-week+ approval process for distributing in the App Store

- Risk of censorship of content and noninclusion by application stores

- $99+ annual Apple Developer membership fee, plus 30% sales fee

- Long waits to push code changes to production, as well as for users to sync and update their application (with HTML5, your changes are live immediately)

What's New(t)? New Elements and APIs

HTML5[4] has been in the works for many years, since efforts began in 2004 on what was originally called Web Applications 1.0. While not finalized, some parts are fairly complete and already supported—oftentimes fully supported—by modern browsers. Modern, or A-grade, browsers include Safari, Chrome, Internet Explorer 10+, Firefox, and Opera. IE8 and older is not in this list. IE9 has some HTML5 support, but is a browser that is holding back the Web. So, while not all browsers provide support for HTML5, it is supported by all WebKit/Blink browsers, Opera Mobile,[5] Firefox OS, and the new Windows phones. It is finally time to start playing with HTML5.

HTML5 is an umbrella term describing the new web API standards, some of which are in the HTML5 specification (e.g., drag-and-drop), and some that aren't (e.g., geolocation).

With HTML5 and the associated APIs, we are no longer limited to native applications. Between the specification for HTML5 and those of the associated APIs, we could kill a tree if we wanted to print it all. I won't describe all of the features in this book, but I will cover some of the more useful ones you can implement today, such as the subjects covered in the following sections.

Semantic Grouping Tags

HTML5 provides new tags used for defining logical groups of tags or sections in your markup. Grouping semantically, instead of using the nonsemantic `<div>` and `<span>` elements to define headers, footers, navigation, etc., assists search engines in defining your site structure. We'll cover the new grouping elements in Chapter 3.

Web Forms

There are millions of forms on the Web, and millions of scripts for each of those forms to validate emails, create pop-up calendars, ensure required elements are filled in before submission, and clear out the placeholder text when a form element receives focus. With HTML5, you may no longer need to validate forms with JavaScript! Form elements have been updated in HTML5 with new features and methods for defining data types.

---

4. HTML5 has become an umbrella term. HTML5 is just a component of the HTML5 "umbrella." Bruce Lawson has suggested the term *NEWT* for this large umbrella, for "New Exciting Web Technologies." I would have thought that term silly, but I loved the newt mascot.

5. Opera Mini does not have good HTML5 support, and never will. It is a different type of browser—a proxy browser—intentionally having limited features in favor of lower bandwidth usage. Opera Mini requests web pages through Opera's servers, which process and compress them before sending them to the mobile phone, dramatically reducing the amount of data transferred. The preprocessing increases compatibility with web pages not designed for mobile phones, but limits the interactivity and features of the site.

In Chapter 4, we'll look at some of these revamped form elements, learning how to create native sliders, placeholder text, and calendar date pickers, plus validating email addresses, ensuring all required fields are entered, and displaying custom keyboards based on input type—all without JavaScript!

SVG and Canvas

With HTML5, images no longer have to be embedded objects. HTML5 adds both <svg> and <canvas> as native HTML elements, which are enhanced with CSS and accessible via the DOM. By adding either element, the browser provides a blank canvas in which you can "draw" programmatically. We will cover <svg> and <canvas> in Chapter 5.

Video and Audio

To date, all browser video and audio have required plug-ins. With HTML5, we now have native browser support for video and audio. And they're scriptable! HTML5 browsers natively support webM and mp4 formats. With the DOM, you can control video and audio, including muting, forwarding, and stopping. With CSS, you can style the players. While iOS devices may never support Flash or Silverlight, all mobile browsers support HTML5 video and audio. We will learn about <video> and <audio> in Chapter 5.

Geolocation API

Geolocation is not part of the HTML5 specifications, but rather an *associated API*, and a very useful module at that. Geolocation is the identification of the geographic location of mobile and desktop devices. The geolocation API is covered in Chapter 6.

Offline Content and Storage

Stating the obvious: phones are mobile devices. Internet service goes in and out (especially for those of us bound to use AT&T). The HTML5 application cache, local storage, and database APIs enable the use and enjoyment of web applications even when AT&T drops you. The APIs that enable your applications to work offline are discussed in Chapter 6.

Other APIs

In Chapter 6, we will also briefly cover microdata, ARIA, and web workers. Though it has no visual or functional effect on your web pages or web application, microdata is a method by which you can add machine-readable semantics to your content to feed the search engine spiders. ARIA, or Accessible Rich Internet Applications, has no visual impact on your content either, but enables better accessibility by providing attributes that explain the role and function of hijacked elements (elements that are used to convey information that is not the default usage of the element). We also briefly cover web workers, which enable you to use additional JavaScript threads to run intensive Java-Script without impeding the UI thread. Chapter 6 is indeed an exciting chapter!

What's New in CSS?

CSS3 provides us with some new great features. CSS3 selectors, described in Chapter 7, provide us with a method of targeting just about every element on the page without adding a single class, including media queries to enable responsive web development. RGBA and HSLA are new alpha-transparent color values, which are discussed in Chapter 8, along with other value types. For designers and prototypers, Chapters 9 and 10 will likely be the most exciting chapters of the book, covering new and not-so-new CSS3 features, including:

- Multiple backgrounds
- Transitions
- Transforms
- 3D transforms
- Gradients
- `background-size`
- `border-image`
- `border-radius`
- `box-shadow`
- `text-shadow`
- `opacity`
- `animation`
- `columns`
- `text-overflow`

Web Fonts

Web fonts allow you to use font faces other than the traditional half dozen *web-safe fonts*. Different browsers have different implementations, including different support for iPhone versus desktop. While all smartphone browsers support `@font-face`, it is a sans-serif font—Helvetica, Roboto, or whatever the default operating system font is—that should be the font of choice when developing for mobile. I can't encourage requiring mobile users to download huge font files. I do encourage using smaller icon fonts in Chapter 11, but web fonts are not largely covered in this book. If you are interested in learning more about web fonts for desktop, there is a link in the online chapter resources to a tutorial I wrote. These resources are available at *http://www.standardista.com/ mobile*, and contain links to external resources, code examples, and all the links referenced in this book.

Mobile-Specific Considerations

With desktop browsers, most people navigate a stationary Web with a mouse and a keyboard. On phones and tablets, we often navigate the Web with our fingers, rotating, shaking, touching, and tapping the device, but we don't—and can't—*click* anything. Even the skinniest, scrawniest of users still has "fat fingers" compared to the precision possible with a mouse. And, with relatively small screens and often with smaller user attention spans, there are different considerations when it comes to the user interface and the limited space for including content.

Mobile tablets are often used at home on WiFi, or other wireless access points. Mobile phones can use these same access points, but generally access the Web via inconsistent and limited shared services. They also have smaller screens, so not much room for developer toolbars, or bandwidth for ginormous JavaScript libraries and images.

Chapter 11 covers responsive web development features. Chapter 12 covers design considerations. We cover mobile and touch screen unique-event handlers in Chapter 13. Mobile performance, debugging, and device limitations are covered in Chapter 14.

Why This Book?

As web developers, we've been stuck in the past. We've been catering to a browser that is over 12 years old. When you don't have to worry about cross-browser compatibility, and you don't have to live within the constraints of CSS2, development gets exciting. Mobile devices ship with advanced browsers that implement cutting-edge technology. Use that technology!

Mobile has opened up this exciting new world. WebKit with HTML5 support is on Android tablets, iPhones, OpenMoko, BlackBerry phones, and more. In addition to BlackBerry, Android, and iOS devices, WebKit is the engine for the Bolt, Dolphin, Ozone, and Skyfire browsers. Firefox, Opera, and IE are also found on cell phones, and the advanced Presto-based Opera browser is still found on a multitude of non-"computer" devices. Opera and Chrome are porting to Blink. Soon, everyone will have a fully fledged web browser on their phone, on their TV, in their car, and even in their refrigerators.

Screen Size

Right now, on the desktop, we may feel held back by Internet Explorer's lack of support for new and upcoming standards. With the proliferation of standards-compliant browsers and the dwindling use of older versions of Internet Explorer, we'll soon be able to rely on CSS3 everywhere. Moving to mobile, we can think past CSS2 constraints. However, we have new issues to deal with: real estate constraints! One size does not fit all. The mobile browser is, obviously, smaller than the desktop browser.

For some sites, you can have a one-size-fits-all approach, but most HTML files and CSS documents do not fit all browser sizes.

Depending on the complexity of the content and design, you may want to serve up different HTML and different CSS depending on the medium.

Sometimes you may just be able to temporarily hide certain content. At other times, you'll want to serve a smaller header and smaller images. You may also want to have a multicolumn layout on a wide screen, and a single column layout on the phone. You will want to alter appearances based on device size: for example, a three-column layout is easiest to read on the desktop. Placing those columns vertically on top of the other makes more sense in the mobile arena.

Mobile web design is all about keeping it simple. You can only fit so much in the small area that the phone provides. Scrolling is only for longer articles, not for home or navigational pages.

You may want to provide separate markup for the mobile version of your website. But you don't have to. And unless you're creating a real web application rather than a simple website, you really shouldn't.

User Goals

Internet access on mobile devices used to be thought of as something only for people on the go. Yes, some mobile browser users are simply quickly looking for access to specific information. They may be checking their online grocery list, looking up the ingredients for a casserole, or trying to find the best Italian restaurant within a five-minute walk.

While perhaps that user is not currently interested in the corporate structure of the food supplier, it doesn't mean that when they are interested in locating that information that they won't try to do so from the same mobile device. While we may perform such in-depth research on a desktop computer, more and more users are only accessing the Internet with their mobile devices.

Perhaps your average mobile user will just want to get an address, a phone number, or a status update on the go, and will not want to delete, reorganize, edit, or research stuff on her iPhone. But she might. The mobile device may be her only computer. So while you should make sure the most necessary information is easily accessible, you do want to ensure your users can perform all tasks that can be done on a widescreen monitor in the mobile space if needed.

You also have to think about usability. Touch screen devices use fingers instead of mice as input devices. Fingers are fatter than cursors. For touch screen devices, action targets need to be large and have padding. We discuss suggested user interface changes for touch devices in Chapter 13.

Nonpresentational images should be removed from mobile device markup: images are generally optimized for the desktop not the mobile device; they take up space that should be reserved for content when real estate is scarce, and bandwidth can be very slow and very expensive. Yes, include content images if the images are contextual, but use (or omit) background images for images that are decorative in nature.

What's in This Book

In Chapter 1, we'll get our development environments set up and discuss the examples used throughout this book.

Chapters Chapter 2–6 discuss what is new in HTML5. We discuss best practices in coding semantic markup that is compatible with all modern browsers, both in the desktop and mobile spaces. We cover the new HTML5 semantic elements, Web Forms 2.0, and several of the HTML5 APIs and related APIs, like geolocation. We'll touch on SVG, canvas, web forms, video, audio, AppCache and database, and web workers.

Chapters 7–11 introduce everything that is up and coming in CSS3, from new color types, to shadows, to border images, to rounded corners, to animation—you will have all the tools you need to create beautiful web applications for both mobile and modern desktop browsers, with responsive web design features highlighted in Chapter 11.

In Chapters 12–14, we focus on the mobile platform, including touch events, user experience design, and mobile performance considerations. Lessons covered will ensure site performance, user experience, and reliability of web pages on all platforms.

Yes, our goal is to develop kickass websites for mobile. The first step to creating a great website for a mobile device is to create a great website! While you should be developing your website in the desktop browser for ease of development, you should design and develop with mobile always in mind. Then, with minimal modifications, your site will look great and perform well on most, if not all, platforms. Our goal is to develop web applications that work on the phone, by creating web applications that work on all modern browsers.

Conventions Used in This Book

The following typographical conventions are used in this book:

Italic
> Indicates new terms, URLs, email addresses, filenames, and file extensions.

`Constant width`
> Used for program listings, as well as within paragraphs to refer to program elements such as variable or function names, databases, data types, environment variables, statements, and keywords.

`Constant width bold`
> Shows commands or other text that should be typed literally by the user.

`Constant width italic`
> Shows text that should be replaced with user-supplied values or by values determined by context.

> This icon signifies a tip, suggestion, or general note.

> This icon indicates a warning or caution.

Using Code Examples

The chapter resources are available at *http://www.standardista.com/mobile*. There you can find links to external resources, code examples, and all the links referenced in this book.

This book is here to help you get your job done. In general, when example code is offered with this book, you may use it in your programs and documentation. You do not need to contact us for permission unless you're reproducing a significant portion of the code. For example, writing a program that uses several chunks of code from this book does not require permission. Selling or distributing a CD-ROM of examples from O'Reilly books does require permission. Answering a question by citing this book and quoting example code does not require permission. Incorporating a significant amount of example code from this book into your product's documentation does require permission.

We appreciate, but do not require, attribution. An attribution usually includes the title, author, publisher, and ISBN. For example: "*Mobile HTML5* by Estelle Weyl (O'Reilly). Copyright 2014 Estelle Weyl, 978-1-449-31141-4."

If you feel your use of code examples falls outside fair use or the permission given above, feel free to contact us at *permissions@oreilly.com*.

Safari® Books Online

Safari Books Online (*www.safaribooksonline.com*) is an on-demand digital library that delivers expert content in both book and video form from the world's leading authors in technology and business.

Technology professionals, software developers, web designers, and business and creative professionals use Safari Books Online as their primary resource for research, problem solving, learning, and certification training.

Safari Books Online offers a range of product mixes and pricing programs for organizations, government agencies, and individuals. Subscribers have access to thousands of books, training videos, and prepublication manuscripts in one fully searchable database from publishers like O'Reilly Media, Prentice Hall Professional, Addison-Wesley Professional, Microsoft Press, Sams, Que, Peachpit Press, Focal Press, Cisco Press, John Wiley & Sons, Syngress, Morgan Kaufmann, IBM Redbooks, Packt, Adobe Press, FT Press, Apress, Manning, New Riders, McGraw-Hill, Jones & Bartlett, Course Technology, and dozens more. For more information about Safari Books Online, please visit us online.

How to Contact Us

Please address comments and questions concerning this book to the publisher:

O'Reilly Media, Inc.
1005 Gravenstein Highway North
Sebastopol, CA 95472
800-998-9938 (in the United States or Canada)
707-829-0515 (international or local)
707-829-0104 (fax)

We have a web page for this book, where we list errata, examples, and any additional information. You can access this page at *http://oreil.ly/mobilehtml5_1e*.

To comment or ask technical questions about this book, send email to *bookquestions@oreilly.com*.

For more information about our books, courses, conferences, and news, see our website at *http://www.oreilly.com*.

Find us on Facebook: *http://facebook.com/oreilly*

Follow us on Twitter: *http://twitter.com/oreillymedia*

Watch us on YouTube: *http://www.youtube.com/oreillymedia*

Acknowledgments

Thank you to Bruce Lawson, Adam Lichtenstein, Jennifer Hanen, Tim Kadlec, Jeff Burtoft, Tomomi Imura, and Justin Lowery.

Bruce Lawson coauthored the first book on HTML5, *Introducing HTML5* (New Riders). He's one of the founders of *HTML5Doctor.com*, and was a member of W3C's Mobile Web Best Practices Working Group. He evangelizes open web standards for Opera, the oldest browser manufacturer, whose mobile, desktop, TV, and embedded browsers are used by 300 million people across the world (see *www.opera.com*). Follow Bruce on Twitter at @brucel, or *www.brucelawson.co.uk*.

Justin Lowery created the look for CubeeDoo. He is a UX architect at his company, Cerebral Interactive, which specializes in the design and development of web and mobile applications. He's been a graphic/print designer since 2001 and a web developer since 2006. He's also an informatics nurse (RN), which lends well to his current focus on revolutionizing information technology for health care education. Follow Justin at @cerebralideas, or *www.cix.io*.

Adam Lichtenstein is a frontend developer and a OOCSS/Sass junkie. He is the creator of FormFace, which focuses on semantic building and styling of HTML5 forms. He is currently the frontend developer and designer at Wufoo and authoring his first book on frontend development. When not coding or writing about coding, his main hobby is thinking about coding. Follow him at @seethroughtrees, or *http://seethrough trees.github.io*.

Jenifer Hanen is a mobile designer, developer, and photographer with a passion to make everyone fall as deeply in love with mobile as she is. Ms. Hanen developed her first public website for a friend's band in 1996 and has had a mobile and web consultancy since 2000, as well as stints as an adjunct web design and art history professor. Follow her at @msjen, or *http://blackphoebe.com/msjen*.

Tomomi Imura is an open web advocate and frontend engineer with mobile focus who has been active in the mobile space since before it was cool. She has been developing mobile web, platform UI/UX, and frameworks at Yahoo! Mobile and webOS at Palm before joining Nokia, to work with the W3C and evangelize HTML5. Follow her at @girlie_mac, or *http://girliemac.com*.

Jeff Burtoft is an HTML5 Evangelist for Microsoft and an avid supporter of the Java-Script/HTML5 community. Mr. Burtoft is a huge proponent of web standards, and loves all programming languages, as long as they are JavaScript. Additionally, he is coauthor of *HTML5 Hacks* (O'Reilly Media) and a founding blogger of *html5hacks.com*. He lives in South Texas with his wife and three kids. Follow him on Twitter at @boyofgreen.

CHAPTER 1

Setting the Stage to Learn Mobile HTML5, CSS3, and JavaScript APIs

If you're anything like me, you've hated older versions of Internet Explorer for years. Those browsers were full of fail. However, they failed the same way everywhere for their entire life spans.[1] We all knew IE6 sucked, but it sucked in the same way. Once we figured out how to polyfill for IE6, we had it figured out.

In the mobile landscape, we also have failure, but we have failure in newer, more diverse, ever-changing ways. Different browser versions on different devices may support many new features, but may do so in different ways. Or, they may support a feature, but that feature may not be usable. For example, a modern device may or may not support localStorage. The devices that support localStorage may or may not allow you to write to it. Even if the browser allows you to read from localStorage, reading from it may take a long time and hinder performance. And, even if the browser generally allows you to write to it, localStorage itself may have reached the storage limit.

We can't cover all the quirks in all the browsers for all operating systems and devices here. Even if I knew all of the quirks (and I don't), the quirks could fill a tome, and said tome would be outdated before I finished writing it. This book is, in fact, out of date. The landscape is ever changing. There is no way to produce a book that is up to date because by the time it goes to print—or even by the time you finish a chapter—the landscape has changed. While some of the browsers, features, phones, and sites mentioned may already be obsolete, the best practices brought forth in this book should be relevant for the next few years. A guiding principle for this book: if you use best practices and code to standards, your code will work in current devices and all future devices.

---

1. IE6 was cutting edge when it was released in 2001. With an almost monopoly on browser market share, there was little competition, and it was never updated.

I included browser support for features, but not lack of support for browser features, as it is expected that all browsers will move forward in the right direction. What is a quirk in a browser today may be resolved tomorrow.

For these reasons, when using a feature, you do need to both feature detect and you need to test to ensure you can successfully use the supported feature.

This book is using device-, OS-, and browser-agnostic markup and no JavaScript libraries. I've gone library free, coding in vanilla JavaScript, to ensure that you learn actual code. By coding in vanilla JavaScript, I've hopefully removed any confusion there may be as to whether a method is native or a framework method.

This doesn't mean you shouldn't use libraries. On the contrary! Open source libraries are some of the best places to find out about browser quirks. Open source projects have hundreds, sometimes thousands, of contributors. These contributors provide for thousands of eyes developing and testing on a multitude of devices, finding the quirks, reporting the quirks, and checking in fixes to the libraries to handle the quirks or provide workarounds and polyfills. These thousands of eyes are also reporting bugs, alerting browser vendors as to what is not working to standards so that these bugs can be fixed in future browser releases.

Popular open source libraries and HTML5 JavaScript API polyfills are the best resources for quickly discovering various browser quirks and solutions. They should be considered an important part of your development tool chest. Even if you don't use them, do read the source code to learn about the mobile browser bugs others have discovered.

The best way to learn HTML5, CSS3, and the associated JavaScript APIs as you read about them is to code. Let's code.

CubeeDoo: HTML5 Mobile Game

The way I learned HTML5 and CSS3 was to mark up a web application for a single mobile browser and push it to its limits. My first foray into CSS3 was a Twitter/Major League Baseball web application mash-up called Pickleview, written the weekend the iPhone first came out in 2007. At the time, Safari for the iPhone was the most advanced browser on the market (except for maybe Opera). By programming it for a single browser, I didn't have to worry about IE6, IE7, or Firefox 2 (Chrome didn't exist yet). Back in 2007, that was the state of the Web.

In 2010, I redid the exercise of coding with the most modern HTML5 and CSS3 in a single browser. A few friends and I created a memory game with animations, storage, offline capabilities, and every new feature that could be found in Chrome 12 on a desktop that wasn't in Safari 3.1 for mobile. By using a single browser and leveraging all of the new technology I could, I was able to learn to code newer HTML5, CSS3, and JavaScript modules that weren't yet usable in production because of the need to support legacy browsers. By 2010, some browsers had come a long way since 2007. Others (IE, I am looking at you here), not so much.

In 2013, most browsers support HTML5 and CSS3. As developers, we are being held back by having to support older desktop browsers, namely Internet Explorer 9 and earlier. On mobile, we have our own "IE6." We are held back by feature phones and by smartphones running Android 2.3 to some extent. But even feature phone browsers and Android 2.3 both support many modern features.

To learn to code HTML5, CSS3, and the associated JavaScript APIs, temporarily forget about older browsers. Together we'll learn what is possible with these newer technologies. I've put the majority of the features that have broad support in modern browsers into the code examples in this book.

CubeeDoo, as shown in Figure 1-1, is a completely frontend-coded memory game. I'll be using code examples from this game, along with a native iPhone settings application replica (as seen in Figure 9-3) throughout the book. The game is marked up with HTML5 elements. Some of the themes include matching icons created with generated content. CSS transforms, transitions, and animations, along with gradients, rounded corners, and other CSS features are used to create the look and feel of the game. The game also includes SVG, JSON, the deprecated but mobile-supported webSQL, localStorage, sessionStorage, data attributes, HTML5 forms, audio, media queries, and data URIs.

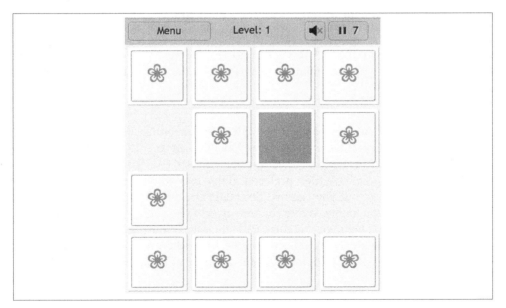

Figure 1-1. Screenshot of CubeeDoo memory game

The code in this book uses no frameworks of any kind. As mentioned earlier, everything is handcoded in vanilla JavaScript, HTML5, and CSS. The goal is to teach you the actual APIs, not polyfills. In production, you will likely want to use polyfills, but to smartly use polyfills, you need to understand what the polyfills do. This book teaches you that.

This book covers CSS3, HTML5, and the associated APIs. The focus is learning the technologies in a mobile landscape. We live in a mobile world, but there is no "mobile web." There is simply the Web. But if you focus on the desktop only, the version of the Web you create may not work for the increasing population that only accesses the Web via mobile devices. And, if you only focus on desktop, you'll only concern yourself with the lowest common denominator of older Internet Explorer versions.

Never push to production an application that only works in a single browser. However, to learn technologies that are nascent, ignoring "older" browsers can provide you the opportunity to learn, to challenge yourself, to think outside the box, and to get to the top of your game. Take what you learn in this book and, using a single browser, code to the limits of what the browser can do. Experiment. You'll fall in love with web development all over again.

All you need is a browser, an IDE, and some time.

Development Tools

Before starting to develop your first mobile web application, you'll want to set up your development environment with the best "tools of the trade." Good news! You already have these tools.

All you need to follow along with this book is a computer with a text editor and browser. You don't even need a phone, though having a mobile device will be hugely helpful.

Text Editor

You should be developing in a plain-text editor or *integrated development environment* (IDE). An IDE is software that generally includes a text editor, debugger, and any other features or plug-ins, such as a file transfer protocol (FTP), that you may need to get the job done. People have their preferred IDEs. Pick whatever suits you. My preference is Sublime Text, but you can use TextMate, Dreamweaver, Eclipse, WebStorm, or whatever makes you happy. While you only need a plain-text editor, you'll discover that using an IDE can help you organize and streamline your development process. I recommend selecting an IDE and becoming best friends with it. IDEs can be hugely powerful tools that make developing pleasant—almost a dream.

Browser

You also need a browser. I prefer developing in Chrome Canary, which is the beta version of Google Chrome. I prefer this browser because of the debugger. All modern browsers have debuggers, but the Chrome debugger is one of the best, and the Canary debugger provides me insight and access to all the new bells and whistles before they even enter into a browser release.

If you don't have an Apple computer, you won't easily be able to develop native iPhone, iPad, or iPod touch applications. If you don't have Windows 8, it would be hard to develop what are formally known as Metro-style applications. No worries! For what we are learning, all you need is a modern browser. The operating system or the device does not matter. You can test all the examples in this book on Windows, Unix, Android phones and tablets, and Macs—you name it.

Your IDE and desktop browser will be your main tool for mobile web development. Your mobile application is previewed and debugged in your desktop browser throughout the development process. There are features that your desktop browser will not succeed at emulating, including mobile rendering accuracy, JavaScript performance, memory and bandwidth limits, and API availability. However, these differences can be overcome with other tools and by testing directly on real or virtual devices.

While you will enjoy developing in your favorite browser, you should have in your toolkit multiple browsers available for testing. You will want access to Internet Explorer for easier testing of the Windows Phone environment. Safari or Google Chrome will enable you to test Android, Bada, Blackberry, and iOS. You'll also want Firefox for Gecko devices. Opera is currently needed for testing all the devices that run the Presto rendering engine, but as Opera Mobile 14 is Chromium-based, and the most recent Opera and Chrome are on Blink,[2] the browsers you need for development need to be updated to match the landscape you are developing in.

If you haven't done so already, download Safari if you're on a Mac, or the latest Internet Explorer if you're on Windows. Download Chrome, Firefox, and Opera on your device as well, even if you're on Unix. You can also download Chrome Canary, Aurora, Opera Next, and WebKit Nightly builds to test in the next releases of the major browsers. These are the current desktop browsers at the time of this writing, but the landscape is ever changing.

Debugging Tools

Browsers come with development tools. Developer tools are built-in browser tools that allow you to inspect and debug your source code. Using the tools, you can manipulate

---

2. Blink is a fork of WebKit's WebCore component made at revision 147503. It is the browser engine in Chrome since version 28, Opera starting with version 15, and other Chromium-based browsers going forward.

the Document Object Model (DOM), edit and debug JavaScript code, edit and debug CSS, analyze resource requests, and audit the performance of web content and web applications on live content.

Developer tools are generally hidden because most users, other than developers, don't utilize these browser features. Mobile browsers often have some debugging capabilities in the device browser. These limited debugging tools are usually available via the device settings interface. Though device-level debugging may be available, it is much easier to debug applications in the much more robust tools you access on your desktop.

Desktop Debuggers

If you've been developing websites for any amount of time, you're likely familiar with Firebug,[3] F12, Web Inspector, and/or DragonFly. Firebug is a Mozilla extension. F12, Web Inspector, and DragonFly ship with Internet Explorer, Chrome/Safari, and Opera, respectively. These developer tools all allow the debugging, editing, and monitoring of a website's CSS, HTML, DOM, and JavaScript, and enable you to analyze features like HTTP requests, local storage, and memory consumption.

Firebug is available from *getFirebug.com*. Safari's developer tools can be found under the Develop menu, but has to be made available via Preferences→Advanced, by checking "Show develop menu in menu bar." In Chrome, you can open the developer tools via View→Developer→Developer Tools.

You can also open Chrome, Safari, Firebug, and Opera debuggers using Command-Option-I or Control-I. F12 and Firebug can also be opened by clicking F12. These tools are the browsers' best tool for debugging CSS, JavaScript, and HTML.

You will want to become familiar with the Web Inspector, Error Console, and User Agent switcher. These debuggers allow you to inspect a web page's CSS, HTML, JavaScript, DOM, and headers. Whether you use Web Inspector, Firebug, DragonFly, F12, Developer Tools, or some combination of these, get to know your debugging tools. Your debugger will become your other best friend.

Likely you have several years of experience using browser-debugging tools for desktop applications, so we won't dive deeply into them here. However, even if you've been using them for five years, chances are you're just scraping the surface of debugger awesomeness. I encourage you to dive deeper on your own, exploring every millimeter with a click and a right-click. We cover the developer tools Timeline tab in Chapter 14.

Mobile viewport

To mimic the mobile viewport, you can simply resize the desktop browser window to the size of the mobile viewport you want to test. The desktop browser viewport is the

---

3. Firefox comes with web developer tools, but most developers use Firebug, a Firefox add-on.

---

browser window. In mobile, the viewport is what you see, but not necessarily what is painted to the screen, but resizing the window should be close enough for most of the testing you'll need to do.

When you resize your browser manually, you can get random sizes. In the Overrides panel of the Settings window, as shown in Figure 1-2, Chrome Developer Tools provides several preset device sizes. Access the Web Inspector settings window by clicking the gear in the bottom right of Developer Tools.

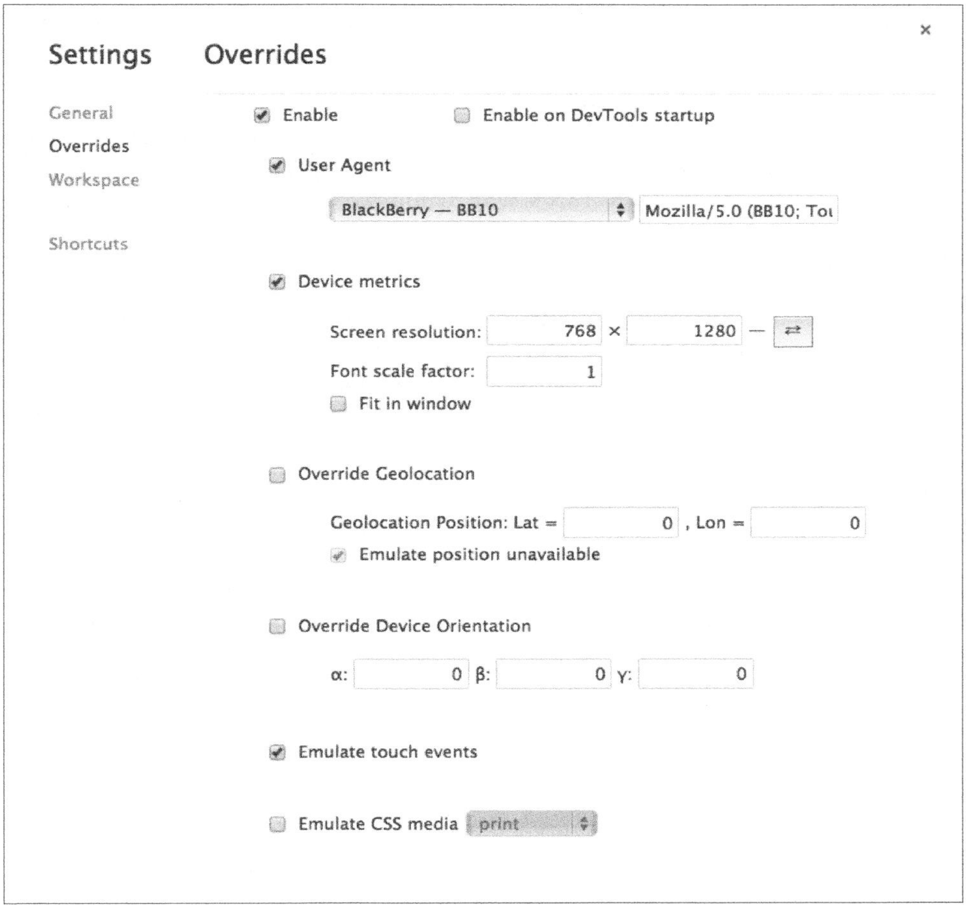

Figure 1-2. Chrome Developer Tools Settings Overrides panel

When you select a device from the User Agent select menu, Chrome switches the user agent to the selected device user agent, and creates a viewport within the browser window that is the size of the selected device. This provides you with a browser viewport that is the same size as the viewport of the selected device.

If your device is not listed, simply enter the device width and height in the two input boxes under device metrics. You can toggle between landscape and portrait mode dimensions by clicking on the toggle button to the right of the device metrics. Check out ScreenQueri.es (*http://beta.screenqueri.es/*) to preview exact device screen sizes. You can also enable touch-event emulation, or use *thumbs.js* as a TouchEvent polyfill.

The Chrome Developer Tools also enable you to override geolocation to emulate a specific longitude and latitude, and, even if your laptop has a gyroscope, you can emulate a specific device orientation.

After you've developed the first stage of your application with your desktop browser, you will want to test it on a mobile device. The main hurdle with testing on a mobile device is that you will not have access to the powerful inspectors that you have grown accustomed to on your desktop. This is why remote web inspectors are awesome.

Remote Debugging

There are tools to remotely debug your mobile browser via your desktop browser. Remote debuggers enable your desktop browser to communicate with external devices to remotely execute and capture code. Just like regular debugging, you can use these remote debuggers to inspect your HTML and CSS, manipulate your DOM and make live edits, and debug your scripts.

The Opera browser engine is being replaced. While I don't know what the future brings, Opera has supported remote debugging of the Opera mobile browser through the Opera desktop Dragonfly debugger since 2008. It has allowed remotely inspecting HTML and CSS, updating the DOM, adding breakpoints, and anything else that could be done with Dragonfly on the desktop.

WebKit began supporting remote debugging via the USB port with Android 4 and iOS 6. To use Chrome to remotely debug, you start Chrome via the command line with a flag, instead of via its icon:

```
chrome.exe --remote-debugging-port=9222 --user-data-dir=remote-profile
```

or

```
/Applications/Chromium.app/Contents/MacOS/Chromium --remote-debugging-port=9222
```

To debug the Firefox mobile browser, add the Debug API, formerly the Crossfire extension, to Firebug.

Of course, the current state is always changing and improving. Keep up to date with Remote Debugging Protocol of the Browser Testing and Tools Working Group (*http://*

www.w3.org/2011/08/browser-testing-charter.html) if this is a discussion you're pas-
sionate about.

Android debugging tools

The Android SDK includes the API libraries and developer tools necessary to build,
test, and debug apps for Android. You can debug web applications directly from your
devices or from emulators the SDK enables you to create, as seen in Figure 1-3.

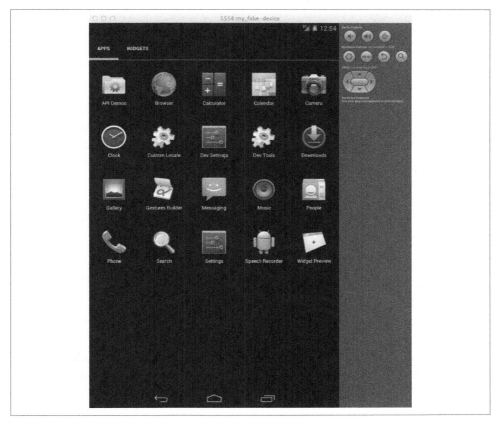

Figure 1-3. Android 4.2.2 emulator running on OS X

Downloading the SDK at *http://developer.android.com/sdk/* will provide you with the
Android Debug Bridge (ADB), debugging, console monitoring, and emulator creating
and launching capabilities.

In the downloaded assets, find the *tool* folder and open *android* to access adb. The
ADB provides various device-management capabilities, including moving and syncing

files to the emulator, running a UNIX shell on the device or emulator, and providing a general means to communicate with connected emulators and devices.

If you prefer, the ADB plug-in (*https://github.com/repenaxa/ADBPlugin*) is a Chrome extension that runs an ADB daemon and enables remote debugging for mobile without needing to download the SDK.

In the same *tools* folder, open *Monitor* to access the Android Debug Monitor. The monitor contains a console by which you can debug your applications, including viewing any `console.log()`s you may have included in your site. The devices being debugged are listed in the device panel on the left in Figure 1-4, and the console log is at the bottom.

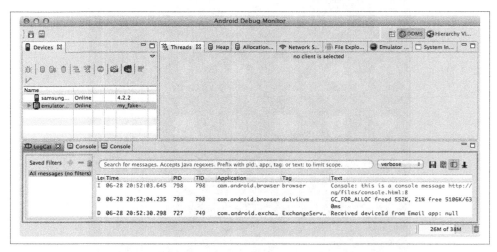

Figure 1-4. The Android Debug Monitor

When the Monitor is open, under the Window menu you'll find the Android Virtual Device Manager, as shown in Figure 1-5. Via this window you can create new emulator testing devices and launch them, as shown in Figure 1-3.

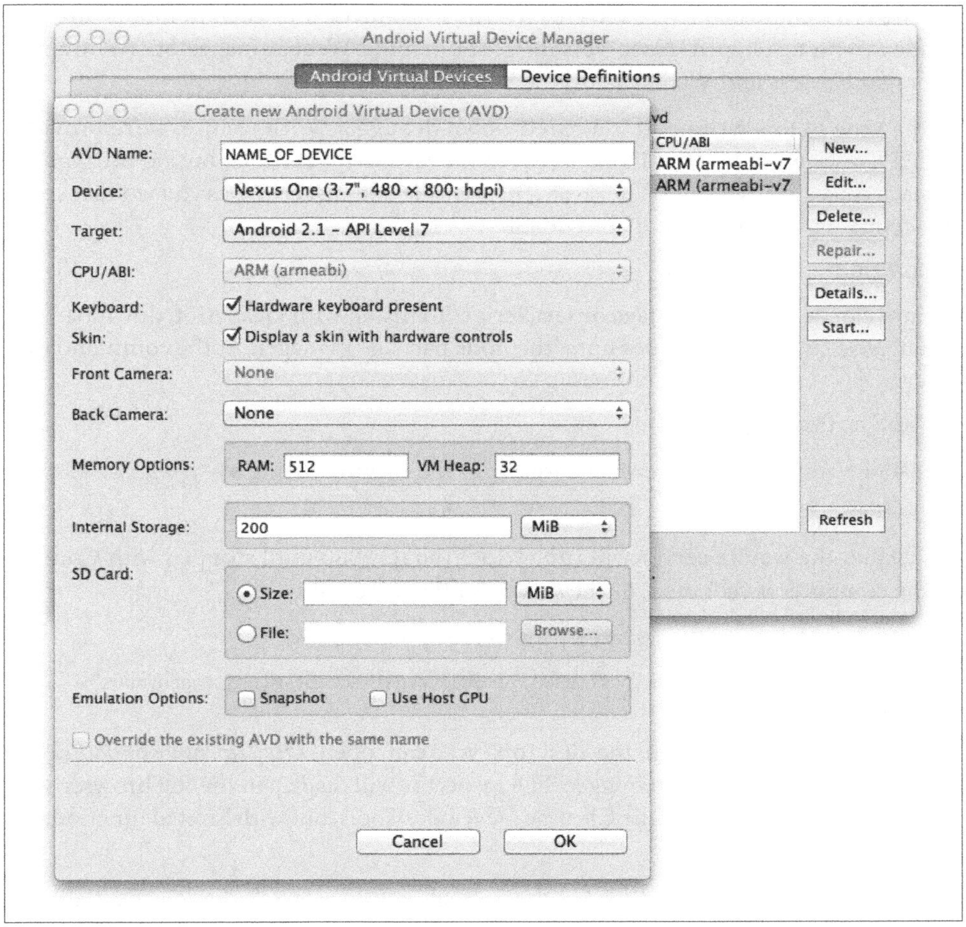

Figure 1-5. The Android Virtual Device Manager provides for the creation of emulators of a limited number of selectable devices, or an unlimited number of independently defined configurations

weinre

Weinre, short for *web inspector remote*, is a powerful remote debugger that lets you inspect and debug JavaScript, HTML, and CSS. Weinre is part of the PhoneGap project; you can use it locally or hosted at *debug.phonegap.com*. Weinre is also the basis of Adobe Edge Inspect, described in the section on page 13.

Weinre is a remote debugger that enables you to connect your current mobile browser window with a stripped-down version of the remote WebKit inspector. Weinre now leverages Node.js and WebSockets.[4]

At the time of this writing, it is a pared-down debugger. With weinre, we're provided with a live view of the DOM and access to the JavaScript console, but no breakpoints or stack traces are available. The JavaScript console does list errors as you would expect, so debugging is more difficult, but doable.

Using weinre

Weinre can be installed via Java or JavaScript. To install with JavaScript, download and install Node.js, which includes npm, the node package manager. At the command line, enter:

```
npm -g install weinre
```

to install weinre. You can now start weinre at the command line by typing:

```
weinre
```

By default, the weinre server will run at localhost:8080 until stopped with Control-C, the computer is rebooted, or the server is otherwise killed.

To be able to debug, add a weinre script to the application with:

```
<script src="http://localhost:8080/target/target-script-min.js#anonymous">
</script>
```

In any WebKit browser on the desktop, you can open *http://localhost:8080/client/ #anonymous* to access the debugger. The inspector will display in the full browser window looking very similar to the Chrome Developer Tools, but with limited functionality and fewer tabs.

In the Remote tab, you'll find a list of the current mobile browser windows available for debugging that are running on the same network as your weinre script. The Elements, Resources, Network, Timeline, and Console tabs, as shown in Figure 1-6, are similar to those of the desktop web inspector. You may note that Sources, Profiles, and Audit tabs are missing from this stripped-down debugger (though these may be added back in the future).

---

4. Originally, it was Java based. Before WebSockets, it leveraged CORS, JSON, and XHR.

Figure 1-6. Weinre debugger

Adobe Edge Inspect and Ghostlab

To simplify the design debugging process, virtually automating the preceding steps for you, Adobe Edge Inspect enables you to debug in a manner similar to weinre, on which it is based. It does this by obfuscating the tasks of starting the server, entering the URL in the browser, and adding scripts to your markup.

You install Adobe Edge Inspect on all of your remote devices and as a Chrome browser extension on your desktop. With both the testing device and the desktop on the same network, you can create a connection with the device.

Opening Edge in your mobile device will provide you with a passcode to the device to be entered into the desktop Edge browser extension. Turn on Edge in your desktop browser by first opening up the application and signing into Adobe.

Once you've signed in, click on the Edge browser extension icon, as shown in Figure 1-7, which tells the browser to look for devices on the network. When it finds your device, add the passcode from the device into the Edge window.

The passcode ensures that you are giving permission to your computer and mobile device to communicate with each other, preventing other unwanted computers from controlling your device and your computer from controlling other people's phones.

Once a connection between your computer and one or many devices is made, you can control which page is loaded in all of your mobile browsers at once. The currently open tab in Chrome will be retrieved and displayed on the mobile device(s) connected via Edge Inspect.

Figure 1-7. Adobe Edge Inspect connecting a Nexus 7 and Google Chrome for debugging

To debug a web page from a device, navigate to the page you want to debug in Chrome or on the device. When you click on the Chrome extension Adobe Edge Inspect menu, click the < > next to the device you want to debug. Weinre will start on your local machine, and the device and web page title will be listed as an active link under the Remote tab in weinre, which is the leftmost tab displayed in Figure 1-6.

The free version of Adobe Edge Inspect only allows for interacting with a single device at a time. The monthly subscription allows you to control all of your devices at the same time. It also helps in taking screenshots.

If you are on a Mac and want to test multiple devices, Ghostlab (*http://vanamco.com/ghostlab/*) enables you to similarly test multiple devices. If you're thinking of purchasing either, Ghostlab's one-time fee may save you money over Adobe Edge's monthly subscription.

JavaScript debugging with Aardwolf

If debugging JavaScript is your main concern, you can try Aardwolf. Aardwolf is a remote JavaScript debugger with which you can execute and capture JavaScript. Aardwolf works by rewriting your code on the server and adding debugging hooks. Similar to weinre with a Node.js backend, it uses synchronous XHR calls to enable breaking on breakpoints. You can use Aardwolf to remotely step through your code, with support for watching objects, breakpoints, and call stacks.

BlackBerry 10 Debugger

While weinre is awesome, the debugger that comes with Blackberry 10 is more powerful.

Like weinre, the BlackBerry Browser uses a client-server architecture to make Web Inspector functionality available. Unlike with weinre, in this case, the BlackBerry

Browser acts as a web server, and serves the web page over HTTP over a USB or WiFi connection. You inspect the content remotely on a desktop browser. You can use any WebKit-based desktop browser on the same WiFi network to navigate to the IP address and port number used by the BlackBerry Browser and begin inspecting the code.

To use the inspector, you must enable debugging under BlackBerry Browser options. Once Web Inspector is enabled, the browser or application displays the IP address and port number it will use to serve the content.

To enable the Web Inspector on BlackBerry 10, from the browser application, swipe down from the top bezel to display the browser's menu bar. Click the settings icon and then Developer Tools to turn the Web Inspector on. If you're using the tablet, this can be found under Options→Privacy & Security instead. The browser displays the IP address and the port number required to connect from your desktop browser. If prompted, type your device password to complete the enabling process. Click Back to save and return to the browser window. You can now open a connection to the BlackBerry Browser to remotely inspect displaying pages.

Testing Tools

It is best to run your sites on actual devices, but it is impossible to test on all devices as there are thousands of devices, with new ones coming out all the time. It is therefore suggested that you test on a representative group of devices, covering different configurations of operating systems, browsers, device sizes, and device capabilities, such as different screen resolutions, memory constraints, and bandwidth access.

It can be expensive and time consuming to test on real devices. In addition to the debugging tools covered in the previous section, there are several tools to help us achieve maximum testing abilities.

Emulators and Simulators

An emulator is software that duplicates or emulates the functions of a mobile device (or devices) on a computer, so that the emulated behavior closely resembles the behavior of the actual device. This focus on exact reproduction of behavior is the difference between emulating and simulating. In simulation, an abstract model of the mobile operating system is simulated.

Emulators allow mobile software to be used on your desktop, enabling you to run and debug your code without having all the devices. Even if you are testing in emulators and simulators, you still can't test in emulators of all the devices. Emulators and simulators simply get you started and quicken the development and debugging process. You should still test on an array of different mobile devices.

When you run your website in a simulator, you are running it in a simulation application on your desktop. Some simulators are for individual devices, and others allow you to choose what device you want to emulate. For example, the iOS Simulator allows you to choose iPhone or iPad. Via menus, you can change the orientation between portrait and landscape. There are virtual buttons to represent the buttons of the device. And, on nontouch devices, you can use your mouse to mimic touch events.

The simulator does not exactly replicate device hardware and there's no guarantee your application will work identically on the actual device. There are certain libraries that will compile and link fine when targeting the simulator (because it is really running on the desktop), but then will not compile when you target the device.

Simulators and emulators generally include a full SDK for testing native applications in a faux native environment. To test our code, we want emulators and simulators that contain a browser, which each emulator and simulator does. You will likely want to download and test your website in the browsers of the following emulators and simulators:

Android Emulator

The free Android emulator for Windows, Mac OS, and Linux is available in conjunction with the SDK from *http://developer.android.com*. As described in "Android debugging tools" on page 9, download the base SDK, then each Android OS separately. The download provides an Android terminal command in Mac/Linux and an SDK *Setup.exe* application for Windows.

The Android emulator enables you to limit memory for the virtual device to better simulate the phone. In the Android Virtual Device Manager, select the device and click Edit (shown in Figure 1-5). On the hardware, click New and select Device RAM size from the Property drop-down menu.

iOS Simulator

Only available for Mac OS X, the iOS Simulator (*http://developer.apple.com/ iphone*) offers a free simulation environment including Mobile Safari. Be warned that the iPhone SDK is about 2 GB, so it will take a long time to download.

This is a simulator, not an emulator. There are no hardware emulation or performance indicators. It looks to see how your code is working and how your website is rendering, but it generally fails to measure website performance.

If you simply want to see what your design looks like, with no emulation or simulation, there are many tools like iPhoney (*http://www.marketcircle.com/iphoney/*) and iPadPeek (*http://ipadpeek.com/*) that simply open your website in a browser that looks like an older device model.

BlackBerry Simulator

BlackBerry simulators (*http://blackberry.com/developers*) for the Windows operating system include the proxy server, plug-ins for Eclipse and Visual Studio for web developers, and the simulators.

Windows Phone Emulator

The Windows Phone Emulator is only available on Windows-based computers. Windows Phone Emulator is a desktop application that emulates a Windows Phone device. You can download the Windows Phone SDK at *http://dev.window sphone.com/en-us/downloadsdk*. The current release and information about installation can be found at *http://bit.ly/16t5utu*.

Currently, the default emulator image in Visual Studio is Emulator WVGA 512 MB, which emulates a memory-constrained Windows Phone 8 phone.

Firefox OS Simulator

The Firefox OS Simulator add-on (*https://addons.mozilla.org/en-US/firefox/addon/firefox-os-simulator/*) for the Firefox browser is the emulator for Firefox OS, providing a Firefox OS–like environment that looks and feels like a mobile phone. Once installed, go to Web Developer→Firefox OS Simulator in your Firefox desktop browser.

Opera Mobile Emulator

The Opera Mobile Emulator for Windows, Mac, and Linux can be downloaded at *www.opera.com/developer/tools*.

Opera Mini Simulator

A full Opera Mini application of the current version of Opera Mini as a Java applet is available at *www.opera.com/mini/demo*.

These are the most prevalent mobile operating systems. Most mobile operating systems, like Symbian and WebOS, have SDKs you can load onto your desktop, enabling you to simulate their environment. Depending on your target market, you should test all of the operating systems your target audience is likely to use. For more emulators, visit *http://www.mobilexweb.com/emulators*.

Online Tools

To quickly assess your device's vital statistics that impact the basic media queries, open up *http://www.quirksmode.org/m/tests/widthtest.html* in your device's browser.

The W3C mobileOK Checker (*http://validator.w3.org/mobile/*) checks your website for best practices, and provides information and links to help make your site more mobile device friendly. mobiReady (*http://mobiready.com*) is an online tool leveraging the W3C mobileOK Checker, displaying the results in a way that is more likely to convince you to take action to make your site more mobile friendly.

Useful for mobile web development, HTTP testing, and privacy, the Modify Headers add-on for Firefox (*http://mzl.la/17bqALt*) enables you to modify—add, replace, and filter—HTTP request headers sent to web servers. Links to these resources (and all other resources listed in this book) are in the online chapter resources.

Phones

Testing on actual devices is an essential step of the development process, but buying a bunch of mobile devices can be quite an investment. Resizing browsers and using emulators won't replicate actual site performance, device capabilities, pixel density, and the impact of the mobile network.

If you are creating native applications, you obviously need to get devices with the operating systems you're developing for. In this book, we are developing with HTML5, CSS3, and JavaScript, not native, so our code will work in browsers on all devices. Although we're developing for the browser, we do need to test in many devices, including some on phone carrier networks. Always test your code in the real devices with real-world connections, including WiFi hotspots, 3G, 4G, and even EDGE. Take a bus or train ride and try accessing your application from various points while moving in the city and in the suburban and rural areas between bigger cities.

Browser labs

Testing on real mobile devices is a part of the development process that can't be omitted. There are many browser labs, so try to find one near you. If there aren't any device labs, get together with others to create one.

If you prefer to have your own device lab, you need devices of different sizes, operating systems, abilities, and browsers. You can create your own device lab with a cross-section of the mobile landscape fairly inexpensively. It is impossible to purchase every device, but you should try to get a sample of different sizes, browsers, and operating systems.

There are also virtual device labs such as DeviceAnywhere, and Nokia Remote Access. These are real devices that you can access remotely. As these are actual devices, if somebody is using one, you need to wait in the queue.

iOS

In North America, iOS devices account for only 5% of Internet traffic overall, with over 50% of mobile traffic.[5] If you don't already have an iOS device in your household, and your application is not solely targeted at impoverished populations in underdeveloped countries, invest in one.

---

5. *http://bit.ly/HaW2PV* and *http://bit.ly/1diKHLb*.

Acquire a device with the latest iOS operating system, and one with an older version of the operating system. You can acquire an older device on Craigslist or eBay for little money. Currently, only 1.8% of iOS users, or 0.13% of Internet users, are on iOS 4.3 or earlier, and 12.5% of iOS users, or 0.93% of Internet users, are on iOS 5.

When acquiring a device, you need the browser to work. That's it. If budget is an issue, cracked-screen devices can be acquired for next to nothing. One device should be a phone. The other can be a phone, iPad, or iPod touch.

Once you've acquired your iOS device(s), download Opera Mini, which is available for free through iTunes.

If all your iOS devices have high-resolution displays, make sure some of your other devices do not. Also, make sure that not all of your devices are phones—include a tablet or two.

Android

Android is the most popular and diverse mobile operating system worldwide. Android runs on a plethora of devices, including phones and tablets. Acquire at least two (preferably more) Android devices: a highly capable smartphone with a recent operating system and a bargain phone running an older version. At the time of this writing, although it's already archaic, Android 2.3 is still being sold in stores on cheap/free devices, and is currently the most popular version of Android, with 34% of the Android market, totaling 2.3% of global Internet users.[6]

In addition to multiple Android OS versions, get devices of different sizes, processing power, resolutions, and makers. On your Android device, you can add other browsers, including Chrome, Opera Mini and Mobile, Firefox Mobile, and Dolphin Mini and HD.

Windows

If you are going to invest in a Windows device, invest in the most recent operating system. The Windows Phone 7 was never hugely popular, but the Windows Phone 8 has the potential to be. Both have the Metro UI interface. In addition to testing your application to make sure your markup works, actually play with the Windows phone. The user interaction of the device is quite different from Android and iOS. You may realize that you will want to adjust some UI interactions to better match the default behaviors developed by using the Windows device.

BlackBerry

The BlackBerry 10 device has the best debugger of any mobile device, but definitely not the largest user base.

---

6. *http://developer.android.com/about/dashboards/index.html.*

There are more of the older BlackBerry devices on the market than the BlackBerry 10. BlackBerry users of both new and older devices surf the Web. I recommend getting a BB6 or BB7. Fortunately, older phones are inexpensive and it is good to have a nontouch device to test your websites on.

Prior to BB6, the browser was not WebKit based. There are fewer users of these really, really old devices. If your target market is likely to be on a BB5 or less, a third BlackBerry device may be in order.

Nokia

By Nokia, I mean the Symbian OS, not the Lumia Windows Phone.

Symbian, Series 40, Samsung, and to a lesser extent Sony Mobile and Motorola, are more common than Android, iOS, BlackBerry, and Windows in some countries. If I suggest a particular device, by the time this goes to print, my suggestion will be outdated. Just realize that internationally, Nokia is a huge player in the mobile market with massive reach. I recommend getting a feature phone that has D-pad input and a small screen so that you can get a sense of what a large percent of the world will see when accessing your site.

Kindle

Don't forget about the Kindle Fire with its WebKit-based Silk browser.

WebOS

WebOS has ceased being made, but is still being used. The Palm Pre or Pixi can be acquired for less than $30.

Automated Testing

The testing tools just listed help you test visually and manually. To really test properly, you have to rotate, zoom, pan, click, and scream in frustration. For appearance, you need to actually look at the rendered page in different device sizes, browsers, and operating systems. For static content, that may suffice, and tools like Adobe Edge can help.

For web applications, you likely need to automate testing. You need to continuously test your application to make sure the code actually works, testing all your events and results. There are several testing libraries for JavaScript.

Jasmine (*http://pivotal.github.io/jasmine/*) is a behavior-driven development framework. PhantomJS (*http://phantomjs.org*) is a headless WebKit, not a testing library, with native support for various web standards, including DOM handling, CSS Selectors, and JSON. You can download a pre-built binary for any OS at the PhantomJS website.

To leverage PhantomJS for automated, frontend tests, download CasperJS (*http://casperjs.org/*). To fake AJAX calls, you can use Sinon.JS (*http://sinonjs.org/*). Each site provides well-written documentation to get you up and running with these libraries for testing in WebKit. It doesn't solve the testing on mobile issue.

There are online testing tools. Some, like SauceLabs (*http://saucelabs.com*), enable you to test against hundreds of mobile and desktop browser/OS platforms.

Pick what is right for you and your application—but always test.

Now let's start coding so we have something to test.

CHAPTER 2

Upgrading to HTML5

HTML takes a few hours to learn and years of experience and discussion to master. Yes, most software engineers, designers, and even large numbers of high school students claim to know HTML, but they likely know only a few elements, and likely use those few elements incorrectly.

In this chapter, we're going to cover many of the sectioning elements of HTML5. By the time you're done reading this chapter, you should have a very good understanding of the semantics of HTML5. I can't teach you everything about HTML in three chapters. Truthfully, I am still learning HTML—and not just because HTML5 is still an unfinished spec. With the specifications being incomplete, there will likely still be several changes. But don't worry about that either. Likely, what has been implemented in browsers will stay the same with just some nuanced differences.

I hope that in addition to learning about the various elements, their attributes, their semantic meaning, and their purpose, you take from this an awareness that you know less about HTML than you thought: the more you learn about HTML, the more you realize how much more there is to learn.

We're going to cover elements, briefly. While a chapter could be written about each element, we do have a lot of ground to cover in a few not-so-short chapters. We'll cover enough for you to know how to use each element, and for you to at least know what you don't know.

The first thing to know is that there is no space in the term HTML5: it is HTML5, not HTML 5.

You see? You've learned something! You're already ahead of the game. Let's dive in.

HTML5 Syntax

HTML5 is very similar to HTML 4 and XHTML. Most of the elements supported in both are still supported in HTML5. Only deprecated tags and attributes have been removed. For the most part, if your document validated as HTML 4 Strict or XHTML, your document will be valid HTML5.[1] The syntaxes of HTML and XHTML are slightly different, but both are supported. Simply change your HTML 4.01 or XHTML doctype to `<!DOCTYPE html>` and it will validate as HTML5 (more on doctype later).

HTML5 improves upon HTML 4 and XHTML, encompassing the elements of previous versions, removing deprecated elements, adding some new elements, and redefining or fine-tuning yet other elements.

The authors of the HTML5 specifications looked into what developers were already doing on the Web: what document sections all sites tended toward, what classes and IDs they gave those components, what scripts most site authors reiterated, and which library features had proliferated to ubiquity.

HTML5 attempts to handle what individual developers have been doing on their own: creating a standard, detailing how browsers are supposed to handle these standards, and how browsers should handle developer markup when their code is, um, less than standard. The HTML5 specifications detail precisely how browsers are supposed to handle, or interpret, every instance of correct and incorrect code. Through this attention to minutiae, one of the goals of HTML5 is to inform browsers how to handle every possible scenario, so browsers construct identical DOMs from the same markup, and so that developers don't continue to waste bandwidth dealing with browser differences.

Personally, I would like to see stricter standards. My view is that instead of browsers leniently interpreting bad code, developers should code correctly. You're reading this, so I assume you're in the "good code" camp. Good! That's what you're going to learn.

Elements

A web page is made up of a series of elements. Some elements are empty, other elements contain text, while others contain other elements (or both elements and text). Most elements can contain child elements or text nodes. Those that can't contain children, such as images and `meta` elements, are called *empty elements*.

---

1. See *http://www.w3.org/TR/html5-diff/* for changed elements and attributes, as well as obsolete elements and attributes.

As shown in Figure 2-1, an element is a construct consisting of an opening tag, some optional (and occasionally required) attributes, usually some content, a closing tag, and, if you're coding XHTML style, an optional forward slash to self-close the tag for empty elements such as `<img>` or `<input>`.

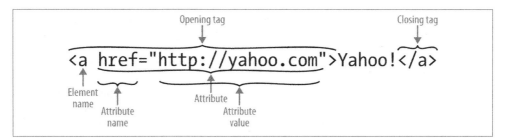

Figure 2-1. The components that make up an element

In prior versions of HTML, inline elements could only contain other inline elements and text. Depending on the element, block-level elements could contain other block-level elements, inline elements, and/or text. Their descendant elements, like the ancestor elements, are also made up of elements, attributes, and text.

 With CSS, you can alter the appearance of any phrase element to display as a block, and force a block or sectioning element to appear inline. (Note that I am using *inline* still. In HTML5, inline refers to presentation, not to element type.)

In HTML5, we've said good riddance to the notion of inline versus block elements—naming conventions based on presentation. In HTML5, elements are defined as sectioning, heading, phrase, embedded, flow, metadata, and interactive elements. Semantically, however, some of the ideas remain the same. For example, sectioning elements should not be located inside of phrase elements.

 When choosing an element, choose the most appropriate element based on semantics, not based on default browser rendering. While you really *can* use any element for any stylistic purpose, you shouldn't. Each element has semantic meaning.

Attributes

All elements can have attributes. Some elements have required attributes. An example of an attribute is the `href` attribute of the `<a>` element, as shown in Figure 2-1. Attributes are typically name/value pairs, with the value optional for Boolean attributes.[2] Attributes provide additional information to the rendering engine about the element, and are found in the opening element tag and not in the closing tag.

There are several attributes that are global to almost all HTML elements—including the core, or global, attributes and the internationalization attributes (covered in the next section)—and others that are more element-specific, which will be described in Chapter 3 when we cover the elements that they are modifying.

Global and Internationalization Attributes

HTML5 has added several internationalization and core attributes that can be applied to almost any element. The id, class, title, style, lang, and dir attributes continue to be supported on all elements. HTML5 adds accesskey, hidden, and tabindex, along with five proposed interactive attributes, contenteditable, contextmenu, spell check, draggable, and dropzone, to the list of core attributes. The attributes are discussed next.

In addition to the global attributes, all elements can also have microdata attributes, WIA-ARIA roles and aria- attributes, and custom data attributes, which are your own attributes that are written as data-*, where * is your own creation. The data- prefix was added to HTML5 to allow developers to create attributes that won't conflict with future versions of HTML. data-* attributes are described in the section on page 33. Microdata and ARIA accessibility attributes are described in Chapter 6.

id

The id attribute is a unique identifier. No two elements should have the same id in a single document, and each element can only have up to a single id. In HTML5, id values must be at least one character long and contain no spaces. This differs from previous versions when the value of the id had to begin with a letter in the range A–Z or a–z and could be followed by letters (A–Za–z), digits (0–9), hyphens (-), underscores (_), colons (:), and periods (.).

I recommend limiting your IDs to letters and digits only, but whichever naming convention you choose to use, the important thing is to be consistent.

---

2. Boolean attributes are attributes that are either true if set or false if not. XHTML examples include readonly="readonly", checked="checked", and disabled="disabled", which in HTML5 can (and should) be written as readonly, checked, or disabled, respectively.

The id attribute is generally optional. However, it is required for internal page anchoring and inside form elements when implementing explicit labels. Explicit labels are associated with form elements via the label's for attribute and the form element's id attribute. Note that the id attribute is not necessary on form elements nested within an *implicit label*. Labels and the id attribute are discussed in Chapter 4.

The id attribute is also helpful, though perhaps used a little too heavily, as an anchor for targeting with JavaScript. The id attribute, if included, can be used in CSS to target elements. However, due to the high value, or specificity, of the id in the CSS cascade, even though id selectors perform a tinge better, id values should be sparsely used in CSS selectors. We'll discuss all of that in Chapter 6. Suffice it to say that by the time you finish this book, you'll understand that you can target any element on a page with CSS3 selectors without the use of id selectors.

class

A class is a name of a classification, or list of names of classifications, to which the element belongs. The class attribute specifies the element to be a member of one or more classes. Unlike the id attribute, any number of elements can share the same class or classes. An element may have multiple, space-separated classes.

In terms of the CSS cascade, the order of class names within the class attribute doesn't matter. The order in the stylesheet, however, does matter (this too will be discussed in Chapter 6):

```
<a href="http://google.com" class="external popup search">link text</a>
```

title

The title attribute provides a human-readable description for any element to which it is applied. The title attribute is often implemented as a "tooltip" on some visual browsers, but other browsers, especially mobile browsers, don't display the title attribute. While screen readers can be set to support the title attribute, most screen readers do not read the title attribute value as a default setting, so the title attribute cannot be relied upon for improving accessibility.

> There are some elements for which the title attribute is required, such as <abbr>, for which the value of the title attribute expands the shortened term. Otherwise, the title attribute is generally optional.

While the title attribute is useful as an attribute for links, images, frames, and multimedia elements, it can come in handy as a method of providing small bits of hidden information that can be displayed based on user interaction. For example, it is possible to extract the content of the title attribute with CSS and create generated content for "tooltip" pop-ups by including the title value as generated content on a ::before or ::after pseudoelement.

While values of the title attribute can be used for nifty tricks for progressive enhancement, due to the inaccessible nature of such a trick, it should not be relied upon for providing important information. And, because the user can access it, only use title if the content of the title is useful and appropriate. If you are adding content to the title attribute to enable your analytics or add codes for use by your JavaScript, don't! Crafty abuses of the rel and title attributes are no longer necessary (and never were appropriate) with the addition of the custom data attributes, described in the section on page 33.

style

The style attribute allows you to specify style rules inline for a single occurrence of an element. This attribute can come in handy for quick prototyping. Other than prototyping, there should never be a need to use this attribute, as web standards dictate to separate content from presentation!

An additional note: when using an inspector to look at code in tools such as Web Inspector for Safari or Chrome, Firebug for Firefox, Dragonfly for Opera, or F12 in IE, styles that are added with JavaScript, or through the debugger interface, will appear inline as the value of the style attribute. This is dynamically generated. The browser may do it. You shouldn't!

lang

The lang attribute is one of the two global internationalization attributes (dir being the other). The primary language of a web page is set using the lang attribute on the <html> element, by using the Content-Language HTTP header, or the http-equiv="language" attribute. Used for internationalization or defining nondefault language sections of content, the lang attribute specifies the language of an element's attribute values and its content, including all contained elements that do not specify their own lang attribute.

The lang attribute enables search engines to index content by its language, and allows screen readers to use international pronunciation rules.

The lang attribute enables styling of text depending on language. The <q> element is supposed to render the appropriate quotation mark for the language defined in the lang attribute, but this is not well supported.

dir

Often used in conjunction with the lang attribute, the dir attribute can be used to change the direction of text when writing Arabic, Hebrew, or other right-to-left languages. The default value of the dir attribute is ltr (left to right). If your web page is

---

primarily in one of those right-to-left languages, set the primary direction using the `dir` attribute on the `<html>` element.

Within the body of the page, if you have content that is in a direction other than the default of the page, you can change the direction of the text with the `dir` attribute. While not explicitly required, I recommend including the `title` and `lang` attributes whenever you include the `dir` attribute on an element. Generally, the `dir` attribute is used for changing parts of your text to right-to-left languages. Including the `lang` attribute is necessary to inform search engines, screen readers, and other assistive technologies that the language has changed. The `title` attribute provides a way for you to include a translation of the content in the main language of your website. These attributes provide ways of making your web content accessible not only to those with disabilities, but also to your main "visually impaired" user: Google!

Note that `dir` is slightly different in HTML5, which has introduced a third value: `auto`. Possible values of the `dir` attribute include `rtl`, `ltr`, and `auto`.

HTML 4 Attributes Made Core in HTML5

The preceding attributes were global, or core, attributes in previous versions of (X)HTML, and continue to be. There are also two accessibility attributes supported on interactive elements that are now global attributes in HTML5. These are covered in the following sections.

tabindex

The `tabindex` attribute was included in prior specifications on interactive elements such as links and form elements, allowing the developer to set the sequence by which these element types receive focus. HTML5 has expanded the role of `tabindex` to include any HTML element.

Many people use mice to navigate through a website, clicking on links and form elements to engage the interactive elements. Others navigate through the page using a keyboard; clicking the Tab key and moving the focus from one interactive element to the next. On nontouch phones, users will navigate through focusable elements in four directions with the navigational or directional pad (D-pad, for short). On smartphones, most users generally touch the links they want to follow or the form elements they want to enter. Once they've finished entering data into a form element, many dynamic keyboards provide for a Next button to forward to the next form element. By default, only links and form fields receive focus through this method. The sequence of the current element to the element receiving focus via the right button on the navigation pad, the Next button, or the Tab key is the order of the form elements in the source code, unless the native sequence has been usurped by the `tabindex` attribute.

In HTML5, the global nature of the `tabindex` attribute adds *focusability* to all elements—not just form elements and links. The attribute takes as its value an integer. As the user tabs, the elements with the `tabindex` attribute will receive focus in sequential order based on the value of the `tabindex` attribute's numeric value—for `tabindex`es that have a positive value.

Don't use `tabindex` with positive values unless you are able to provide `tabindex` values to every interactive element on the page *plus* have good reason to rearrange the order, *plus* be certain that you will be able to maintain the correct order through the life of the application. Instead, mark up the page in the correct order. The default tab order is the same as the source order. Rearranging the tab order of a page can be very confusing to the user, and can lead to very bad user experiences. It's best to lay out the page in an order that makes sense, and never use the `tabindex` attribute. Using the default tab (and therefore source) generally creates the best user experience.

So, if you're not supposed to change the order of the page, why has `tabindex` become a global variable? The `tabindex` attribute has become global to enable programmatic focus on all elements, including noninteractive elements, generally via JavaScript and/or keyboard focus.

Since we don't want to actually change the tab or keyboard focus order from the source order of the page, the only values of `tabindex` should be 0 or −1. The value of `tabindex="-1"` (any negative value works, but −1 is the convention) can be used for programmatic focus and `tabindex="0"` for accessibility reasons only, if you want to provide keyboard access to an element other than a link or form element without changing the order of the page.

 You may be wondering what `tabindex` has to do with the mobile realm, where you don't generally tab to navigate. Note that when you fill out a form element, the displayed keyboard on some devices includes a Next button at the top. Also, just like you want to enable focus via JavaScript on the desktop, you may want to do so on the phone. And, just like on the desktop, not all users have a pointing device. Many visually impaired people use smartphones, especially the iPhone in the United States. In that way, `tabindex` helps with accessibilty.

accesskey

The `accesskey` is similar to the `tabindex`, except instead of navigating the page by tabbing through to the element with the next higher `tabindex` value in sequential order, the focus moves directly to the element for which the activated access key has been set. Think of it as a keyboard shortcut.

The `accesskey` attribute's value creates keyboard shortcuts. For example, `<input ac cesskey="s" name="search" type="text"/>` creates a search input box with an accesskey of s. When the user presses on the letter "s," the focus moves to the search input.

The value of the accesskey attribute is one or more characters separated by a space. Generally, it's just one character, but the specifications allow for more than one keyboard shortcut for an element. The syntax for the value of accesskey is similar to the class attribute in that the value of this attribute is an ordered set of space-separated tokens. However, here the order matters; tokens beyond the first are considered fallbacks for user agents that can't support the initial values.

While tabindex and accesskey were originally highly regarded as possible solutions for accessibility concerns, they aren't the accessibility solution that everyone had hoped for. As mentioned previously, tabindex can create a bad user experience by altering the expected sequence of the focus of the page. Similarly, accesskey can interfere with default behaviors and shortcuts set in the client's browser.

As of yet, I have found no use for the accesskey on smartphones, but because we're learning HTML5, I've included it here. The accesskey used to be helpful before the advent of smartphones, when navigating websites on tiny old mobile device browsers was a chore.

New to HTML5: Global Accessibility and Interactive Attributes

HTML5 includes several new attributes, including some new global attributes, which are included in this section. We'll cover some of the new element-specific attributes and values when we discuss the elements to which they relate in the next two chapters.

hidden

When included, the hidden attribute indicates that the element is not yet, or is no longer, relevant. Supporting browsers do not display elements with the hidden attribute, including display:none; in the user-agent stylesheet. It is best not to use this attribute simply to *hide* elements from the user since it has semantic meaning: it indicates that the content encompassed in this hidden attribute is either outdated or otherwise not relevant.

contenteditable

The contenteditable attribute indicates whether an element is editable or not. When included, user changes to your content are not saved, but they do change the DOM, so you can capture the changes and send them back to the server to be saved. The contenteditable attribute is supported in all of the desktop browsers and all mobile devices except Opera Mini, with support starting in Android 3.0 and iOS 5.

When an element has the contenteditable attribute set, the dynamic keyboards on touch devices should pop open to enable editing.

contextmenu

The contextmenu enables the linkage of the element with a <menu> that provides more context to that element or <command>. It takes as its value the value of the id of the <menu> you want associated with it. This attribute has yet to be supported in any browser other than experimentally in Chrome, so the <menu> and <command> elements are not part of this book.

draggable

The draggable attribute indicates whether an element is draggable or not. You may have noticed that you can drag images in most desktop browsers, but you can't drop them. This is the default draggable behavior in action. For the draggable attribute to be useful, it should be used in conjunction with JavaScript event handlers such as dragstart, drag, dragenter, dragleave, dragover, drop, and dragend. Mobile browsers, other than IE10, don't support drag-and-drop, so the API is not covered in this book.

dropzone

It's one thing to drag an element, but what do you do after dragging it? HTML5 provides us with a dropzone attribute that specifies what types of content can be dropped on an element. You can move, copy, or create a link to the originally dragged content using the move, copy, and link attribute values, respectively. Since drag-and-drop is not well supported on mobile browsers, we won't be discussing it further in this book.

spellcheck

The spellcheck attribute indicates whether an element is to have its spelling and grammar checked or not. By default, most smartphones and tablets autocorrect text areas as you type, but not always well—there are several sites making fun of some of the "corrections." While they don't support the spellcheck attribute, they do support autocorrect.

Interestingly, although the default behavior of iOS is to autocorrect text, if the autocorrect attribute is added to an input of type text, it actually does not spell check; it will autocorrect only if the attribute is not included.

ARIA accessibility attributes

HTML5 supports the Accessible Rich Internet Applications (ARIA) accessibility module attributes of role and aria-*. ARIA is a separate module, and not part of the HTML5 specifications. With live regions, roles, and ARIA states and properties, WAI-ARIA can help improve the accessibility of dynamically updating content and hijacked elements.

When interacting with rich Internet applications, the user visiting with a screen reader may be having one part of the page read aloud while another part of the page is dynamically updated. ARIA live regions can help indicate to the user that a part of the page—a part that doesn't currently have focus—has updated. With the arialive values of `assertive`, `polite`, or the default `off`, ARIA provides a way for the site author to interrupt the screen reader to inform the user that part of the page has been updated. Associated attributes include `aria-atomic,` `aria-busy` and `aria-relevant`.

The ARIA `role` attribute enables the creation of a semantic structure on repurposed elements—for example, elements repurposed into a `grid`, `listbox`, `menu`, `menubar`, `tablist`, `toolbar`, `tree`, or `treegrid` can be identified as such—making seemingly nonsemantic markup accessible, usable, and interoperable with assistive technologies. While full support of the new HTML5 elements (see Chapter 3) by screen readers may make some of the ARIA structure roles irrelevant, adding the `role` values of `article`, `application`, `banner`, `complementary`, `contentinfo`, `document`, `form`, `heading`, `main`, `navigation`, and `search` to your pages now can help with screen readers that are supportive of ARIA, but not yet HTML5.

Two notes about roles: (1) once set, a `role` should not be dynamically changed, since this will confuse the assistive technology, and (2) roles take precedence over element default semantic meaning.

In addition to the `role` attribute and its many values, ARIA also provides for state and property attributes. There are state attributes `aria-disabled`, `aria-busy`, `aria-expanded`, `aria-hidden`, and property attributes such as `aria-describedby`, `aria-haspopup`, and `aria-labelledby`, which provide additional information on dynamic widgets and repurposed elements. It is best practice to use the most semantic existing element for the job, but when you must absolutely use a specific element for a nonintended purpose (such as a tree menu), ARIA should be used.

Custom data attributes with data-*

In HTML5, you can create your own attributes. While you could create your own attributes before, your markup would not validate. HTML5 introduces the custom data attributes, where, as an author, you can define the name of the attribute.

Developers have been including invalid attributes and/or abusing the `title` and `rel` attributes to provide data for interactivity. Instead of misusing HTML 4 attributes like `rel` and `title`, simply create an attribute with the `data-` prefix, and your code will validate.

For example, in our CubeeDoo game, we want to maintain the position and value of every card so that when we compare them, we can see if the first flipped card matches the second flipped card, and also to maintain state, in conjunction with localStorage, when we pause the game and leave the screen. We could keep track of every card as an array in our JavaScript. Instead, we created the `data-position` and `data-value` attributes in our markup, dynamically updating the `data-value` for each new board setup:

```
<div id="board" class="level1">
    <div data-value="0" data-position="1">
        <div class="face"></div>
        <div class="back"></div>
    </div>
    <div data-value="0" data-position="2">
        <div class="face"></div>
        <div class="back"></div>
    </div>
    <div data-value="0" data-position="3">
        <div class="face"></div>
        <div class="back"></div>
    </div>
    <div data-value="0" data-position="4">
        <div class="face"></div>
        <div class="back"></div>
    </div>
    ...
    <div data-value="0" data-position="24">
        <div class="face"></div>
        <div class="back"></div>
    </div>
</div>
```

When the user selects two cards, the `data-value` values are compared. If they match, we have a match. The `data-position` attribute enables us to track the location of each card, changing the `data-value` of the two cards to 0 when matched. We also use the value of the `data-value` attribute to style the front of the cards using attribute selectors, covered in Chapter 7.

Prior to having the `data-*` attributes, we may have structured our cards with `<div class="..." rel="15" title="4">` or similar. While that `title` might have validated, it was unhelpful and would even allow people to easily cheat (you can still cheat with an element inspector in this game, but showing a tooltip would have made the game a bit too easy) when hovered on the desktop. The `data-` prefix has been reserved for this purpose to avoid clashes with future versions of HTML. Custom data attributes are intended to store custom data private to the page or application. The only requirement on these attributes is that they are not used for user-agent extensions like `-moz-` or `-webkit-`.

Dataset API. The custom data attributes come with the `dataset` API. With the `dataset` API, you can capture the attribute/value pairs even if the custom data attribute name is dynamically generated (i.e., you don't know what the attribute name is after the dash):

```
1          // get all the cards values and positions
2          // use dataset to get value for all the cards.
3          currCards = document.querySelectorAll('#board > div');
4          for (i = 0; i < qbdoo.cards; i++) {
5              cardinfo.push(currCards[i].dataset);
6          }
7          currentState.cardPositions = JSON.stringify(cardinfo);
```

While we know what attributes we've set, we are using the `dataset` API instead of `getAttribute()` to teach the API when we extract the values to pause the game. The snippet from the `qbdoo.pauseGame` method uses a query selector to capture all the cards (line 3), then iterates through the cards using the `dataset` API to capture the key/value pairs of any dataset attributes present as a `DOMStringMap` as an array value. The last line (line 7) converts the key/value pairs we've captured into a JSON string. Instead, we could have also iterated through the deck :

```
1          for (i = 0; i < qbdoo.cards; i++) {
2              for (key in currCards[i].dataset) {
3                  deck[key] = currCards[i].dataset[key];
4              }
5              cardinfo[i] = deck;
6          }
```

itemid, itemprop, itemref, itemscope, and itemtype

There are five other global attributes related to *microdata* that have been removed from the main part of the HTML5 specification and are now part of the microdata specifications (*http://www.w3.org/TR/microdata/*), including `itemid`, `itemprop`, `itemref`, `itemscope`, and `itemtype`. I've included them here so you have all the global attributes listed together. These attributes are explained in "Microdata API" on page 187.

HTML Element/Attribute Syntax

We've talked about elements and attributes, but we haven't discussed how to include them. Syntax is important, so let's dive in.

To include an element in your web page, you include an opening and closing tag. Opening tags start with a left angle bracket (or less-than sign, <), followed by the element name, followed by the right angle bracket (or greater-than sign, >).

Correct:

```
<a>
<p>
<div>
```

Incorrect:

```
<m> <!-- there is no 'm' element' -->
< div><!-- there can be no space before the element name -->
```

If there are any attributes, they are included in the opening tag, after the element name, separated by a space. All attributes are name/value pairs. Unlike XHTML, HTML5 Boolean attribute values don't need to be explicitly declared. The browser defaults to true when a Boolean attribute is present but the value is omitted.

Even though HTML5 does not require it, for ease of legibility and best practices, the attribute should be in all lowercase and the value should be in quotes. Depending on the type of attribute, the value may be case-sensitive.[3]

An attribute can only appear once for each element's opening tag. While you likely know that, and don't include an attribute multiple times in elements on purpose, it is a common cause of validation errors, so take this as a friendly reminder.

Correct:

```
<a href="http://www.standardista.com">
<p class="racket-tailed drongo">
<div id="content">
```

Valid, but not best practices:

```
<a href=http://www.yahoo.com>
<!-- best to quote all attribute values -->
```

Not valid:

```
<p class="racket-tailed" class="drongo">
 <!-- no duplicated attributes allowed. -->
<p class=Racket-Tailed Drongo>
 <!-- while HTML5 does not require quotes around all attributes, it is
best practice. And, if there is a space in the attribute value, the
quotes are required to unambiguously delineate the start and end of
the attribute's value! -->
```

To end, or close, the element, you include a left angle bracket and a forward slash, followed by the element name (that matches the element in the opening tag) and a right angle bracket. If the element is an empty element (see the section "Self-Closing Elements" on page 37), you can end the element by adding the optional forward slash immediately before the right angle bracket in the opening tag:

```
<a href="http://standardista.com/mobile/ch2">Files for this chapter</a>
<p class="racket-tailed drongo">Exotic Asian Bird</p>
<div id="content">. . .</div>
```

In between the opening and closing tags you put the content of the element, which may include other elements and/or text nodes. Nest your elements correctly! If you include

---

3. Values defined in the specifications are generally not case-sensitive, but strings that you define, such as IDs and class names, are case-sensitive.

an element as a child of another element, the nested child element must be both opened and closed before the closing tag of the parent element:

```
<div id="content">
 <p class="files">
  Examples in the <a href="http://standardista.com/mobile">
  online chapter resources</a>
 </p>
</div>
```

In this example, the <div> element contains everything from the first < to the last >, including the descendant paragraph and anchor element. Notice that the <a> is both opened and closed within the opening and closing <p> tags, and, in turn, the <p> element is both opened and closed within the <div>.

Self-Closing Elements

All elements have closing tags, except self-closing elements, also known as empty or void elements, which, in XHTML syntax, we self close with a trailing backslash.

Empty elements cannot contain nested elements or text. Being self-closing, they don't include an end or closing tag. You can include a slash before the right angle bracket of the opening tag if you wish. While HTML5 does not require elements to be closed, XHTML syntax does require it via the trailing slash. Self-closing, or empty elements, include:

`<img/>`	Image
` `	Line break
`<meta/>`	Metadata
`<hr/>`	Thematic break
`<base/>`	Base URL and default target for resources and links
`<link/>`	Link
`<keygen/>`	Cryptographic key/pair generator form control
`<area/>`	Image map area
`<col/>`	Table column
`<command/>`	Menu command
`<embed/>`	Plug-in
`<input/>`	Form control
`<param/>`	Parameter for object
`<source/>`	Audio or video media source
`<track/>`	Timed media tracking
`<wbr/>`	Linebreaking opportunity

Best Practices

There are several coding rules required for XHTML that were optional or even unsupported in HTML. While HTML5 supports both coding formats, here are some nonrequired best practices:

Use lowercase for markup

In XHTML, the element tags must all be lowercase as must all the attribute names. While HTML5 supports camelCase and everything else, please use all lowercase markup. Nothing in the W3C states that attribute values need to be lowercase, but some, like id, are case-sensitive, so stick to lowercase.

Quote all attributes

In XHTML, all attribute values must be encased in single or double quotes. In HTML5, only attribute values with spaces or special characters are required to be in quotes. Make me happy: quote all attributes.

Close all elements

In XHTML, every opening tag must have a closing tag. Empty elements such as <img/> and <br /> must be self-closing. In HTML5, some tags can be left unclosed. While omitting the closing element reduces the number of characters on a page, it can make your markup harder to read and therefore harder to maintain. Some speakers/blog posts recommend omitting end tags to reduce the number of characters to make smaller files for mobile. The few bytes saved are not worth the risk. Reducing the number of DOM elements will have more of an impact than reducing the number of characters in this way. Make me happy: close all elements.

In terms of trailing slashes to close elements, you can include them or you can omit them. Whichever you choose, however, be consistent.

Nest all elements

All tags must be properly nested: if you start tag <a> and then start, or nest, a , you must close the tag before you close the </a> tag. Nest your tags correctly: your markup will render as expected, it will be easier to troubleshoot, and your markup will be valid (plus, you'll make me happy).

Provide values for all non-Boolean attributes

In XHTML, all attributes must be coded as attribute/value pairs, even Boolean values. The default selected option in XHTML should be written selected="selected". In HTML5, the same can simply be coded as selected. In HTML5, providing values for Boolean attributes is not necessary, since including the attribute property makes a Boolean value true even if the value of the attribute is false in most browsers. Whether you choose to include or not include Boolean values, be consistent with your decision. If you include Boolean values, always include them. If you omit them, always omit them.

Don't include an empty string, ="", for a Boolean (or even non-Boolean) attribute; rather, always include the value.

 Note that if you include a Boolean value, it will be true even if you set the value to the empty string. If you want it to be false, you will have to use removeAttribute(attributeName) and not se tAttribute(attributeName, '') since the empty string will result in the Boolean attribute being true.

Note that the empty string can have unintended consequences, especially when it comes to the form attribute as will see in Chapter 3.

Use the most semantically correct element for the job
In XHTML, elements need to be coded in a semantic manner. Tables and forms cannot be included in paragraphs. Form elements, being phrase elements, need to be contained within a semantic block-level element, such as a paragraph or table cell. Yes, you can use spans and divs to contain everything on your page, but if a header is a header, use an <h1-6> tag.

The Required Components

Elements are the building blocks that make up the Web. Without the content of a site, CSS and JavaScript would have nothing to enhance. But, in reality, for a web page to be valid XHTML it only requires five components:

- The document type declaration, or DTD
- The HTML root element: <html></html>
- The head of the document, a direct child of html: <head></head>
- The document title, found in the head: <title></title>
- The body of the document, a direct child of html: <body></body>

In other words, the minimum required for a valid HTML5 document using XHTML syntax is:

```
<!DOCTYPE html>
<html>
  <head>
   <meta charset="utf-8"/>
   <title>Blank Document</title>
  </head>
  <body>
  </body>
</html>
```

I've included the `charset` `<meta>` element, which is not required if you have the correct HTTP headings set on your server. If you don't have control over your server, consider it required as well.

In truth, HTML5 doesn't even require that many elements for a document to be valid. Browsers implicitly include `<html>`, `<head>`, and `<body>` if omitted. The shortest possible HTML5 document is actually:

```
<!DOCTYPE html>
<title>blank document</title>
```

Notice in Figure 2-2 that the browser includes the missing tags. When you omit `<html>`, `<head>`, `<body>`, or closing tags, the browser will render the document correctly, adding the nodes as rendered into the DOM and adding closing tags.

Figure 2-2. When you omit <html>, <head>, and <body>, the browser will render the document correctly, adding the nodes as rendered into the DOM (the HTML provided is above; the rendered document is below)

Yes, you can fit an entire HTML5 document inside a 140-character tweet. Just because you can omit what were once three of the only five required elements on a page doesn't mean you should. For ease of legibility and maintenance, especially by others, pick a coding style and stick with it: preferably code in XHTML-style syntax, and include the five elements.

Let's look at the five "required" components in greater detail.

The Document Type Declaration

The Document Type Declaration, doctype or DTD, informs the browser what markup syntax you are using so that the browser knows what to expect and how to handle it.

This is always the first line that should be sent to the browser, with the exception of the XML prologue, if parsing as XML. The previous example uses HTML5's DTD, which is the shortest, and the point of this book, but there are others as shown in Table 2-1.

Table 2-1. HTML 4, XHTML, and HTML5 doctypes

Page type	Document Type Declaration (DTD)
HTML 4.01 Transitional	`<!DOCTYPE HTML PUBLIC "-//W3C//DTD HTML 4.01 Transitional//EN" "http://www.w3.org/TR/HTML 4/loose.dtd">`
HTML 4.01 Strict	`<!DOCTYPE HTML PUBLIC "-//W3C//DTD HTML 4.01//EN" "http://www.w3.org/TR/HTML 4/strict.dtd">`
XHTML 1.0 Transitional	`<!DOCTYPE html PUBLIC "-//W3C//DTD XHTML 1.0 Transitional//EN" "http://www.w3.org/TR/xhtml1/DTD/xhtml1-transitional.dtd">`
XHTML 1.0 Strict	`<!DOCTYPE html PUBLIC "-//W3C//DTD XHTML 1.0 Strict//EN" "http://www.w3.org/TR/xhtml1/DTD/xhtml1-strict.dtd">`
XHTML 1.1	`<!DOCTYPE html PUBLIC "-//W3C//DTD XHTML 1.1//EN" "http://www.w3.org/TR/xhtml11/DTD/xhtml11.dtd">`
HTML5	`<!DOCTYPE html>`[a]

[a] Like the rest of HTML5, the doctype is not case-sensitive.

While you may have been using an XHTML DTD for 10 years, chances are you still copy and paste it into your documents, because you have yet to memorize it. Me too! After typing the HTML5 doctype once, I've never had to look it up again.

All modern mobile browsers support all of the HTML and XHTML DTDs, including the new, shorter HTML5 doctype declaration.

If you're concerned about how your old code will fare with the new HTML5 doctype, don't worry.[4] If your web page validated as HTML 4 or XHTML Strict, your markup is valid HTML5. HTML5-supporting browsers should provide for backward compatibility of all previous HTML and XHTML versions, including deprecated elements. However, just because the formerly deprecated elements are supported by the browser doesn't mean you should use them! While <center> and <font> may render as intended, it doesn't pass as valid or as good code![5] To ensure consistent, clean, and extensible code, I recommend using XHTML syntax including quoting all attribute values and closing all elements. HTML5 allows for lazy coding practices, but don't be a lazy coder!

The <html> element

The <html> element is the root element of an HTML document. While it is optional in HTML5, it's required when using XHTML syntax. HTML 4 transitional does not require

---

4. The HTML5 DTD throws older IE desktop browsers into quirks mode.

5. Obsolete features are listed at *http://bit.ly/16t5Z6L*.

the <html> element, and neither does HTML5, but we want to write good, clean, standards-compliant code: so, for all intents and purposes, it is required and is written as shown in Table 2-2.

The <html> element has two children nested in it: <head> and <body>. It's good practice (but not required) to include the lang attribute in the HTML element.

Table 2-2. HTML element and required by page type

Page type	HTML element
HTML 4.01 Transitional	`<html>`
HTML 4.01 Strict	`<html lang="en">`
HTML5	
XHTML 1.0 Transitional	`<html xmlns="http://www.w3.org/1999/xhtml">`
XHTML 1.0 Strict	`<html lang="en" xmlns="http://www.w3.org/1999/xhtml">`
XHTML 1.1	

HTML5 provides for a new attribute on the <html> element. The manifest attribute, when included, takes as its value the URL of the manifest file. Application cache, the manifest file, and offline applications are discussed in Chapter 6.

Some HTML5 script tools like modernizr add classes to the opening <html> element. This is completely legal. With the application cache, modernizr script for feature detection, and a language declaration, my opening <html> tag often looks like this:

```
<html lang="en" manifest="cache.appcache" class="no-js">
```

We covered the lang attribute earlier. We'll cover the manifest attribute in offline and storage in Chapter 6. The no-js class should be included if you are using modernizr[6] to test for native implementation of the various web technologies discussed in this book.

The <head> element

The <head> of the document contains important information that, other than the <title> element, is not displayed directly in the browser window.[7] While the contents of the <head> are generally not displayed, most browsers display the title, which is the only required element for a valid HTML5 document, in the tab or other browser chrome. The other contents of the <head> element inform the browser how to render the page and "speaks" to search engine spiders about the content of the page. In terms of changes between HTML 4 and HTML5, the never used profile attribute of the <head> element is not included in the proposed HTML5 specifications.

---

6. modernizr (*http://modernizr.com/*) is a JavaScript library that feature detects HTML5 and CSS3 browser support in your users' browsers.

7. It is possible to display the contents of the <head> to the user with CSS.

`<head>` is the parent element for the required `<title>`, and the optional `<style>`, `<script>`, `<link>`, `<meta>`, and `<base>` elements.

The `<title>` element

The `<title>` element is *required* and must include the closing `</title>` tag. Your page can validate without `<head>`, `<body>`, or even `<html>` tags, but will not validate without the required `<title>`, and won't parse if the closing tag is missing. Your `<body>` can be empty, and you can display no content to the user. Even the `<title>` can contain no text, but it's still required!

The contents of the `<title>` tag should define the overall content of your document. While the `<title>` may seem unimportant to the layout of your web page, the `<title>` is the most important element of your document when it comes to search engines.

Note how the contents of the `<title>` tag appear in the browser chrome, as seen in Figure 2-3. While this may be a nonfactor as compared to the `<title>`'s importance in search engine optimization (SEO) on the desktop, when you're looking at the tiny screen of a cell phone, it can get ugly fast, so choose your title wisely.

Figure 2-3. The content of the `<title>` element displayed in the browser chrome of iOS Safari and Firefox OS

The `<body>` element

We've added a `<title>`, but we still have a blank web page. All the content that you want to display on your website needs to be in the body of the page, encompassed in a single `<body>` element. The `<body>` is the second and last of the two child elements of the root `<html>` element.

There are several presentational attributes for the body element that were deprecated in XHTML. HTML5 goes along with that ingenious XHTML tradition: HTML5 has none of the presentational attributes that were in HTML 4, like `align`, `bgcolor`, and background and link coloring, since their functions are better handled by CSS. The only attributes you will likely be adding to the `<body>` element are `id` and `class`, and `lang` and `dir` if necessary.

When viewing the source of a web page, you'll often encounter event handlers in the opening <body> tag, such as onload="doSomething();". In general, you should only be adding global attributes, such as class or id, to the opening <body> tag. Event handlers should be in your external JavaScript file, and styling should be in your external CSS file.

Our first, bare-bones HTML5 document could be coded like the following, with the only noticeable differences being the character set (described later) and the document type declaration:

```
<!DOCTYPE html>
<html>
<meta charset="UTF-8"/>
 <head>
  <title>My First HTML5 Web Page</title>
 </head>
<body>
</body>
</html>
```

And with those six components (DTD, <html> root, <head>, <meta> character set, <title> element, and the <body> element), we've created a web page—a blank web page, but a web page nonetheless. And, with relevant contents in the <title> element, our blank web page is more findable by search engines than many sites on the Web.

As I mentioned earlier, you don't even need that many elements:

```
<!DOCTYPE html>
<meta charset="utf-8">
<title> My First HTML5 Web Page </title>
<p> Hello World
```

While this is a valid HTML5 document, it's not good practice. By being more explicit in your code, developers that maintain your code later, including yourself, will be better able to grok your code's original intentions.

Elements Found in the <head>

The <head> may be the least sexy part of the web page markup, as it's not visible to the user by default. But just because it's not sexy doesn't mean you're allowed to neglect it. The head of the web document is where you, as a developer, tell the browser how to render your page, and where you can give hints to the printer, the search engine, and parser on how the content should be handled.

In the <head>, you will always find the <title>, but you may also come across <meta>, <base>, <link>, <script>, <style>, <command>, and <noscript> tags.

Here is what a really busy head section could look like:

```
<head>
<meta charset="UTF-8"/>
<title>Mobile HTML5</title>
<meta name="author" content="Estelle Weyl"/>
<meta name="publisher" content="O'Reilly"/>
<meta name="copyright" content="Copyright 2013"/>
<meta http-equiv="date" content="Mon, 18 Nov 2013 16:15:30 GMT"/>
<meta http-equiv="date-modified"
    content="11/18/2013" scheme="MM/DD/YYYY"/>
<meta name="keywords" content="html5 css3 svg
    border-radius canvas audio iphone android ipad"/>
<meta name="description" content="Moving from desktop to mobile:
    Learning CSS3 and HTML5."/>
<meta name="pagetopic" content="Internet"/>
<meta name="page-type" content="Instruction"/>
<meta name="audience" content="all"/>
<meta name="robots" content="index,follow"/>
<meta name="generator" content="Sublime"/>
<meta name="apple-mobile-web-app-capable" content="yes"/>
<meta name="apple-mobile-web-app-status-bar-style" content="black">
<base href="http://www.standardista.com/"/>
<script src="/js/application.js"></script>
<link rel="apple-touch-icon" href="touch-icon-iphone.png"/>
<link rel="apple-touch-icon" sizes="72x72"
    href="touch-icon-ipad.png"/>
<link rel="apple-touch-icon" sizes="114x114"
    href="touch-icon-iphone4.png"/>
<link href="/css/prettification.css" media="all" rel="stylesheet"/>
<link href="/css/tinylittledevice.css" media="only screen and
    (max-device-width: 480px)" rel="stylesheet"/>
<link href="/css/print.css" media="print" rel="stylesheet"/>
<style>
    p {color: #333333;}
</style>
</head>
```

That is a verbose header, and yours should *never* look like this, but you should understand it. So, what does it all mean? Let's take a look…

<meta>: Adding Metadata

The <meta> element allows web developers to include various types of metadata on their pages by specifying a property and a value. There are four attributes specific to <meta>: charset, http-equiv, content, and name.

<meta charset="UTF-8">

The first <meta> element we'll cover is the one you're likely to use in every HTML5 document you create:

```
<meta charset="utf-8"/>
```

You've likely been adding:

```
<meta http-equiv="Content-Type" content="text/html; charset=utf-8"/>
```

to your documents for years, telling the browser to treat the page as HTML and to use the UTF-8 character set in case your server's HTTP headers are not configured to set the charset.

While the `<title>` element was supposed to be the first element after the opening `<head>` tag, we made an exception for the character set declaration, as we wanted to be sure the rendering agent knew which `charset` to render before characters got rendered. While new to HTML5, this is supported in all major browsers, since browsers have been supporting the erroneously unquoted `meta`:

```
<meta http-equiv=Content-Type content=text/html; charset=utf-8>
```

Note that in this incorrectly written `<meta>` tag, due to the lack of quotes and the space in the value of the content attribute, the browser sees `charset` as a separate attribute. This former "error," supported by all browsers because the error was so prevalent, is now an implemented part of the HTML5 proposed specifications.

You can (and should) serve all your files as UTF-8 from the server. If you're running Apache, add `AddDefaultCharset UTF-8` to your *.htaccess* file.

With the exception of `charset`, the type of `<meta>` tag is defined by the value of either the `name` or the `http-equiv` attribute value. Other than `charset`, each `<meta>` tag must contain either the `name` *or* `http-equiv` attribute *and* the `content` attribute.

Generally, unless you're trying to generate an HTTP response message header, a `<meta>` tag has the `name` attribute and a `content` attribute, yet the values of both are basically freeform: you create the value for the name and the value for the content. We'll cover the ubiquitous `<meta>` types first, and then delve into the more mobile-specific ones.

Description meta tag

There are some standard values, including the most important nonmobile-specific one: *description*. The content of the `"description"` `<meta>` tag is what many search engines return when your web page is included in search results. So, make sure your description `content` value is a well-formed, descriptive sentence about the contents of the page, including your keywords for the page (see Figure 2-4):

```
<meta name="description"
  content="CSS3, JavaScript and HTML5 as explained by Estelle Weyl">
```

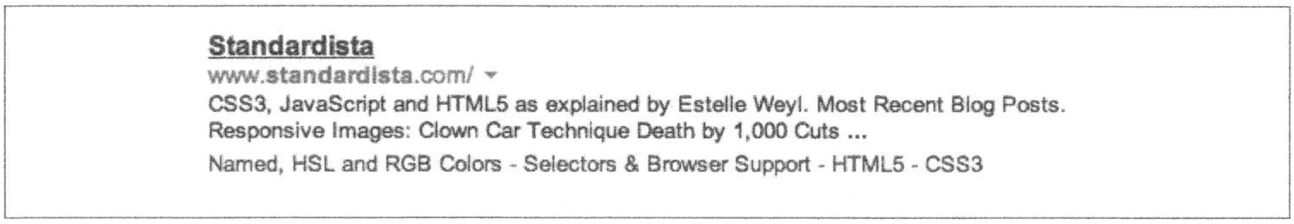

Figure 2-4. The content of the description <meta> tag displayed in Google search results

Keyword meta tag

Of all the `<meta>` tags, the `"keyword"` is the most famous. However, since the abuse of the `"keyword"` meta tag by spammers last millennium, search engines don't place high value on its content. You can feel free to include keyword metadata, but don't rely on it for your search engine efforts:

```
<meta name="keyword" content="CSS3, HTML5, JavaScript">
```

<meta http-equiv=". . .">

While the `<meta>` element with `name` attribute is fairly freeform, the `http-equiv` attribute is not. The `http-equiv` attribute, used instead of `name`, can replace the server creation of an HTTP response message header. The values of the `http-equiv` attribute mimic the HTTP response headers. I created a list of the `http-equiv` `<meta>` tag values at *http://www.standardista.com/html5/http-equiv-the-meta-attribute-explained/*. If you have access to the *.htaccess* file on your server, use that file to set up your headers. Relying on the `<meta>` tag to set your headers should be your last, not first, resort:

```
<meta http-equiv="cache-control" content="no-cache" />
```

Mobile Meta Tags

There are several `<meta>` tags that are specifically geared to mobile devices. Among them are `<meta>` tags that tell the browser to take up the entire viewport and disable scaling, and to change the status bar color, which we will cover in the following section.

Viewport meta tag

On the desktop, unless you've expanded your browser window size beyond the bounds of your monitor, the viewport size is the size of the browser window. On most mobile devices, the scale of the page can be controlled, but the viewport size remains the same, determined by the size of the device's screen.[8]

---

8. On most smaller devices, the browser is automatically fullscreen and not user changeable. On some devices, like the Slate tablet, the browser is resizable.

The "viewport" <meta> tag allows us to dictate the logical dimensions and scaling of the browser viewport window on mobile. In CubeeDoo, our web application, we've used the following meta tag:

```
<meta name="viewport"
 content="user-scalable=no, width=device-width, initial-scale=1.0"/>
```

This viewport <meta> tag is supported on all smartphones and mobile devices, including iOS, Android, webOS, Windows Phone, and Opera Mobile. By setting the viewport width equal to device-width, we're telling the browser to set the document width to the device width. Duh!

The viewport <meta> tag supports a comma-delimited list of directives allowing us to dictate the width, scale, and height of the browser viewport. You can tell the browser to not allow scaling, or to scale up to a maximum or down to a minimum value.

width=<*num*>|device-width
> Generally, you'll want to use the key term device-width to set the viewport width to the width of the device, though numeric values are also valid. The default value differs by browser, but is generally around 980. The minimum value is 200, the maximum 10,000.

height=<*num*>|device-height
> Set to device-height, or a value like 480 for an iPhone 4 or older, defines the viewport height. This value is generally omitted in favor of using only width. For reference, the minimum value is 223.

user-scalable=no|yes
> Determines whether or not the user can zoom in and out to change the scale of the viewport. Set to yes to allow scaling and no to disallow scaling. The default is yes. Setting to no also prevents scrolling on data entry. User scaling, if allowed, can be limited by the minimum-scale and maximum-scale properties of the viewport <meta>.

initial-scale=<*float*>
> Sets the initial scaling or zoom factor (or multiplier) used for viewing a web page. The default value of 1.0 displays the web page unscaled.

maximum-scale=<*float*>
> Sets the user's maximum limit for scaling or zooming unless user-scalable is set to no. The maximum value is 10, but can be a float value of 0.25 or larger.

minimum-scale=<*float*>
> Sets the user's minimum limit for scaling or zooming a web page. The minimum value is 0.25.

The default width rendered by most mobile browsers is 980 px. By setting the width to device-width, the user doesn't need to zoom in on page load because you served them

980 px width on a 320 px device. We could have set the viewport width to 320 for 320 px instead of `device-width`, but then it would only work correctly on mobile devices of exactly 320 px width. We are setting the width of the window to the width of the device, which is optimal: it scales the page proportionally to the device without the author having to know the width of the device the user may be using.

However, this isn't necessarily optimal for all websites, but rather just for mobile sites and mobile web applications. Then, when `user-scalable` is enabled, the user can zoom in to make the page more legible for those who can't read small print.

With CubeeDoo, we are creating a mobile game. When playing, the user will be touching the screen. We do not want our users to accidentally scale the page up or down while trying to flip a tile, so we told the browser to make the game the full width of the screen and to not allow scaling. Had we been creating a website instead of an app, we would have allowed user scaling without limits for better usability, which we do in our language picker:

```
<meta name="viewport" content="user-scalable=yes,
    width=device-width, initial-scale=1.0"/>
```

The function of the viewport `<meta>` tag really is presentation, and was never part of any specifications; rather, it's a feature initiated by Apple. The specification to convert the functionality from HTML markup to CSS with `@viewport` is well under way, and is partially supported in IE10.

Mobile Vendor-Specific Values

There are also some mobile vendor-specific values: for example, Google and Apple have created their own meta name/value pairs for integrating with some of their services/ APIs. There are three such tags that we have used in our project, which we cover in the following sections.

apple-mobile-web-app-capable

This `<meta>` tag reads "apple" but is also supported on Android; it sets whether a web application runs in fullscreen mode. When run in fullscreen mode, none of the browser chrome shows. The browser takes up the whole screen, with just the phone's status bar showing. This `<meta>` tag only affects the web application if the site has been bookmarked. We've included this `<meta>` tag in our web app so that if the user chooses to bookmark our application, we can take up as much real estate as possible:

```
<meta name="apple-mobile-web-app-capable" content="yes"/>
```

If content is set to `yes`, the web application runs in fullscreen mode; otherwise, it does not.

You can use JavaScript to determine whether a web page is displayed in fullscreen mode by using the Boolean `window.navigator.standalone` read-only property.

apple-mobile-web-app-status-bar-style

As noted previously, even when you enable full-screen mode with `apple-mobile-web-app-capable`, the status bar still shows. It is the one element on the mobile device that developers cannot remove, even with native web applications. Few people know, however, that you do have some control over the status bar's appearance, even if that control is minimal: we can impact its color and transparency with the `apple-mobile-web-app-status-bar-style` `<meta>` tag:

```
<meta name="apple-mobile-web-app-status-bar-style" content="black"/>
```

If your web app is mostly black, making the status bar match may enhance your design and make your web app look more like a native application. The iOS values for this are `default`, `black`, and `black-translucent`. Unfortunately (or fortunately, considering some people's lack of taste), these are currently your only options.

format-detection

The `format-detection` mobile `<meta>` tag enables or disables automatic detection of possible phone numbers in a web page:

```
<meta name="format-detection" content="telephone=no"/>
```

By default, some devices automatically detect strings formatted like phone numbers, creating links where none existed that allow for direct calling, or at least the launch of the phone application with the phone number pre-entered. Specifying `telephone="no"` disables this feature. We have no phone number in our application, or anything that resembles a phone number, so we are not employing this `<meta>` tag in our application.

The <base> of Your Web Page

Almost never used, `<base>` can be really helpful when it comes to local testing. The `<base>` element gives a base URL for de-referencing relative URLs. For example, suppose you have a relative image in your code such as `<img src="image/drongo.gif" alt="Meandering Racket-Tailed Drongo"/>`. By including the `<base src="http://RacketTailedDrongo.com"/>`, the browser will go to the image directory on the *RacketTailedDrongo.com* server to find *drongo.gif*.[9]

The base URL may be overridden by an HTTP header, but it's generally helpful for local testing. Try saving a file from the Web onto your hard drive. Add a `base` pointer to the originating server in the `<head>` of the file. When you open the page locally, the page will likely render correctly on your desktop, even though the file is local and you never downloaded images or changed the path of a file in the body of your page. The syntax is:

```
<base href="http://www.mydomain.com"/>
```

---

9. If you're wondering why I keep referencing the Racket-tailed Drongo, it's the bird on the cover of this book.

`<link>`s Aren't Just for Stylesheets

The `<link>` element gets no credit. It's a powerful, often included but rarely considered element. The `<link>` element provides the ability to define relationships among your HTML document and other documents and resources. `<link>` can be used to control print rendering, to link stylesheets and scripts, to define favicons, or to provide alternative forms of the current document.

We have four link tags in our web application:

```
<link rel="icon" href="/appleicon.png"/> ❶
<link rel="apple-touch-icon" href="/appleicon.png"/>
<link rel="apple-touch-startup-image" href="startup.png"/>
<link rel="stylesheet" href="styles.css"/>
```

❶   Add `rel="shortcut icon"` for IE, which requires the "shortcut" term when favicon is not named *favico.ico* or not stored at site root.

The `<link>` element can include several attributes: `href`, `rel`, `type`, `sizes`, `hreflang`, `media`, and `title`. The `rev` and `charset` attributes have both been removed from `<link>` in HTML5. Here's the syntax:

```
<link href="url to resource" rel="type of relationship" title="title"/>
```

The `rel` attribute specifies the named relationship from the current document to the resource specified by the `href` attribute. Both the `rel` and `href` attributes are *required*.

Of our four `<link>` tags, the first three are for imagery and the fourth you are likely most familiar with: linking to stylesheets.

Add `<link>`s for your stylesheets

This powerful little `<link>` element can be used to send different stylesheets to a phone, tablet, and desktop. It can be used to serve up different stylesheets depending on the tilt of any type of mobile phone or the width of the user's browser.

While we've only included one stylesheet in our web application, we could have included several, each targeting differing or overlapping media, browser sizes, DPIs, or even browser orientations:

```
<link href="/css/styles.css" media="all" rel="stylesheet"/>
<link href="/css/tinylittledevice.css"
  media="only screen and (max-device-width: 480px)" rel="stylesheet"/>
<link href="/css/print.css" media="print" rel="stylesheet"/>
```

These examples should look familiar, with perhaps two exceptions. Note that the `type="text/css"` attribute/value pair is missing. There is currently no other type of stylesheet language (nor do I see any forthcoming), so HTML5 assumes that the type is `text/css`, and explicitly stating it is not necessary. Also, `media="only screen and (max-device-width: 480px)"` may be new to you. We'll quickly cover that attribute, along with the other attributes of the `<link>` tag, in the following sections, and go into deeper detail on media queries in Chapter 7.

Attributes of the `<link>` tag

Like almost all elements, the `<link>` tag accepts all of the global attributes. Shown in Table 2-3 are the other attributes of the `<link>` element.

Table 2-3. Attributes of the `<link>` element

Attribute	Description
href	Required. The "hyperlink reference" is the URL for the destination file of the `<link>`.
media	Describes to which media the contents of the link will be included.
rel	Specifies relationship of `<link>` to current document.
hreflang	Language of the linked media.
type	MIME type of the linked media. Optional unless the value is not of type expected by the `rel` relationship.
sizes	New. If media is an icon, it defines the size of the icon.

The media attribute

The `media` attribute describes for which media the contents of the link will be included. If not declared, the default is `all`, indicating that the source described by the `href` attribute will always be present.

Values used to be fairly limited, with values such as `screen` for desktops and `print` for printers, etc. Values for media included: `screen`, `tty`, `tv`, `projection`, `handheld`, `print`, `braille`, `aural`, and `all`. Now you can include `@media` queries. The `media` attribute value has been greatly expanded with CSS3. We can now serve up different stylesheets based on more esoteric values of the `media` property. For example, mobile device flipping and desktop browser resizing will change the screen aspect ratio from portrait to landscape and back again, so you can serve different CSS files when in portrait versus when in landscape mode:

```
<link rel="stylesheet" media="all and (orientation:portrait)" href="prtrt.css"/>
<link rel="stylesheet" media="all and (orientation:landscape)" href="lndscp.css"/>
```

The `@media` queries that are new in CSS3 are acceptable values for the `media` attribute. Newly accepted key terms in the attribute values include:

- `(min/max)-width`: Viewport width
- `(min/max)-height`: Viewport height
- `(min/max)-device-width`: Screen width
- `(min/max)-device-height`: Screen height
- `orientation`: Portrait(h>w) | landscape(w>h)

- `(min/max)-aspect-ratio`: Width/height
- `(min/max)-device-aspect-ratio`: Device-width/height

Several `<link>` attributes that were in HTML 4 have since been removed from the HTML5 spec, including the `coords`, `shape`, `urn`, `target`, `charset`, `methods`, and `rev` attributes. Also, the `title` attribute has special semantics on this element.

The rel attribute

The `rel` attribute specifies the named relationship from the current document to the resource specified by the `href` attribute. The `rel` attribute is stated as being optional, but if you don't include it, your browser will not correctly link the resource to your document. A stylesheet link without `rel="stylesheet"` will not correctly render any styles: your browser will just download the file and think "Well, that was a waste of bandwidth." (Yes, browsers can think, and they make fun of us all the time.) Table 2-4 lists some values of the `rel` attribute along with the value's definition.

Table 2-4. The rel attribute

rel attribute value	Definition of rel attribute value of link element
stylesheet	The most commonly used value of the `rel` attribute, informing the browser that the linked file should be used to render the presentation of the current document. When including `stylesheet`, `type="text/css"` is no longer a required attribute/value pair, as `text/css` is the only type of stylesheet language, and is therefore inferred.
next	The link references the next document in a guided tour or next document in an ordered series. The spec was originally meant to aid in the preloading of the subsequent file, improving user experience.
prev	The link references the previous document in a guided tour or previous document in an ordered series.
index	Index for the document.
help	The link references a document offering help, (e.g., describing the wider context and offering further links to relevant documents). This is aimed at reorienting users who have lost their way.
contents	Links to a document containing a table of contents for the document or site.
alternate	Specifies an alternate version of the document. When used in conjunction with the `hreflang` attribute, it implies the linked file is a translation of the document. When used in conjunction with the `media` attribute, it implies a media-specific version, such as for a printer. When combined with `stylesheet`, it indicates that there is an alternate stylesheet for the user to select.
copyright	References a copyright statement for the document or site.
glossary	A document with definitions of terms used in the current document.
icon	The favicon for the page or website.
apple-touch-icon	Defines which icon is displayed on the user's screen when a web application is bookmarked and added to the screen.
apple-touch-startup-image	A startup image that is displayed while the web application launches. This is especially useful when your web application is offline. If not included, some browsers will display a screenshot of the web application the last time it was accessed.

Android and iOS both support the `apple-touch-icon` and `apple-touch-startup-image`. Windows Phone has tiles instead of icons. To include tile information, include:

```
<meta name="msapplication-TileColor" content="#<color>"/>
<meta name="msapplication-TileImage" content="<image reference>"/>
```

`<style>`

The `<style>` element provides a method for you to add styles to a document. Unlike styles imported via the `<link>` element, the styles included in the `<style>` tag in the head of the page are applied to the current page only, and are therefore not natively accessible in the cache for other documents to use. Unlike styles added using the `style` attribute on an element, which only impact the element on which the attribute is placed until the `scoped` attribute is supported, styles included within `<style>` are applicable to the matched selectors in the entire document.

The `<style>` element used to require the `type` attribute (generally, `type="text/css"`). It can be omitted in HTML5, in which case its presence with the value of `"text/css"` is implied. Like the `<link>` tag, the `<style>` accepts the `media` attribute.

New in HTML5, but not yet supported in any browser, is the `scoped` attribute. Adding the `scoped` attribute to the `<style>` element tells the rendering agent to apply that CSS only within the scope, or section, in which that style is found. This will be useful when creating widgets appearing on sites over which you may have no control, ensuring that the CSS for your widget doesn't accidentally overwrite the hosting website's CSS.

`<style>` and mobile performance: standards anti-pattern. For the past 12 years, it has always been recommended to use `<link>` to include site-wide styles instead of `<style>`. Including CSS via `<style>` may reduce the number of HTTP requests, but it does not allow for caching. This is obviously not optimal.

Due to latency issues of extra HTTP requests, a mobile anti-pattern has emerged.

To reduce latency, the site CSS is included inline in the main response inside one or more style tags. With JavaScript, the content of the `style` blocks are extracted and saved in localStorage, and the key values are added to the cookie string. Additional HTTP requests include the cookie with the names of the styles (and other resources) that are stored in localStorage. Server side, the server reads the cookie, checks which resources (if any) are still needed, then sends along only the files that are not yet in localStorage embedded in the one response. This results in a large download on first request, and much smaller downloads on subsequent requests, with the original site load and all subsequent site reloads being a single HTTP request and response.

While this is an anti-pattern, reducing the number of HTTP requests can greatly improve performance. The improvement in performance can well outweigh the costs of sending a fairly large file (with content that was required anyway) and the cost of accessing data stored in localStorage.

Adding a <script> to your web page

The <script> tag allows you to include blocks of JavaScript or link to an external Java-Script (or other script type) file. The type attribute was required in XHTML and was almost always type="text/javascript". In HTML5, the type is assumed to be text/javascript. As long as your script is JavaScript, the type attribute should be omitted. Also, the language attribute has been made obsolete.

When src is included, it may seem like the element is empty, since there is no text between the opening and closing tags. Include a full closing tag anyhow, and do *not* put any JavaScript between those tags.

JavaScript performance tips. Although we are discussing elements within the <head> of the document, the <script> element can be found inside the <body> or <head> of the document, and sometimes (usually, really) the end of the body is the best suited location for the <script> element.

Why? JavaScript is generally parsed immediately when downloaded, halting the down-load of the document in its tracks until the JavaScript has finished being downloaded, parsed, and executed. This can greatly slow down the perceived download time of the page. For this reason, it is recommended to include scripts toward the end of the docu-ment, instead of in the <head>.

Consider your visitors to be non-JavaScript users during the time it takes to download, parse, and execute all the components of your web page. Wouldn't you prefer them to be looking at some content rather than a blank screen? This is why JavaScript perfor-mance and source order matters.

There are two attributes that can alter the order of execution of the JavaScript: the defer and async attributes. Both are Boolean, with async being a new addition in HTML5. async indicates that the script should execute asynchronously, when it becomes avail-able. defer indicates that the script should execute after the document has finished parsing. If neither attribute is present, the JavaScript is parsed when encountered. Both are only valid for external scripts and invalid for inline scripts.

As stated earlier, JavaScript is parsed immediately when encountered (unless async and/or defer are included and supported by the browser). Browsers stop downloading ad-ditional elements from the server until the JavaScript is fully downloaded, parsed, and executed. By including the JavaScript at the end of the document instead of the head, the *perceived* download time is much shorter. When the script is in the <head>, the page "hangs" while it loads and executes the JavaScript. With the <script> in the footer, while it actually takes the exact same amount of time to download and execute the script, the perceived download time is much faster as there is no visible halting in the download.

There is a new solution to the issue of the hanging UI due to slow JavaScript in HTML5. Web workers, described in Chapter 6, enable multiple threads of JavaScript to execute concurrently. Dynamically generating the script tag is another trick to improving performance.

When a user has JavaScript turned off, <noscript>

You can include a <noscript> element with content that is made visible only if the user has JavaScript disabled. Generally, it's best to progressively enhance static functionality of a page, making the <noscript> obsolete. However, there are some project managers that insist on sites completely reliant on JavaScript. In these cases, you can use <no script> in the body of the document to include directions to your user to turn JavaScript back on. JavaScript is by default enabled in all mobile browsers and other modern browsers, including mobile WebKit, Blink, Opera Mobile, Windows, and Firefox.

A <body> of elements

The <body> is always the second and last child of the <html> element, the first child being the <head>. Everything displayed to the user within the main window of the browser is found within the <body> element. While the <head> contains all the metadata for the page, the <body> contains all the visible (and occasionally some nonvisible) content.

The next chapter discusses the elements that are actually displayed to the client: the <body> element and all of its children. As mentioned earlier in the discussion of required elements, the <body> has no element-specific attributes, but has many event handlers, including:

- onafterprint
- onbeforeprint
- onbeforeunload
- onblur
- onerror
- onfocus
- onhashchange
- onload
- onmessage
- onoffline
- ononline
- onpopstate
- onredo
- onresize
- onstorage

- onundo

- onunload

It is best to include these event handlers within your external JavaScript and *not* within the <body> element. I've included them here so that you know what is available, but I highly recommend and completely encourage you to keep content separate from presentation separate from behavior.

Now it is time to focus on the actual content of our pages.

CHAPTER 3

Elements That Are New in HTML5

HTML5 provides us with new and mostly semantic elements; it redefines some existent elements and makes other elements obsolete (think of "obsolete" as the new, politically correct version of "deprecated"). As we saw in Chapter 2, we have the root `<html>` element, document metadata described in the `<head>` section, and scripting elements. HTML5 provides us with sectioning elements, heading elements, phrase elements, embedded elements, and interactive elements. Interactive form elements are covered in Chapter 4. The media-related embedded elements will be discussed in Chapter 5. We won't discuss table elements, since, for the most part, they haven't changed in HTML5. The other elements are discussed in the next section.

In prior specifications, elements were described as being either *inline*, for text-level semantics, or *block*, for flow content. HTML5 doesn't use the terms block or inline to describe elements anymore. The HTML5 authors correctly assume that CSS is responsible for the presentation, and all browsers, including all mobile browsers, come with stylesheets that define the display of elements. So, while HTML5 no longer defines elements in terms of block or inline, the default user-agent stylesheets style some elements as block and others as inline, but the delineation has been removed from the specification.

With HTML5, we have most of the HTML 4 elements and the addition of a few new ones. HTML5 also adds several attributes and removes mostly presentational elements and attributes that are better handled by CSS. In Chapter 2, we covered the new global attributes. In this chapter, we cover many of the new elements of HTML5, and some of the existent elements that have had major changes. Other elements such as form and embedded content elements will be discussed in their own, separate chapters.

Sectioning Elements in HTML5

The sectioning root is the `<body>` element. Other HTML 4 sectioning elements included in the HTML5 spec are the rarely used `<address>` element and the leveled headings from `<h1>` to `<h6>`. HTML5 adds several new sectioning elements, such as:[1]

- `section`
- `article`
- `nav`
- `aside`
- `header`
- `footer`

It also maintains support for these older sectioning elements:

- `body`
- `h1-h6`
- `address`

The new sectioning elements encompass content that defines the scope of headings and footers. The new sectioning elements, like `<footer>`, `<aside>`, and `<nav>`, do not replace the `<div>` element, but rather create semantic alternatives. Sectioning elements define the scope of headings and footers: does this heading belong to this part of the page or the whole document? Each sectioning content element can potentially have its own outline. A sectioning element containing a blog post, for example, can have its own header and footer. You can have more than one header and footer in a document. In fact, the document, each `section`, and even each `blockquote` can have its own `footer`. Because each section has its own scope for headings, you are not limited to a single `<h1>` on a page, or even limited to six heading levels (`<h1>` through `<h6>`). Let's cover the new sectioning elements.

The authors of HTML5 scanned billions of documents, counting each class name, to determine what web developers were calling the various sections of their page. Opera repeated the study, including the names of IDs in addition to class names. Due to Dreamweaver and Microsoft Word, `style1` and `MsoNormal` were very, very popular. Ignoring the software-generated classes and obviously presentational class names like `left` and `right`, they discovered that web developers were using semantic sectioning

---

1. The `hgroup` element that was originally added to HTML5 was made obsolete. It has not yet been removed from the WHATWG spec, but has been removed from the W3C HTML5 and W3C HTML5.1 specifications.

names like `main`, `header`, `footer`, `content`, `sidebar`, `banner`, `search`, and `nav` almost as if they were included in a default Dreamweaver template (they weren't).

Reflecting what developers were doing, more than 25 new elements have been added to HTML5. Originally missing was the "main" or "content" elements. The reason? Anything that is not part of a navigation, sidebar, header, or footer is part of the main content. The `<main>` element is a late addition to the specification, and is described on page 67.

Using the new elements, like `<header>` and `<footer>`, which replace and make more semantic the semantically neutral `<div id="header">` and `<div id="footer">`, we can create the standard web layout in a more semantic way. These new elements, shown in Figure 3-1 in what is a common page layout, enable including semantics to the layout of a document.

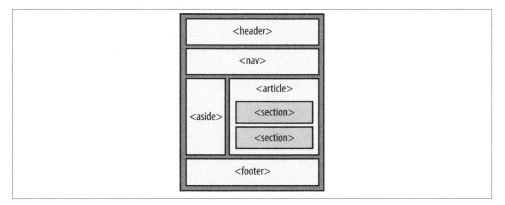

Figure 3-1. Typical web page layout using HTML5 sectioning elements

`<section>`

The `<section>` element can be used to thematically group content, typically with a heading. The `<section>` element represents a generic document or application section, but is not a generic container element: it has semantic value. If you are simply encompassing elements for styling, use the nonsemantic `<div>` instead:[2]

```
<section>
 <header>
    <h1>Mobile Web Applications with HTML5 and CSS3 </h1>
 </header>
```

---

2. Because of its semantic value, screen readers announce the beginning and end of each `<section>`. Unless your page is comprised of semantic sections of content, use the nonsemantic `<div>`, which is not called out by the screen reader.

```
<h2>HTML5</h2>
<p>Something about HTML5.</p>
<h2>CSS3</h2>
<p>Something about CSS3.</p>
<footer>Provided by Standardista.com</footer>
</section>
```

\<article\>

The \<article\> element is similar to \<section\>, but like a news article, it could make sense independent of the document or site in which it is found. The \<article\> is a component of a page that consists of a self-contained composition in a document, page, application, or site that is intended to be independently distributable or reusable, such as for syndication:

```
<article>
  <header>
     <h1> Mobile Web Applications with HTML5 and CSS3 </h1>
     <p><time datetime="2013-11-11T12:31-08:00">11.11.13</time></p>
  </header>
  <h2>HTML5</h2>
  <p>Something about HTML5.</p>
  <h2>CSS3</h2>
  <p>Something about CSS3.</p>
  <footer>
     <p>Provided by Standardista.com</p>
  </footer>
</article>
```

Originally, the HTML5 specifications included a Boolean pubdate attribute, but that has been removed from the specification, as microdata vocabulary can be used to provide such information.

\<section\> Versus \<article\>

There is some debate in the spec-writing community that these two elements are too similar. You should use \<article\> versus \<section\> when the encapsulated content is a discrete item of content. It is often a judgment call. The only difference in the two code snippets given in the previous two sections is that I've added an optional \<time\> to the \<article\> example.

In terms of explaining the similarities, differences, and functionalities of these two elements, use the analogy of the Sunday newspaper (for those of you too young to remember what a newspaper is, it's that thing you recycle or start chimney fires with). The Sunday newspaper has several sections: the front page, news, real estate, classified, weekly magazine, comics, and so on. Each of these sections has articles. Those articles have headers, and some, especially in-depth news reports, have nested sections. Similar to the Sunday paper, articles and sections can be nested within each other and within themselves.

An `<article>` can be a forum post, a magazine or newspaper article, a blog entry, a user-submitted comment, an interactive widget or gadget, or any other independent item of content.

The general rule is that the `<section>` element is appropriate only if the element's contents can be listed explicitly in the document's outline, such as saying "the '`<section>` versus `<article>`' section is in this book." The HTML5 sections grouping you are reading right now would be in a `<section>` tag if it were online.

Examples of sections would be chapters, the various tabbed pages in a tabbed dialog box, or the numbered sections of a thesis. A website's home page could be split into sections for an introduction, news items, and contact information.

Authors are encouraged to use the `<article>` element instead of the `<section>` element when it makes sense to syndicate the contents of the element.

`<nav>`

The `<nav>` element is used for major navigational blocks within a document, providing for a section of a page that links to other pages or to parts within the page. By major or main navigation, think drop-down menus or other large groups of links that a visitor to your site using a screen reader may want to skip listening to on their way to hearing the main content of your page.

Small groups of links, like legalese and other links often found in the footer, can be encapsulated in the `<footer>`. If your `<footer>` has a large navigational section, you can nest a `<nav>` in it.

By encapsulating your site navigation in the `<nav>` element, you are telling sightless readers (think visually impaired, but also think searchbots like Google's spiders) that this is the navigation to your site. When the `<nav>` element becomes well supported by screen readers, we will be able to stop including "skip navigation" links that we've been using for accessibility. If you want to provide for additional accessibility right now, use the WAI-ARIA `role="navigation"`:

```
<nav role="navigation">
    <ul>
        <li><a href="/">Home</a></li>
        <li><a href="/css/">CSS3</a></li>
        <li><a href="/html/">HTML5</a></li>
        <li><a href="/js/">Javascript</a></li>
        <li><a href="/access/">Accessibility</a></li>
    </ul>
</nav>
```

<aside>

The <aside> contains content that is tangentially related to the main content: related enough to be taken out of the flow, but not actually part of the content. The <aside> content is separate from the main content, and can be used for typographical effects like pull quotes or sidebars, for advertising, for groups of navigational elements, and for other content that is considered separate from, including tangentially related to, the main content of the page. Basically, if you can pull the <aside> out of the page, and the main content still makes sense, you're using the element correctly.

<aside> content does not need to be relegated to the sidebar. For example, when the bottom section of your document contains more than footer-type content, creating what is called a *fat footer*, you can put your <aside> at the bottom of the page instead of or in addition to a <footer>:

```
<section>
  <h1>......</h1>
  <!-- main content of page -->
<section>
<aside>
  <dl>
    <dt>HTML5</dt>
    <dd>The next major revision of the HTML standard.</dd>
  </dl>
</aside>
```

<header>

The <header> groups introductory or navigational aids and contains the section's heading (an <h1>–<h6> element), but this is not required. The <header> element can also be used to wrap a section's table of contents, a search form, or any relevant logos: basically, anything that makes up a header.

There can be more than one <header> on a page: the main <header> for the document, containing the logo, the main navigation, and the titles of your site and login, and separate <header> elements for each <section> and/or <article> code blocks. For example, your blog may have a document header with logo, search, tagline, and main navigation in the main <header>, with a separate <header> element for each blog post for the post title, author, and publication date.

 Think of the <header> as a semantic replacement for the main <div id="header"> and the multiple section headings <div class="heading"> of yore.

<footer>

The <footer> element typically contains information about its section or article, such as who wrote it, links to related documents, copyright data, and more. Like the <header>, you can have more than one <footer> in a document: one representing the global footer, and other <footer> elements for each individual <section> and/or <article>, such as social networking links and a link to comments at the bottom of each post in a blog.

The <footer> element should encompass the footer for the nearest ancestor sectioning content. Similar to the <header>, each <footer> will be associated with the nearest ancestor <article>, <section>, or <body>. If the closest parent sectioning content is <body>, then the <footer> represents the footer for the whole document, replacing the formerly ubiquitous <div id="footer">, and adding semantic meaning.

Author contact information belongs in an <address> element (described momentarily), which can be in a <footer>. Footers don't have to be at the end of a document or article, though they usually are. Footers can also be used for appendixes, indexes, and other such content:

```
<footer>
  <p>Copyright 2013
    <address>estelle@standardista.com</address>
  </p>
</footer>
```

Note that the footer and aside are slightly different sectioning elements: the headers of your <footer>s and <aside>s will not be included in the outline for your document.

CubeeDoo Header and Footer

With games on mobile devices, we want to provide as much room as possible for the board. However, if our users have a desktop screen, we have all this extra room! So, depending on browser size, we include a header and footer above and below the game in larger screens:

```
1    <article>
2    <header>
3        <h1>CubeeDoo</h1>
4        <h2>The Mobile Memory Matching Game</h2>
5    </header>
6    <section id="game" class="colors">
7      <div id="board" class="level1">
8      <!-- game board goes here -->
9      </div>
10      <footer> <!-- footer for the section -->
11        <div class="control scores">Scores</div>
12        <div class="control menu" id="menu">Menu</div>
13        <ul>
```

```
14              <li id="level">Level: <output>1</output></li>
15              <li id="timer">
16               <div id="seconds"></div>
17              </li>
18              <li><button id="mutebutton">Mute</button></li>
19              <li id="score">Score: <output>0</output></li>
20            </ul>
21         </footer>
22       </section>
23       <footer><!-- footer for the article -->
24        <ul>
25           <li><a href="about/estelle.html">About Estelle</a></li>
26           <li><a href="about/justin.html">About Justin</a></li>
27        </ul>
28       </footer>
29     </article>
```

We've contained our page in an `<article>` with the game (lines 6–22) a `<section>` nested within that article. The document has a `<header>` (lines 2–5) and `<footer>` (lines 23–28). In the article header, we have a title and a subtitle marked up as an `<h1>` and `<h2>`. The page has two footers. In addition to the document footer that is relevant and is visible in all the pages on our site, there is also a `<footer>` (lines 10–21) for the game's main screen that is encapsulated in a `<section>`.

Not New, but Not Often Used: <address>

The `<address>` element is not new to HTML5. It's been around for a while, and is well supported, being rendered in italic by most user agents. Almost no developers implement it, so I'm reminding you about its existence here. And, no, the `<address>` element is not for your contact information.

Unlike many elements, the semantics of `<address>` aren't completely obvious. Actually, it's quite nuanced. The `<address>` element represents the "contact information for its nearest article or body element ancestor." If that is the `<body>` element, then the contact information applies to the document as a whole. If it is an `<article>`, then the address applies to that article only. Basically, it's not meant for your street address on your contact page, which would seem to make sense.

Grouping Content: Other New HTML5 Elements

Most of the formerly block-level elements have been divided into sectioning and grouping elements. The grouping set of elements includes lists, `<p>`, `<pre>`, `<blockquote>`, and `<div>`. We have three new elements, `<main>`, `<figure>`, and `<figcaption>`. The `<hr>` element has been provided with semantic meaning in HTML5, so has been included under the new category because the old `<hr>` had no semantic meaning and didn't group anything (see Table 3-1).

Table 3-1. Grouping elements

New grouping elements	Older grouping elements
main	p
figure	pre
figcaption	blockquote
hr (changed)	ol
	li
	ul
	dl
	dd
	dt
	div

We'll only cover the new grouping elements and changes to the older grouping elements, as you should already be familiar with the existent ones.

<main>

The <main> element defines the main content of the page. Because it's the main content of the page, the <main> must be unique to the page. The <main> element is not sectioning content like the elements just described, and therefore has no effect on the document outline. <main> should encompass the content that is unique to the page and exclude site-wide features like the site header, footer, and main navigation.

Being the main content, it can be the ancestor but not the descendant of articles, asides, footers, headers, and navigation sections. No, I did not just contradict myself. Using the example of a blog, the <main> would encompass the blog posts, along with the post's header and footer, but would not encompass the site-wide header, footer, navigation, and aside.

<figure> and <figcaption>

The <figure> element encompasses flow content, optionally with a <figcaption> caption, that is self-contained and is typically referenced as a single unit from the main flow of the document.

OK, that was totally W3C-speak. Lay terms? You know how you're always struggling with how to include an image with a caption? You now have a semantic way to do it.

The <figure> element should be used on content that, if removed, would not affect the meaning of the content. For example, most of the chapters in this book have had tables and figures with captions. Had we removed those images, this content might be more difficult to digest, but the flow of the text would not be affected. Those figures would be perfect candidates for the <figure> element:

```
<figure>
  <img src="madeupstats.jpg" alt="Marketshare for chocolate
    in the USA is 27% dark chocolate, 70% milk chocolate,
    and 3% white chocolate." />
  <figcaption>Browser statics graph by chocolate type</figcaption>
</figure>
```

In the preceding example we used both `<figure>` and `<figcaption>`, and bogus statistics.

Only found as the first or last child of a figure element, the `<figcaption>` is a caption or legend for the rest of the contents of the `<figure>` it's nested in. The inline contents of the `<figcaption>` provide a caption for the contents of its associated `<figure>`.

`<hr>`

The empty `<hr>` element has garnered new semantic meaning in HTML5. Whereas it used to be defined purely in presentational terms, a horizontal rule, it has been given the semantic purpose of representing a "paragraph-level thematic break" or "hard return." The `<hr>` is useful to delineate scene change, or a transition to a new topic within a section of a wiki.

The element-specific attributes of the `<hr/>` element have all been deprecated.

`<li>` and `<ol>` Attribute Changes

In addition to the global and internationalization changes described in Chapter 2, the `value` attribute on list items and the `type` attribute on ordered lists, deprecated in previous specifications, have returned. In addition, the Boolean `reversed` attribute has been added to ordered lists, reversing the order of the numbers and enabling descending order.

Text-Level Semantic Elements New to HTML5

There are more than 20 text-level semantic elements in HTML5. Some of these elements are new, some have been repurposed, some have attribute changes, some have remained the same, and a very few, like `<acronym>`, have been removed from the specification altogether. The elements are shown in Table 3-2.

Table 3-2. Text-level semantic elements

New	Changed	Unchanged	Obsolete
mark	a	q	acronym
time	small	samp	big
ruby	s	kbd	center
rt	cite	sub	font
rp	i	sup	strike
bdi	b	bdo	tt
wbr	u	span	
data		br	
		em	
		strong	
		dfn	
		abbr	
		code	
		var	

\<mark\>

The \<mark\> element is used to mark text due to its relevance in another context. "Huh?" you may ask. Think of \<mark\> as "marking text," rather than giving strong or emphasized importance to it. A good use is highlighting search terms in search results, or text in one block that you reference in the next.

Have you ever used native search in Safari desktop? You know how it grays out the page, highlighting occurrences of the term you were seeking?

Were you to create that effect, or the effect of viewing a cached page in Google search, it would be correct to use \<mark\> for all the results that were found, with:

```
mark {background-color: yellow;}
mark:focus {background-color: blue;}
```

in your CSS. This would give you an effect similar to the results shown in Figure 3-2.

While presentational in explanation, it does have semantic meaning. Text that is marked gets semantically (and with CSS, visually) highlighted to bring the attention to a part of the text that might not have been considered important in its original unmarked presentation.

Figure 3-2. Searching for a string in Opera Mobile highlights occurrences of matching text

<mark> can be used to indicate a part of the document highlighted due to its current, though not necessarily permanent, relevance. For example, when searching for "HTML5," to highlight the search term in the resulting page, the most semantic method would be to code it as follows, styling <mark> with CSS:

```
<p><mark>HTML5</mark> is currently under development as the
    next major revision of the HTML standard. Like its
    immediate predecessors, HTML 4.01, and XHTML 1.1,
    <mark>HTML5</mark> is a standard for structuring and
    presenting content on the World Wide Web.</p>
```

You can add scripts to your search functionality to encapsulate search term results with the <mark> tags, and then you can style the marks with CSS to show how many search results were found and where they are.

<time>

The <time> element is used to define a specific time or date, providing a precise, machine-readable time that may get parsed by user agents to be reused for other purposes, such as entry into a calendar. In your average game, appropriate uses of the <time>

element would be the date and time that high scores were achieved, and even the duration of the game or time left.

The `datetime` attribute enumerates the date. If the `datetime` attribute is present, then its value must be a valid date string.[3] If the `datetime` attribute is not present, then the element's text content must be a valid, machine-readable date.

"I play CubeeDoo on Saturday mornings" would not be a good candidate for inclusion of the `<time>` element. "Let's play next Saturday at 11:00 a.m. (I like to sleep in)" would be a better place to include the element, since it is an exact date and time that can be specified:

```
<time datetime="2013-11-30T11:00-8:00">next Saturday at 11:00 a.m.</time>
```

In CubeeDoo, we could use the `<time>` element to encapsulate the times that the highest scores were achieved if you list the dates: while the user sees a human-readable time, the `datetime` attribute provides a machine-readable time.

`<rp>`, `<rt>`, and `<ruby>`

The `<ruby>`, or ruby annotation, element allows spans of phrasing content to be marked with ruby annotations. This has nothing to do with the Ruby programming language. Rather, ruby annotations are notes or characters used to show the pronunciation of East Asian characters (Figure 3-3).

The `<rp>`, or ruby parenthesis, element can be used to provide parentheses around a ruby text component of a ruby annotation, to be shown by browsers that don't support ruby annotations, hidden when the browser does support it. The `<rt>`, or ruby text, element marks the ruby text component of a ruby annotation.

君子は和して同ぜず。

Figure 3-3. `<ruby>` and `<rt>` used to write Japanese (Translation: [Confucius says] One must draw the line somewhere[4])

Use together with the `<rt>` and/or the `<rp>` tags: the `<rp>` element provides information, an explanation, and/or pronunciation of the `<ruby>` contents. The optional `<rp>` element defines what to show browsers that do not support `<ruby>`. We don't use this in CubeeDoo and ruby is only partially supported on mobile devices. If you are interested

---

3. Date values must be machine-readable dates. Date strings are defined at *http://www.w3.org/TR/NOTE-datetime*.

4. From *https://dl.dropboxusercontent.com/u/1330446/tests/ruby.html*.

in more information, there is a link to a good explanation of these three elements and their implementations in the online chapter resources.

<bdi>

The <bdi> element (in contrast to the existing <bdo> element, which overrides the direction of text) isolates a particular piece of bidirectional content. It is needed because of the way the Unicode bidirectional algorithm deals with "weak" characters. <bdo dir="rtl"> will invert a whole line even if only a span is encompassed. <bdi> ensures that only the contents between the opening and required closing </bdi> tag are reversed. The CSS3 Writing Modes specification has added some properties, like text-combine-horizontal, to help move presentational aspects of content out of the HTML content layer and into CSS, where it belongs.

<wbr>

The <wbr> element represents a line break opportunity within content that otherwise has no spaces. For example, sometimes URLs can be very, very, very long. Too long to fit in the width of your column:

```
<p>
<a href="http://isCubeeDoo.partofhtml5.com/">Is<wbr/>CubeeDoo.<wbr/>
Part<wbr/>Of<wbr/>HTML5.com</a>?
</p>
```

To ensure that the text can be wrapped in a readable fashion, the individual words in the URL are separated using a <wbr> element. Add the <wbr> element to indicate where the browser can break to a new line. The <wbr> is an empty element with no element-specific attributes.

Changed Text-Level Semantic Elements

A few elements from HTML have been modified in HTML5, including a, small, s, cite, i, b, and u.

<a>

As you well know, the <a> element represents a hyperlink. While not new, we include a description here since there are changes to the element in HTML5, and there are special mobile actions depending on the value of the now-optional href attribute.[5]

First, note that some attributes of the <a> element are now obsolete, such as the name attribute. To create an in-page anchor, put the id attribute on the closest element to your

---

5. If the href attribute is not specified, the <a> represents a placeholder hyperlink.

target in the document and create a hyperlink to that element using the id. For example, `<a href="#anchorid">` is an anchor link that targets the element with an id of anchor id. Also obsolete are the shape, coords, charset, methods, and rev attributes.

The target attribute of `<a>`, which was deprecated in XHTML Strict, is back. There are a few new attributes, including download, media, and ping.[6] The download attribute indicates the hyperlink is intended for downloading. The value, if included, is the name the filesystem should use in saving the file. The media attribute takes as its value a media query list for which the destination of the hyperlink was designed. The ping attribute accepts a space-separated list of URLs to be pinged when a hyperlink is followed, informing the third site that an action was taken, without redirecting through that site.

Also different in HTML5 is that the `<a>` element can encompass both inline and block-level content, or in HTML5 parlance, sectioning and phrase elements. For example, this is now a valid HTML5 hyperlink:

```
<a href="index.html" rel="next" target="_blank">
  <header>
   <h1>This is my title</h1>
   <p>This is my tagline</p>
  </header>
</a>
```

Mobile-specific link handling

Mobile devices have a few link types that receive special treatment when displayed in a browser or in the mobile device's email client.[7]

You're likely familiar with mailto: links. When clicked, it opens your computer's or mobile device's email application, creates a new message, and addresses it to the target of the link. You can also include the *subject* and *content* for the email.

The tel: link will open the mobile device's calling application and calls the number used as the link's target. In iOS, a confirmation dialog pops up before redirecting to the phone application and dialing the number for you. When a tel: link is clicked in Android, users are brought directly to the phone application with the telephone number from the link pre-entered, but doesn't dial for you. Similarly, the sms: link will open up messaging.

If you are unfamiliar with SMS links, the syntax is:

```
sms:<phone_number>[,<phone-number>]*[?body=<message_body>]
```

---

6. The media, ping, and download attributes are under discussion, but are expected to be included in the specifications.

7. Skype can also be launched from the browser. Check out *http://dev.skype.com/skype-uri* for more details.

Clicking on the following hyperlink will open an alert that asks if you want to call the number in the link or cancel in iOS, and brings up the key pad with the number pre-populated on Android. The SMS link opens up the messaging application. Remember that not all devices have SMS capabilities:

```
<a href="tel:16505551212">1 (650) 555-1212</a>
<a href="sms:16505551212">Text me</a>
```

Telephone number detection is on by default on most devices. For example, Safari on iPhone automatically converts any number that takes the form of a phone number of some countries to a phone link even if it isn't a link, unless you explicitly tell the device not to (see "format-detection" on page 50 in Chapter 2).

Other links handled differently are Google Maps, YouTube links, iTunes links, and Google Play. When a regular link to a Google Maps page is included in a web page or an email, some mobile devices will open the device's map application, rather than opening the map in the current or new browser window. Recognizing the link, the phone will launch the Maps application instead:

```
<a href="http://maps.google.com/maps?q=san+francisco,+ca"> Map of SF</a>
```

Links to YouTube and to the iTunes store (in iOS) will launch the YouTube widget and iTunes respectively. Links on Android for Android applications will open a pop-up that asks if you want to follow the link or open the link in Google Play.

There are examples of these link types in the online chapter resources.

Text-Level Element Changes from HTML 4

We all thought the presentational elements of <i>, <b>, <s>, <u>, and <small> were destined to become deprecated, or made obsolete. Instead, they have newfound glory with semantic meaning.

The <i> element should be used instead of a <span> to offset text from its surrounding content without conveying any extra emphasis or importance, such as when including a technical term, an idiomatic phrase from another language, a thought, or a ship name.

The <b> element represents a span of text to be stylistically offset without conveying any extra importance, such as keywords in a document abstract, product names in a review, or other spans of text whose typical typographic presentation is bold.

The <s> element encompasses content that is no longer accurate or relevant and is therefore "struck" from the document. The <s> element has been around for a long time, but before HTML5 only had a presentational definition. HTML5 provides <s> with semantic value.

Similarly, the <u> element has been given semantic value. The <u> element represents text offset from its surrounding content without receiving any extra emphasis or importance, and for which the typographic convention dictates underlining, such as misspelled words or Chinese proper names.

The <small> element should be used to represent the "fine print" part of a document. While <small> text doesn't need to be displayed in tiny print, it should be reserved for the fine print, such as legalese in a sweepstakes or side effects in a pharmaceutical ad (which, if you think about it, should really be in a huge font).

While I didn't think <cite> was heading for the realm of distant memories, it too has acquired new meaning. The <cite> element now solely represents the cited title of a work; for example, the title of a book, song, film, TV show, play, legal case report, or other such work. In previous versions of HTML, <cite> could be used to mark up the name of a person: that usage is no longer considered conforming.

Unchanged Elements

While you likely know the usage of all the text elements that preceded HTML5 and haven't had any semantic updates, some may be used less often. Table 3-3 shows a quick summary.

Table 3-3. Unchanged elements

Element	Description
em	Text with emphatic stress.
strong	Text with strong importance.
q	Text quoted from another source.
dfn	The defining instance of a term.
abbr	Abbreviation or acronym. Note that acronym has been made obsolete. Include a title attribute with the full term.
code	Fragment of computer code.
var	Math or programming variable or placeholder meant to be replaced with another value.
samp	Sample output from a program or computing system.
kbd	Representation of user (keyboard) input.
sub	Subscript.
sub	Superscript.
bdo	Directionality formatting control providing a way to specify a direction override.
span	Generic, nonsemantic wrapper for phrasing content.
br	Line break.

There are also the <ins> and <del> elements, which are considered editing elements, representing insertion and deletion, respectively.

Embedded Elements

The 12 embedded elements include six new elements and six old elements. The new elements include the following:[8]

- embed
- video
- audio
- source
- track
- canvas

And these are the existing elements:

- img
- iframe
- object
- param
- map
- area

The embedded elements include the media elements, <video>, <audio>, <source>, <track>, and <canvas>, which we will discuss in Chapter 5. The other "new" element is <embed>, which has been implemented for years but was never part of the HTML 4 or XHTML specifications. We'll discuss this new element and visit the previously existent elements, as some attributes have been made obsolete.

Changes to Embedded Elements

<iframe>

The <iframe> element is not new to HTML5, but it does have different attributes than before. <iframe> lost longdesc, frameborder, marginwidth, marginheight, scrolling, and align attributes, and gained srcdoc, sandbox, and seamless.

The srcdoc attribute value is HTML that is used to create a document that will display inside the <iframe>. In theory, any element that can be used inside the <body> can be used inside the srcdoc. You should escape all quotes within the srcdoc value with

---

8. The <picture> element for responsive images is currently under consideration. The draft specification is at *http://www.w3.org/TR/html-picture-element/*.

" or your value will end prematurely. If a browser supports the `srcdoc` attribute, the `srcdoc` content will be used. Browsers that do not support the `srcdoc` attribute will display the file specified in the `src` attribute instead:

```
<iframe srcdoc="<p>Learn more about the
<a href=&quot;http://developers.whatwg.org/the-iframe-element.html
#attr-iframe-srcdoc&quot;>srcdoc</a> attribute."
src="http://developers.whatwg.org/the-iframe-element.html
#attr-iframe-srcdoc"></iframe>
```

The `sandbox` attribute enables a set of extra overrideable restrictions on any content hosted by the `<iframe>`. The effect of adding the attribute is to embed the externally sourced content as if it were served from the same domain, but with severe restrictions. Plug-ins, forms, scripts, and links to other browsing contexts within the `<iframe>` are disabled. The content of the `<iframe>` is treated under a unique origin and cannot traverse the DOM or read cookie information. These features are overwritable by setting a value to the `sandbox` attribute that conforms to a specific syntax.

The `allow-same-origin` keyterm allows the content to be treated as being from the same origin instead of forcing it into a unique origin. The `allow-top-navigation` keyword allows the content to navigate its top-level browsing context; and the `allow-forms`, `allow-pointer-lock`, `allow-popups`, and `allow-scripts` keywords re-enable forms, the pointer-lock API, pop-ups, and scripts, respectively. Include zero or more space-separated values depending on your needs, but realize that each value can create a security risk:

```
<iframe sandbox="allow-same-origin allow-forms allow-scripts"
    src="http://maps.google.com" seamless></iframe>
```

The `seamless` attribute makes the `<iframe>` appear seamless: as if it's a native part of the parent document. When supported, it is expected that it will allow CSS rules to cascade from parent through to the contents of the `<iframe>`, enable links to navigate the parent, and grow and shrink as necessary to expand to fit the parent, all on same origin only.

`<img>`

The empty `<img>` element lost the `border`, `vspace`, `hspace`, `align`, `longdesc` and `name` attributes. There is discussion around adding a `srcset` attribute to provide for alternative images based on width, height, or pixel density.

Unless an image is part of the content of your page, and necessary for context, you will want to use background images instead. We cover background images, and how to serve different background images for different screen sizes and devices of differing DPIs in Chapter 9.

If you do want to support responsive foreground images, until browsers natively support the srcset attribute, the <picture> element, or client hints, the Clown Car Technique[9] <object> tag can be employed to serve SVG files (discussed in Chapter 5) that provide a single raster image based on media queries.

<object>

The <object> element requires the data and type attributes. Several attributes, including align, hspace, vspace, and border were made obsolete in favor of CSS. Also obsolete are the archive, classid, code, codebase, and codetype, which should be set in the <param> instead. Instead of using the old declare attribute, repeat the <object> at each occurrence. Instead of using the now-obsolete standby attribute, optimize the resource so it loads quickly, and incrementally if applicable. While not often used, <object> is well supported.

<param>

The empty <param> element lost the type and valuetype attributes in favor of the name and value attributes.

<area>

The empty <area> element lost the nohref attribute, and gained the rel, ping (see the section "<a>" on page 72 for a description), media, and hreflang attributes.

<embed>

The <embed/> element is likely not new to you. It's just new to the specifications. The <embed> element is an integration point for content that will be displayed with a third-party plug-in (e.g., Adobe Flash Player) rather than a native browser control like <video> and <audio>. Like the <img> element, it is an empty element and should be self closing. Include the URL of the embedded source with the src attribute and MIME-Type of your source with the type attribute.

Interactive Elements

The interactive elements currently include form elements, the changed <menu> element, the new <detail>, <summary>, and <command> elements.

<details> and <summary>

Have you ever created a node that, when clicked on, opens up more details about the content of the node? And, when clicked on again, the details disappear? When supported, the <details> and child <summary> enable doing this natively in HTML5 without any JavaScript (Figure 3-4).

---

9. The Clown Car Technique is described in full detail at *http://github.com/estelle/clowncar/*.

Figure 3-4. Clicking on the always visible <summary> toggles the visibility of the <details>

The <details> element can be used to encompass a disclosure widget from which the user can obtain additional information or controls, such as content that may best fit into footnotes, endnotes, and tooltips. The <details> element has an open attribute that is also new in HTML5. With the open attribute, the content of the <details> will initially be visible. Without the open attribute, the details will be hidden until the user requests to see them.

The <summary> element should be included as a child element of the <details> element, with its text node providing a summary, caption, or legend for the rest of the contents of the <summary> element's parent details element. The contents of the <summary> show by default whether the open attribute is set or not. By clicking on the <summary>, the user can show and hide the rest of the content of the `<detail>` element. This interactivity is a default behavior of the `<details>`/`<summary>` element combo and, when supported, requires no JavaScript:

```
<details>
  <summary>5 of 5 stars from three reviews</summary>
  <ul>
      <li>5 stars from Amazon</li>
      <li>5 stars from Costco</li>
      <li>5 stars from Barns &amp; Noble</li>
  </ul>
</details>
```

When supported, the contents of `<details>` (except for the `<summary>`) are hidden, as the optional open attribute is not included (the default is to hide everything other than the summary). The rest of the contents should display when the `<summary>` is clicked. The `<summary>`, not to be confused with the summary attribute of the `<table>` element, a child of the `<details>` element, is the control that toggles the rest of the `<details>` content between visible and hidden (as if `display: none;` was set). The `<summary>` element represents a summary, caption, or legend for the rest of the contents of the parent `<details>` element.

Because the `<summary>` is the control to open and close the `<details>` element, it is always visible (in both the details open and not open states). Until all browsers support this functionality, it's easy to replicate with JavaScript. Simply add an event listener to the summary element that adds and removes the open attribute on the parent `<details>` element, and add the following styles to your CSS:

```
details * {display: none;}
details summary {display: auto;}
details[open] * {display: auto;}
```

If that last line doesn't make sense to you yet, don't worry! We cover attribute selectors in Chapter 8.

`<menu>` and `<menuitem>`

The `<menu>` element, deprecated in HTML 4.01 and XHTML, has resurfaced. Originally, it was defined as a "single column menu list." In HTML5, the `<menu>` element has been redefined to represent a list of commands or controls.

The `<menu>` element has been redefined in HTML5 to list form controls. The value of the `<menu>`'s id attribute can be included as the value of a `<button>`'s menu or `<input>`'s menuitem attribute to provide a menu or context menu for a form control. A menu can contain `<menuitem>` elements that cause a particular action to happen. The type attribute set to toolbar should be used when using `<menu>` to mimic a toolbar or when using context to create a content menu. The value of the label attribute determines the menu's label. They can be nested to provide multiple levels of menus.

`<menuitem>`

The `<menuitem>` element, found only inside the `<menu>`, defines a command button or context menu item. The type of command is defined by the `type` attribute, which can have as its value `radiobutton` for selecting one from a list of items, `checkbox` for options that can be toggled, or `command` to create a button upon which you can add an action. Though it sounds like a typical form control, it is not intended for the submission of information to a server. `<menuitem>` is an interactive element included to enable interactivity with the current contents of a web page.

The `<menuitem>` is an empty element with no closing tag. You should make sure to include a *label* attribute whose value is what will be displayed to the user. Other attributes include *icon*, *disabled*, *checked*, *radiogroup*, *default*, and *command*. The *command* attribute's value is the command definition. The *title* attribute, if included, should describe the command.

When implemented, you can create menu controls similar to the right-click menu controls that display in the Windows environment. So far, there is only experimental support for this on desktop, and no support on mobile.

All of XHTML Is in HTML5, Except...

Almost all of the elements from XHTML are still available and valid in HTML5. The elements that are obsolete include the following:

- basefont
- big
- center
- font
- strike (use `<del>`)
- tt
- frame (`<iframe>` is still valid)
- frameset
- noframes
- acronym (use `<abbr>`)
- applet (use `<object>`).
- isindex
- dir

As mentioned earlier, a few elements, instead of being made obsolete, have gained more semantic meaning. `<b>`, `<hr>`, `<i>`, `<u>` and `<small>`, while completely presentational in prior specs, now have semantic meaning and are defined beyond their appearance. <menu> has gained a purpose to be useful for toolbars and context menus. <strong> now means "important" rather than "strongly emphasized." <a> can now encompass blocks instead of just inline content, and doesn't need to have the href attribute present.

Some attributes are now obsolete. Some attributes have been added. Most of the changes are in web form elements, which we'll cover in great detail in Chapter 4. Otherwise, a few things to note that have not been previously detailed include:

- <table> no longer has the width, border, frame, rules, cellspacing, and cell padding attributes.
- <ol> has regained the reverse and start attributes.
- <col> and <colspan> lost all their element-specific attributes except for span.
- <td> and <th> had their attributes narrowed down to headers, rowspan, and col span, obliterating abbr, axis, width, align, and valign. Scope was removed for <td> but remains for <th>.
- <tr> and <thead> are attribute-less other than the global attributes.

In Conclusion

The HTML5 spec is *huge*. This section has introduced you to the syntax and semantics of HTML5, and to some of the new elements. This chapter was intended as a quick (or not so quick) explanation of the new elements in HTML5.

We're not done with HTML5. We are going to cover some wonderful features of web forms in Chapter 4, and show you how the Web Form features of HTML5 can help you quickly develop fantastic user interfaces with minimal JavaScript.

HTML5 Web Forms

If you're a web geek like me, perhaps the coolest new features of HTML5 are the new form features. Yes, Canvas is fabulous. SVG is wonderful. JavaScript APIs provide for targeting DOM nodes with selectors; matching with media queries; and easily adding, removing, and toggling class names all without needing to include a JS framework (if you don't believe me, wait; we'll cover these topics later). CSS3 enables quick prototyping of any designer's whimsy. So, why are HTML5 forms my favorite? Because HTML5 web forms provide enhanced usability and reduced reliance on JavaScript validation.

With HTML5, we are able to do form validation and several other tricks in a more declarative way. HTML5 allows developers to provide enhanced form usability features such as validation and error messaging without JavaScript. Reduced reliance on Java-Script can reduce development and maintenance time, making our lives much easier.

For example, instead of adding a setFocus() method on onload to provide focus to a form element, we now have an autofocus attribute (which you still shouldn't use).[1] Instead of providing multiple JavaScript functions to require, validate, and provide focus on error to email addresses, HTML5 web forms enable labeling form controls as required, provides native validation of multiple input types (both standard types like email format, and formats the developer can define with regular expressions), and provides useful error messaging for the user as to what the error was.

In the past, we've been adding a plethora of attributes and event handlers to our form elements. With default values and behaviors provided by HTML5, when universally supported and used, we might just be able to write <form>!

---

1. When you set focus on a form element, the page jumps to that form field, skipping over the preceding associated label for that input; this is bad for accessibility and can negatively impact user experience, especially on small devices where the label may get cut off. Due to accessibility issues with both these methods, you may want to avoid using either one.

Before, we were very limited with what type of data we could specify. The `type` attribute of the `<input>` element was limited—with `'text'` used for most data entry form fields no matter what type of data was expected—showing the QWERTY keypad for data entry on mobile devices. With HTML5 web forms, we can tell the browser what data types to accept, dictate the data entry patterns that are acceptable, and provide suggestions or tips to the user. Mobile browsers are providing improved HTML5 web form support, including displaying relevant virtual keyboards based on expected input type (like a phone keypad if the input type expects a phone number), and enhanced UI features, like calendars and color pickers.

Before HTML5, developers used CSS for appearance, JavaScript for validation, and backend code for ensuring a required element was completed. While you should definitely continue separating the three concerns and *always* validate user data on the backend, with HTML5 we will eventually be able to omit the frontend JavaScript layer, or at least simplify it greatly.

With HTML5, the browser can check that required elements are completed with the correct datatype, in the correct range, with the correct syntax, etc., preventing the form from submitting if data is incorrect. These features are über cool and are nearing full browser support. In this chapter, we'll discuss all the new features and whether they are already or soon to be supported.

Mobile devices have been supporting some of the HTML5 web form features for a while, and other features are just beginning to get support. On most touch devices with virtual keyboards, browsers will present users with the correct minimal keyboard, showing the keypad most relevant to completing the web form input type. Other mobile browsers handle most of the new web form UI features and native validation. No matter what level of support mobile devices have the day you are coding your forms, you should definitely be using all of the HTML5 web form features, as all the features are progressive enhancements. Newer browsers will have advanced features, but even the oldest of mobile browsers from the mid-1990s would present your HTML5 form elements in an accessible manner.

To indicate that a form control expects a particular type of input, you can specify the types using the `type` attribute. Before, we were limited to a small group of input types and we had to jump through hoops to validate them client-side before allowing submission to the server. With HTML5, not only are we provided with more input types, but now we also have native validation of many datatypes. Soon, the thousands of Java-Script validation scripts we've programmed will be obsolete as we rely on the browser's native form validation. Until we have full native support of the features described in the next section, we can fake support for all of them with minimal JavaScript. With a little JavaScript—and taking advantage of the new attributes and input types, while still using UI Selectors (see the section "Styling to enhance usability" on page 122), attribute selectors (see Chapter 7), and input-specific dynamic keyboards, we can improve usability in all modern browsers while HTML5 web form support improves.

Attributes of <input> (and Other Form Elements)

Before diving into the old and new input types, you should understand some of the new and old attributes of the <input> element.

The type Attribute

We just discussed the only required input attribute: the `type` attribute. Although required, it will work if omitted, defaulting to `type="text"`:

```
<label>Phone: <input type="tel" name="phone"></label>
<label>Website: <input type="url" name="website"></label>
```

With HTML5, there are 23 possible values of the `type` attribute. They are covered in the section "<input> Types and Attributes" on page 94. Note that if a browser doesn't support a new input type, the `type` defaults to the `text` type. These new types are an enhancement. Forms are fully accessible if the browser doesn't understand the new types, so don't wait for full browser support before implementing the new input types.

The required Attribute

To mark a form field as required, the `required` attribute can be used. When a user tries to submit a form, if a form field is `required` and is left empty or contains an invalid value, the form should not submit, and focus will move to the first invalid form element. Supporting browsers provide the user with an error message, such as "You have to specify a value" if left empty or "12-12 is not in the format this page requires" when the pattern is wrong (the `pattern` attribute is described on page 89), or other similar message.

The `required` attribute is valid on any input type except `buttons`, `range`, `color`, and `hidden`:

```
<label>Email: <input type="email" name="email" required="required" /></label> ❶
<label>Phone: <input type="tel" name="phone" required /></label>
```

 The syntax is either simply `required` or `required="required"` if you are coding with strict XHTML syntax.

Form elements with no value selected do not need to match the appropriate format expected for their type unless they are required controls. An email type with no value selected is empty, and therefore doesn't need to match any email format. However, if the `required` attribute is present, it will stop submission for being empty or being of the wrong format.

Pro Tip: Browsers that support the `required` attribute also support the `:required` and `:invalid` pseudoclasses. You can provide visual cues to the user to indicate which fields are required, indicating successful data entry with CSS:

```css
input:focus:invalid {
  background-color: #CCCCCC;
}
input:valid {
  background-color: #00FF33;
}
input:required {
  border: 2px solid #0066FF;
}
```

We discuss CSS3 UI selectors in Chapter 7.

Accessibility Tip: For improved accessibility, whenever the `required` attribute is included, include the ARIA attribute: *aria-required="true"* (we discuss ARIA, or Accessible Rich Internet Applications, in Chapter 6):

```html
<input type="tel" name="phone" required aria-required="true"/>
```

Minimum and Maximum Values: The min and max Attributes

To set the range of values that are allowed, the `min` and `max` attributes can be used.

The `min` and `max` attributes can be applied to the date/time inputs, `number` and `range` only. If the browser provides a UI widget for the input type, it disables selecting a value outside the `min`/`max` range by not showing values below and above the allowable range set by the `min` and `max` attributes.

On browsers that fully support the `number` input type, the browser displays a spinner that is limited in range, and will go down to the `min` and up to the `max` values. In UIs that provide for free form data entry, like the `number` input type, if the form element is required, the form will not submit if the value is outside of the range set by `min` and/or `max` in supporting browsers.

In the `range` input type, the leftmost value will be set to the `min` value and the right value will be set to `max` if it is larger than `min`. These attribute features will be discussed with the `number` and `range` input types in the next section.

Minimum and maximum values have often been incorporated into form validation, which makes these attributes very helpful for web developers. For example, if you're writing a reservation system, you already know what times you have available to seat people. You can encode this information in the page's form itself, so the user never ends up submitting an invalid time, avoiding the dreaded error message. Instead, the page already knows when the available slots are, and only lets the user select a valid time:

```
<label>Reservation Time:
  <input type="time" min="17:00" max="22:00" name="dinner" required>
</label>
```

In the online restaurant reservation system example, you serve dinner starting at 5:00 p.m., with your last seating at 10:00 p.m. In supporting browsers, without any JavaScript, you can ensure that your system only accepts reservations during those hours.

The step Attribute

The step attribute is implicitly included in date/time input types, range and number, but can also be explicitly defined on those input types. For example, if you have a five-and-dime store, where every price is divisible by 5, and the maximum price is $1.00, you can include the following in your price-setting GUI:

```
<p>
 <label for="cost">Price </label>
 <input type="number" min="5" max="100" step="5" name="cost" id="cost"/>
</p>
```

If the UI provides a widget, such as the range slider, moving the slider will increment the value by the value of the step attribute. Similarly, the number type's spinner will increase and decrease by the value of the step.

In UIs that provide for freeform data entry, like the number input type, supporting browsers will not submit the form if the value is not a valid step greater than the minimum value. For example, in the preceding example, 7 would not be valid. Had the minimum been 2 and the step 5 (as in the following code sample), 7 would have been valid, but 100 would not have been:

```
<p>
 <label for="cost">Price </label>
 <input type="number" min="2" max="100" step="5" name="cost" id="cost" required/>
</p>
```

In the online chapter resources, the number, range, month, and time examples include examples using the step attribute.

 In the step examples, I used explicit labels with the for attribute. Prior to this, I employed implicit labels. The for attribute is explained later in this chapter.

The placeholder Attribute

Possibly the most common JavaScript form feature is including placeholder text inside a form control, providing a hint or instruction on expected datatypes. Originally on focus but now on data entry, the placeholder text disappears. On data deletion, if the input is empty, the placeholder text reappears. User-agent stylesheets style the placeholder text as background text so as to make it apparent that the form element is still empty. HTML5 provides us with this functionality natively with improved accessibility. The placeholder attribute does what our oft-coded, rarely accessible placeholder function used to do, greatly improving form accessibility without the need for JavaScript.

One difference between our inaccessible scripts and the accessible placeholder attribute is the placeholder text disappears on change rather than on focus. In most modern browsers, the placeholder text remains in place as long as no text has been entered into the input field.

The placeholder attribute is a short hint for the user about what data should be entered. If a long hint is needed, describe the input type in a title attribute or in text next to the <input> element, but not in place of the <label> or placeholder. To ensure that your forms are accessible, include labels for your form elements: <label>s, not <title>s or <placeholder>s, provide for form accessibility.

While the placeholder attribute is only relevant to the text, search, url, telephone, email, and password types, until all browsers correctly support date and color types, it makes sense to include a placeholder value so the user knows what format to enter, especially if the pattern attribute, described next, is included. We've included placeholder values in most of the chapter code examples and online chapter resources.

The :placeholder-shown UI pseudoclass has been added to the CSS Selectors Level 4 specification. When supported, this pseudoclass will enable the styling of <input> elements based on the presence, or lack of presence, of the placeholder text (see Appendix A):

```
input:placeholder-shown {}
input:not(:placeholder-shown) {}
```

Include the attributes discussed in this chapter even if they aren't fully supported in all browsers. Attributes that aren't understood are ignored. These "ignored" attributes are still useful when used in conjunction with JavaScript to fake support for browsers.

You can use JavaScript to capture the contents of the unsupported attributes such as placeholder, min, max, pattern, and unsupported input types to polyfill support.

The pattern Attribute

The `pattern` attribute is supported wherever the `placeholder` attribute is allowed, which makes sense. The `pattern` attribute contains a JavaScript-style regular expression that the `<input>`'s value must match before the form can be submitted.

The `pattern` attribute allows for specifying a regular expression against which the control's value is to be checked. The `pattern` attribute is currently case-sensitive and must be a complete match. The regular expression language used for this attribute is the same as that used in JavaScript, except that the `pattern` attribute must match the entire value, not just a subset. If you want to allow the user to add more characters than provided by your regular expression, add * at the end to allow for more characters.

Table 4-1 provides the very basics of regular expressions.

Table 4-1. Some of the metacharacters of regular expressions used in pattern matching for the value of the pattern attribute

Metacharacter	Meaning
?	Match the preceding character 0 or 1 times only.
*	Match the preceding character 0 or more times.
+	Match the previous character 1 or more times.
{n}	Match the preceding character n times exactly.
{n,m}	Match the preceding character at least n times but not more than m times.
[]	Match anything inside the square brackets for one character position once and only once. [123] will match 1, 2, or 3.
[n-m]	The dash inside square brackets is the *range separator* and allows us to define a range; [123] could be written [1-3].
[^n-m]	The caret inside the brackets is a negation character, and will match any character except n through m.
\d	Match any digit. Equivalent to [0-9].
\D	Match any nondigit character. Equivalent to [^0-9].
\s	Match any whitespace characters (space, tab, etc.).
\S	Match any nonwhitespace character.
\w	Match any letter or number. Equivalent to [0-9A-Za-z].
\W	Match any character that is not a letter or number. Equivalent to [^0-9A-Za-z].
()	Parentheses can be used to group (or bind) parts of the expression together.
|	The vertical bar or pipe means find the lefthand or righthand values: gr(a|e)y will find "gray" or "grey."

Note that explaining regular expressions is beyond the scope of this book, but several code examples in the online chapter resources have regular expressions that you can learn from. Just realize that if you make a mistake (if your `pattern` is not a valid regular expression), it will be ignored for the purposes of validation, as if it were not specified.

When including a `pattern`, it's good practice to include a `title` attribute to give a description of the pattern. To use our color pattern and credit card number examples:

```
<label for="col"> Color: </label>
<input pattern="#[0-9A-Fa-f]{6}"
  name="col" type="color" placeholder="#ffffff "
  id="col" title="A hash sign followed by 6 hexadecimal digits"/>
<label for="cc"> Credit Card: </label>
<input type="text" pattern="[0-9]{13,16}"
  name="cc" id="cc" title="13 to 16 digit credit card number"
  placeholder="credit card #"/>
```

Some mobile browsers support the `color` input type, providing a color widget for color selection. This is covered later in the chapter. Other browsers support the `pattern` attribute, but have yet to support the `color` input type. While we wait for full support, we can employ the `pattern` attribute, as shown in the preceding code, to require the correct input format in these semi-supporting browers.

In supporting browsers, if the user's input does not match the pattern provided via the `pattern` attribute, the form will not submit and the browser will put focus on the first invalid input type, providing a validation error message, as shown in Figure 4-1, in browsers that already support native validation.

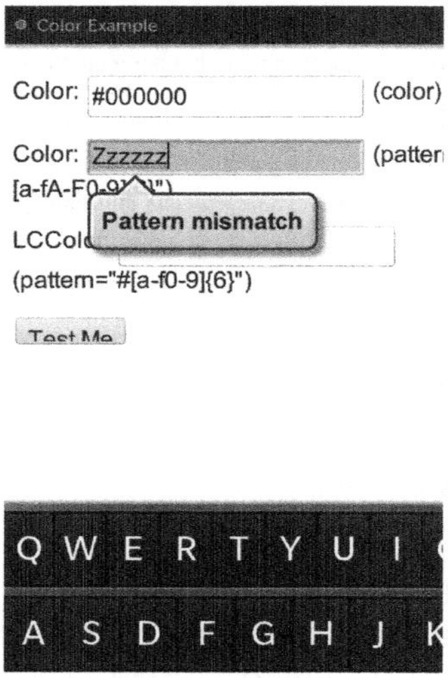

Figure 4-1. Native validation displays an error message when a pattern mismatch occurs (BlackBerry 10)

CSS Tip: Use the `:invalid` pseudoclass to target elements for styling that have content that does not match the pattern attribute, or is otherwise invalid. The `:valid` pseudoclass will match when the content matches the pattern, or is otherwise a valid entry.

The readonly Attribute

This `readonly` attribute, when present, makes a form control not editable. The attribute applies to text, password, email, URL, date/time, and number input types, as well as the `<textarea>` element. It does not apply to radio buttons, checkboxes, file upload controls, range controls, select elements, or any of the button types, since they are not editable anyhow. It's not a new attribute, so it is supported in all browsers, including older versions of IE. The `readonly` attribute is Boolean, so can be written either of these two ways:

```
<input type="text" value="Not Editable" readonly/>
<input type="text" value="Not Editable" readonly="readonly"/>
```

The disabled Attribute

The `disabled` attribute disables a form element. It can be applied to any form control except the `<output>` element. In HTML 4, the `disabled` attribute did not apply to the `<fieldset>` element. Now, when applied to a `<fieldset>` element, it overrides the `disabled` attributes of any child form controls, even if they are part of a different form (see the section "The form Attribute" on page 92). In other words, a form control will be disabled if it has its `disabled` attribute set, or if it has a parent `<fieldset>` that has its `disabled` attribute set.

CSS Tip: Use the `:disabled` pseudoclass to target disabled elements for styling.

So, what is the difference between `readonly` and `disabled`? Neither can be modified, but the `readonly` attribute can be tabbed to and is submitted along with the form. The `disabled` form control cannot receive focus, nor is it submitted with the form.

The maxlength Attribute

The `maxlength` attribute applies to `text`, `password`, `url`, `search`, `telephone`, and `email` input types, and `<textarea>` elements, but not to date/time or `number` input types. In HTML 4, this attribute only applied to the `text` and `password` types.

While you can include `maxlength` on email and URLs, I generally recommend that you don't use `maxlength` unless necessary for a compelling reason. While supported in all browsers, why should the user interface be allowed to determine that an email address or URL is too long? Understandably used for security reasons and if there are real character limits, for good user experience you should consider the consequences before adding this attribute. Even Twitter doesn't use it, as users want to enter more than 140 characters sometimes, and then omit words or delete characters where they can to fit into the 140-character limit.

The size Attribute

The `size` attribute is another older attribute. It historically had two functions: to define the number of options meant to be shown by a form control like a `<select>`, and to define the number of characters to display in a form control by controlling the width of the control. The `size` attribute of the `<input>` element should be deprecated in favor of using CSS to specify the layout of the form.

The `size` attribute was actually deprecated for a time, but was put back into the draft HTML5 specifications. The `size` attribute does not determine how many characters can be entered (use `maxlength` instead) or how many options can be selected (use `multiple` instead).

The form Attribute

New in HTML5, form controls don't have to be nested within a form. The new `form` attribute allows a form element to be associated with any form on the page. They can also be nested in one form but submitted with another.

A form control can have a `form` attribute with the `id` of the `<form>` with which the form control is associated. In this way, you can put form controls anywhere on a page, including outside of the form with which it should be submitted.

This is a bit complex to explain, so let's take a look at an example:

```
<form id="form1">
 <!-- all nested form content here -->
</form>

<p>
 <label for="userid">User ID</label>
 <input type="text" id="userid" name="user" form="form1"/>
</p>
```

The `#userid` `<input>` is not a descendant of `#form1`. In previous versions of HTML, the `name` and `value` of `#userid` would *not* be sent with the form upon form submission. In browsers that support the HTML5 `form` attribute, because the `id` of the form is included as the value of the #userid form attribute, when #form1 is submitted, #user id will be sent along with the form even though it is not a descendant of the form.

Before HTML5 web forms, form controls had to be nested within an ancestor <form>. With HTML5, form controls and fieldsets are associated with the forms given in their form attribute, or, if they don't have one, with the nearest ancestor <form>.

 Note that an empty string, form="", will disassociate the element from all forms, even the form for which the form element is a descendant, which can have unintended consequences. Generally, you will want to use removeAttribute('form') rather than setAttribute('form', ''); to avoid disassociating a form field from the <form> element in which it is nested.

The autocomplete Attribute

Autocompletion is a native feature in many browsers.[2] When a browser enables auto-complete functionality, it may store the value entered by the user so that if the user returns to the page, the browser can pre-fill the form. The autocomplete attribute is the method by which the site author (you) can suggest to the user agent that you do or don't want the autocomplete feature turned on for a particular form field. autocomplete takes one of three values: on, off, or default. The on keyword will map to the on state, and the off keyword maps to the off state.

The off state indicates that the form control's data is sensitive, like a password, or that it will never be reused, like a CAPTCHA. The user will have to enter the data each time, and the browser should not pre-fill the value. Conversely, the on state indicates that the user can expect to be able to rely on their browser to remember previously entered values for that control. Omitting the value puts the form control in the default state, which means the form control should have the same autocomplete value of the form it is associated with:

```
<p>Login: </p>
<p>
  <label for="user">Username: </label>
  <input type="text" name="user" id="user" autocomplete="on"/>
</p>
<p>
  <label for="pwd"> Password:</label>
  <input type="password" name="pwd" id="pwd" autocomplete="off"/>
</p>
```

---

2. Google is working on a requestAutocomplete() API as a web standard to allow form fields to request form completion information the browser knows.

The autofocus Attribute

The `autofocus` attribute specifies that the form control should have focus when the page loads. Only one form element can have autofocus in any given page. The Boolean `autofocus` attribute can be included in a single `<input>` (except type hidden), `<button>`, `<select>`, or `<textarea>` per page. If more than one element is assigned the `autofocus` attribute, the *last* element with the `autofocus` attribute set will get focus.

As mentioned earlier, for usability and accessibility reasons, I recommend against using the `autofocus` attribute. If you were using jQuery as an exact shim for the attribute, it would read:

```
$('[autofocus]').last().focus();
```

That line of code reads, "Find all the elements with the `autofocus` attribute, get the last one and give that focus." This is likely not what you would want. For better usability, you want to highlight the first element, not the last, which is the opposite of what this does.

Note that focusing on a text field on onload is disabled in iOS because the keyboard will show up.

HTML5 has added a plethora of very useful input types and attributes. There are now 23 input types, and even more input attributes. As we've already seen, some attributes belong to only certain input types. Browsers that don't support a specific input `type` attribute may still support other attributes in the `<input>`. A browser may support attributes on the `text` input type (such as `maxlength` or `size`), and will therefore support those attributes on a type it doesn't support, as the input will default to `text` type. For example, as displayed previously, while not all browsers support the `color` input type, they all support the `disabled` attribute on all input types.

`<input>` Types and Attributes

There are now 23 values for input `type`. Some are old. Some are new in HTML5. We'll cover them all.

Re-introduction to Input Types You Think You Know

Let's first recap the input types we've been able to use prior to HTML5. While you may think "I've been coding HTML for years; I already know this stuff," most developers haven't really thought about all the different `<input>` types. This recap may be helpful even if you're a pro.

Pro Tip: Generally, you will want to style buttons differently than text and other input types. You can use attribute selectors to target form input fields based on their `type` value. This code snippet makes the borders of all input elements except those of input type `submit` have a dark gray border:

```
input:not([type=submit])){
    border: 1px solid #666666;
}
```

We discuss attribute selectors and the `:not` pseudoclass in Chapter 8.

Text: <input type="text">

Displayed as a data entry box, the `text` input type, `type="text"`, often called "text box" or "text field," allows the user to input one line of text. This is also the default value for the required `type` attribute: if the `type` is omitted or not supported, it will default to `text`.

 `text` is the default value for the `<input>` element. If the `type` attribute is missing or the value is misspelled or unsupported, the browser will treat the input as `type="text"`. This means that if a browser does not support a new HTML5 input type, it will display the default `text` type. So, feel free to use all the HTML5 input types even if you're still supporting Netscape 4.7. In the worst case, your users will see text boxes.

The `value` attribute is optional. If included, the value of the `value` attribute will display inside the text box on page load. Only include a value for the `value` attribute if you are pre-filling a form for the user using data you would like to receive back.

Other attributes include `name`, `disabled`, `form`, `maxlength`, `readonly`, `size`, `autocom plete`, `autofocus`, `list`, `pattern`, `required`, and `placeholder`. The new attributes we discussed are what make the `text` input type so interesting and useful in HTML5:

```
<label for="username">Username</label>
<input type="text" name="username" id="username"/>
```

It is *not* a good idea to include instructions as the value of the `value` attribute, as users most likely will submit the instructions you provided instead of filling out the form field. The values submitted on form submit will be whatever is contained in the input box at the time of submission. So, unless the form is pre-populated, do not include the `value` attribute. The `placeholder` attribute should be used to provide a hint, supplying the correct solution to this very old problem.

If you want to include instructions as the default value displayed in your text box, do so using the `placeholder` attribute.

As mentioned earlier, it *is* a good idea—generally good user experience—to pre-populate the text input boxes with values from a database if your user is registered, the information is available, and the information poses no security issues.

Password: <input type="password">

The `password` input type, `type="password"` or "password" field, is like the text field just described except the value entered by the user or the default value entered via the `value` attribute is obfuscated in the UI. Instead of displaying "pAssW0rd," the user will see "●●●●●●●●." Although hidden from the user interface, the password value is sent to the server as plain text.

 Note that if you're requesting a user password, use the form's `POST` method over SSL. While the password is obfuscated in the browser window, the password is sent to the server as plain text. If you were to use `GET`, the URL of your form confirmation page might read:

```
https://www.website.com/index.php?user=Estelle&password=pAssW0rd
```

When requesting a password in a form, use the form's `POST` method over the HTTPS protocol. While using the `POST` method still submits the password value in plain text, it is sent behind the scenes so is not as blatant of a security risk:

```
<label for="password">Password</label>
<input type="password" name="password" id="password"/>
```

Also note that in WebKit you can make nonpassword types look like password input types with the CSS `-webkit-text-security` property. Set `-webkit-text-security` to `circle`, `square`, `disc`, or `none` to alter the presentation and control the appearance of the icons that are obfuscating the value entered by the user.

By default and for better usability with tiny smartphone keyboards, some mobile devices temporarily display the last character entered in a password field.

Checkbox: <input type="checkbox">

The checkbox input type, type="checkbox", better known as a "checkbox," has as a default presentation a small square: with a checkmark if selected, empty if not selected, or a horizontal line through the middle if the state is indeterminate. Checkboxes are great for yes or no type answers, or when multiple answers can be checked: for example, you have either read and agree to the web form's associated privacy policy or you haven't and don't. On a travel site, you may be willing to fly out of San José or San Francisco, but not Oakland.

Remember to always include a name and value for each of your checkboxes. On form submission, if a checkbox is checked, the name and value attribute values will be submitted as a name/value pair. Unchecked checkboxes are omitted from the data submitted by the form:

```
<input type="checkbox" name="remember" value="true">
<label for="remember">Remember me</label>
```

 Pro Tip: You can style checkboxes based on whether the checkbox is checked or not with the CSS :checked pseudoclass selector. In the following example, the label immediately following a checkbox will turn gray when the checkbox preceding it is checked:

```
input[type=checkbox]:checked + label {
  color: #cccccc;
}
```

If that CSS doesn't make sense to you, don't worry! We discuss attribute selectors, the + adjacent sibling selector, and the :checked pseudoclass in Chapter 8.

Radio: <input type="radio">

The radio input type, type="radio", better known as a "radio button," has as a default presentation a small circle: either filled if selected or empty if not selected.

Radio buttons are generally presented in groups of related values where only one value can be selected, such as multiple-choice questions that accept only one answer. If you have a multiple-choice question that can take more than one answer, use checkboxes. If you only have one option and not a group of buttons, use a checkbox instead of a radio button.

The various radio buttons presented in a related group should all have the same value for the name attribute and differing values for the value attribute. There are a few things to remember about radio buttons:

- Only one radio button of a group of same named radio buttons can be selected.
- Upon form submission, only the value of the value attribute of the selected radio button is sent to the server, along with the name. So, remember to include a unique value attribute for each radio button.
- Users can select radio buttons, but cannot change their values.
- A radio button can only be deselected by selecting another radio button in the same group. In other words, once a radio button in a same named group is selected, it is impossible to unselect all of the radio buttons in that group: you can click on a different radio button to deselect what was previously selected and select the new radio button instead. However, there is no way outside of JavaScript or resetting the form to bring it back to the state of no radio buttons in that group being selected.

```
<p>What is your favorite color (pick one):</p>
<ul>
  <li>
    <label>red:
    <input type="radio" name="favoritecolor" value="red"/>
    </label>
  </li>
  <li>
    <label>green:
    <input type="radio" name="favoritecolor" value="green"/>
    </label>
  </li>
  <li>
    <label>blue:
    <input type="radio" name="favoritecolor" value="blue"/>
    </label>
  </li>
</ul>
```

Note that all of the radio buttons in this group have the same name value. name values should be identical for all radio buttons in a group. IDs, if included, must be unique.

 Note that we are using implicit labels in this example. For accessibility reasons, always include a label—whether implicit or explicit—for each input. For explicit labels, make the for attribute of the label match the id of the form element. <label> is detailed later in this chapter.

Submit: <input type="submit">

The submit input type, type="submit", more commonly known as a "submit button," submits the form when clicked. The submit button sends the form data unless prevented by having the disabled attribute set or prevented with JavaScript by return false or preventDefault() on its event handler. When the `disabled` attribute is set, the "disabled" state has the disabled UI and is not clickable by the user. The JavaScript method of `preventDefault()` or `return false` does not change the appearance or the clickability:

```
<input type="submit" value="Submit this Form"/>
```

 Note that if included, the onsubmit event should be associated with the `<form>` element, not the submit button, as it is the form being submitted, not the button.

The default presentation of the `submit` input type is a button displaying the content of the `value` attribute, centered. If the `name` attribute is included, the name/value pair will be submitted along with the rest of the form on submit.

In HTML5, the submit button does not need to be contained within the `<form>` that it will be submitting. You can associate a form element with a `<form>` that is not its ancestor with the `form` attribute: `form="id_of_form_to_submit"` will submit the form indicated by the value of the `form` attribute.

And with our submit button, we have covered enough HTML to complete the Cubee-Doo sign-in form:

```
<form>
<ul>
<li>
 <label for="username">Username</label>
 <input type="text" name="username" id="username"/>
</li>
<li>
 <label for="password">Password</label>
 <input type="password" name="password" id="password"/>
</li>
<li>
 <input type="checkbox" name="remember" value="true"/>
 <label for="remember">Remember me</label>
</li>
<li>
 <input type="submit" name="submit" value="Sign in"/>
</li>
</ul>
</form>
```

Reset: <input type="reset">

The reset input type, `type="reset"`, is better known as the "reset button." The reset button restores the form data to the original default values unless prevented by the disabled attribute or through JavaScript. If included, the onreset event should be associated with the <form> element, not the reset button, as it is the form being reset, not the button.

Since accidentally clicking the reset button instead of the submit button on form completion is one of the most annoying user experiences, don't include a reset button. If you must, place it relatively far from the submit button and far from where user experience design suggests the submit button should be located to help avoid accidental resets.

The reset button used to be popular, but you'll almost never see it anymore due to the horrendous user experience of accidentally obliterating everything you entered:

```
<input type="reset" value="Reset this Form"/>
```

The only time that you really do want to use the reset button is if you have radio button groups that you want to enable the user to deselect.

The default presentation of the reset button is a button displaying the content of the value attribute. Unlike the submit button, the name/value pair of the reset button is *not* sent to the server on form submission.

File: <input type="file">

The file input type, type="file", is different from the other input types. Its purpose is to enable the user to upload, attach, or otherwise interact with a local file from their computer or network. The input of file type is disabled on iOS prior to 6.0 (on Safari for iPhone/iPad). Older versions of the iPhone, iPod, and iPad display the input file type as disabled. The file type is also disabled on IE10 on Windows Phone 8, but enabled on Windows 8 RT for tablets.

Most browsers allow for only limited, if any, styling of the input box and button, and don't allow for styling or text changes of the associated browse/choose button. However, browsers are now beginning to expose the shadow DOM. It is actually possible to style the form elements, including the file input type in some browsers:

```
input[type="file"] {
  /* Style of "choose file" text here */
}
input[type="file"]::-webkit-file-upload-button {
    /* style the choose file button here */
}
```

The file input type's attributes can include name, disabled, accept, autofocus, multiple, required, and capture. If a value is included, it is ignored.

The accept attribute may be used to specify a comma-separated list of content types that a server processing the form will handle correctly. The file input type doesn't have the min or max attributes to set the number of files that must be uploaded, but logically it defaults to 0 and 1 respectively, with the ability to overwrite by including the `multi ple` attribute.

In some mobile browsers the `accept` attribute allows for accessing the camera, microphone, and camcorder on some devices:

```
<input type="file" name="image" accept="image/*;capture=camera">
<input type="file" name="video" accept="video/*;capture=camcorder">
<input type="file" name="audio" accept="audio/*;capture=microphone">
```

These are not universally supported, but will work in some browsers, including Android 3.0 browser, Chrome for Android (0.16), FF Mobile 10.0, and Opera Mobile 14.

The specifications have recently been modified.[3] The `capture` component that used to be part of the accept attribute is now a seperate Boolean attribute. The preceding code has become the following:

```
<input type="file" name="image" accept="image/*" capture>
<input type="file" name="video" accept="video/*" capture>
<input type="file" name="audio" accept="audio/*" capture>
```

It is up to the device to decide on which supported media capture mechanism to use, or to act as if no `capture` attribute had been included if there is no appropriate capture control mechanism available.

Hidden: <input type="hidden">

The `hidden` input type, `type="hidden"`, only needs three attributes: `type="hidden"`, `name="somename"`, and `value="some value"`. The `hidden` type is not displayed to the user, but rather is used to communicate information to the server. `hidden` types are often used to maintain session IDs, user IP addresses, or data garnered from previous pages of a multipage form.

Many developers also take advantage of the `hidden` type to maintain state or otherwise help handle their frontend JavaScript voodoo. HTML5 provides us with alternative options like `<output>` and localStorage, and good old-fashioned cookies that can make this misuse of `hidden` types obsolete. I say "misuse" since you only want to use `hidden` types for name/value pairs that you want to send to the server.

Image: <input type="image">

The `image` type input, `type="image"`, is similar to the `submit` type in behavior, and takes all the `<img>` attributes, namely `src` and `alt`. If the `value` and `name` attributes are included, the name/value pair of the image button will be submitted along with the form.

---

3. The media capture draft (*http://www.w3.org/TR/html-media-capture/*) is in the last call.

If you are looking to take a picture or upload a picture, see the section "File: <input type="file">" on page 100.

Button: <input type="button">

The button input type, type="button", referred to as "button," does absolutely nothing without event handlers, and therefore should generally only be added to the form with JavaScript as progressive enhancement. The default presentation of the button is a button displaying the content of the value attribute:

```
<input type="button" value="I do nothing"/>
```

 Many people confuse the button input type with the <button> element, which is more easily styled than the input of type="button", and can actually do something, like submit or reset the form, without JavaScript. Use input type="button" if you want to match a form control with the appearance of a submit button. Otherwise, you'll generally want to use <button> instead, as it is more readily styled.

Styling Input Types

Each browser provides default styling to the various form elements. In WebKit and Mozilla browsers, we can affect the default appearances with the not yet standard appearance property. The vendor prefixes -webkit-appearance and -moz-appearance enable us to change the appearance of buttons and other controls to resemble native controls, and provide us with a better ability to override default appearance of form controls.

There are too many supported values for appearance to mention them all. Just realize that any feature for which the user agent presents a default UI, from checkboxes to buttons to ranges, the default stylesheet will include appearance values such as checkbox, button, and slider-horizontal (nesting a shadow DOM <div> with sliderthumb-horizontal). You can control appearance values with CSS.

Resources on the various values of the appearance property can be found in the online chapter resources.

New Values for <input> Type

Now comes the cool stuff!

In the past, we were using the text input type for everything: dates, email addresses, phone numbers, and URLs. Then we had to validate client-side before sending to the server. No more! (Well, "no more" when HTML5 is fully supported and you implement everything you've learned in this chapter.) The <input> element has been greatly expanded. HTML5 defines 13 new values for the type attribute of the HTML <input> element:

- search
- tel
- url
- email
- datetime
- date
- month
- week
- time
- datetime-local
- number
- range
- color

Mobile and desktop browser support for HTML5 forms has greatly improved. Just like with radio, checkbox, and button input types, the graphical representation of these new input types will often reflect the type. In addition, if the browser is on a touch device with a dynamic UI keyboard (rather than a physical keyboard), the keyboard provided will reflect the input type.

For example, when on phones with dynamic keyboards like the BlackBerry 10, if the type is tel, when the user gives focus to the input, the telephone keypad is displayed instead of the full keyboard, as shown later in Figure 4-4.

Most browsers support the user interface :invalid pseudoclass CSS selector. Instead of (or in addition to) using JavaScript to do client-side validation and error messaging, you can indicate invalid input values with CSS:

```
input:focus:invalid {background-color: #CCCCCC;}
```

Email: <input type="email">

The email type displays similar to a text field, and is used for specifying an email address.

On a touchscreen, focusing on this element will bring up a keyboard optimized for email address entry. The email type has been supported on the iPhone since iOS 3.1, providing a keyboard with A–Z, @, period, and a button reading _123 that leads to a modified numeric keyboard, as seen in Figure 4-2:

```
<p>
  <label for="email">Email: </label>
  <input id="email" type="email" name="email"
         placeholder="name@domain.com" required multiple/>
</p>
```

The email input type supports the Boolean multiple attribute, allowing for multiple, comma-separated email addresses.

 To include more than one address, separate email addresses with a single comma, or a comma and space(s).

Other attributes the email input type should support according to the current draft of the spec include name, disabled, form, autocomplete, autofocus, list, maxlength, pattern, readonly, required, size, and placeholder. There are examples in the online chapter resources.

Figure 4-2. An email field in a form with dynamic keyboards on Blackberry 10, iPod, Windows Phone, and Firefox OS

URL: <input type="url">

Like the email type, the url type displays similar to a text field, and is used for specifying a web address. On a touchscreen, focusing on this element will bring up a keyboard optimized for web address entry on many devices. On iOS devices, the url type provides the smartphone user with a keyboard with A–Z, period, forward slash, and ".com," but no colon, as shown in Figure 4-3. The BlackBerry is similar, but with no slash, and no colon either.

Figure 4-3. Dynamic keyboards for the URL input on Firefox OS, iPod, Blackberry 10, Windows Phone and Chrome on an Android tablet

Browsers supporting the url input type report the input as valid if the URL begins with an Internet Protocol, any Internet Protocol—even made-up ones like **Q:**. (**Q://** works just as well as **ftp://**.) A web address without a protocol, like *www.yahoo.com*, will not validate.

Browsers currently do not check the actual URL, as the HTML5 specifications suggest, because there is no code to check for a valid URI/IRI according to the current URL specifications. A bug has been reported for the W3C on this. In the meantime, at least we get a slightly more relevant keyboard (Figure 4-3), though they really should add the colon in the default keyboard state.

To allow only specific protocols, you can employ the `pattern` attribute:

```
<p>
  <label for="url">Web Address: </label>
  <input id="url" type="url"
    pattern="^(http|https|ftp)\://[a-zA-Z0-9\-\.]+\.[a-zA-Z]*"
    placeholder="http://www.domain.com" required />
</p>
```

Telephone: <input type="tel">

`tel` is short for telephone. Unlike the `url` and `email` types, the `tel` type does not enforce a particular syntax or pattern. Letters and numbers, or any noncarriage return characters for that matter, are valid. Different countries have different types of valid phone numbers. Different systems prefer different ways of writing the number. For example, in the United States, +1(415)555-1212 is just as well understood as 415.555.1212.

So, why have a `tel` input type? The default keyboard displayed for the `tel` input type is a telephone keypad, as shown in Figure 4-4. Use the best input type for the data type you want: your users will thank you for it!

You can encourage a particular phone format by including a `placeholder` with the preferred syntax and a comment after the form field with an example. You can require a format by using the `pattern` attribute and you can use the `setCustomValidity()` method (see the section "Form Validation" on page 118) to provide for custom error messaging during client-side validation:

```
<p>
  <label for="tel">Telephone: </label>
  <input id="tel" type="tel" placeholder="XXX-XXX-XXXX"
        pattern="[0-9]{3}-[0-9]{3}-[0-9]{4}" required />
</p>
```

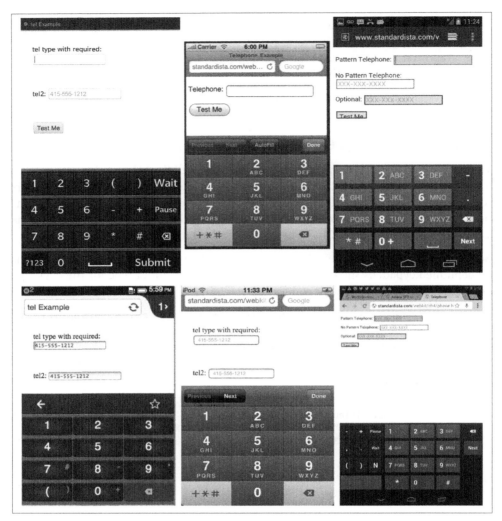

Figure 4-4. The telephone input type and associated keypads

Number: <input type="number">

The number type provides a text field for specifying a number. When supported on a touch pad, focusing on an input element of type number will bring up a number pad keyboard like the ones shown in Figure 4-5. The attributes of min, max, and step can be included.

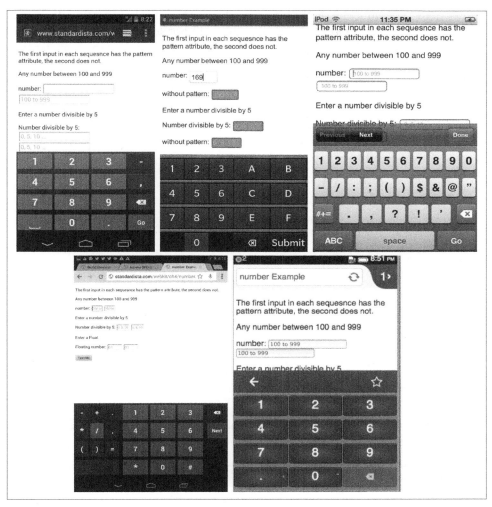

Figure 4-5. Entering numbers into a numeric form field

The `min` attribute is the minimum value allowed. The `max` attribute value is the maximum value allowed. The `step` attribute indicates the step between available values. The default `step` value is 1, allowing for floats if the `min`, `max`, or `step` attributes have a float set as a value.

The user interface of desktop browsers that fully support this feature provide for incrementing or decrementing the counter without keyboard entry. This spinner is not yet seen on mobile browsers. Even when the number input type provides a spinner UI with up and down arrows, it also accepts freeform keyboard data entry. When using the spinner (currently only supported in some desktop browsers), clicking or touching the arrows steps the number up or down by the value of `step`, displaying only valid values. If the form element is a required field, the form will not submit if there is a nonvalid entry. Invalid entries include a nonnumber, a number less than the `min` or greater than the `max`, or an invalid number of steps above the `min`. Instead, when an attempt is made to submit the form, the incorrect value gets focus:

```
<input type="number" min="0" step="5">
```

To be valid, the value must be a number equal to `min + n * step` where n is any integer value with a result within the `min`/`max` range. For example, if `min=2`, `max=10`, and `step=5`, 7 is valid and 10 is not:

```
<p>Any number between 100 and 999</p>
<p>
 <label for="number">number: </label>
 <input id="number" type="number" placeholder="100 to 999"
    pattern="[1-9][0-9]{2}" min="100" max="999" required />
</p>
<p>Enter a number between 0 and 1,000 that is divisible by 5</p>
<p>
 <label for="even">Number divisible by 5: </label>
 <input id="even" type="number" placeholder="0, 5, 10 &hellip;"
    pattern="[0-9]*[05]" min="0" max="1000" step="5" required />
</p>
<p>Enter a positive Float less than 10.0</p>
<p>
 <label for="float">Floating number: </label>
 <input id="float" type="number" placeholder="0.1"
    pattern="[0-9](?\.[0-9])?" min="0.1" max="9.9" step="0.1"/>
</p>
```

With the new HTML5 form input types, we also get new APIs. For the `step` attribute, we have the `stepUp()` and `stepDown()` methods:

```
input.stepUp(x)
input.stepDown(x)
```

These two methods change the form control's value by the value given in the `step` attribute, multiplied by x, or 1 if no parameter is passed, within the values provided by the `min` and `max` attributes.

The `pattern` attribute is not supported in the `number` type, but I have included it as it is more widely supported than the `number` input type. The `pattern` attribute can be considered a graceful degradation for browsers that support the `pattern` attribute but don't fully support an input type.[4]

---

4. For example, at the time of this writing, Safari on iOS 6 supports `pattern`, but does not support `number` and does not provide for validation on submission.

If a browser supports the number type, that supersedes the pattern. A pattern of `pattern="[0-9]*"` or `pattern="\d+|\d+\.\d+"` is almost equivalent to the number type, though matching the ability to have `min`, `max`, and `step` can lead to an unwieldy regular expression.

Range: <input type="range">

The `range` input type displays as a slider, like those in Figure 4-6, that lets the user drag or tap along its length to select a value. As with the number type, its minimum value is set with the `min` attribute, its maximum value with the `max` attribute, and its discrete step size with the `step` attribute. While the `range` input type has been around since Safari 2.0, only with the release of Safari 5 have `min`, `max`, and `step` been fully supported, so it is finally usable in mobile WebKit. Opera, Blackberry, IE10, and Chrome support `range` as well. Mobile Firefox began to support `range` with version 23. Android has partial support.

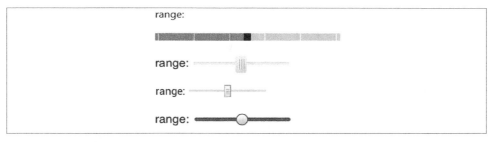

Figure 4-6. Sliders created by a range control on Windows Phone, Blackberry 10, iPhone, and Chrome

The default value of the slider is the midpoint between the minimum and the maximum. You can change where the thumb lands on the slider with the `value` attribute. If the range is 20 to 30, the default value will be 25. If you don't set a min, max, or step, they'll default to 0, 100, and 1, respectively. As there is a default value, when supported, a `range` input type always returns a value.

One question I get is: "Can you make the slider vertical instead of horizontal?" The answer is: "Yes, in some browsers." The way to do it in WebKit is:

```
input[type=range]{-webkit-appearance: slider-vertical;}
```

You can also declare a height that is a larger value than the width, which will create a vertical range in older Presto-based versions of Opera.

Search: <input type="search">

Input type `search` provides for a search field. While the specifications don't mandate a particular UI for new form types, the search field often looks like a round-cornered text box. In many browsers, though not all, when the search is nonempty, a `search-cancel-button` appears in the right of the box that, when clicked, clears the field, as shown in Figure 4-7.

Figure 4-7. The search input type on Blackberry 10 (note the delete icon in the filled out search field) and iOS 6.1 (note the "search" key)

Some devices will display a keyboard with the word "search" or the magnifying glass where the "go" or "enter" button normally is on the keyboard field.

Color: <input type="color">

When fully supported, the `color` input type displays a color picker widget, such as the "color well" shown in Figure 4-8. The `color` input type, like all new input types, will display as a regular text box when not fully supported. The values of selected colors are submitted in lowercase hexadecimal color format. The default value of color pickers is #000000, which means, when supported, a `color` input type always returns a value.

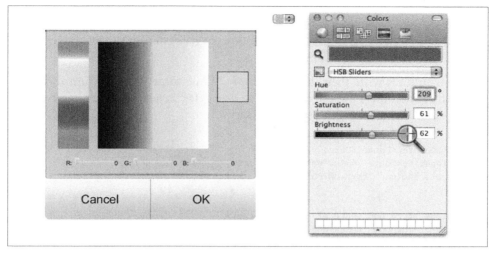

Figure 4-8. Color picker on the BlackBerry 10 and in Opera on Mac

For a while, some browsers supported named colors, such as "indianred." Named colors support is not in the specifications and support has been removed.

Native color picker UI interfaces in supporting browsers are nifty but not ubiquitous yet. To "fake" support for hex color values, only accept values that match the regular expression #[a-zA-Z0-9]{6} by using the `pattern` attribute with a `placeholder` indicating that hexadecimal color values are required. Neither of these attributes is supported by the `color` input type as per the specifications, but they are simply ignored in browsers that fully support the `color` input type:

```
<label for="clr">Color: </label>
<input id="clr" name="clr" type="color" placeholder="#000000"
    pattern="#[0-9A-Fa-f]{6}" required />
```

Date and Time Input Types

There are several new date and time input types including `date`, `datetime`, `datetime-local`, `month`, `time`, and `week`. All times are based on ISO 8601 dates. Supporting browsers provide interactive widgets replicative of the device's native calendar widget. All of the date/time types have a code sample in the online chapter resources. The value for `date` is better supported across browsers than any of the other date and time input types.

Date: <input type="date">

The date input type provides a date with year, month, and day (no time or day or time zone). The expected user interface presentation is a date control. When supported, the browser provides a calendar control.

Different cultures write their dates differently. While some browser controls put the month first and others put the day first, the date gets converted to the same syntax of YYYY-MM-DD before getting sent to the server:

```
<p>
  <label for="date">Date: </label>
  <input id="date" name="date" type="date"
    placeholder="YYYY-MM-DD" required />
</p>
<p>
  <label for="dob">Date of Birth: </label>
  <input id="dob" name="dob" type="date"
    placeholder="YYYY-MM-DD" min="1900-01-01" required />
<p>
```

Until date is supported in all browsers, you can use pattern matching. However, if pattern matching is relied upon, the users won't get a native calendar widget. Also, you might want to use JavaScript validation to account for leap years and the like, as a regular expression for dates is kind of horrific.

Supporting browsers, as shown in Figure 4-9, provide a date picker and don't allow direct data entry, ensuring the user submits a valid date (perhaps not the correct date, but a valid date).

The date type is the full date, with no time or time zone. This is the best supported of the various date/time input types. We'll cover the others briefly for when they are supported.

Figure 4-9. The date picker that appears on iOS, BlackBerry, Android, and Firefox OS when the input of date type receives focus

Datetime: <input type="datetime">

The datetime input provides two fields: one for the date (year, month, day) and one for the time (hour, minute, second, fraction of a second) with the time zone set to UTC with minutes and seconds, but not fractions of a second. You can include the min, max, and step attributes to limit the possible values, such as min="2012-03-01T12:00Z".

You may prefer to use pattern matching, but again, you'll need to validate the input for true times and valid dates:

```
<p>
  <label for="datetime">datetime: </label>
  <input id="datetime" name="datetime" type="datetime" placeholder="YYYY-MM-DD"
      min="2010-01-01T00:00Z"max="2011-12-31T23:59Z" required />
</p>
<p>
  <label for="dte">datetime: </label>
  <input id="dte" name="dte" type="text" placeholder="YYYY-MM-DDT00:00Z"
      pattern="\d{4}\-\d{2}\-\d{2}T\d\d\:\d\dZ" required />
</p>
```

Datetime-local: <input type="datetime-local">

The datetime-local value is identical to datetime, except it is not UTC time. (The Z is not included.)

Month: <input type="month">

The month input type is supposed to include the month and year, with no day of month and no time zone. Default values differ by device, with defaults such as a min value of 0001-01 and default max value of 2147483647-12. Therefore, I recommend including a min and max value. You can also include the step attribute. For example, use step="6" to limit your month choice to January or July:

```
<p>
  <label for="month">Month: </label>
  <input id="month" name="month" type="month" placeholder="YYYY-MM" required
      min="2010-01" max="2020-01" step="6"/>
</p>
```

Unlike JavaScript, which indexes starting with 0, January is represented as 01.

Time: <input type="time">

The time input type provides a mechanism for inputting time in military (24 hour) format. Times must be greater than or equal to 0 and must be less than 24 hours, with tighter restrictions imposable by the min and max attributes.

The time increments in seconds, not minutes. Including a step of 60 for 60 seconds, will create a better user experience. In our example, the `step` attribute is set to 900, for 60 sec × 15 min, or 15-minute increments:

```
<p>
  <label for="time">Meeting time: </label>
  <input type="time" min="09:00" max="17:00" name="time" id="time"
    step="900" placeholder="12:00" required />
</p>
```

This `type` is not for elapsed time, but rather for time of day. When supported, browsers are expected to show a time widget, such as a clock, with no time zone.

Week: <input type="week">

The `week` input type allows for a date consisting of the number of the week within the year, with no month, day, or time. The value will range from 01 to 52, with a year. For example, the first week of the year will output 2014-W01.

The week calendar does not start with January 1. Rather, week 01 is the week that contains January 4th, which may not necessarily include January 1st:

```
<input type="week" name="week" id="week" min="2010-W01" max="2020-W02" required />
```

The `week` input type is the least supported of the date/time input types. We'll get there eventually...

In all, we now have 23 input types to play with. The various input types include:

- button
- checkbox
- color
- date
- datetime
- datetime-local
- email
- file
- hidden
- image
- month
- number
- password
- radio

- range
- reset
- search
- submit
- tel
- text
- time
- url
- week

Form Validation

Currently, web developers use JavaScript scripts to perform form validation on the client side. We're getting closer and closer to the day when we can simply write the following simple form, and the browser will prevent submission when invalid with no need for client-side JavaScript validation (you must always do server-side validation). The user won't be able to submit this form unless all three inputs have values, with the latter two needing to be of a single email address and a single URL, respectively:

```
<form>
  <ul>
    <li>
      <label>
        Name: <input name="name" required"/>
      </label>
    </li>
    <li>
      <label>
        Email: <input name="email" type="email" required />
      </label>
    </li>
    <li>
      <label>
        Website: <input name="website" type="url" required />
      </label>
    </li>
    <li>
      <input type="submit" value="Send"/>
    </li>
  </ul>
</form>
```

On submit, the browser checks if all conditions are met: if all the fields are completed and the email and url are correctly formatted, the form will successfully submit. If there is a mistake or omission of a required form control, an error message will be displayed to the user, like the one shown in Figure 4-10.

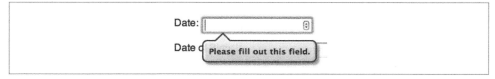

Figure 4-10. Error messaging for required fields that were not completed before an attempt was made at form submission

When required fields are left empty, or an input's value does not match its `type` or `pattern` attribute, error messages will be shown like the ones shown in Figure 4-11. Most browsers support native form validation, with iOS and Android support lagging at this time.

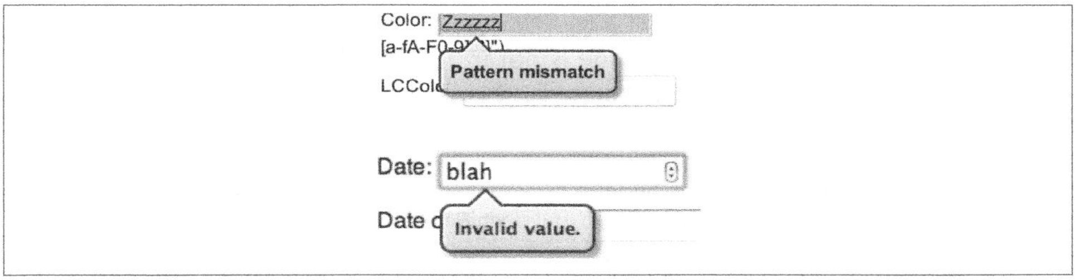

Figure 4-11. Form fields with messaging signaling that validation failed

Native browser form validation detects invalid data, and flags those errors with focus and error messaging. Native validation in HTML5-supporting browsers occurs before submitting the form to the server, submitting the form only if all rules set by attributes in the form fields pass native browser validation tests.

By preventing invalid data from being submitted, the browser saves a round trip to the server. While native validation will eventually be used to supplant client-side JavaScript validation, it will never supplant server-side validation. Browser validation is not sufficient to handle all errors. Always include server-side validation because malicious users will always be able to forge HTTP requests or otherwise mess with data submission.

When form validation is natively provided, the first invalid form element will display the error message and receive focus when the user tries to submit a form that is not fully valid. Eventually with native client-side validation, it may be possible to ensure correct form completion client-side with no JavaScript. HTML5 greatly minimizes the need for client-side form validation, but we still have a ways to go.

The HTML5 specifications provide for DOM methods and properties to enable validating without the cross-browser hoops we've been jumping through. HTML5 introduces eight form control properties via the `validity` state object.[5]

`Validity` is part of the validity constraint API. It is accessible from all form controls that support validation, and can be accessed with the form controls `validity` property:

```
var element = document.querySelector('#form_control_id');
var validityStateObject = element.validity;
```

or

```
var validityStateObject = document.form_id.form_control_id.validity;
```

The `validityStateObject` contains references to several `validity` properties:

`element.validity.valueMissing`
> If a required element, as set with the `required` attribute, has no value set, the `valueMissing` property is `true`; `false` otherwise. The `valueMissing` property looks at whether a value is missing or not, not whether it is valid or not.

`element.validity.typeMismatch`
> Returns `true` if the element's value is not in the correct syntax; `false` otherwise. For example, if the type is `number`, `email`, or `url` and the value is not a number, email, or URL respectively, then that `typeMismatch` will return `true`.

`element.validity.patternMismatch`
> If a form control requires a certain pattern as set with the `pattern` attribute, and the value of the form control does not match the pattern, the `patternMismatch` property is `true`; `false` otherwise. The `pattern` attribute limits the value to specific formats as defined by the `pattern` value's regular expression. The `patternMis match` is basically the property that enforces any `pattern` rule set on a form control.
>
> As mentioned earlier, when including the `pattern` attribute, also set a `title` describing the rules of the format for improved accessibility.

`element.validity.tooLong`
> When the `maxlength` attribute is set on a form control, the `tooLong` property returns `true` if the element's value is longer than the provided maximum length; `false` otherwise, ensuring that a value does not contain too many characters. The `max length` attribute should actually prevent the user from entering too many characters. This property double-checks to ensure that the `maxlength` was adhered to.

---

5. To be precise, there are ten validity properties, but the specification is evolving. We've included the original eight that are relevant to this chapter and already have browser support.

`element.validity.rangeUnderflow`

rangeUnderflow enforced the minimum value of a form control when the min attribute is set. rangUnderflow returns true if the element's value is lower than the defined minimum.

`element.validity.rangeOverflow`

rangeOverflow is the counterpart to rangeUnderflow: it enforces the maximum value of a form control when the max attribute is set.

`element.validity.stepMismatch`

Returns true if the element's value doesn't fit the rules given by the step attribute; false otherwise. The stepMismatch ensures that the form controls value conforms to the step value in conjunction with the min value. The value must be a multiple of the step added to the minimum value.

`element.validity.valid`

If the form control has no validity problems, the ValidityState object's valid property will return true; otherwise it will return false. Think of this property as a summary of the preceding seven properties and the customError (described next): if all return false, valid will be true. If any fail (are true), valid is false.

`element.validity.customError`

In addition to these validity properties, we have a customError property that returns true if the element has a custom error enabling the handling of errors, but doesn't actually check for validity.

By default, all form controls have customError of an empty string: empty strings are falsey. To be truthy, you have to call setCustomValidity(*message*) onto a form control, where *message* is the text that will be placed in the validation bubble as shown in Figures 4-1, 4-10, and 4-11. Setting a message puts the form control into the customError state of *true* as the custom error message is no longer empty. Until it is falsey, you will be unable to submit the form.

When the custom validity message is set, the control will be invalid and return the customError constraint as true. To clear the error, simply call setCustomValidity("") on the control, passing an empty string value.

 If you set customError to true by setting a custom validity message the form will *not* submit even if the form is otherwise valid. Make sure to reset the value to an empty string to enable valid forms to submit.

Easy UI Improvements with CSS

In addition to changing the content of the error messaging, in some browsers you can also control the appearance of those error messages. The preceding error and other UI features of web forms are styleable to some extent.

Controlling validation bubbles

WebKit provides a native look and feel for their validation error speech bubbles. The error bubble is made up of four containing elements that are part of the shadow DOM. These four elements are styleable via pseudoelements that apply to separate sections of the bubble:

```
::-webkit-validation-bubble
::-webkit-validation-bubble-arrow-clipper
::-webkit-validation-bubble-arrow
::-webkit-validation-bubble-message
```

The containing element is the absolutely positioned ::-webkit-validation-bubble. The ::-webkit-validation-bubble-arrow-clipper child clips the ::-webkit-validation-bubble-arrow at 16 pixels high, creating a tail for the bubble. The ::-webkit-validation-bubble-message contains the text node of the actual error message. The default styling is in the user style agent (*http://bit.ly/1idOlUH*), and can be overwritten with your own CSS.[6]

Styling to enhance usability

Like the error messaging, HTML5-supportive browsers stylize all the form controls to some extent. As a developer, you are a pro-user (hopefully) and likely know the subtleties of how a cursor changing over disabled versus active form controls indicates expected user behavior. Most of your users are not pro-users, so use styling to improve the usability of your forms.

For example, to make the user understand that a form control was required, you may have included an asterisk, perhaps encased in a class, to make the asterisk appear more prominently. This mandated including extra markup, such as:

```
<span class="required">*</span>
```

This required adding content for presentational reasons, and did nothing other than inform some sighted users that the element might be required. The asterisk provided no useful information to the actual form control.

With HTML5 attributes being included to create differing states of form controls, you can use CSS to stylize the required, disabled, checked, read-only, valid, invalid, focused,

---

6. This feature is in WebKit, but not in Blink. As this book is going to print, this feature has been removed from Chrome. I expect we will be able to style the validation bubbles with Web Components, and will update the status of this feature in the online chapter resources.

---

hovered, etc., form controls. There are various pseudoclasses by which you can style form elements based on state, including:

```
input:required,
input:invalid {
  background-color: #FFFFFF;
  border: 1px solid #FF0000;
}
input:valid {
  border: 1px solid #999999;
}
input:read-only {
  background-color: #DDDDDD;
  border: 1px solid #666666;
}
input:checked + label {
  color: #666666;
  font-style: italic;
}
```

We'll cover CSS in Chapters 6, 7, and 8, so if you are not familiar with pseudoclasses and elements feel free to skip ahead and come back to this section after you've mastered those chapters.

Adding the ARIA attribute `aria-required="true"` and data entry instructions via the `title` or `aria-labeledby` attributes provides for even better accessibility support.

New Form Elements

There are several form elements we haven't mentioned yet. We have five new form elements in HTML5: `<datalist>`, `<output>`, `<keygen>`, `<progress>`, and `<meter>`. We'll also cover differences in a few other elements that predate HTML5.

The `<datalist>` Element and the list Attribute

For the `text`, `email`, `url`, date-related, time-related, and numeric types of the `<input>` element, the new `list` attribute points to a list of values that the browser should offer to the user in addition to allowing the user to pick an arbitrary value.

The `list` attribute takes as its value the `id` of its associate `<datalist>`. `<datalist>` is a new HTML5 element.

The `<datalist>` element represents a set of `<option>` elements that represent predefined options for the `<input>` elements that associate themselves with that `<data list>` via the form field's `list` attribute. Several form controls can use the same `<data list>`, but each form control that supports the `list` attribute can be associated with only one `<datalist>`.

The `<datalist>` provides a list of data values, in the form of a list of `<option>` elements. When the form element has a `list` attribute, the options in the `<datalist>` provide author-specified autocompletion values for the control. The user can still enter freeform, but options are provided like a `<select>`, as shown in Figure 4-12:

```
<p>
<label for="url">Animals: </label>
<input id="animals" type="text" placeholder="animals and sounds"
  requiredlist="animalnames" name="animals"/>
</p>
<datalist id="animalnames">
        <option value="quack">duck</option>
        <option value="banana slug" label="sssss"/>
        <option value="sheep" label="bah"/>
        <option value="horse" label="neigh"/>
</datalist>
```

Figure 4-12. The appearance of the `<datalist>` in supporting browsers (Opera 10.6 is displayed in this screenshot)

Think of it as similar in functionality to the Google autosuggest. In the case of `<data list>`, the list of suggested terms is hardcoded or dynamically generated. When the user starts typing, options from the data list that match the characters typed are suggested via a drop-down of the `<datalist>`'s `<option>` values or labels, if present. Similar to Google search autocomplete, it can be dynamically updated via an AJAX request. There is an example of the `<datalist>` element in the online chapter resources.

Graceful degradation of the `<datalist>`

The element's contents can include fallback content for browsers not yet supporting `<datalist>`, providing users of older browsers with the choice to enter freeform data or select from an list of options made up of `<option>` elements that represent the predefined or suggested values for the form elements linking to it. Each suggestion has a value and a label. The default rendering of `<datalist>` and its children is hidden.

The `<datalist>` provides options for the form control, but still allows for freeform data entry. This is a very nice enhancement that you may not want legacy browsers to miss. To enable users of user agents that don't support `<datalist>`, which includes most mobile browsers, encompass the options within a `<select>`. Supporting browsers will ignore everything other than the options within the `<datalist>` and nonsupporting browsers will ignore the `<datalist>` tag, showing the descendant content it understands (see Figure 4-13):

```
<p>
  <label for="url">Web Address: </label>
  <input id="url" type="url" placeholder="http://www.domain.com"
      requiredlist="mydatalist" name="url"/>
</p>
<datalist id="mydatalist">
 <p><label>Or select from the list</label>
   <select name="url2">
     <option value=http://www.standardista.com label="Standardista"/>
     <option value="http://www.oreilly.com" label="O'Reilly"/>
     <option value="http://www.evotech.net" label="Evolution Technologies"/>
   </select>
 </p>
</datalist>
```

Figure 4-13. With this gracefully degrading implementation of <datalist>, the noncompliant browser shows the children of <datalist>, ignoring the element it doesn't understand (notice the URL keyboard configuration, and the <p> and <datalist> are visible: touching the Next button will activate the select menu in the datalist)

The fallback content will only be shown in browsers that don't support <datalist>, as shown in Figure 4-13. Supporting browsers will ignore <p>, <label>, and <select>, and all other elements within a <datalist> other than <option>, as displayed in Figure 4-12. When using the JavaScript-less method of graceful degradation, make sure the server is set to receive data from both form fields.

There is an even better fallback that requires a little bit of JavaScript. The HTML looks like:

```html
<input type="text" name="animal" list="dl_animals" id="animals" />
<datalist id="dl_animals">
 <select id="slct_animal">
  <option value="moo">Cow</option>
  <option value="sssss">Banana Slug</option>
  <option value="bah">Sheep</option>
 </select>
</datalist>
```

The JavaScript that makes it work is:

```javascript
var select = document.getElementById('slct_animal'),
    input = document.getElementById('animals');
select.addEventListener('change', function() {
 input.value = this.value;
}, false);
```

The CSS looks like:

```css
input[list],
datalist select {
 float: left;
 height: 1.4em;
 position: relative;
}
input[list] {
 z-index: 2;
 width: 20em;
}
datalist select {
 width: 1.2em;
}
```

In the preceding example, we've added a select with no name attribute, so the select will not be submitted with the form. We've also styled the select to appear as a select spinner to the right of the input with the list attribute.

The <output> element

The <output> element acts like a <span> element, except that it is considered to be a form control for the purposes of the DOM. The <output> element, which is new to HTML5, can have the form, name, and for attributes, and the onchange, onforminput, and onformchange events in addition to the universal attributes and event handlers.

The output does not have a value attribute. Rather, the value is defined by its inline contents between the opening and closing tag. As such, the <output> element must have both a start tag and an end tag. The value can be set and retrieved via the DOM.

The for attribute value is a bit different for the <output> element than the <label> element: the for attribute takes as its value a space-separated list of the IDs of other elements associated with the output.

The <output> element should be used when the user will never directly manipulate the value, and when the value can be derived from other values, such as the result of an equation based on the values of the elements listed in the for attribute.

CubeeDoo

In CubeeDoo, we use the <output> form element to store the score, level, and seconds left in the current round. In our code example, the current score, current level, and time left are contained in <output> and are updated via DOM manipulation. The HTML is very simply marked up with:

```
<output name="score">0</output>
<output name="level">1</output>
<output name="time">120</output>
```

We pre-populate the values because when the page loads at game start, the score is zero, the user is on the first level, and the default time on the clock is 2 minutes. In our JavaScript, we dynamically maintain and update the values.

<meter>

The <meter> is generally used as a gauge to provide a measurement within a known range. The <meter> is used to indicate the current value in relation to the minimum and maximum values, like a needle gauge. Possible implementations include displaying password strength during user entry and similar visual feedback indicators.

The <meter> element's attributes, which take floats as their value, include min, max, high, low, and optimum. The optimum attribute provides the value for the point that marks the optimal position for the meter. The min and max are the minimum and maximum values respectively. The high and low attributes should be the lowest value that can be considered a high value, and the highest value that can be considered a low value, respectively.

For example, grades may go from 0% to 100%, so you would have a min of 0 and a max of 100. Using the typical American system as an example (with A being 90% and better, a B being between 80% and 89%, etc.), it is generally considered to be good to have a B + (87%) or better and bad to have a C– (73%) or lower. If you're not doing so well in school (getting a 61%), your grade meter could look something like this:

```
<p>Grade: <meter value="61" min="0" max="100" low="73" high="87">D-</meter></p>
```

The UI provides a meter with the left side being the minimum value and the right being the maximum value. A colored bar fills the meter from the left to right, proportionally, based on the value. Depending on the attributes and the current value (and the browser), the bar may be red, green, or yellow. The bar should be green if the value falls between the high and low value, and red or yellow if it falls outside of those values, depending on the optimum value (as shown in Figure 4-14).

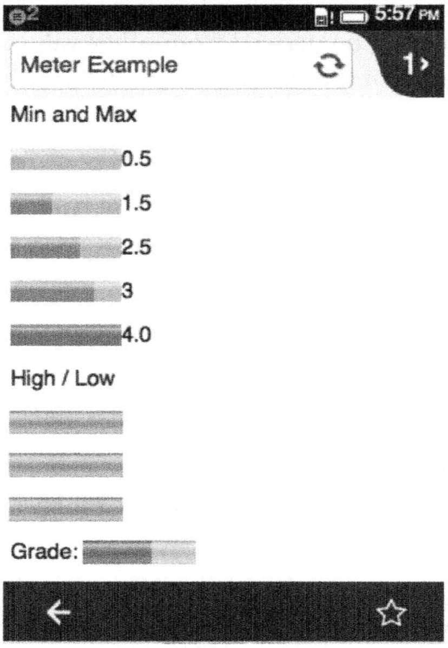

Figure 4-14. The UI and colors of <meter>

The <meter> element should not to be used to show progress. Instead, use the <pro gress> element for that purpose. Use the <meter> when you know what the minimum and maximum values are, such as grades (max="100"), and when the values go both up and down, like blood pressure or a gas tank. Otherwise, if the value is only going in one direction, use <progress>.

There is an example in the online chapter resources.

<progress>

The <progress> is similar to <meter> but is used to indicate progress toward a goal or task rather than as a gauge. Unlike the <meter> that shows the current value in relation to a minimum and maximum value, the <progress> indicator represents how far a task has progressed between the start of the task and the estimated completion of it. For example, the `<progress>` element, as shown in Figure 4-15, can be employed to display the progress of a time-consuming function in JavaScript.

The `<progress>` element takes a `value` and `max` attribute, with both being positive floats, and the `value` being less than the `max`. There is an example in the online chapter resources.

Figure 4-15. The `<progress>` element in Firefox OS and Chrome for Android

`<keygen>`

The self-closing `<keygen>` provides for a key/pair generator/input control. Useful to client-side application developers for authorization protocols, the `<keygen>` element represents a control for generating a public-private key pair and for submitting the public key from that key pair. Accepting the attributes of `challenge`, `keytype`, `autofocus`, `name`, `disabled`, and `form`, the `keytype` value is `rsa` and the `challenge` attribute takes as its value a challenge string that is submitted along with the public key. Opera, WebKit, and Firefox all support this element, rendering it as a select menu generating encrypted keys, though all provide different options.

There is an example in the online chapter resources.

Other Form Elements

The following sections provide quick descriptions of the various form elements. We are including these elements that you are most likely familiar with to delineate new features of HTML5.

The <form> element

The `<form>` element has had a few changes. The form now automatically validates the input types on submission. The new Boolean `novalidate` (novalidate="novali date") attribute was added to enable the form to not be natively validated upon submission.

The form controls no longer need to be children of an ancestor `<form>`: instead the `form` attribute on the form controls can be included to dictate with which form the control is associated. The `autocomplete` attribute has also been added to the `<form>` element.

In addition, the `action` attribute is no longer required. If omitted, the form will submit to itself, as if `action` were set to the current page.

<fieldset> and <legend>

The `<fieldset>` groups form controls together. The remainder of the `<fieldset>`'s children form the group. The optional first child of the `<fieldset>` is the `<legend>`, which gives the `<fieldset>` group its name. The `<legend>` element is the title or caption for the rest of the contents of the `<fieldset>` in which it finds itself. The `<legend>` can only be found as a child of a `<fieldset>`, and must have a closing tag.

The Boolean `disabled` attribute, if specified, causes all the form control descendants of the `<fieldset>` element, excluding children of the `<legend>`, to be disabled. The `form` attribute can be used to associate the `<fieldset>` element with a specific form (see the description of the `form` attribute). The `name` attribute represents the element's name.

<select>, <option>, <optgroup>

The `<select>` tag specifies a selection menu. A `<select>` must contain one or more `<option>` elements or one or more `<optgroup>` containing `<option>`s. In Safari, if the `size` attribute is explicitly set for this tag, the input box resembles a combo box, otherwise it will resemble a pop-up menu.

<textarea>

The `<textarea>` is a free-form text field, nominally with no line-break restrictions. This tag specifies a scrollable, multiline text-input block.

New in HTML5 is the wrap attribute. The <textarea> element may have a wrap attribute specified with the values of soft (default) and hard: soft means the text is submitted without line breaks other than explicitly entered line breaks, and hard includes explicit line breaks. If setting the wrap to hard, specify a cols attribute.

In HTML 4, we were required to specify the <textarea>'s size onscreen by specifying values for rows and cols. In HTML5, the rows and cols attributes of the <textarea> element are no longer required attributes as they were in HTML 4, unless you set the wrap attribute to hard, then the cols attribute is required. Otherwise, cols and rows are now optional. CSS should be used to define width and height instead. The closing tag is required.

<button>

The <button> element comes with three types: submit, reset, and button (the default is submit). Unlike the <input type="button"/>, the <button> element is not self-closing: you must include the </button> closing tag. This element remains unchanged from previous versions.

The <label> Element

The <label> element is not new to HTML5, but since it is often misused, it's worth reviewing.

The <label> provides a caption in the user interface for a form control. The caption is associated with a specific form control by using the for attribute for an explicit label, or by putting the form control inside the <label> element itself creating an implicit label.

The value of the for attribute in the explicit label must match the value of the form control's id.

It is important to note that the form control/label relationship is not just for improved accessibility for screen readers. Clicking or touching the label provides a click event on the associated form control: touching on the label of a checkbox toggles the checkbox's state, making the form field more accessible to all users, not just those using screen readers or voiceovers. Clicking or touching the <label> associated with a radio button toggles the checked status of that radio button. Touching a <label> associated with a text field gives focus to that field, prompting the user to enter data.

In Conclusion

When HTML5 input elements and attributes are fully supported, sites will require less JavaScript client-side validation as the browsers will be doing most of the heavy lifting. However, servers should still perform data validation, as malicious users will be able to bypass any client-side type-checking and validation, and legacy user agents will likely not disappear completely for the foreseeable future.

SVG, Canvas, Audio, and Video

We've covered most of the new elements of HTML5, with the exception of elements uniquely associated with web APIs currently under development and the well-supported media-related elements of SVG, Canvas, Audio, and Video. The former are subject to change, so aren't covered in this book. The latter are covered here.

We've covered the main features you're likely to use in your day-to-day work as a frontend web developer, enabling you to use modern features when developing for mobile browsers. All modern mobile browsers (with the exception of Opera Mini) support `<canvas>`, `<video>`, and `<audio>`, as well as web APIs like geolocation, localStorage, offline web applications, etc.

A book could be written about each of the individual topics covered in this chapter, and, for the most part, already have been written. We'll provide you with enough information, hopefully, to decide, "Hey, I do need to read the book on that" or to decide, "Hmmm, not interested quite yet." While we won't deep dive into any of these topics, you'll have enough knowledge to get started. And, more importantly, you'll understand the benefits and drawbacks of these technologies in the mobile arena.

HTML5 Media APIs

The original HTML specification was purely for textual content and did not even include the `<img>` element. We've come a long way since then. HTML5 provides for creating scalable, vector-based graphics with SVG and blank drawing space with `<canvas>`. In addition to supporting graphics, HTML5 supports `<video>` and `<audio>` inclusion without third-party plug-ins.

SVG

With SVG, you can create complex *scalable vector graphics*. Introduced in 2001, SVG is an open standard for defining two-dimensional vector graphics. The "scalable" aspect of SVG means the same graphic can look equally sharp on a large monitor as it does on a small mobile screen, without any modifications.

The SVG spec defines an XML grammar for shapes, lines, curves, images, and text, including features such as transparency, arbitrary geometry, filter effects (shadows, lighting effects, etc.), scripting, and animation.

Because it is a text-based image format, the file size can be very small. Because it has an object model, it can be changed with scripting. Because it is vector based, it can scale without pixelated or jagged edges. Because it is declarative, it is easy to understand. Because SVG supports animation, it can be animated.

There are various forms of SVG, with various levels of browser support. Basic support of standalone *.svg* files exists in all mobile devices and modern browsers, with support in Android beginning with Android 3. SVG as a source for the <img> element has been supported since iOS 3.2, Android 3.0, and mobile IE8.

The SVG file format as a value for the CSS background-image property has been supported since Android 3 and iOS 3.2, and it has been long supported in Opera Mobile. We've even been able to use the <svg> element in HTML5 pages since iOS 5, Android 3, and IE9 (along with all other modern browsers). Android 2.3.3 and below, Amazon Silk, and HP's now defunct WebOS are the only mobile browsers lacking full SVG support. Static SVG is even supported in Opera Mini (as is <canvas>, which is supported in all mobile browsers), but can't be animated, as Opera Mini's JavaScript support does not allow for that.

As it's an XML-based language, SVG's root element is not <html>. Rather, it's <svg>. Like all XML documents, SVG begins with an XML prologue and an SVG DTD. The <svg> root element contains all of the document's content. SVG does not have a <head> and <body>. Rather, all of the content, including nested <svg> elements, are contained in the root <svg>.

A good starter SVG is the Japanese flag, which is simply a white rectangular flag with a red sun or disc in the center, as shown in Figure 5-1.

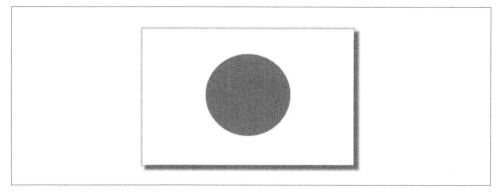

Figure 5-1. The Japanese flag made with SVG

```
1 <!DOCTYPE svg PUBLIC "-//W3C//DTD SVG 1.0//EN"
2       "http://www.w3.org/TR/2001/REC-SVG-20010904/DTD/svg10.dtd">
3 <svg xmlns="http://www.w3.org/2000/svg" height="220" width="320" version="1.0">
4   <title>Japanese Flag</title>
5   <desc>Red circle on white flag</desc>
6   <rect x="10" y="10" width="300" height="200"
7       style="fill: #ffffff; stroke: #e7e7e7;"/>
8   <circle cx="160px" cy="107px" r="60px" fill="#d60818"/>
9 </svg>
```

So what does that all mean? Lines 1–3 are the SVG DTD and then the root `<svg>` element, respectively. Something to note about the root element is that the size of the vector graphic is declared. To be able to use the CSS `background-position` when the background image is of type SVG, the size of the SVG must be declared. This is important if you are creating an SVG sprite file.

You can use `<title>`, line 4, if the SVG file is used independently of other resources. The `<desc>` in line 5 is where you can put a text-only description that will not be natively displayed when the SVG is rendered. Including good content in your `<desc>` or `<title>` provides for accessibility. As not all screen readers support SVG, adding the `aria-label` attribute can improve accessibility.

The `<rect>` in line 6 provides for a rectangle. Available shapes and lines include `<path>`, `<rect>`, `<circle>`, `<ellipse>`, `<line>`, `<polyline>`, and `<polygon>`. We provided four attribute values, `x`, `y`, `width`, and `height`, for the x-offset, y-offset (both for positioning), width, and height, respectively. We have also included a `style` attribute.

Like a regular HTML document, you can use CSS to provide style to elements in your SVG document. You can declare your styles inline using the `style` attribute, as I did in the previous example, or you can include an embedded or external stylesheet, targeting elements with selectors, just as you would in an HTML file.

The property names are slightly different than the CSS you may be used to, but they are human readable. The `fill` property is similar to the `background` property. In this case, we provided a background color. The `stroke` property is similar to the CSS `border` property. We could have provided a gradient or pattern.

While you can use most CSS properties and values in your SVG files, for content security reasons, some browser manufacturers[1] prevent SVG file types from importing raster images or scripts when included as a foreground image with `<img>`.

The `<circle>` in line 8 provides for a disc with a solid red background. Instead of a height and width, the `<circle>` has the `r` attribute, for radius. Instead of being positioned based on a top-left corner, like the `<rect>`, the `<circle>` is positioned based on the center of the circle, the `cx` is the x-axis coordinate of the center of the circle, and the `cy` is the y-axis coordinate of the center of the circle.

If you look at the circle attributes, you'll note that we used `fill` as CSS property on the `<rect>`, and as an attribute on the `<circle>`.

Including SVG in Your Documents

You can include SVG directly in your document with the `<img>`, `<object>`, and `<embed>` tags:

```
<img src="flag.svg" alt="Japanese Flag"/>
```

or:

```
<embed type="image/svg+xml" src="flag.svg" width="320" height="220"/>
```

or:

```
<object data="flag.svg" type="image/svg+xml" width="320" height="220"></object>
```

Note that although the `<embed>` and `<object>` don't have the *alt* attribute, SVG can be made accessible. You can improve accessibility by describing the illustration with `<desc>` or `<title>`, and adding an `aria-label` attribute with a value that matches the SVG title. By including the height and width in the `<svg>`, you shouldn't need to include them on the `<img>`, `<embed>`, or `<object>` elements, but do include them in your CSS.

Clown Car Technique: SVG for Responsive Foreground Images

SVG can be used to create and serve responsive images. We can leverage browser support for SVG and SVG support for both media queries and raster images to create responsive images, using media queries within SVG to serve up the right image.

---

1. Currently, WebKit and Mozilla prevent importing scripts and raster images in SVG via the `<img>` tag, even when the raster images are from the same origin.

We know from CSS background images it is indeed possible to only download needed images. Similarly, to prevent the SVG from downloading all the included images, we use CSS background images instead of foreground images in our SVG file. In our responsive SVG, we include all the images that we may need to serve and show only the appropriate image based on media queries (media queries are discussed in more depth in Chapter 7):

```
<svg xmlns="http://www.w3.org/2000/svg"
  viewBox="0 0 300 329" preserveAspectRatio="xMidYMid meet">

<title>Put the alt attribute here</title>

<style>
 svg {
  background-size: 100% 100%;
  background-repeat: no-repeat;
 }

 @media screen and (max-width: 400px) {
  svg {
   background-image: url(images/small.png");
  }
 }

 @media screen and (min-width: 401px) and (max-width: 700px) {
  svg {
    background-image: url(images/medium.png);
  }
 }

 @media screen and (min-width: 701px) and (max-width: 1000px) {
  svg {
   background-image: url(images/big.png);
  }
 }

 @media screen and (min-width: 1001px) {
  svg {
   background-image: url(images/huge.png);
  }
 }
</style>
</svg>
```

To preserve the aspect ratio of the containing element and ensure that it scales uniformly, we include the viewbox and preserveAspectRatio attributes. The value of the view box attribute is a list of four space- or comma-separated numbers: min-x, min-y, width, and height. By defining the width and the height of our viewbox, we define the aspect ratio of the SVG image.

Because of the security issues with `<img>` and SVG importing raster images, we use the `<object>` to include the responsive image in our site. The `<object>` element allows an external resource to be treated as an image:

```
<object data="awesomefile.svg" type="image/svg+xml"></object>
```

By default, the `<object>` will be as wide as the parent element. However, just as with images, we can declare a width or height with the `width` and `height` attributes or with the CSS `width` and `height` properties. Because of the `viewbox` and `preserveAspectRatio` declarations in our SVG file, the `<object>` will by default maintain the declared aspect ratio if only one dimension (height or width) is declared.

Because this technique uses `<object>` instead of `<img>`, we have no `alt` attribute. To make this technique accessible when and if screen readers support SVG,[2] ensure the contents of the SVG `<title>` contain what you would have included as the `alt` attribute.

The `<object>` embeds the SVG. The SVG pulls in the background image that matches the `@media` query based on the size of the `<object>`, not the viewport. With the preceding code, two HTTP requests are made: one for the SVG and one for the appropriate image. To reduce it to a single HTTP request, include an escaped data URI[3] for the `<object>`'s `data` attribute.

I call this the Clown Car Technique since we are including many large images (clowns) into a tiny single SVG image file (car).

Learning SVG

We've just touched the surface of SVG. SVG can be made accessible, scales to any screen resolution, and supports animation via the SVG syntax or via JavaScript, with full control over each element using the SVG DOM API. There is so much more that can be done with SVG, which is beyond the scope of this book. The W3C spec (*http://www.w3.org/TR/SVG/*) provides more information about all the elements, attributes, and animation API.

The Japanese flag is a very simple SVG. SVG can get very complicated very fast. If you are familiar with Adobe Illustrator, you may have noticed that you can export your illustrations as SVG. While this is a good way to create exacting SVG files, it creates a lot of code and the program is expensive.

Amaya is free software that supports a subset of SVG, including basic shapes, text, images, foreignObject, alpha transparency, transformations, and animations. You can

---

2. *http://www.iheni.com/just-how-accessible-is-svg/*.

3. The data URI needs to be escaped for IE9 and later. This is just a brief overview of the Clown Car Technique. More details and examples, along with fallbacks for browsers that don't support SVG, can be found at *http://github.com/estelle/clowncar*.

download Amaya (*http://www.w3.org/Amaya*) directly from the W3C. Amaya is helpful in learning SVG, as the source can be inspected and edited. You may also want to check out Inkscape (*http://inkscape.org*), which is an open source vector graphics editor, with capabilities similar to Illustrator, CorelDraw, or Xara, using the W3C standard SVG file format.

CubeeDoo SVG

In CubeeDoo, we employ SVG twice. We have an SVG sprite for the background image of our game's "shapes" theme, and as an SVG data URI for the mute icon.

We offer the user a few themes. We have numbers, colors, and shapes, among others. We are able to produce our shapes with a simple SVG sprite. The code we used to create the SVG sprite, as seen in Figure 5-2 for the face side of one of our decks of cards, is as follows:

```
1  <!DOCTYPE svg PUBLIC "-//W3C//DTD SVG 1.0//EN"
2       "http://www.w3.org/TR/2001/REC-SVG-20010904/DTD/svg10.dtd">
3  <svg xmlns="http://www.w3.org/2000/svg" height="400" width="400" version="1.0">
4   <desc>Squares, circles, diamonds and triangles sprite</desc>
5
6   <!-- Color squares -->
7   <rect x="10" y="10" width="80" height="80" style="fill: #d60818;"/>
8   <rect x="10" y="110" width="80" height="80" style="fill: #ffff33;"/>
9   <rect x="10" y="210" width="80" height="80" style="fill: #00FF00;"/>
10  <rect x="10" y="310" width="80" height="80" style="fill: #0000FF;"/>
11
12  <!-- Color Circles -->
13  <circle cx="150" cy="50" r="40" style="fill: #d60818;"/>
14  <circle cx="150" cy="150" r="40" style="fill: #ffff33;"/>
15  <circle cx="150" cy="250" r="40" style="fill: #00FF00;"/>
16  <circle cx="150" cy="350" r="40" style="fill: #0000FF;"/>
17
18  <!-- diamonds -->
19  <polygon points="250,10 210,50 250,90 290,50"  style="fill: #d60818;"/>
20  <polygon points="250,110 210,150 250,190 290,150" style="fill: #FFFF33;"/>
21  <polygon points="250,210 210,250 250,290 290,250" style="fill: #00FF00;"/>
22  <polygon points="250,310 210,350 250,390 290,350" style="fill: #0000FF;"/>
23
24  <!-- Triangles -->
25  <polygon points="310,10 350,90 390,10" style="fill: #d60818;"/>
26  <polygon points="310,110 350,190 390,110" style="fill: #FFFF33;"/>
27  <polygon points="310,210 350,290 390,210" style="fill: #00FF00;"/>
28  <polygon points="310,310 350,390 390,310" style="fill: #0000FF;"/>
29 </svg>
```

Line 1 is the DTD. In line 3, we declare the root element, and include the height and width of the SVG image. While not required by the specifications, you must include these attributes if you plan on using an SVG image as a background image. Line 4 provides a description, which helps both in accessibility and in search engine optimization.

Figure 5-2. SVG sprite of shapes

Lines 7 through 10 provide the declarations for four squares. Line 9 reads: "Create a rectangle starting 10 px from the left, 210 px from the top. Make the rectangle 80 px wide and 80 px tall. Fill this shape in with #00FF00."

```
<rect x="10" y="210" width="80" height="80" style="fill: #00FF00;"/>
```

Lines 13 through 16 define four circles or discs. Line 16 reads: "Find the point 150 px from the left and 350 px from the top, and make that the center of our 40 px radiused circle that has a background color of #0000FF."

```
<circle cx="150" cy="350" r="40" style="fill: #0000FF;"/>
```

Lines 18 to 28 declare eight polygons: four diamond shaped and three triangles. Polygons are declared by defining the corners. Line 19 reads: "This shape has four corners, with the top point at 250 px from the left and 10 px from the top. The second point is at 210 px from the left and 50 px from the top. The bottom point is 90 px from the top, and the right-most point is 290 px from the left and 50 px from the top. The area within those four points should be filled in with #d60818, which is a shade of red."

```
<polygon points="250,10 210,50 250,90 290,50" style="fill: #d60818;"/>
```

We chose to make squares, circles, diamonds, and upside-down triangles.

We could also have included these small images as data URIs directly in our CSS file, or as foreground images. For example, you can include encoded SVG as data URIs:

```
background-image: url(data:image/svg+xml,%3Csvg%20xmlns%3D%22http%3A%2F%2F
www.w3.org%2F2000%2Fsvg%22%20version%3D%221.0%22%3E%3Crect%20x%3D%220%22%20y
%3D%220%22%20fill%3D%22%23abcdef%22%20width%3D%22100%25%22%20height
%3D%22100%25%22%20%2F%3E%3C%2Fsvg%3E);
```

In CubeeDoo, we also include a mute icon. The data URI for that icon is:

```
background-image:
    background-image:
    url("data:image/svg+xml;utf8,%3Csvg%20xmlns=
'http://www.w3.org/2000/svg'%20width='100'%20height='100'%3E
%3Cpolygon%20points='39,13%2022,28%206,28%206,47%2022,48%2039,63
%2039,14'%20style='stroke:#111111;stroke-width:5;stroke-linejoin:round;
fill:#111111;'%20/%3E%3Cpath%20d='M%2048,50%2069,26'%20%20style='fill:none;
stroke:#111111;stroke-width:5;stroke-linecap:round'%20/%3E%3Cpath%20
%20d='M%2069,50%2048,26'%20style='fill:none;stroke:#111111;stroke-width:5;
stroke-linecap:round'%20/%3E%3C/svg%3E");
```

The paths in this example are barely human readable. They were created using Amaya. However, the syntax should be familiar. We are using the CSS `background-image` property. Instead of using `url(path/mute.jpg)`, or even `url(path/mute.svg)`, we employ `url("data:image/svg+xml;utf8,<svg... /></svg>");`, putting the entire SVG file, escaped, within the quotes.

For versions of Internet Explorer that support SVG (currently IE9 and IE10), data URIs should be escaped, as per the specifications.

Canvas

The HTML5 Canvas specification is a JavaScript API for creating drawings. The canvas API allows the definition of a canvas context object as the `<canvas>` element on your HTML page, inside which we can draw. We can even include canvas drawings in your CSS as background images.

We can draw in both 2D and 3D (WebGL) context. 2D is available in all of the modern web browsers. WebGL is gaining ground in the mobile space, and should only be included when hardware is accelerated (if at all) for performance reasons.

2D context provides a simple yet powerful API for performing quick drawing operations on a 2D bitmap surface. There is no file format, and you can only draw using script. You do not have any DOM nodes for the shapes you draw—with `<canvas>` you're drawing pixels, not vectors. The single node makes canvas appear mobile friendly, but the high CPU usages of JavaScript animation can quickly drain a mobile battery (though battery usage performance is improving with hardware acceleration).

Your first <canvas>

Being a very basic introduction to canvas, we are only going to cover basic shapes and lines. If you are unfamiliar with JavaScript, the syntax may at first seem a bit confusing. If you are familiar, it should make sense.

The first step is adding the <canvas> element to your document. In terms of HTML, the only step is adding the <canvas> element to your document:

```
<canvas id="flag" width="320" height="220">
  You don't support Canvas. If you did, you would see a flag.
</canvas>
```

That is it for the HTML part of canvas. I could simply have written <canvas></canvas>. The id was included for ease of JavaScript targeting, though I could also target it via the DOM. I have also included alternative content for users that don't support or otherwise can't see the <canvas> content.

 Other than the aria-label attribute, <canvas>, as currently implemented, is a completely non-accessible API.

With that, we've created our blank drawing board, or canvas. Everything else takes place in our JavaScript. In this example, we are creating the Japanese flag again, as seen in Figure 5-3.

The next step is drawing to our canvas. From now on, everything is in JavaScript. We target the <canvas> node with basic JavaScript in one of three ways:

```
document.getElementById('flag')
document.getElementsByTagName('canvas')[0]
document.querySelector('#flag')
```

We then initialize a 2D context and start drawing using 2D context API commands. Again, we draw the Japanese flag:

```
1  <script>
2  var el= document.getElementById("flag");
3
4  if (el && el.getContext) {
5    var context = el.getContext('2d');
6      if (context) {
7          context.fillStyle   = "#ffffff";
8          context.strokeStyle = "#cccccc";
9          context.lineWidth   = 1;
10         context.shadowOffsetX = 5;
11         context.shadowOffsetY = 5;
12         context.shadowBlur  = 4;
13         context.shadowColor = 'rgba(0, 0, 0, 0.4)';
14         context.strokeRect(10, 10, 300, 200);
15         context.fillRect(10, 10, 300, 200);
16         context.shadowColor='rgba(0,0,0,0)';
17         context.beginPath();
18         context.fillStyle = "#d60818";
19         context.arc(160, 107, 60, 0, Math.PI*2, false);
```

```
20          context.closePath();
21          context.fill();
22      }
23 }
24 </script>
```

Line 2 finds the `<canvas>` element by matching the element's `id` attribute. Before creating the 2D context, we check to make sure that the canvas element has been found *and* that the browser supports canvas, checking for the existence of the `getContext` method in line 4.

 You can use feature-detection scripts like Modernizr to feature detect whether a browser supports canvas and other modern features. Modernizr provides for feature detecting all features, or single features that you are actually employing. We're not using Modernizr here because we're showing you how to feature detect directly. Other than minimizing external scripts and HTTP requests, there is actually no reason to not use Modernizr if it otherwise makes sense.

In line 5, we create a reference to a context using the `getContext(contextId)` method of the canvas element: `2d` is the correct context for `<canvas>`. If context creation is successful, checked in line 6, we are finally free to draw in our canvas, which we do in the rest of the script.

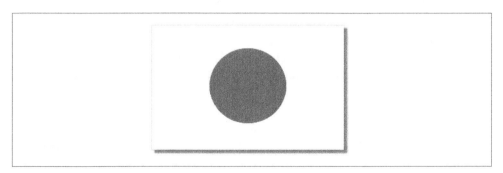

Figure 5-3. Japanese flag created as a canvas

While still experimental, if we want to include the canvas drawing as a background in a WebKit (*http://bit.ly/1cXjICc*) browser via CSS,[4] instead of calling the canvas element within our DOM, we could include it as a background image:

---

4. Firefox 4+ supports canvas in CSS as well, dynamically creating a virtual canvas element with JavaScript and with `-moz-element('#myCanvas')` in the CSS.

```
background: -webkit-canvas(theCanvas);
```

in our CSS, and:

```
var context = document.getCSSCanvasContext("2d", "theCanvas", 320, 220);
```

in our JavaScript, where the 2nd parameter is the name of the canvas that we use, un-quoted, in our CSS.

Through line 6, and even through line 13, we haven't drawn anything yet. All we have done up through line 6 is to define a canvas context in which we can draw and redraw pixels.

Before drawing a shape, we must define the look and feel of the shape we want to draw by setting properties on the context object. We define the look of the border (stroke and linewidth) properties, the background color (fill) and the shadow (shadowOff setX, shadowOffsetY, shadowBlur, and shadowColor) of our first rectangle, which we draw with the strokeRect() method in line 14. We pass the same parameters as our SVG example: (10, 10, 300, 200). The four values are the x-offset, the y-offset, width, and height, respectively.

Once the script executes a command, the script forgets about what it has done, and moves onto the next line of code. Unlike our SVG example in the preceding section, the rectangle we've drawn on our canvas is not part of the DOM. Being properties, the stroke, fill, linewidth, and border properties are still remembered, but the browser and script are not aware of what has been drawn. If you do want to capture what is drawn on the canvas and where, use the getImageData()method on the context to capture the red, green, blue, and alpha transparency values of your pixels.

When we draw our second rectangle using the fillRect method in line 15, which paints rectangles using the previously set fillStyle property, we need to pass the coordinates again, as the DOM does not remember our first rectangle (though it can access pixel information).

Both rectangle method calls (lines 14 and 15) have the same parameters—10, 10, 300, 200—we've drawn our fill rectangle directly on top of our drop shadow rectangle. We could have created an object with those coordinates and passed it to both methods, but we can't tell the canvas to access the first rectangle's coordinates and copy to the second after the method call.

We first stroked the rectangle, then we filled it. Had the reverse order been the case, the shadow would have been on top of the background color. As the origin coordinates are the same, and the border width is only 1 pixel, the final border will only be 0.5 pixels wide, as the fill covers the inner half of the border stroke.

As mentioned earlier, as we start the process of drawing the disc or sun on our flag, once you paint onto the canvas, the DOM has no recollection of what you've painted. Yes, it's true that the JavaScript remembers the values of the properties you've set, like our shadowColor. It also remembers the most recent drawing steps whether or not they have been drawn. However, the pixels that are places on the canvas are just pixels of color. As we don't want a shadow on the red circle, we must set the shadowColor to transparent before drawing it, which we do in line 16.

We start our instructions for our circle with beginPath() (line 17) and end with close Path()(line 20). The script remembers the drawing steps whether or not they have been drawn. If we drew a circle, and then some lines without opening and closing the context, when we drew the lines, the steps to draw the circle would still be in memory, and your new line may cut through that circle, cutting it in half. We avoid this by opening and closing the drawing paths with beginPath() and closePath(), respectively.

We define our circle: context.arc(x-offset, y-offset, radius, startAngle, endAngle, anticlockwise) adds points to an arced path creating a virtual circumference of a circle described by the arguments context.arc(160, 107, 60, 0, Math.PI*2, false);. Starting at the given start angle, in our case 0, which is on the right horizon, and ending at the given end angle, going in the given direction, which in our case is clockwise. Had our *end angle* been less than 2Π, our circle would have been flattened: the start and end points connected by a straight line. Π would have created a half circle.

We also redefine the fill color, from white to red (line 18). We then paint the circle we created using the fill() method (line 21) that fills the described arc in the fillStyle color.

We haven't even touched the surface of what <canvas> can do. *http://ie.microsoft.com/ testdrive/Graphics/CanvasPad/Default.html* is a fun page where you can learn simple shapes, colors, shadows, text, images, transformation, animation, and mouse movement with <canvas>.

<canvas> code example

In our game example, to make higher levels a little more difficult, we can include a changing background for the game board. We can include shapes that are on the front side of the cards in our animation just to make the higher levels insanely difficult.

In the online chapter resources, I've included a few canvas code examples. Try drawing the Japanese flag. Then convert your flag into a static Pac-Man, making the red circle yellow, with a mouth, a black circle for an eye, and three little edible dots. The online chapter resource examples also include some text to provide you with code that is beyond the scope of this book, including a function to invert the colors of the Pac-Man so that you may learn how to access the pixels already drawn to your canvas and other methods of drawing to the page.

While we've included an example of <canvas> in CubeeDoo for this book, we currently would not include a dynamic canvas element for production for mobile web applications. The battery consumption of running canvas animation via JavaScript with the current state of implementation would make your users very, very sad, but support for hardware acceleration of <canvas> is improving.

Canvas Versus SVG

HTML5 Canvas and SVG have several similarities and are often compared and contrasted. They are both web technologies that allow you to create rich graphics inside the browser, but they are fundamentally different.

As we've seen, in SVG, you "draw" with XML. For canvas, you draw with JavaScript. Canvas is the painting of pixels onto a canvas: once painted, each pixel is forgotten. SVG, on the other hand, creates DOM nodes, accessible until deleted or until the user navigates away from the page. They both have their advantages and disadvantages.

SVG drawings are resolution independent, making SVG an excellent choice for user interfaces of all sizes, as it allows scaling for all screen resolutions. SVG is an XML file format enabling easy accessibility. SVG can be animated using a declarative syntax, or via JavaScript. Each element becomes part of and is accessible via the SVG DOM API in JavaScript. However, anything that accesses the DOM repeatedly slows the page down, which is especially important and noticeable in the mobile environment.

Canvas is all drawn in pixels. Zooming can lead to pixelation. Canvas is inherently not accessible: accessibility is limited mainly to including fallback content should canvas not render. Interactivity requires redrawing of each pixel. There are no DOM nodes for anything you draw. There's no animation API. Instead, timers or requestAnimation Frame are generally used for updating the canvas at quick intervals. Canvas gives you a surface to draw onto with the API of the context you choose. Canvas, however, is very well suited for editing of images, generating raster graphics such as for games or fractals, and operations requiring pixel-level manipulation. Drawings created with the canvas API can also be exported as images.

The <canvas> 2D context is well supported in all browsers (since IE9). SVG is also well supported, but in varying formats (since IE9 and Android 3). While both SVG and Canvas are well supported, they both have their drawbacks.

SVG may not perform well. Mobile browsers have difficulty handling increased DOM elements. Each additional DOM node uses up memory, and needs to be recalculated when the page is reflowed. For these reasons, you should limit the number of DOM nodes added to your web applications when developing for mobile. SVG is made up of DOM nodes, and these increased number of DOM elements can harm performance and, in more extreme cases, can crash some mobile browsers. Canvas, on the other hand, when animating (versus drawing a single image), can drain your users' battery. Canvas has been hardware-accelerated in all major browsers, making the draw time and update time much faster, as well as improving battery consumption.

Weigh the pros of cons of both before deciding to use either (or neither).

WebGL

3D, or WebGL, support is still nascent, with major performance issues, excessive battery consumption, and limited implementation on mobile devices. (Try the Blackberry 10 at the time of this writing for the best implementation. WebGL was also recently implemented in Firefox OS.) When available on older mobile devices, because CPU usage eats up battery life, and JavaScript makes for heavy CPU usage, you may want to think twice before including WebGL: you don't want to drain your users' batteries. Devices that support WebGL, like BlackBerry 10, put WebGL on the GPU, which performs better and consumes less power than if it were on the CPU, but I am still hesitant to recommend its use. If you do choose to implement WebGL, always be aware of performance, such as memory usage and battery consumption.

Audio/Video

Prior to HTML5, there was no standards-based way to embed video in a web page. Instead, web videos were displayed through third-party plug-ins like Flash or Quick-Time. In addition, without an easy way of creating accessible media, when video files were included, they were often inaccessible to the visually and hearing impaired.

HTML5 defines a standard way to embed video and audio into web pages, using the `<video>` and `<audio>` elements. Both `<audio>` and `<video>` are supported in all mobile browsers (except Opera Mini), but not all browsers support the same video formats at this time. Before we discuss how to include video and audio into a document, we need to discuss media file codecs and browser support, since we'll need to include different media types for different browsers, and fallbacks for browsers that don't support your media type.

Media Types

With browser support of the HTML5 `<video>` and `<audio>` elements and standard media types, there will no longer be a requirement for third-party plug-ins for this type of media. At this time, however, different browsers support different video and audio codecs. As you likely know, the iPad and iPhone do not support Flash. They do support the `<video>` and `<audio>` elements, supporting the H.264 video and AAC audio formats (described in the next section). Modern browsers all support HTML5 video, but do so with different video formats. Firefox, Chrome, Android, and Opera support Ogg/Theora (*.ogv*). IE9, Safari, Chrome, Android, and iOS support MPEG4/h.264 (*.mp4*). Firefox 4+, Chrome, Opera, and Android (2.3+) support WebM/VP8 (*.webm*), as does IE9 if the required codecs are installed on the system. See Table 5-1.

Table 5-1. Browser video codec support (Ogg and WebM can be separately installed in IE9)

	iPhone/iPad	Android	BlackBerry	Opera Mobile	Opera Mini	Windows/IE	Chrome Android	Firefox Android
\<video\>	Yes	Yes	7	11		9	yes	yes
Ogg		2.		11		(9*)		yes
H.264	Yes	3.0[a]	7			9	yes	yes*
WebM		2.3		14		(9*)	yes	yes

[a] See *http://www.broken-links.com/2010/07/08/making-html5-video-work-on-android-phones/*.

There are several video codecs. The three most relevant codecs are Theora/Ogg, VP8, and H.264. Theora/Ogg (*.ogv*) is an open standard natively supported by Firefox 3.5, Chrome 4, and Opera 10.5+, and works in IE only after installing a plug-in. WebM, used with the VP8 video codec, is a newer format that is supported natively in the newest versions of Chrome, Mozilla Firefox, and Opera 10.6.

VP8 is currently royalty free. There is a patent, but Google, the owner, provides for royalty-free licensing. Unfortunately, while well supported in modern browsers, WebM/ VP8 video codec faces patent issues with Nokia that may make it unlikely to be adopted as an Internet standard anytime soon.

H.264 provides for low, medium, and high bandwidth devices, is playable through Adobe Flash, and mobile devices including Android and iPhone, but is not an open standard. Licensing can be quite costly. Originally, Chrome stated that it would drop support for it, but hasn't yet. Firefox added support in 2013 if it is installed in the operating system. Opera on mobile does the same.

At this time, there is no format that works in all browsers, as demonstrated in Table 5-1. To make your video work everywhere, you have to encode your video in more than one format.

For right now, for mobile phones in the United States, H.264 is the way to go. Just keep yourself updated for the possibility that support may change. If the "mobile" devices you support include GPS systems, video games, etc., remember that Opera is the most popular mobile browser around the world, and even in the United States for other-than-phone-and-PC devices.

Adding \<video\> to Your Website

While simply including H.264 for mobile may work if you are targeting the US smartphone market, for maximum device compatibility, two versions of the video need to be produced. Make a WebM version (VP8 video and Vorbis audio) and an MP4 version (H.264 video and AAC audio). Link to both video files using the HTML5 \<video\>

element and the child `<source>` tags, and include a Flash-based video player as a default option.

Attributes of `<video>` and `<audio>`

There are several attributes for `<video>` and `<audio>` elements that control the appearance and behavior of the embedded media.

The `<video>` and `<audio>` elements support:

src
> The `src` attribute, or "source attribute," takes as its value the URL for the video or audio file. It can be replaced by multiple `<source>` child nodes.

autoplay
> The Boolean `autoplay` attribute, if present, tells the browser to start playing the video automatically, not waiting for the user to press play. This should only be included on web pages where the primary content of the page is the video.

loop
> If the Boolean `loop` attribute is present, the video or audio will loop, once started it will play continuously until paused or stopped. When the video or audio clip reaches its end, if the `loop` attribute is present, it will start from the beginning again.

controls
> If the Boolean `controls` attribute is included, the browser should display the media controls (timing, play, pause, etc.).

preload
> The `preload` attribute hints to the browser how much it should download before the video starts playing. If omitted or included and set to `none`, the media does not preload. If included or included and set to `auto`, the media will be downloaded. If set to `metadata`, the dimensions, length, and other metadata should be retrieved, but the whole media object need not be downloaded.

The following attributes apply to `<video>` only, not to `<audio>`:

poster
> The `poster` attribute takes as its value the URL of an image to be used as a visual placeholder until the video starts playing. If not included, the video player will show the first from of the video, which generally appears as a black rectangle.

width
> The `width` attribute takes as its value the width of the video container (in pixels).

height
> The `height` attribute takes as its value the height of the video box (in pixels).

Here is a sample `<video>` declaration (a description of each component is given in Table 5-2):

```
<video autoplay controls loop poster="poster.jpg" preload="metadata"
src="video.mp4" height="360" width="480">Fallback Text</video>
```

Table 5-2. The components of a sample <video> declaration

Component	Description
`<video>`	The video tag.
`autoplay`	If set, the video starts when page loads.
`controls`	If set, a control bar is shown.
`loop`	If set, the video continuously loops.
`poster="/img/poster.jpg"`	If set, a preview image is shown.
`preload="metadata"`	Can be none, metadata, and auto.
`src="/video/video.mp4"`	Link to the video file.
`height="360"`	Height of the video.
`width="480">`	Width of the video
`Fallback Text`	Can be any valid HTML code. Linking to the video is standard practice.
`</video>`	The closing `</video>` tag is required

HTML5 `<audio>` and `<video>` allow for associating captions with the embedded media. These elements are part of the HTML5 DOM that allows for CSS styling and provides for a powerful API giving developers control over movie playback through a whole slew of new JavaScript methods and properties, including `play()`, `pause()`, `muted`, and `ended`.

When HTML5 video is fully supported, with all browsers supporting the same codec, the code will be as simple as this:

```
<video src="myVideo.mp4" width="400" height="300"
        controls poster="myImage.jpg">
    You don't support HTML5, but you can still
    <a href="myVideo.ogv"> download the video here</a>.
</video>
```

Unfortunately, that code won't work cross-browser quite yet. As explained previously, not all browsers support the same codec: we have to provide different sources to different browsers.

To enable that, HTML5 provides us with the `<source>` element. The `<source>` element allows the specifying of more than one media resource. The `<source>` element has three attributes (other than the global attributes) including `src`, `type`, and `media`.

To dynamically change the media being played, modify the src attribute of the <video> and <audio> tags. Modifying the src attribute of a <source> element will not work. Use the canPlayType() method to select a type that the browser supports.

The type attribute denotes the type of the media resource, so that the browser can determine if it understands the media type before downloading it. If specified, its value must be a valid MIME type.

Until all browsers support a single codec, the code is still not too complicated. In our game example, we could add an instructional video explaining how to play the game. We didn't include this video, but we could have. Had we opted to include a video, supporting video for all browsers would currently look something like this:

```
<video width="400" height="300" preload="none" poster="posterImg.jpg"
        controls>
  <source src="myVideo.mp4" type="video/mp4; codecs=avc1.42E01E, mp4a.40.2"/>
  <source src="myVideo.webm" type="video/webm; codecs=vp8, vorbis"/>
  <source src="myVideo.ogg" type="video/ogg; codecs=dirac, speex"/>
  <object width="400" height="324" type="application/x-shockwave-flash"
          data="myVideo.swf"/>
   <param name="movie" value="myVideo.swf"/>
   <param name="flashvars"
          value="image=posterImg.jpg&amp;file=myVideo.mp4"/>
  <!-- fallback -->
  <a href="linktovideo">
    <img src="posterImg.jpg" width="400" height="300"
         alt="Awesome Video"/>
  </a>
  </object>
</video>
```

If your browser supports it, HTML5 video is used. If the browser does not support the first media type and the code if included, it will try the next. If HTML5 video is not supported, Adobe Flash is used. If neither Flash nor <video> are supported, the placeholder image will be displayed. You may also want to include video download links.

The preceding Flash file source is declared to be 24 px taller than the other versions: this is because the Flash controls take up 24 px of height below the video instead of overlaying the video like HTML5 video formats.

If we were targeting just modern mobile devices, we could have omitted Flash and added tracks (described in the section "The <track> element" on page 152):

```
<video width="400" height="300" preload="none" poster=
        "posterImg.jpg" controls>
  <source src="myVideo.mp4" type="video/mp4;
        codecs=avc1.42E01E, mp4a.40.2"/>
  <source src="myVideo.webm" type="video/webm;
        codecs=vp8, vorbis"/>
  <source src="myVideo.ogg" type="video/ogg;
        codecs=theora, vorbis"/>
    <img src="posterImg.jpg" width="400" height="300"
            alt="Title of Video" title="Your browser does
            not support video"/>
  <track kind="subtitles" label="English" src="en.vtt"
        srclang="en" default></track>
  <track kind="subtitles" label="Deutsche" src="de.vtt"
        srclang="de"></track>
</video>
```

Video files usually contain both audio and video tracks. Audio tracks contain markers to synchronize the audio with the video. Individual tracks can have metadata, such as the aspect ratio of a video track, or the language of an audio track. Containers can also have metadata, such as the title of the video itself, cover art for the video, episode numbers (for television shows), and so on.

Similarly, you can add `<audio>` to your documents:

```
<audio id="sound">
  <source src="music.mp3" type="audio/mp3"/>
  <source src="music.ogg" type="audio/ogg"/>
  <!-- flash version of the audio for non supporting browsers -->
</audio>
```

An article on Dev.Opera (*http://dev.opera.com/articles/view/everything-you-need-to-know-about-html5-video-and-audio/*) provides very detailed instructions on detecting support.

The <track> element

To make videos and audio files accessible to users with hearing impairments, or even accessible to nonnative speakers, you can add captions to your video with a `<track>` element linking to a subtitling file.

Included as the child of a `<video>` or `<audio>` element, `<track>`'s src attribute links to a timed track, or time-based data. The `kind` attribute sets what kind of data is included by the src attribute. Values of the `kind` attribute include `subtitles`, `captions`, `de scriptions`, `chapters`, or `metadata`.

You can include multiple track elements as children of a media element, but they must be of unique kind and language combinations:

subtitles
> The default value of the kind attribute, indicates a translation of the dialogue and is displayed over the video or audio by default. This is most useful when the conversations are inaudible or in a foreign language.

captions
> Denotes a track file that provides a transcription or translation of the dialogue similar to subtitles, but includes sound effects, musical cues, and other audio information that could fully replace the soundtrack if the audio is unavailable. This is most useful when videos are muted or the user is hearing impaired.

descriptions
> Tracks are descriptions of the video component of the media resource, intended for audio synthesis when the video is unavailable. This is helpful for the visually impaired and for those who otherwise can't see the video or read track text.

chapters
> Denotes a track defining chapter titles, intended to be used for navigating the media.

metadata
> Denotes a track that is intended for use by scripts and is not displayed to the human user.

Include the source of the track file with the required src attribute. The srclang attribute gives the language of the text <track> data. The label attribute gives a user-readable title for the <track> used by the browser to list subtitle, caption, and audio description tracks in their user interface.

The default attribute, if specified, indicates that the <track> is to be enabled if the user's preferences do not indicate that another <track> would be more appropriate. There can only be one default <track> element.

HTML5 <audio> and <video> allow for associating captions with the embedded media. These elements are part of the HTML5 DOM, which allows for CSS styling and provides for a powerful API giving developers control over movie playback through a whole slew of new JavaScript methods and properties, including play(), pause(), muted, and ended.

Video and Audio and JavaScript

If you're going to use JavaScript to control the <audio> and <video> elements, you will need to use feature detection to ensure support and avoid throwing a JavaScript error:

```
if (createElement('audio').canPlayType) { /* audio is supported */}
```

You can include native controls, or create your own. <audio> and <video> support the play() and pause() methods. To create your own, you can add HTML for the controls and JavaScript to play and pause the audio, with code similar to this:

```
<div id="controls" style="display: none">
 <button id="playButton">Play</button>
 <button id="pauseButton">Pause</button>
</div>

<script>
 if (document.createElement('audio').canPlayType) {
  if (document.createElement('audio').canPlayType('audio/mp3') ||
    (document.createElement('audio').canPlayType('audio/ogg'))) {
   // HTML5 <audio> and an included audio type is supported
   document.getElementById('player').style.display = 'block';
  } else {
  ... Include flash or other audio here ...
 }
</script>
```

To create your own controls, you can include the following:

```
var videoClip = document.querySelector('#clip');
var playButton = document.querySelector('#playButton');
var pauseButton = document.querySelector('#pauseButton');

playButton.addEventListener('touchEnd', function() {
  playVideo();
});
pauseButton.addEventListener('touchEnd', function() {
  pauseVideo();
});


function playVideo() {
   //play the video
   videoClip.play();
   // update the controls
   playButton.disabled = true;
   pauseButton.disabled = false;
}

function pauseVideo() {
   //pause the video
   videoClip.pause();
   // update the controls
   playButton.disabled = false;
   pauseButton.disabled = true;
}

function MuteUnMute() {
   //change the button value
   document.getElementById('mute').value = videoClip.muted ? 'Mute' : 'Unmute';
```

```
    //change the state of the video
    videoClip.muted = videoClip.muted ? false : true;
}
```

CubeeDoo

In our game example, we have a few sounds. In addition to optional annoying background music, when someone gets to the next level, makes a match, fails to make a match, etc., the game makes a sound indicating if there was a success or failure.

A background sound, if included, would use the actual <audio> tag, since the background music is user controllable. The feedback sounds are based on user action and success, so I dynamically generated them with JavaScript.

Here are the two methods we can employ to include sound. We can include the audio directly in our HTML:

```
<audio id="nonmatchsound" preload src="notmatch.mp3"></audio>
<audio id="matchsound" preload src="match.mp3"></audio>
```

We've preloaded the audio, but do not autoplay or loop our audio files. Instead, we use JavaScript to initiate playing the matched or nonmatched sound:

```
playSound: function(matched) {
        if (qbdoo.mute) {
            return false;
        }
        if (matched) {
            qbdoo.matchfound.play();
        } else {
            qbdoo.failedmatch.play();
        }
    },
```

Alternatively, we don't have to put the audio in our HTML. Instead, we add the audio to the DOM with JavaScript, without appending the audio files to the page:

```
playSound: function(matched) {
        //if sound is off for game, skip
        if (qbdoo.mute) {
            return false;
        }
        // if we haven't created the audio node, create it.
        if (!qbdoo.audio) {
            qbdoo.audio = document.createElement('audio')
        }
        if (matched) {
            qbdoo.audio.src = qbdoo.matchedSound;
        }
        else {
            qbdoo.audio.src = qbdoo.failedMatchSound;
        }
```

```
            qbdoo.audio.play();
    },
```

We've only included audio to demonstrate the use of `<audio>`. Never autoplay music; it is bad user experience. You'll note the game includes a mute button. If you do include sound and it is on by default, if the user selects to mute the sound, remember this selection in localStorage, which we cover in Chapter 6.

Styling Video

The `<video>` element is an HTML element. Like all elements, `<video>` is styleable. You can use CSS to define the width and height of the video. You can mask it, round the corners, and even reflect its contents. With canvas you can sample the pixels and invert them (which we may also be able to do with CSS Filters).

Responsive video sizing

More importantly, you may want to resize videos based on device size and aspect ratio. Thierry Koblentz proposed an effective method (*http://www.alistapart.com/articles/ creating-intrinsic-ratios-for-video/*) for allowing browsers to determine video dimensions based on the width of the containing block (or the width of the page) using intrinsic dimensions. A width change, such as an orientation change, triggers a new height calculation, allowing videos to resize and giving them the ability to scale the same way images do.

To create the resizable video, you create a resizable box with the proper ratio (4:3, 16:9, etc.), then make the video inside that box stretch to fit the dimensions of the box by using padding, percentages, and absolute positioning. The padding is generally set as a percentage of either 56.25% or 75% of the width, depending on the aspect ratio. Taking advantage of the box model, the `<video>` is absolutely positioned to take up the entire height and width of the padding area.

If you need to include a resizable video for your responsive website:

```
.wrapper {
    position: relative;
    height: 0;
    width: 100%;
    padding-bottom: 56.25%;
    / * or */
    padding-bottom: 75%;
}
video {
    position: absolute;
    width: 100%;
    height: 100%;
    left: 0;
    top: 0;
}
```

Things to know about <video> implementation

Unlike Flash, which is a plug-in controlled by one company, and therefore behaves similarly everywhere, different browsers and operating systems have slightly different quirks when it comes to <video>. On the iPhone, Android, and Windows Phone 8, videos are always fullscreen. On the iPad, the controls have a fullscreen button, and it even works with the pinch gesture. Video uses GPU on iOS and Windows, but Android played video off the CPU until Android 4:

- Make sure that your server is supporting the video mime types or Firefox may fail. Add `AddType video/ogg.ogv` and the like to the *.htaccess* file if not already supported.
- iPhone and iPad will not `autoplay`, even if the attribute is included.
- The appearance of the controls are based on the native browser controls. As mentioned earlier, the look and feel can be overwritten with JavaScript. Check out *http:// videojs.com/* if you would like to skin your controls.
- If you want to start including your own videos, there is an open source, GPL-licensed, multiplatform, multithreaded video transcoder, available for Mac OS X, Linux, and Windows called Handbrake (*http://handbrake.fr/*).

Remember that video and sound uses a lot of battery power. While both are supported on all smartphones, with great power comes great responsibility: it is your job to ensure that your web applications don't drain your users' batteries. Use caution when including battery-draining features.

Other HTML5 APIs

Offline Web Applications

Until now, users of web applications have only been able to use applications while connected to the Internet. When offline, web-based email, calendars, and other online tools have been unavailable, and for the most part, continue to be.

While offline, users may still access some portions of sites they have visited by accessing what is in the browser cache, but that is limited and difficult to manage. If a user gets bumped offline in the middle of a process, like writing an email or filling in a form, hitting submit can lead to a loss of all the data entered.

The HTML5 specification provides a few solutions, including local and session storage for storing data locally, and an offline application HTTP cache for ensuring applications are available even when the user is offline. HTML5 contains several features that address the challenge of building web applications that don't lose all functionality while offline, including indexDB, offline application caching APIs, connection events, status, as well as the localStorage and sessionStorage APIs.

Am I Even Connected to the Internet?

One thing you may want to know when implementing offline features is if the user is indeed connected to the Internet. HTML5 defines an `onLine` property on the Navigator object so you can determine whether the user is currently online:

```
var isOnline = navigator.onLine;
```

This will return true or false. Note that if it returns true, it could mean the user is on an intranet and does not necessarily mean the user has access to the Internet.

Application Cache

If you want to create web-based games that are able to compete with native games on mobile devices, you have to ensure that players can access your game even when they are not online. We want CubeeDoo players to be able to play whether they're at home on their WiFi, camping in the Mojave desert (why enjoy nature when you could be flipping cards?), or even flying over the Pacific. *Application cache* enables you to create web-based applications that are accessible even when the user is not currently online.

In the past, desktop browsers have only been able to save the HTML file and associated media to a local folder. This method works for static content, but it never updates and is generally a bad user experience.

With the ubiquity of web-based applications, it is more important than ever that web applications are accessible when the user is offline. While browsers have been able to cache the components of a website, HTML5 addresses some of the difficulties of being offline with the application cache ("AppCache") API.

AppCache allows you to specify which files should be cached and made available offline, enabling your website to work correctly when your user is offline even if they reload a page. Using the AppCache interface gives your web application the following advantages: (1) offline browsing, (2) faster reloads, and (3) reduced server load. With application cache offline browsing, your entire site can be navigable even when a user is offline.

AppCache on most mobile browsers enables the local storage of up to 5 MB (or limits you to 5 MB, depending on your perspective). Different browsers may have different limits. While users can change these limits in their browser preferences, you should always code to browser default values, unless all your users are power users.

For AppCache to work, you must include the `manifest` attribute in the opening `<html>` tag, the value of which is the URL of a text file listing which resources should be cached. In your HTML file, include `manifest="URL_of_manifest"`:

```
<!doctype HTML>
<html manifest="cubeedoo.appcache">
<meta charset="utf-8"/>
<title>....
```

With the inclusion of the `manifest` attribute on the `<html>` element linking to a valid manifest file, when a user downloads this page, the browser will cache the files listed in the manifest file, the manifest file itself, and the current document, making them available even when the user is offline. Even though the current document is by default cached, it is best to list it among the cached files in the manifest.

The document linking to the manifest file is cached by default.

So how does it work? When a browser sees a `manifest` attribute, it downloads the manifest file and attempts to cache the files listed in that manifest. If the user opens a locally stored website when offline, it uses the already cached files. If online, the browser accesses the cached site first, and only then does it check to see whether updates have been made to the cache manifest file and therefore the cache.

If changes have been made to the cache manifest file, the browser will download the entire cache before making updates to the cache in memory. The browser looks for changes in the manifest file, not the rest of the files on the server, to determine whether the cache should be refreshed. In other words, to get the cache to update, you need to edit the manifest file itself. Updating your other assets is not enough. Remember this when the "comment" is detailed in the section "Updating the cache" on page 162.

After loading the site from the cache, it fetches the manifest file from the server. If the manifest has changed since the page was last visited, the browser re-downloads all the assets and re-caches them. If the browser fails to re-download all of the assets, it continues to use the old cache. However, if the browser successfully downloads all the required files, it still continues to use the old cache, switching to the newer cache the next time the user accesses the site.

The cache manifest file

The *.appcache* file is a text file that lists the resources the browser should cache to enable offline access to your application. The file must start with the following string: CACHE MANIFEST. The required string is then followed by a list of files to be cached, and optional comments and section headers.

Your *.appcache* file should be served with the MIME-type `text/cache-manifest`. Add:

```
AddType text/cache-manifest .appcache
```

to your *.htaccess* file or server configuration. This used to be required, but is now optional. The manifest file is permanently stored in the browser cache. An *.appcache* may look something like this:

```
CACHE MANIFEST
#version01

#files that explicitly cached
CACHE:
index.html
css/styles.css
scripts/application.js
```

```
#Resources requiring connectivity
NETWORK:
signin.php
dosomething.cgi

FALLBACK:
/ 404.html
```

Note that the files listed in the cache manifest file are relative to the manifest file.

To create a comment, include a # as the first character of the line and the remainder of the line will be ignored.

Section headers add more control to how AppCache treats your web files and assets. There are four possible section headers: CACHE, FALLBACK, SETTINGS, and NETWORK, each followed by a colon.

The files following the CACHE header are explicitly cached. If no header is defined, or if files are listed above the headers, those files are cached as if they followed the CACHE header. Note that secure (HTTPS) files can only be cached if from the same origin as the manifest.

The file containing the cache manifest file in the <html> element is always added to the cache whether or not it's listed under the CACHE header.

Do not list the manifest file itself, or the site may never update.

The files following the NETWORK heading are explicitly *not* cached, and are therefore only accessible when the user is online.

FALLBACK files include paired files: files to show, and fallback files to backfill if the former file is not available. (If the first file in the pair is not available, the second file listed on the line will be served.) If included, the SETTINGS header should be last and list the single line value prefer-online.

 Do not list the *cache.appcache* file as a file to be cached in your manifest file, or your site may never update.

Updating the cache

The browser cache is not updated or overwritten until a change is made to the manifest file or by using applicationCache JavaScript methods. Making an update to a file listed in the manifest, such as your JavaScript, CSS, or HTML, is not sufficient: a change needs to occur in the manifest file itself.

A standard practice is to add a comment within the manifest file to force a file update. In the preceding snippet, changing the comment #version01 to #version02 will inform the browser that the cache should be updated. Using a timestamp instead of a version number may be more intuitive for you. Note that what you put in the comment is not important, only that it creates a change in the file that the browser will detect.

The version number for our cache is basically the comment on the second line. When the user requests that web page, the browser first loads the site from the cache if the cache is present. Then it downloads the *.appcache* file from the server and compares it with the one in memory. If there is a change to the manifest file—such as a change in that version number—it will download the rest of the cache. This is why we add a comment. It is much easier to change a comment than to change a filename (and all the files linking to it). Changing the comment with a version number or timestamp has become the standard way of informing the browser that the manifest file should be considered updated.

Once an application is offline it remains cached until the user clears their browser's data storage for your site, the *.appcache* file is modified, or the application cache is programmatically updated.

The browser first loads the site from the cache. Only then does it check to see if there are changes in the manifest file. When a change is noted, all the files listed in the manifest file are downloaded. The cache is not updated, however, until all the files are successfully retrieved from the server. If the manifest file or a resource specified in it fails to download, the entire cache update process fails—there is no risk of your user seeing a partially updated version of your web application.

You can force an update to the cache without altering the manifest file programmatically. To explicitly update the cache, call `applicationCache.update()`. When the status is ready, swap the old cache for the new one:

```
var appCache = window.applicationCache;

if (appCache.status == appCache.UPDATEREADY) {
  appCache.swapCache();
}
```

The possible status values include `UNCACHED`, `IDLE`, `CHECKING`, `DOWNLOADING`, `UPDATE READY`, and `OBSOLETE`. If the manifest file or a resource specified in it fails to download, the entire cache update process fails and the browser will keep using the old application cache.

While these steps update the cache, they do not update what the user is currently viewing. The user will continue viewing the previously cached version of the site until the next time he or she tries to access the web application. It thus takes two loads of your site for the user to get the new content.

You can force the new site on the user by reloading the site based on an `updateready` event handler, but having the site reload while the user is interacting with it could be bad user experience; do so thoughtfully.

In terms of CubeeDoo, we can add all of the files to the manifest file. We would have excluded the secure login form if we had one. We also include a comment with the version number (or the date, or something that makes sense to you), which we will update if we ever make changes to any of the files listed under the CACHE: or FALL BACK: headers:

```
CACHE MANIFEST
#version01

CACHE:
index.html
css/cubeedoo.css
scripts/cubeedoo.js
assets/matched.mp3
assets/notmatched.mp3
images/shapes.svg

NETWORK:
login.html

FALLBACK:
/ 404.html
```

When we are ready to deploy our application, we will add the manifest attribute to our index page's <html> tag. But *don't do it now*. There is very little that is more annoying than developing and testing a web application that is completely cached in the browser:

```
<html lang="en-us" manifest="cubeedoo.appcache">
```

Browsers will also clear the cache if they are unable to find the cache manifest file on the server. Linking to a nonexistent file, thereby returning a 404 Not Found response, will cause the browser to clear the cache.

Local and Session Storage

With application cache, we can get our web applications saved onto devices so they're available offline. Application cache enables you to store the files, but sometimes you also need to store data. For example, when our CubeeDoo player is offline (and online), we want to maintain our high scores with the names, times, and scores of these over-achievers along with the current game state when a player pauses the game. For these features, we could use localStorage, IndexedDB, or the deprecated Web SQL Database.

We're going to use localStorage to pause the game and use the deprecated (and yet still pervasive) Web SQL Database to save high scores. We could have done the inverse. We can't, however, use IndexedDB, since it is not yet supported on iOS or Android (though IE10, Blink, and Firefox added support in recent releases).

LocalStorage and sessionStorage are easy-to-use key/value stores. You may be thinking "but we have cookies, so what is the big whoop-dee-doo?" There are a lot of drawbacks to cookies, which localStorage solves.

The cookie comparison

The main uses for cookies are session management, personalization, and tracking. Server cookies are strings sent from the web server to the browser and back again with each HTTP request and response. The browser can return an unchanged cookie to the server, introducing state into an otherwise stateless HTTP transaction. Client-side cookies are JavaScript-generated strings that can be used to enable state, pass information back and forth to the server, or even simply to maintain values client-side, such as items in a shopping cart.

Browsers can store 300–400 cookies with a maximum size of 4 KB per cookie, and a limit of 20 cookies per server or domain. All cookies are sent with each HTTP request. While this automatic sending of information may be used to your favor, one of the big downsides in terms of mobile is the increased bandwidth. Also, passing cookies back and forth can be a security risk.

Whereas cookies are limited to 20 cookies at 4 KB each for a total of 80 KB per domain, the new local and session storage standards allow for more space. The size depends on the browser, but is generally in the MB rather than KB range.

LocalStorage is used for long-term storage of lots of data for a particular domain within a single browser. LocalStorage data persists after the browser or browser window is closed. LocalStorage data is accessible across all browser windows.

SessionStorage data is confined to the browser window that it was created in, and gets deleted when the session ends. SessionStorage is accessible to any page from the same origin opened in that window. If you open a window and navigate from page to page in the same site in the same window, every page navigated to within that same browser window will have access to the sessionStorage. If the user has multiple windows opened —for example, viewing your site in three separate browser windows—each browser window would have its own individual copy of the sessionStorage, but would share the same localStorage key/value pairs.

Long-term and session cookies are both sent to the server with every HTTP request. If you need to send information to the server, cookies may be the right solution. However, saving state via cookies, like many of us did before HTML5, meant sending lots of useless information to and from the server, wasting bandwidth. LocalStorage and sessionStorage both save bandwidth.

SessionStorage and localStorage both have the same five methods and a single property, as shown in Table 6-1.

Table 6-1. SessionStorage and LocalStorage methods and properties

Method/property	Description

setItem(key, value)	Sets the value for the given key. For example, define the session variable with:
	`sessionStorage.setItem('keyname', 'data value')`
	`localStorage.setItem('keyname', 'data value')`

getItem(key)	Retrieves the value for the given key. Returns null if the key does not exist:
	`sessionStorage.getItem('keyname')`
	`sessionStorage.keyname`
	`localStorage.getItem('keyname')`
	`localStorage.keyname`

removeItem(key)	Removes the key and its associated value. Unset the value with:
	`sessionStorage.removeItem('keyname')`
	`localStorage.removeItem('keyname')`

clear()	Removes all key/value pairs. Clear all the key value pairs with:
	`sessionStorage.clear()`
	`localStorage.clear()`

key(position)	Returns the key for the value in the given numeric position:
	`sessionStorage.key(position)`
	`localStorage.key(position)`

length	The read-only length property indicates how many key/value pairs are currently stored in sessionStorage:
	`sessionStorage.length`
	`localStorage.length`

Using sessionStorage and localStorage is extremely easy. It is like a regular object with a predefined name: sessionStorage and localStorage, respectively.

There is an argument as to the speed or performance of these storage APIs. While hitting the hard drive to retrieve data is slower than hitting a JSON value in the browser, hitting the hard drive on a mobile device is generally more performant than making an HTTP request.

LocalStorage to enhance mobile performance

Some websites, like *http://m.bing.com*, have taken advantage of localStorage to reduce the number of HTTP requests a page load makes. As briefly described in "<style> and mobile performance: standards anti-pattern" on page 54, they include the scripts and styles in the first hit to the server, then extract the JavaScript and CSS into separate localStorage name/value pairs. Each script has a unique identifier as the name in the name/value pair, which is stored inside a cookie.

When the user makes a request for a new page, the cookie gets sent along with the request informing the server which files are already stored in the user's browser. The server then only sends the needed files. This reduces a page request to a single HTTP request.

While the first request may have a large file size, subsequent requests are small as all of the assets are stored locally in localStorage. While including scripts and styles within a page is an anti-pattern of performance and standards, it has been used effectively to improve the performance on some mobile web applications and sites.[1]

Data and user settings persistence is not just helpful in terms of user experience, but can also benefit web users whose data or WiFi may not be consistent, be it due to overloaded cell towers, lack of data, or the user wanting to limit their data usage.

Because application cache isn't the panacea we are all hoping for, developers have developed their own best practices for offline application storage, generally mixing application cache with localStorage. The *Financial Times* has a good article explaining their process, reasoning, and code (*http://bit.ly/1aFW4Xu*).

CubeeDoo

In CubeeDoo, we use localStorage to save state for pausing the game, and sessionStorage to store the username and the game's default values. You can use sessionStorage or localStorage for all three, or any combination of the two. I chose to use both to demonstrate both.

We are leveraging the storage APIs to reduce the need to save state server-side. In fact, there is no server backend for CubeeDoo. Our server only needs to store and serve static files. All of the features such as high scores that generally sit on a database in the cloud are on the user's device.

LocalStorage is used to maintain state when the game is paused. When the user pauses the game, we use the custom data attributes and the dataset API to set and get the values and locations of each card. We store the card values in localStorage, along with all the other relevant data—such as time left, current level, current score, etc.—required to continue the game where and how we left off. Had we used sessionStorage, pausing the game would have worked just as well, but the information would have been cleared when the user closed the browser window, as sessionStorage key/value pairs are cleared when a browser session is terminated.

SessionStorage is used to temporarily store the user's name. The benefit of using sessionStorage instead of localStorage for the username is that a separate player's username can be maintained in a second tab in the same browser. The drawback (or benefit) is that when the user closes the browser, the username (used for listing and storing high scores) is cleared.

We stored the original state of the game—the default values—with sessionStorage. It's employed to save the default game settings when the game is initially loaded. When the

---

1. For more information on sessionStorage, see *http://www.nczonline.net/blog/2009/07/21/introduction-to-sessionstorage/*.

user progresses through the game, the levels increase, then the time allowed per level decreases, and so on. When the user starts a new game, instead of refreshing the page, we pull the original values out of sessionStorage. In this way, starting a new game does not require a page reload to access the game settings, which may have changed during the previous game. We could have saved these variables as properties on a global object in our script, but reloading would have reset the values to the default values set in our JavaScript.

I've chosen to store these default values in sessionStorage because, with HTML5, I can! I used sessionStorage instead of localStorage so those values don't maintain state between sessions.

I've included the following functions (among many others):

storeValue
: Stores default game values.

alterValue
: Updates stored default values.

pauseGame
: Pauses game. Stores current state in localStorage.

playGame
: Resets the game to pre-paused state, putting the cards back in their place and restarting the timer.

reset
: Clears localStorage set up when game was paused, clearing the saved paused state of the game.

Note qbdoo is the top-level namespace for CubeeDoo, and has several properties you can control:

```
 1    var qbdoo = {
 2        //game settings
 3        currentLevel: 1,
 4        currentTheme: "numbers",
 5        gameDuration: 120,
 6        score: 0,
 7        matchedSound: 'assets/match.mp3',
 8        failedMatchSound: 'assets/notmatch.mp3',
 9        mute: true,
10        cardCount: 16,
11        iterations: 0,
12        iterationsPerLevel: 2,
13        possibleLevels: 3,
14        maxHighScores: 5, ...
```

You can set the default values such as the number of cards, iterations per level, initial duration of a round, and so on. You, as the developer, can alter any of these default values. As the user plays the game, some of these values get altered. We store the original values, and restore these values as they get altered in sessionStorage.

The storeValues() function stores the initial game values:

```
1    storeValues: function(newgame) {
2        var currentState = {};
3        //capture values for play
4        currentState.currentTheme = qbdoo.currentTheme;
5        currentState.timeLeft = qbdoo.timeLeft;
6        currentState.score = qbdoo.score;
7        currentState.cardCount = qbdoo.cardCount;
8        currentState.mute = qbdoo.mute;
9        currentState.iterations = qbdoo.iterations;
10
11       // get all the cards values and positions
12       // use dataset to get value for all the cards.
13       if (newgame == 'newgame') {
14           currentState.currentLevel = qbdoo.currentLevel;
15           currentState.score = 0;
16           currentState.gameDuration = qbdoo.gameDuration;
17           sessionStorage.setItem('defaultvalues',
                   JSON.stringify(currentState));
18           return;
19       } else {
20           return currentState;
21       }
22   },
```

The storeValues() function is called when the game is initialized to store the default values set in our JavaScript file. As the user plays the game, some of these values change. By storing these values, when the user starts a new game by clicking on the new button, we do not need to reload the page. Instead, the default values are captured in lines 4–9, and updated in 14–16 if the user is starting a new game (without reloading the page).

When the function initially called, we set the values on the locally scoped current State object. In line 17, we use JSON's stringify() method to turn that object into a JSON string. We then save that string in sessionStorage with the key defaultvalues using sessionStorage's setItem() method. We use the key defaultvalues to retrieve the value with the getItem() method, which we do in our playGame() function.

We've included an alterAValue() function to update or return the default values set with storeValues(), should a user choose to change settings or should the progression of the game change the user's settings.

```
23   alterAValue: function(item, value) {
24       var currentState = JSON.parse(sessionStorage.getItem('defaultvalues'));
25       if (value) {
26           currentState[item] = value;
```

```
27          } else {
28              qbdoo[item] = currentState[item];
29          }
30          sessionStorage.setItem('defaultvalues', JSON.stringify(currentState));
31          return value;
32      },
```

The parameter of the `alterAValue()` function is the item to be set or retrieved and an optional value for the item, if the item is to be set. When the user changes the theme of the cards or mutes/unmutes the audio, the item and value are sent as arguments with the function call. The `alterAValue()` function fetches the item from sessionStorage, alters the object property required, then re-saves the default values for the game in sessionStorage to reflect the new value.

The function retrieves the default setting from sessionStorage with the `getItem()` method in line 24. The return value is the JSON string we had stored in sessionStorage with the `setItem()` method earlier with the `storeValues()` function. Because we stored a JSON string, when we retrieve the value with the `getItem()` method, a JSON string is returned. We parse it with the `JSON.parse()` method to define our locally scoped `currentState` object.

If two values are passed to the `alterAValue()` function, the first parameter is the game property to be altered. The second parameter is the new value of that game property. The `currentState` object is updated to reflect that change. If only one parameter is passed, the `alterAValue()` function returns the value of that game property.

We've included `pauseGame()`and `playGame()` functions, to pause and play the game, along with associated functions:

```
33      pauseGame: function(newgame) {
34
35          var currentState = {}, i, cardinfo = [];
36          if (qbdoo.game.classList.contains('paused')) {
37              qbdoo.playGame();
38              return false;
39          }
40
41          qbdoo.pauseOrPlayBoard('pause');
42          currentState = qbdoo.storeValues();
43          currentState.currentLevel = qbdoo.currentLevel;
44
45          for (i = 0; i < qbdoo.cardCount; i++) {
46              cardinfo.push(qbdoo.cards[i].dataset);
47          }
48
49          currentState.cardPositions = JSON.stringify(cardinfo);
50          localStorage.setItem('pausedgame', JSON.stringify(currentState));
51
52          qbdoo.clearAll();
```

```
53
54        },
```

The pauseGame() function is called when the pause/play button is clicked in the upper righthand corner of our game, toggling between paused and play states. The current state of the game—whether paused or in play—is determined by the class on the game. In lines 36–38, we note that if the game is already paused, as indicated by the presence of the paused class, the playGame() function, described in the next section, is called. If the game is not already paused, we call the pauseOrPlayBoard() method in line 41 that toggles the game's class and clears the timer interval.

To pause the game, we need to store the current state of the game. We need to store the remaining card face values and locations as well as the state of the game. We capture some of the stored state of the game values with a call to the storeValues() method in line 42, which we described earlier. We add the current level with the currentLevel property to the state object in line 43.

We then iterate through all the cards, pushing the dataset key/value pairs into the cardinfo array in lines 45–47. We turn that array into a JSON string, adding the card positions into the state object in line 49. We then stringify the entire currentState object and store the JSON string we've created in the browser as the pausedgame key's value in line 50 in localStorage.

In the last line, we clear the board by calling the clearAll() method. That function clears the cards from view by changing the value of the custom data attribute data-value to 0 for all cards. We hide all of the cards that have a data-value value of 0. We discuss CSS selectors and how we target based on attributes in Chapter 7.

classList. Note that we used the term classList on line 36. The classList object, added to all nodes within the DOM, provides us with the ability to add, remove, toggle, and query the existence of classes on any DOM node. classList returns a token list of the class attribute of the element:

node.classList.add(class)
> Adds the class to the node.

node.classList.remove(class)
> Removes the class from the node's list of classes if it was present. If the class was not present, it does not throw an error.

node.classList.toggle(class)
> Adds the class to the node's list of classes if the class was not already present, and removes it if it was.

node.classList.contains(class)
> Returns a Boolean: true if the DOM node's list of classes contains a specific class; false otherwise.

`classList` has been supported since iOS 5, Android 3, and IE10.

When the user pauses the game, the pause button becomes a play button. This change is done with CSS based on the `paused` class we added with the `pauseGame()` function. When the user then clicks on that same button again, the conditional in line 36 returns true, calling the `playGame()` function:

```
55        playGame:  function(newgame) {
56            var cardsValues, cards, i, currentState = {};
57
58            if (newgame == 'newgame') {
59            currentState = JSON.parse(sessionStorage.getItem('defaultvalues'));
60            qbdoo.timeLeft = qbdoo.gameDuration = currentState.gameDuration;
61            } else {
62            // get state via local storage
63            currentState = JSON.parse(localStorage.getItem('pausedgame'));
64
65            if (qbdoo.game.classList.contains('paused')) {
66                qbdoo.game.classList.remove('paused');
67            }
68            qbdoo.timeLeft = currentState.timeLeft;
69            }
70            qbdoo.reset('pausedgame');
71
72            qbdoo.currentTheme = currentState.currentTheme;
73            qbdoo.mute = currentState.mute;
74            qbdoo.currentLevel = currentState.currentLevel;
75            qbdoo.score = currentState.score;
76            qbdoo.cardCount = currentState.cardCount;
77            qbdoo.iterations = currentState.iterations;
78
79            qbdoo.setupGame(currentState.cardPositions);
80        },
```

The `playGame()` function is called when the user restarts a game from pause and when the user starts a new game after losing a previous game. If the user is restarting the game, we want to continue the game from where we left off. If we want to start a new game, we want to reset the default values of the game. The `playGame()` function handles both.

If starting a new game, with lines 58–60, the function retrieves the default values for the game from sessionStorage with the `getItem()` method, parsing the string and assigning it to the `currentState` object. We also reset the `gameDuration` to its appropriate value, and change the `timeLeft` to that value.

Otherwise, if the game is started from pause, we get the saved state with card positions and values from localStorage with the `getItem()` method, passing the `pausedgame` key instead of the `defaultvalues` key, which is a sessionStorage key, getting the `paused` state and parsing the JSON string into the `currentState` object. The function also changes the class of the board to drop the `paused` class.

The end of the function sets the game properties based either on the `defaultvalues` captured from sessionStorage or the paused values captured from localStorage, before calling the `setupGame` method to start the game.

In line 70, we call the `reset()` function, which deletes the paused game values stored in localStorage, using the `removeItem()` method, which has as its only argument the key name for the localStorage key/value pair we want to delete:

```
81        reset: function(item) {
82              localStorage.removeItem(item);
83        }
```

In CubeeDoo, when we pause the game, we use custom data attributes and a custom dataset to extract the card position and values, the `JSON.stringify()` method to turn the game object into a JSON string, and then store that string in localStorage.

In terms of sessionStorage, the important line here is line 30. We created a sessionStorage entry with a key of `defaultvalues` and a value of a JSON string representing our current state object. Lines 6 through 25 (in the earlier code snippet) create the properties of that object, with lines 18 through 25 using custom data attributes and the dataset API (covered in Chapter 2) to capture the key/value pairs showing each card's position and value.

When we restart the game, we get the item from localStorage:

```
gameState = localStorage.getItem('cubeedoo');
```

And then we delete the stored state from memory with:

```
localStorage.removeItem('cubeedoo');
```

Items that are stored in localStorage and sessionStorage are visible in the various debuggers, as shown in Figure 6-1.

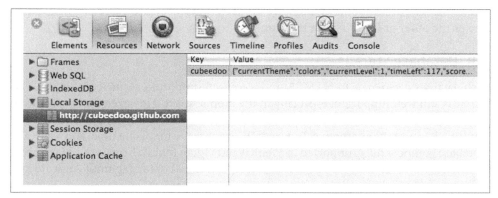

Figure 6-1. Contents of localStorage and sessionStorage are visible via the browser's debugging/web inspector tools

Note that while you can see the localStorage and sessionStorage items in your debugger, some debuggers don't automatically update the view. You may have to close your debugger and reopen to see the current state of your resources.

Our other use of sessionStorage is fairly simple as well.

If the username doesn't exist, we prompt the user for their username and add it both to the namespaced `player` property and to sessionStorage:

```
if (!player || player == 'UNKNOWN') {
        player = qbdoo.player = prompt('Enter your name') || 'UNKNOWN';
        sessionStorage.setItem('user', player);
    }
```

We assign the player name on page load with:

```
player: sessionStorage.getItem('user') || '',
```

If the user refreshes the page, the username is captured from sessionStorage. Otherwise, it defaults to blank. While we could have used cookies, this information doesn't need to be sent back and forth to the server. I could also have used localStorage, but for the case of this book example, I wanted the "security" of when the user closes the browser and the username is deleted, as is what happens with sessionStorage.

The quirk with CubeeDoo is that whoever loses the game gets credit for the full game: if one user starts the game, and pauses it, the cards and current score status are saved in localStorage. Since the username is in sessionStorage, if the browser is closed out after a pause, any username stored in sessionStorage is lost. When a user continues on from the paused state, they can enter a name. If you don't want a second user to continue on from where the first user left off, even if they are the same person, use sessionStorage instead of localStorage to store the paused state of the game. If you don't want to bug the user for their username, even if they haven't played in a month or two, use local-Storage instead of sessionStorage to store the username. If you don't care, still implement one or the other or both. This stuff is fun!

SQL/Database Storage

Web databases were new to HTML5, and were well supported. Actually, Web SQL Database is still well supported, especially in the mobile space. However, the specification was abandoned, and will not be supported in browsers that never supported it (IE and Firefox). Because the alternative, IndexedDB, is not ready for prime time, and Web SQL Database is almost fully supported in WebKit and Opera Mobile browsers, I'm covering it! Realize, however, that Web SQL is obsolete, and is just a stopgap until Android and iOS support IndexDB.

So, what is it? Web databases are databases that are hosted and persisted inside a user's browser. The client-side SQL database allows for structured data storage: tables with rows and columns, not just name/value pairs. This can be used to store emails locally for an email application or for a cart in an online shopping site. The API to interact with this database is asynchronous, which ensures that the user interface doesn't lock up (localStorage is synchronous). Because database interaction can occur in multiple browser windows at the same time, the API supports transactions.

Just like SQL, Web SQL has several methods and properties, detailed in the following sections.

Web SQL methods

openDatabase method. An `openDatabase()` method of the window object takes four parameters: the database name, version, display name, and database size. `openData base()` creates a database object. The database needs to be opened before it can be accessed. You need to define the name, version, description, and the size of the database:

```
window.openDatabase(database_name, database_version, display_name, db_size);
```

This method returns a reference to the database, which is referenced for all database transactions.

In CubeeDoo, the high scores can be maintained in two ways: either localStorage or Web SQL. We check to see if Web SQL is supported, and if so use it. If not, we set the script to use localStorage. We fork our code based on the `qbdoo.storageType` property:

```
storageType: (!window.openDatabase)? "WEBSQL": 'local',
```

Because Web SQL is currently supported but will forever be obsolete, don't use it without first checking for support!

To maintain the high scores in a database, we need to create that database:

```
var dbSize = 5 * 1024 * 1024; // 5MB variable for dbSize
if (!qbdoo.db) {
  if (window.openDatabase) {
   qbdoo.db = openDatabase("highscoresDB", "1.0", "Scores", dbsize);
  }
}
```

transaction method. The `transaction()` method of the database object takes up to three arguments: the transaction, error, and success callback functions. `transaction()` is a method of the database object we created using the `openDatabase()` method, not a window object like the `openDatabase()` method that created the database. You pass it a SQL transaction object on which you can use the `executeSQL()` method:

```
db.transaction(transaction_callback, error_callback, success_callback)
```

executeSQL() method. The executeSQL() method takes one to four arguments: a SQL statement, arguments, a SQL statement callback, and a SQL statement error callback. The SQL statement callback gets passed the transaction object and a SQL statement result object that gives access to the rows:

```
db.transaction(function(trnactn) {
  trnactn.executeSql('SELECT * FROM scores', [], callbackFunc,
    db.onError);
});
```

In CubeeDoo, we combine the two to get and set scores:

```
saveHighScores: function(score, player) {
  qbdoo.db.transaction(function(tx) {
    tx.executeSql("INSERT INTO highscoresTable (score, name, date)
    VALUES (?, ?, ?)", [score, player, new Date()], onSuccess, qbdoo.onError);
  });
  function onSuccess(tx, results){
    // not needed
  }
},
```

With offline SQL database storage, you can create tables, delete rows, and basically run any SQL command that you might run on your database server. Client-side SQL database storage (Web SQL Database) is supported in Safari, Chrome, and Opera, but will never be supported in Firefox or Internet Explorer. However, since it is supported in WebKit and Opera, it can be used for mobile web applications for improved performance, with localStorage as a fallback until IndexDB is well supported.

CubeeDoo high scores code

As noted earlier, in CubeeDoo we use Web SQL to store the high scores, with a localStorage backup in case Web SQL is not supported. I feature detected, and set the storageType on the qbdoo object:

```
storageType: (window.openDatabase)? "WEBSQL": 'local',
```

I then included functions to create the table, save high scores, load the high scores, render the high scores, and to delete the scores from the database. I included a method for sorting high scores for the local storage scores method of retrieving high scores. I didn't need to sort the Web SQL scores when saving, as I can retrieve sorted scores with SQL using ASC or DESC on the column by which I want to sort.

We have to create the table in our database with the SQL create statement:

```
createTable: function() {
  var i;
  qbdoo.db.transaction(function(tx) {
    tx.executeSql("CREATE TABLE highscoresTable (id REAL UNIQUE, name TEXT,
    score NUMBER, date DATE )", [],
      function(tx) {console.log('highscore table created'); },
```

```
          qbdoo.onError);
      });
    },
```

We save high scores with the SQL `insert` statement, or we store in localStorage with the `setItem()` method if the browser doesn't support Web SQL:

```
saveHighScores: function(score, player) {
    if (qbdoo.storageType === 'local') {
      localStorage.setItem("highScores", JSON.stringify(qbdoo.highScores));
    } else {
      qbdoo.db.transaction(function(tx) {
        tx.executeSql("INSERT INTO highscoresTable (score, name, date)
        VALUES (?, ?, ?)", [score, player, new Date()],
          onSuccess,
          qbdoo.onError);
      });
      function onSuccess(tx,results){
      // not needed
      }
    }
},
```

We have two functions to load high scores depending on whether we're using local-Storage or Web SQL. We use the SQL `select` statement to select the high scores from the database, sorting in descending order:

```
loadHighScoresLocal: function() {
    var scores = localStorage.getItem("highScores");
    if (scores) {
      qbdoo.highScores = JSON.parse(scores);
    }
    if (qbdoo.storageType === 'local') {
      qbdoo.sortHighScores();
    }
},

loadHighScoresSQL: function(){
    var i, item;
    qbdoo.db.transaction(function(tx) {
      tx.executeSql("SELECT score, name, date FROM highscoresTable
      ORDER BY score DESC", [], function(tx, result) {

        for (i = 0, item = null; i < result.rows.length; i++) {
          item = result.rows.item(i);
          qbdoo.highScores[i] = [item['score'], item['name'], item['date']];
        } //end for
      }, onError);    // end execute
      function onError(tx, error) {
        if (error.message.indexOf('no such table')) {
          qbdoo.createTable();
        } else {
          console.log('Error: ' + error.message);
```

```
      }
    }
    qbdoo.renderHighScores();
  }); // end transaction
},
```

The `renderHighScores()` function creates a list of the high scores:

```
// put the high scores on the screen
renderHighScores: function(score, player) {
  var classname, highlighted = false, text = '', i;
  for (i = 0; i < qbdoo.maxHighScores; i++) {
    if (i < qbdoo.highScores.length) {
      if (qbdoo.highScores[i][1] == player && qbdoo.highScores[i][0] == score) {
        classname = ' class="current"';
      } else {
        classname = '';
      }
      text += "<li" + classname + ">" + qbdoo.highScores[i][1].toUpperCase() +
      ": <em>" + parseInt(qbdoo.highScores[i][0]) + "</em></li> ";
    }
  }
  qbdoo.highscorelist.innerHTML = text;
},
```

The SQL `drop` statement can be used to delete the table if the user chooses to delete the scores. If Web SQL is not supported, the `reset()` function uses the localStorage `removeItem()` method:

```
eraseScores: function() {
  if (qbdoo.storageType === 'local') {
    qbdoo.reset("highScores");
  } else {
    qbdoo.db.transaction(function(tx) {
      tx.executeSql("DROP TABLE highscoresTable", [],
        qbdoo.createTable,
        qbdoo.onError);
    });
  }
  qbdoo.highscorelist.innerHTML = '<li></li>';
},


onError: function(tx, error) {
  console.log('Error: ' + error.message);
},

reset: function(item) {
  localStorage.removeItem(item);
}
```

IndexedDB

For client-side storage of structured data, we will soon have IndexedDB. IndexedDB, when finalized and supported, will provide for high-performance data searches using indexes. While DOM Storage is useful for storing smaller amounts of data, IndexedDB provides for an asynchronous solution for storing larger amounts of structured data. Since it is not currently widely supported in mobile browsers, we are not covering it here. If you prefer to use APIs that are actually moving forward as specifications, there is a polyfill to enable using IndexedDB syntax in Web SQL supporting browsers (*https:// github.com/axemclion/IndexedDBShim*).

As support improves, I will add IndexedDB to the online chapter resources. At the time of this writing, the only support in the mobile space is in IE10, and prefixed with different syntax in BlackBerry 10.

Enhanced User Experience

In addition to providing for offline web applications and uniform support for media, HTML5 includes several APIs that enable developers to enhance user experience. HTML5 includes a geolocation API enabling browsers to determine user location (with user consent, of course), web workers to improve script runtime of web applications, microdata to improve the semantics of web content, cross-document messaging API should allow documents to safely communicate with each other regardless of their source domain, and ARIA, to enable developers making the rich Internet applications accessible.

Geolocation

Geolocation allows users to share their physical location with your application if they choose to. Especially useful in social networking, geotagging, and mapping (but applicable to any type of application), geolocation enables developers to enhance the user experience, making content, social graphs, and advertisements more relevant to the location of the user.

The browser will request the permission of the user before accessing geolocation information (see Figure 6-2). Geolocation is an opt-in feature: when your web application requests geolocation information, the browser will ask the user if permission to share geolocation information is granted via banner or alert. The user can grant permission or deny it, and optionally remember the choice on that site. If permission is granted, the geolocation information will be accessible to your scripts and any third-party scripts included in the page, letting your application determine the location of the user, and capable of updating location information as the user moves around.

Figure 6-2. Permission must be granted for a website to receive a user's geolocation information

Location information is approximate, garnered from IP addresses, cell towers, WiFi networks, GPS, or even getting the information through manual data entry by the user. While approximate, you'll notice that it can be freakishly accurate.

The geolocation API does not care how the client determines location as long as the data is received in a standard way. The geolocation API is asynchronous.

To determine browser support for geolocation, use:

```
if (navigator.geolocation) {
    //geolocation is supported
}
```

The geolocation object provides for the `getCurrentPosition()` and `watchCurrentPosition()` methods that asynchronously return the user's current location, either once or continuously. The `watchCurrentPosition()` method can be used for active location applications such as GPS/navigation applications. For our web application, we don't need direction information, so the `getCurrentPosition()` method would suit our needs, and wouldn't drain the battery by repeatedly seeking location information. We don't need location information for CubeeDoo, but we can still learn it:

```
if (navigator.geolocation) {
    navigator.geolocation.getCurrentPosition(handle_success, handle_errors);
}
```

If successful, the callback function returns the current position with the coords object containing the more commonly used latitude and longitude properties, as well as the altitude, accuracy, altitudeAccuracy, heading, and speed properties. The following script will return the alert with the current latitude and longitude, and is available in the online chapter resources:

```
if (navigator.geolocation) {
    navigator.geolocation.getCurrentPosition(handle_success,handle_errors);

  function handle_success(position) {
      alert('Latitude: ' + position.coords.latitude + '\n Longitude: '
      + position.coords.latitude);
    }

  function handle_errors(err) {
    switch(err.code) {
      case err.PERMISSION_DENIED:
        alert("User refused to share geolocation data");
        break;
      case err.POSITION_UNAVAILABLE:
        alert("Current position is unavailable");
        break;
      case err.TIMEOUT:
        alert("Timed out");
        break;
      default:
        alert("Unknown error");
        break;
      }
  }

}
```

If successful, both the getCurrentPosition() and watchCurrentPosition() methods success callbacks will return a location object with the coords object, with the following properties:

- position.coords.latitude
- position.coords.longitude
- position.coords.altitude
- position.coords.accuracy

The watchCurrentPosition() method also returns the following properties:

- position.coords.heading

- `position.coords.speed`

The properties are kind of self-explanatory. Other than the Kindle and Opera Mini, geolocation is supported everywhere, and has been for a while (since IE9 on desktop).

We don't need location information for CubeeDoo, but we did include pinpointing current location on a map as an example in the files:

```
1    function getLocation() {
2    if (navigator.geolocation) {
3        navigator.geolocation.getCurrentPosition(success, error);
4        console.log('got position');
5        } else {
6        error('not supported');
7        }
8    }
9    function error(text) {
10        text = text || 'failed';
11        console.log(text);
12    }
13    function success(location) {
14        var lat = location.coords.latitude;
15        var long = location.coords.longitude;
16        var url = "http://maps.google.com/maps?q=" + lat + "," + long;
17    }
```

The `getLocation()` function feature detects in line 2 to see if geolocation is supported by the browser. Note that geolocation is on the `navigator` object (rather than window or document, like most method and properties we use). We get the current position with the `getCurrentPosition()` method of the `geolocation` object in line 3. If successful, the success callback uses the returned `coords` object's `latitude` and `longitude` properties to add a pinpoint to a Google map in lines 14–16. We included an error callback function on line 9. The message is usually a timeout, permission denied, or position unavailable if there is a failure.

Web Workers

All of the JavaScript, including page reflows and repaints, runs on the single UI thread that also handles repainting of user interactions, non-hardware-accelerated animations, etc. If there is a task with a heavy script load, the browser may slow to a crawl, greatly harming user experience. Web workers allow JavaScript to delegate heavy tasks to other processes so that scripts run in parallel. This enables the main thread to do the exciting UI stuff while the web worker does any heavy lifting you pass to the worker without slowing the main script thread. Web workers are useful in allowing your code to perform processor-intensive calculations without blocking the user interface thread.

Workers enable web content to run scripts in background threads, even AJAX. The worker thread can perform tasks without interfering with the user interface.

You know how sometimes web applications take a long time and you have to wait for the hourglass or rainbow beach ball to disappear before being able to interact with the page? Web workers are a solution. Workers perform JavaScript on a background thread leaving the main UI thread free to manipulate the DOM and repaint the page, if necessary. Web workers cannot manipulate the DOM. If actions taken by the background thread need to result in changes to the DOM, they should post messages back to their creators to do that work. The `postMessage()` method can be employed.

If your JavaScript includes some resource-intensive calculations, you can pass this to a web worker to process while the main thread continues running. Before creating a worker, ensure that the browser supports web workers. Web workers support heavy JavaScript processing that might crash a non-web-worker–supporting browser:

```
if (window.Worker) {
    //browser supports web workers
}
```

To create a web worker, you call the `Worker()` constructor, specifying the URI of a script to execute in the worker thread. The URI is relative to the file calling the script:

```
if (window.Worker) {
    var webWorker = new Worker('subcontractor.js'); //create it
}
```

Communicating with the web worker is accomplished via the `postMessage()` method. Once created, set the worker's `onmessage` property to an appropriate event handler function to receive notifications from the web worker. You terminate a worker with the `terminate()` or `close()` method. The `terminate()` method is immediate, stopping all current processes:

```
if (window.Worker) {
    var webWorker = new Worker('subcontractor.js'); //create it
    webWorker.postMessage(some_message);
}
```

In the worker (in this case, the *subcontractor.js*), receive the message from the main thread and act on it:

```
//in the subcontractor.js file
self.onmessage = function(event) {
        // handle the message
        var stuff = event.data;
        // and send it back to the main thread
        postMessage(stuff);
};
```

Workers can use timeouts and intervals just like the main thread can. This can be useful, for example, if you want to have your worker thread run code periodically instead of nonstop. You can control the worker by employing the `setTimeout()`, `clearTimeout()`, `setInterval()`, and `clearInterval()` methods.

Worker threads have access to a global function, importScripts(), which lets them import scripts or libraries into their scope. It accepts as parameters zero or more URIs of resources to import:

```
/* imports two scripts */
importScripts('scripts/jquery-min.js', 'application.js');
```

Web workers do not have access to the DOM. They don't have access to the console either. You may also get a security error when testing locally, which can make developing with web workers a little more difficult than regular JavaScript.

In CubeeDoo, we have no intensive JavaScript that we need to run, or background AJAX processes. While we don't employ the benefits of web workers in CubeeDoo, there is a Fibonacci sequence example in the online chapter resources. Also, we've included a web worker to handle our high score sort function. Sorting five numbers is certainly doable without the need of a web worker. However, if we kept the top 1,000,000 scores, sorting that many values would be a good use of a web worker (but a bad use of localStorage).

Were we to have used web workers for sorting the high scores, we would have replaced our sorting function with a web worker call:

```
var webWorker = new Worker('js/sort.js');
    webWorker.postMessage(qbdoo.highscores);
    webWorker.onmessage(function(event) {
        qbdoo.highscores(event.data);
    });
```

The web worker script, in turn, needs to expect and accept the highscores via the onmessage property, and needs to post back the sorted scores via postMessage:

```
self.onmessage = function(event) {
        var sortedScores = sortScores(event.data);
        self.postMessage(sortedScores);
};
```

Microdata

Another feature of HTML5 is *microdata*. While microdata will not impact your site in any visible way, it is an increasingly relevant feature when it comes to search engine optimization and data scraping.

Microdata will replace the need for *microformats*. Microformats are standardized sets of vocabularies that are both human and machine-readable. They are web page conventions used to describe common information types including events, reviews, address book information, and calendar events via class attributes. Each entity, such as a person, event, or business, has its own properties, such as name, address, and phone number.

Microdata lets you create your own vocabularies beyond HTML5 and extend your web pages with custom semantics. Microdata uses the new to HTML5 attributes of item scope, itemprop, itemref, and itemtype.

The itemscope attribute is used to create an item, indicating that the scope of the item begins in the opening tag in which the attribute is included, and ends at that element's closing tag. The itemprop, or item property attribute, is used to add a property to an item. If an itemprop has associated properties that are not descendants of that item prop, you can associate those properties with that itemprop by using the itemref, or item reference attribute. The entity that has the itemscope attribute also accepts the itemref attribute that takes as its value a space-separated list of IDs of entities that should be crawled in addition to the itemprop's descendants.

Microdata is most useful when it is used in contexts where other authors and readers are able to cooperate to make new uses of the markup. You can create your own types of microdata or use predefined data vocabularies. Some predefined vocabularies can be found at *http://www.data-vocabulary.org/*.

Microdata versus microformats

Microformats are very similar to microdata. In fact, microdata can be viewed as an extension of the existing microformat idea, which attempts to address the deficiencies of microformats without the complexity of the often preferred systems like RDFa. Instead of using the new itemscope, itemprop, itemtype, etc., attributes, Microformats repurpose the class attribute to provide human and machine-readable semantic meaning to data—in essence, microdata.

In general, microformats use the class attribute in the opening HTML tags (often <span> or <div>) to assign brief, descriptive names to entities and their properties. Unlike microdata, microformats are *not* part of the HTML5 specification.

Here's an example of a short HTML block showing my contact information for myself:

```
<ul>
 <li><img src="http://standardista.com/images/estelle.jpg"
    alt="photo of Estelle Weyl"/></li>
 <li><a href="http://www.standardista.com">Estelle Weyl</a></li>
 <li>1234 Main Street<br />San Francisco, CA 94114</li>
 <li>415.555.1212</li>
</ul>
```

Here is the same HTML marked up with the hCard (person) microformat.

```
<ul id="hcard-Estelle-Weyl" class="vcard">
 <li><img src="http://standardista.com/images/estelle.jpg"
    alt="photo of Estelle Weyl" class="photo"/></li>
 <li><a class="url fn" href="http://www.standardista.com">Estelle Weyl</a></li>
 <li class="adr">
 <span class="street-address">1234 Main Street</span>
 <span class="locality">San Francisco</span>, <span class="region">CA</span>,
```

```
    <span class="postal-code">94114</span>
    <span class="country-name hidden">USA</span>
  </li>
  <li class="tel">415.555.1212</li>
  </ul>
```

In the first line, `class="vcard"` indicates that the HTML enclosed in the `<ul>` describes a person: in this case, me. The microformat used to describe people is called hCard but is referred to in HTML as vCard. While confusing, it isn't a typo.

The rest of the example describes properties of the person, including a photo, name, address, URL, and phone, with each property having a class attribute describing the property. For example, `fn` describes my "full name."

Properties can contain other properties. In the example, the property `adr` encompasses all the components of my fake address, including street address, locality, region, and postal code. With a little CSS, we can hide elements with class `hidden` and add a line break between street address and locality. To create your own hCard, visit *http://micro formats.org/code/hcard/creator*.

The same content could be written with microdata:

```
  <ul id="hcard-Estelle-Weyl" itemscope
      itemtype="http://microformats.org/profile/hcard">
  <li><img src="http://standardista.com/images/estelle.jpg"
      alt="photo of Estelle Weyl" class="photo"/></li>
  <li><a href="http://www.standardista.com" itemprop="fn">Estelle Weyl</a></li>
  <li itemprop="adr">
      <span itemprop="street-address">1234 Main Street</span>
      <span itemprop="locality">San Francisco</span>,
      <span itemprop="region">CA</span>,
      <span itemprop="postal-code">94114</span>
      <span class="hidden" itemprop="country-name">USA</span>
  </li>
  <li itemprop="tel">415.555.1212</li>
  </ul>
```

Or you can combine the two:

```
  <ul id="hcard-Estelle-Weyl" class="vcard" itemscope
      itemtype="http://microformats.org/profile/hcard">
  <li><img src="http://standardista.com/images/estelle.jpg"
      alt="photo of Estelle Weyl" class="photo"/></li>
  <li><a class="url fn" href="http://www.standardista.com"
      itemprop="fn">Estelle Weyl</a></li>
  <li class="adr" itemprop="adr">
      <span class="street-address" itemprop="street-address">1234 Main Street</span>
      <span class="locality" itemprop="locality">San Francisco</span>,
      <span class="region" itemprop="region">CA</span>,
      <span class="postal-code" itemprop="postal-code">94114</span>
      <span class="country-name hidden" itemprop="country-name">USA</span>
  </li>
```

```
<li class="tel" itemprop="tel">415.555.1212</li>
</ul>
```

Microdata does not alter the appearance of a document. Rather, it just enhances the semantics of that document. Search engines will not display content that is not visible to the user. Providing search engines with more detailed information, even if you don't want that information to be seen by visitors to your page, can be helpful. To enable the Web to be a single global database, being able to parse the available data into meaningful data points is required. Microdata and microformats help make otherwise nondescript data meaningful to parsers.

Microdata API

Not yet well supported, the microdata DOM API provides access to the microdata items. The document.getItems(itemType) returns a nodeList containing the items with the specified types, or all types if no argument is specified. The document.getItems() method returns a nodeList containing all the microdata items on a page when no argument is passed. You can specify a specific itemtype URL as the argument to return only items of that type.

Once you've returned your nodeList, you can then access the different properties with the properties attribute:

```
var allMicrodata = document.getItems();
var firstItemName = allMicrodata.properties['name'][0].itemValue;
```

Each item is represented in the DOM by the element on which the relevant item scope attribute is found.

Cross-Document Messaging

Cross-document messaging allows documents to communicate with each other regardless of their source domain, in a way designed to protect us from cross-site scripting attacks.

Web applications often include services from several different domains. The current way of doing mash-ups has many security risks. When you include third-party JavaScript on your website, those external scripts, over which you have no control, have access to your domain's cookies and can forge requests that appear to come from the user. Iframes are not the solution to the problem, since your document cannot communicate with the contents of an iframe embedded within the page if that iframe comes from a different domain.

The HTML5 cross-document messaging API attempts to solve both of these issues by enabling the registration of event handlers for incoming messages from other domains, and sending messages to other domains.

To verify that the message is coming from the expected domain:

```
window.addEventListener('message', function(e) {
  if (e.origin == 'http://the_domain.com') {
    // the origin of the message is verified. Test to see if
    // it's in the correct format before using
  }, false);
```

Send a message to another domain:

```
var theFrame = document.getElementById("myIFrame").contentWindow;
theFrame.postMessage("The message", "http://www.the_domain.com");
```

CORS: Cross-Origin Resource Sharing

As CubeeDoo is a small, self-contained application with limited visitors and no third-party app integration, we aren't using any cross-document messaging or cross-origin resource sharing (CORS). If you are creating more popular applications, you'll likely be using content delivery networks (CDN) or integrating third-party applications. For example, if we were hosting our font on a CDN, we would need to use CORS to tell Firefox and Internet Explorer that it is OK to render fonts from a different domain.

Security

Security is a major concern in cross-domain messaging. Always check the `origin` property to ensure that messages are only accepted from domains that you expect to receive messages from. After you've confirmed that the message is coming from the expected server, confirm that the data received is in the expected format. You should never rely on someone else's server not being compromised.

Accessible Rich Internet Applications (ARIA)

Accessibility

HTML5, just like prior versions, can be made to be completely accessible. It just requires a little bit of planning. ARIA, or Accessible Rich Internet Applications, is the first part of HTML5 that is supported by all modern browsers. Most popular JavaScript libraries also provide support for ARIA implementation. In addition to ARIA, HTML5 provides the ability to enhance accessibility in the fact that it does not use Flash (yes, they talk the accessibility talk, but no one has figured out how to make Flash walk the accessibility walk) or other embedded objects. It uses <video>, <audio>, <svg>, and <canvas>, HTML elements that, with the exception of <canvas>, are inherently accessible. As part of the DOM, they are easily targetable to increase accessibility.

As we create more and more dynamic web applications, the content becomes less and less inherently accessible to differently abled users. You can use ARIA properties to provide the basic type, state, and changes created via JavaScript widgets to screen readers and other assistive technologies. For example, when checking for airfares, selecting a checkbox entitled "nonstop only" may lead to a dynamic response that updates the airfare rates without reloading the page. If a user is visually impaired, how do they know that part of the page was updated since they can't actually see the update? On a finance page, how does a user know that the stock ticker is continually updated? The ARIA API provides for unobtrusive (and obtrusive) ways of providing such information to the user.

As previously stated, ARIA stands for Accessible Rich Internet Applications. With the proliferation of Internet applications, there has been an increase in the number of sites requiring JavaScript and that update without page refreshes. This imposes accessibility issues that weren't addressed by Web Content Accessibility Guidelines, or WCAG 1, as those specifications were written when "sites must work without JavaScript" was a reasonable accessibility specification.

With the increase of web-based "applications" (versus "sites") requiring JavaScript, and improved support of JavaScript in assistive technologies, new accessibility issues have emerged. ARIA attempts to handle some of those issues. Through the inclusion of roles, states, and properties, your dynamically generated content can be made accessible to assistive technologies. Additionally, static content can be made more accessible through these additional, enhanced semantic cues.

By including ARIA accessibility features on your website, you are enhancing the accessibility of your site or application. By including roles, states, and properties, ARIA enables the developer to make the code semantically richer for the assistive technology user. ARIA enables semantic description of element or widget behavior and enables information about groups and the elements within them. ARIA states and properties are accessible via the DOM.

Similar to including the `title` attribute, ARIA is purely an enhancement and will not harm your site in any way. In other words, there is no valid reason to not include these features! Most JavaScript libraries, such as jQuery and Dojo, already support ARIA. Modern browsers, including IE8, support ARIA.

The easiest to include and most important properties of ARIA are the inclusions for the `role` attribute, and inclusion of states and properties:

- Only use ARIA roles, attributes, and properties when regular HTML markup does not support all of the semantics required.
- Apply the ARIA `role` attribute in cases where the markup needs to be semantically enhanced and in cases where elements are being employed outside of their semantic intent. This includes setting up relationships between related elements (grouping).
- Set the properties and initial state on dynamic and user-changing elements. States, such as "checked," are properties that may change often. Assistive technology that supports ARIA will react to state and property changes.

- Support full, usable keyboard navigation. Elements should all be able to have keyboard focus.
- Make the user interface visually match the defined states and properties in browsers that support the ARIA CSS pseudoclasses.

The `role` attribute enables the developer to create semantic structure on repurposed elements. While to a sighted user, the example of a span repurposed as a checkbox is not noticeable, the `role` attribute makes this seemingly nonsemantic markup accessible, usable, and interoperable with assistive technologies. Once set, however, a `role` attribute's value should not be dynamically changed, since this will confuse the assistive technology.

Example: your designer insists that they want the checkboxes on your page to look a certain way. "Impossible," you say. You know that you can use CSS to make a span look like a checkbox. The sighted user would never know that you weren't using `<input type="checkbox"`..., but for accessibility concerns, you know a screen reader user will not know it's a checkbox. With the ARIA `role` attribute included in your code, and both a browser and screen reader that support ARIA, you can make your repurposed span accessible with:

```
<span role="checkbox" aria-checked="true" tabindex="0"/>
```

It's not enough to simply use `role` in the preceding example. If you include spans transformed into checkboxes, you will need to include equivalent but unobtrusive touch, keyboard, and mouse events for each interaction. Best practices dictate that you should use the most semantically appropriate element for the job, so in practice you should not do this.

There are currently over 60 roles, including:

alert	dialog	listitem	option	spinbutton
alertdialog	directory	log	presentation	status
application	document	main	progressbar	tab
article	form	marquee	radio	tablist
banner	grid	math	radiogroup	tabpanel
button	gridcell	menu	region	textbox
checkbox	group	menubar	row	timer
columnheader	heading	menuitem	rowgroup	toolbar
combobox	img	menuitemcheckbox	search	tooltip
complementary	link	menuitemradio	scrollbar	tree
contentinfo	list	navigation	separator	treegrid
definition	listbox	note	slider	treeitem

There is no need to include `role` if an element is employed as intended (you don't have to include `role="checkbox"` on `<input type="checkbox"/>`). However, if you use a span to appear and function like a checkbox, include the ARIA `role` attribute: `<span role="checkbox">`. Choose the role type from this list that is most similar to the role you are assigning to the element you are employing in a nonsemantically correct manner.

If you are interested in learning more about WAI-ARIA, Web Accessibility Initiative—Accessible Rich Internet Applications, *http://www.w3.org/WAI/intro/aria.php* is the place to start.

In Conclusion

This chapter is intended to give you an idea of the APIs that are being included in HTML5. Each of these sections merit books of their own. In fact, some, like microformats, already have their own books. In other cases, such as cross-document messaging, the issue is too nascent to write about. Please check out the online chapter resources for links to more in-depth articles on each of these topics.

Upgrading to CSS3

CSS3 has been in the works for over a decade. WebKit/Blink, Opera, and Firefox have been supporting some features for a long time now. With IE10 and IE11, we're almost there! It's time we took advantage of some awesome new (and sometimes not so new) features. Especially when it comes to CSS selector support, mobile browsers are there.

When you don't have to worry about older versions of Internet Explorer (IE8 and earlier), you can use any CSS3 selector. All of them are supported in all modern browsers, and all of them are supported on all smartphone and tablet browsers.

The CSS2 specifications were adopted in 1998. CSS3 has been in development since then. The CSS3 specifications are still in development, and will likely never be finalized.

"Huh?" you ask. CSS 2.1 and earlier specifications were monolithic specifications. CSS3 is an umbrella term for all specifications after CSS 2.1. Instead of a monolithic specification, there are now modules for each CSS component, and new modules and new features keep getting added. Some of these specifications, like colors and selectors, are level 3, with work having commenced on level 4. Other specifications are at level 1. All of these modules, whatever the level, are under the umbrella called "CSS3." Each module goes through the spec writing and finalization process at its own pace.

WebKit/Blink, Opera, and Mozilla have not waited for module specifications to be finalized. With Internet Explorer 9, Microsoft finally joined the game. Most of the recommended features have been part of the draft specifications for years. In most areas, the recommended specifications are stable enough that most browser developers have begun implementing these CSS3 features.

While web developers may still have to ensure graceful degradation of our websites on the desktop for the various IEs, the ubiquity of CSS3 and HTML5 support in the mobile market and on non-Windows operating systems (think PlayStation, Wii, etc.) means we're not just playing with these technologies, we can implement them. We are reaching millions, even billions, of people through HTML5 and CSS3 supportive browsers, which are the default browsers of most mobile phones, tablets, and almost all other non-Windows desktop OS-based devices.

In this chapter, we'll cover CSS selectors, and how to use selectors to target DOM nodes in JavaScript (without jQuery).

We'll first give a brief overview of the CSS3 syntax, which is the same as the syntax of previous CSS recommendations. Then we'll take an in-depth look at CSS3 selectors, selectors that enable semantic targeting of elements in HTML documents, including targeting any element in your document without touching the HTML or adding a class or ID, before diving into query selectors.

CSS: A Definition and Syntax

Before diving into CSS3, you need to know the basics of creating a CSS rule set. We will cover the syntax briefly for those who may be new to CSS, and then dive into some very advanced element targeting with CSS selectors.

First off, we need to know what CSS means.

Cascading Style Sheets, or CSS, make up the presentational layer of the Web. With CSS, you can define the look and feel of your site in one location, and that one file can impact the look and feel of your entire site. If there is a design change, with CSS, you can make a change to the one presentational file, and that change will be immediately apparent site wide. When your boss or other client says, "You know what, I changed my mind ... let's make the links purple instead of green," with a correctly coded site using an external CSS file, that change can take one minute. It doesn't matter if your site has one page of HTML or one million. Change one line in your CSS file, and you can successfully update the appearance of all your web pages.

In earlier versions of HTML there were a series of presentational elements, such as <font> and <center>, which were used to enable webmasters to design sites. For proper web standards, however, the content layer, or HTML, should be separate from the presentational layer (the CSS) and from the behavioral layer (the JavaScript). Had you used <font color="green">, the request to change to purple would be a challenge. You would have to update every occurrence of color="green" in every web page.

Using elements for presentation is so 1996! In fact, many of these presentational elements that were commonly used in 1996 have been deprecated or made obsolete in favor of using CSS for presentation. Don't use <center>, <b>, <i>,[1] <font>, <tt>, or other presentational elements for presentational effect, even if not obsolete. Instead, use CSS. Here's how...

---

1. As noted in Chapter 3, <i> and <b> have received new semantic meaning in HTML5. Use these elements sparingly, when semantically appropriate.

CSS Syntax

Before implementing rules with selectors, properties, and values, we need to learn the syntax. Stylesheets are made up of rules, which are selectors followed by a block statement with properties and values. Most CSS rules look similar to this:

```
selector {
  property1: value1;
  property2: value2;
}
```

The *selector* tells the browser what element(s) to match. The *property* is the feature of the element that you want to affect, and the *value* is a value that you want to set for that property of that element.

Properties support specific value types and/or value keywords, which we discuss in Chapter 8.

CSS selectors enable you to target elements in your markup with the styles you define in the style declaration block. The *style declaration block* consists of the properties and values between the curly braces. All the properties and values for a rule are encased in curly braces, creating a declaration block:

```
p {
  color: blue;
  margin-bottom: 12px;
}
```

The statement reads: "paragraphs should have blue text and have a margin of 12 pixels below it."

Note that in this example, values and properties are separated by a colon and each declaration ends with a semicolon.

The semicolon on the last declaration in a block is officially optional, but don't omit it! You may save a few characters by not including the optional final semicolon, but since a single missing required semicolon, parentheses, or curly brace can make the rest of your stylesheet fail, I highly recommend always including the final optional semicolon. The bandwidth cost of including it is chump change compared to the time you may have to spend troubleshooting failing CSS caused by a missing character.

CSS styles impact the element that is targeted by the selector. Elements can be targeted generally, by their element name, or with exacting precision by defining elements based on their relationships to other elements, their position in the document flow, their attributes, attribute values, current state, or through unique IDs. We'll cover all the selectors in the next section.

A style like this one can be put into one of three locations: inline, in embedded styles, or in an external stylesheet.

Styles can be declared as an *inline* style as part of the opening `<p>` tag using the style attribute:

```
<p style="color:blue; margin-bottom: 12px;">
```

Styles can be *embedded* within the head of the document:

```
<style>
  p {
    color: blue;
    margin-bottom: 12px;
  }
</style>
```

 Note that we write `<style>` and not `<style type="text/css">` in the examples given here. In HTML5, `type="text/css"` is implied and therefore omittable.

Styles can, and *should*, be included in an *external stylesheet*, linked to using the `<link>` element:

```
<link rel="stylesheet" src="styles.css"/>
```

Best practices recommend using external stylesheets. By using an external stylesheet, you can link all of your web pages to a single stylesheet, ensuring that all your pages have the same look and feel, and reducing site maintenance as design changes can be made to the whole site by editing a single file. Use `<link>` rather than `@import` to download your stylesheets in parallel for faster load time.

By using an external stylesheet, the styles for the site only have to be downloaded once: on the users' initial visit to any page within your site. The CSS file is generally cached by the client browser. Therefore, the bytes of the CSS are only downloaded once. Also, keeping your style information in a separate document separates your content from your presentation. Separating content from presentation from behavior is a key tenet in web standards.

While best practices dictate using external stylesheets, due to issues of mobile network latency, the anti-pattern of including embedded styles and storing the style in local storage have the benefit of reducing HTTP requests. This topic was discussed in Chapter 2 when we covered the `<style>` element. Whether you link to your styles or you embed them as part of the anti-pattern, do ensure that you reduce the number of lookups and HTTP requests.

Using External Stylesheets: <link> Revisited

To include an external stylesheet, we employ the `<link>` element. We discussed the `<link>` tag in Chapter 2, so I won't reiterate all the attributes and values. Instead, let's look at the attributes and values that are relevant to CSS. The points that do require emphasis include the attributes found in the external stylesheet link:

```
<link type="text/css" rel="stylesheet" src="styles.css" media="all"/>
```

In XHTML, the `type` attribute defining the MIME type as `type="text/css"` was required. This supposedly informed the browser that the linked file is text (not an application or binary), with CSS markup. As noted previously, this attribute is not required in HTML5, unless you are using something other than CSS, which you won't likely be doing. Ever. When the relation, or `rel`, is set to `"stylesheet"`, the `type` is assumed to be `test/css` unless otherwise indicated, and the default of `media` is `"all"`:

```
<link rel="stylesheet" src="styles.css"/>
```

Don't forget to include the `rel` attribute written as the `rel="stylesheet"` attribute/value pair. Without this attribute, the browser won't know the purpose of your file and will not render it as CSS. If your CSS fails to render, check to make sure you included this attribute. This is the cause of many headaches: hard to spot but easy to resolve. The `rel` attribute value tells the browser what relation the linked file has to the file.

When present and set to `"stylesheet"`, the *type* is implied, and the browser knows to parse the content of the file as `text/css`.

The `src` (or source) attribute should have a URL as its value, pointing to the external stylesheet containing your CSS.

The `<link>` element is an empty element. If you are using an XHTML-styled markup, you can self-close it with a slash before the closing bracket.

The media attribute

The `media` attribute, if not included, defaults to `media="all"`, which means all media. The main values that have been part of CSS for years are:

`all`
> Rendered for all devices, including all types listed here.

`braille`
> Rendered only for Braille tactile-feedback devices.

`embossed`
> Paged Braille printers.

handheld
> Intended for handheld devices, usually with small screen and limited bandwidth. Note that although smartphones and the iPad are handheld devices, they have full-featured browsers and respond to screen and all, and not to handheld.

print
> Rendered by printers, PDFs, and the "print preview" mode of most browsers.

projection
> Intended for projectors and other projected presentations.

screen
> Color computer screens, including laptop, desktop, and smartphone browsers, including devices like phones, tablets, and phablets.

speech
> Intended for speech synthesizers. Note: CSS 2 had a similar media type called aural for this purpose.

tty
> Intended for media using a fixed-pitch character grid (such as teletypes, terminals, or portable devices with limited display capabilities).

tv
> Intended for television-type devices, when there is sound but no ability to scroll.

As noted earlier, smartphones have full browsers, and therefore implement linked stylesheets that have the attribute media="screen", media="all", and no media declarations, as the default is all.

You can use a single stylesheet without the media declaration, and target different types using @media:

```
@media screen {
 p {
  color: blue;
 }
}

@media print {
 p {
  color: red;
 }
}
```

Media Queries

In CSS3, the `media` attribute is not limited to the values in the preceding list. Media queries allow us to target CSS to a device or browser based on the height, width, resolution, and orientation of the browser window or device, or, in the case of SVG, to the parent container. If you want to use the same HTML page but different stylesheets for smartphones, tablets, and desktop web browsers, you can use the `media` attribute to indicate which CSS file should be rendered in different-sized screens:

```
<link media="only screen and (max-device-width: 480px)"
    href="mobile.css" rel="stylesheet"/>
```

While there are many device properties with which we can target devices and browsers to style, the most common properties are shown in Table 7-1.

Table 7-1. The more relevant @media properties in the mobile landscape

Property	Minimum property	Maximum property	Description
`width`	`min-width`	`max-width`	viewport width
`height`	`min-height`	`max-height`	viewport height
`device-width`	`min-device-width`	`max-device-width`	screen width
`device-height`	`min-device-height`	`max-device-height`	screen height
`orientation`			portrait(h>w) landscape(w>h)
`aspect-ratio`	`min-aspect-ratio`	`max-aspect-ratio`	width/height
`device-aspect-ratio`	`min-device-aspect-ratio`	`max-device-aspect-ratio`	device-width/height

You can target a device specifically; for example, you can target an iPhone in portrait mode specifically with:

```
<link media="only screen and (width: 320px) and (orientation: portrait)"
    href="iphone.css" rel="stylesheet"/>
```

However, this is a *bad* idea. Mobile devices come in all shapes and sizes...well, at least all sizes. Instead of defining a separate stylesheet for every possible device of every pixel width and height, create media queries with ranges of sizes, creating breakpoints where a change in layout might make sense. For example, it may make sense to put your extended navigation bar on top for a tablet user, but better to put the content above the extended navigation on a very small device so the user doesn't have to scroll to get the important content.

Media queries can be used to provide different CSS property values based on device and viewport size and orientation. For example, media queries can (and often should) be used to serve different media to different screen sizes. There is no reason to serve a 1,400 px wide image to a 320 px wide phone:[2]

```
@media screen and (min-width: 440px) {
    #content { background-image: url(/images/small/bg.jpg);
}
@media screen and (min-width: 1000px) {
    #content { background-image: url(/images/large/bg.jpg);
}
```

Note that in these @media blocks we used two widths that are not necessarily standard device widths. When choosing breakpoints in your designs and markup, don't pick breakpoints based on popular device sizes. Rather, pick breakpoints that make sense in terms of your user interface design. The quickest method for choosing breakpoints is to test them in browsers. Slowly grow or shrink your screen on your desktop. When the design starts to look bad, that is a good place for a breakpoint.

We'll discuss @media and responsive features further in Chapter 11.

In addition to targeting based on size and orientation, you can also target based on a browser's support of animation, transitions, and 3D transforms with:

```
@media screen and (transform-3d) {
  .transforms {}
}
```

Here the property in the parentheses may need to be vendor prefixed in browsers that still require prefixing from the aforementioned three properties.

Browsers will eventually support @supports:

```
@supports (display: table-cell) and (display: list-item) {
  .query .supports { display: block; }
}
```

Where the supports query, similar to the media query, can target CSS to different devices based on browser CSS feature support. However, at the time of this writing, this feature has some desktop browser support, but no mobile browser support.

---

2. If you need to figure out the width and height of your viewport with JavaScript, you can do so, but you will force a layout:

    ```
    width = window.innerWidth;
    height = window.innerHeight;
    ```

window.matchMedia

CSSOM, the CSS Object Model, provides us with extensions to the window interface. `window.matchMedia`, when supported,[3] returns a new `MediaQueryList` (mql) object representing the parsed results of the specified media query string that has a `matches` property:

```
var mql = window.matchMedia(mediaquery);
if (mql.matches) {
    //if it matches the media query
}
```

Where *mediaquery* is a media query.

For example, you can test to see if the viewport is less than 500 px wide:

```
var mqobj = window.matchMedia('(orientation: portrait)');
if (mqobj.matches) {
    document.querySelector('body').classList.add('portrait');
}

if (window.matchMedia("(max-width: 500px)").matches) {
 // the view port is no more than 500 pixels wide
} else {
 // the view port is more than 500 pixels wide
}
```

We are also provided with a way to listen to media change events. We can test to see if the orientation is currently in portrait or landscape mode, and listen for changes:

```
var mqobj = window.matchMedia('(orientation: portrait)');
mqobj.addEventListener('orientationchange', bodyOrientationClass);

function bodyOrientationClass() {
 if (mqobj.matches) {  // orientation is portrait
    document.querySelector('body').classList.remove('landscape');
    document.querySelector('body').classList.add('portrait');
 } else {
    document.querySelector('body').classList.remove('portrait');
    document.querySelector('body').classList.add('landscape');
 }
}
```

We first create a media query list object and include an `addEventListener` listener method of the media query list object, which calls a function to respond to the event. I've included a function that checks to see if it matches the media query, and handles it.

We can remove the listener with:

```
myobj.removeEventListener('orientationchange', bodyOrientationClass);
```

---

3. `window.matchMedia` is supported in all mobile browsers except IE, starting with iOS 5 and Android 3.

CSS Best Practices

In order to maintain quality and improve download speed for your site, here are five tips (or rules!) to put in your tool belt that will enable you to write better CSS.

1. Minimize HTTP requests

To improve download speed, minimize the number of separate stylesheets to minimize the number of HTTP requests. The overhead of an HTTP request can be extreme. Reducing the number of requests can dramatically reduce a page's download time.

HTTP requests are often the largest time consumer in terms of download time, especially over mobile networks. As such, it is generally better to include one longer stylesheet that includes all the styles for your site rather than several smaller stylesheets, each styling a component of your site.

While it may be beneficial to modularize your styles within your stylesheet, with styles for each "module" of your website grouped together, in production, serve all of your CSS in one longer file. Instead of having *style.css*, *home.css*, *about.css*, *footer.css*, *side bar.css*, etc., include a single *all.css*.

Downloading and caching one larger CSS file will generally create a better user experience than having the client download page-specific stylesheets, even if those page-specific stylesheets are smaller. The cost of making an extra HTTP request is oftentimes greater than the cost of having a few lines of unused CSS. Additionally, by using a single CSS file, all of your styles for the entire site are cached when the first page's content is downloaded: no waiting for additional CSS files to download as the user navigates through your website.

That being said, note that mobile memory is more limited than desktop device memory, so don't go crazy with super large file sizes. While I recommend server-side preprocessors, like Sass, to help make writing CSS easier and faster, if you don't know what you're doing, your CSS files can become much larger than necessary. If you know what you are doing, these tools can help you modularize and minify your CSS, greatly reducing the bytes needed. Use these tools wisely.

2. Use external stylesheets

Use an external stylesheet, linked to within the <head> of your files. The benefits of including this single external stylesheet include:

- You change your styles for the whole site in one location.
- Users download and cache the stylesheet once on their first visit (and don't have to download it again when they visit a second, third, and fourth page).
- Users only have to download your stylesheet once, saving HTTP requests on secondary page visits.

- You're preserving the separation of content from presentation.

While rule number 1 (minimize HTTP requests) may lead one to believe that it is better to embed the CSS and save an HTTP request, the price paid of adding a single HTTP request is generally well worth the benefits of having an external stylesheet (though there is an anti-pattern exception, as noted in Chapter 2). The browser can cache the external stylesheet references by all your pages, so it only has to be downloaded once. Embedded styles, on the other hand, are downloaded with every page.

While the download time cost associated from a single HTTP request is generally less than the cost associated with downloading the bytes of in-page CSS when the second, third, and fourth pages of your site are downloaded, HTTP requests over 3G networks can have a lot of latency. For websites accessed over a tethered network, the extra HTTP request for an external stylesheet is worth it. This isn't always the case with mobile.

As noted in Chapter 2, some mobile sites use an anti-pattern. They embed the CSS, and even the JavaScript, into the first server response. Then they use JavaScript to extract the embedded scripts and put them into local storage using the localStorage API. By providing each script with a unique ID, the script can be stored, retrieved, and referenced with that unique key. The script identifier is also added to a cookie. On following page loads, as with all HTTP requests, cookies are sent along with the HTTP request, informing the server which scripts the user already has, allowing the server to decide which scripts, if any, to send on subsequent requests. This anti-pattern can lead to a very large download on first page load, with much smaller subsequent requests. While localStorage has some drawbacks, such as the time it takes for the device to access the localStorage data, it can be a viable tool in minimizing HTTP requests, which helps with latency issues in mobile. We discussed localStorage in Chapter 6.

3. Normalize browsers with a CSS reset or normalizer

Browsers come with their own stylesheet called a user agent (UA) stylesheet. This native stylesheet sets up default styles, such as italics for `<em>`, bolding, and font size increases for `<h1-h6>`, indenting and bullets on `<li>`s. Unfortunately, not all browsers and not all browser versions come with the same UA stylesheets. For example, margins on paragraphs and the body change from browser to browser. It is recommended to start with a reset[4] or normalizer CSS file to make all browsers behave similarly: to remove or normalize many of the default styles in favor of a uniform styling for all browsers.

To normalize, begin your stylesheet with a low specificity setting of baseline styles to remove cross-browser differences in UA stylesheets. By setting defaults, you avoid browser inconsistencies of both current and future browsers.

---

4. Yahoo! provides an excellent CSS reset file at *http://developer.yahoo.com/yui/reset/*. Add `background-repeat: no-repeat;` to it, and you're golden.

Even if you are developing your website purely for a single browser—for example, a single version of WebKit (which, of course, I recommend against doing)—I still recommend using a CSS reset/normalizer.[5] I include `margin: 0; padding: 0;` and `background-repeat: no-repeat;` in my reset on most elements. By including these three lines of markup in my reset, I save hundreds of lines of code by not having to repeat any of them.

 If you use * in your reset, do so with caution, as you likely don't want to remove default styling on some elements, like form fields. In addition, it increases memory usage and rendering time.[6]

4. Use the weakest specificity for ease of overwriting

Another recommendation is to use elements and classes in your selectors, rather than IDs. Decreased specificity reduces the number of selectors needed to override a rule. The weaker your specificity, especially when creating your reset and original template, the easier it will be to override a value for one-off styles. Begin by styling the basic HTML tag selectors.

Avoid IDs, as IDs have the greatest value in the cascade. Although ID'd selectors may perform slightly better when it comes to rendering time, the time savings is small. Using IDs limits the target of your CSS to a single subset area, and overriding ID'd styles requires even stronger ID'd specificity. So, although there is a miniscule performance hit, use the least amount of specificity needed in a selector to create more general rules and to better enable overwriting a property value.

Then you can create specific styles for the sections to override the defaults.

For example:

```
<p id="myP" class="blue">This is
    <strong class="warning">important</strong></p>
```

Could be targeted with:

```
body p#myP.blue strong.warning {
 color: red;
}
```

---

5. *Normalize.css (http://necolas.github.io/normalize.css/)* is a small CSS file providing for cross-browser consistency of default styling (rather than resetting) of HTML elements. Created by Jonathan Neal and Nicolas Gallagher, it targets only the styles that need normalizing.

6. The documentation of the source code of HTML5BoilerPlate on GitHub (*https://github.com/h5bp/html5-boilerplate*) provides lots of useful tips.

Or simply:

```
.warning {
 color:red;
}
```

We often come across CSS with selectors as specific as the former, but the latter does the trick.

You're not only saving bytes of code with the latter, but it's easier to code, read, maintain, and, mostly, override. Imagine if your designer adds a caveat: "If that paragraph is in the sidebar, I want the red to be more chartreuse." There are two issues here: one, I have no clue what "chartreuse" is. At least I can Google it. The main issue is that to change the color, you have to be even more specific! So:

```
body aside.sidebar p#myP.blue strong.warning {
color: #7FFF00;
}
```

Or, if you were less specific to begin with:

```
aside .warning {
color: #7FFF00;
}
```

If you're using Sass or another compiler, you may find yourself with selectors that are 10 rules deep. As a general rule, I limit my selectors to three deep, which feels like a good balance between performance, specificity, and ease of maintenance.

For more information on CSS Specificity, see "Specificity Trumps Cascade: Understanding CSS Specificity" on page 237 and Appendix A.

5. Don't use inline styles or the !important modifier

That's it. No explanation required. Inline styles and the !important key term are bad practices. Don't use them (other than for prototyping).

If you need an explanation: the !important keyword overrides the cascade for the property in which the !important declaration is included. A property value for a selector with low specificity that includes the !important modifier in a declaration, that value has greater specificity than any other value for that same property and cannot be overwritten. For example:

```
p {color: green !important;}
p#myP {color: blue;}

<p style="color: red" id="myP">
```

In this case, the paragraph text will be green no matter what, because the !important modifier was used.

The !important modifier was added to CSS to enable users to override web author styles. For all intents and purposes, assume that the !important key term is the domain of your power users, not you as a developer.

The only time I use !important is for debugging. I add !important temporarily to see if my selector is hitting my element at all. When the addition of !important doesn't alter my element as intended, I realize I have a typo in my selector, or I thought my <span> was a link <a>, or some similar error.

 No matter how specific you are, even with the addition of !impor tant, you cannot overwrite an !important in a property declaration in the UA stylesheet. There aren't many in most UA stylesheets, but those property values that include them cannot be overwritten by your own styles.

The tips listed here are best practices and simplify the efforts of writing CSS. There are several other best practices for creating maintainable stylesheets, such as grouping selectors by section, commenting for future readability, and indenting for current readability, but we won't delve into the best practices for human readability,[7] as there are "different strokes for different folks."

The best advice I have is to pick your best practices and stick with them. For example, I don't care if you use spaces or tabs for indentation, but whatever you choose, stick with it: consistency rules!

CSS Selectors

If you're familiar with CSS, skip to the section "More CSS3 Selectors" on page 210. If not, we'll cover the basics. And, even if you are a pro, don't skip "More CSS3 Selectors." You may be surprised at how powerful CSS selectors have become.

Selectors are CSS patterns used to determine which style rule blocks apply to which elements in the document tree. Selectors range from simple element types to rich contextual patterns targeting DOM nodes based on attributes, source order, or family tree relations. If all conditions in the pattern are true for a certain element or pseudoelement, rules are applied to that element.

---

7. Chapter 9 of *Advanced CSS* by Moscovitz and Lewis, published by Friends of Ed, dedicates an entire chapter to optimizing CSS for performance.

All mobile browsers support the CSS 2.1 and CSS3 selectors discussed in this chapter, as do all desktop browsers, with the exception of IE8 and earlier.

Basic Selectors

If you have any experience with CSS, you likely know how to target elements using element, class, and ID selectors, or a combination of them. These are the most often used type, class, and ID selectors: the basic CSS selectors that were provided to us in the original versions of CSS.

You'll discover that with CSS3, you can target with incredible precision almost any node in your document, generally without even having to add a class or ID. But first we need to ensure full understanding of the building blocks of CSS.

Type selector

The *type selector* or element selector will target all elements of a particular type:

```
a {
    color: blue;
}
p {
    color: pink;
}
strong {
    color: green;
}
```

The preceding CSS dictates that your links will be blue, your paragraphs will be pink, and your strongly emphasized text will be green.

```
<p>This is a paragraph with an
    <a href="..."><strong>emphasized</strong> link</a>
</p>
```

In this example, due to nesting, the word "emphasized" will be green, the "link" will be blue and the rest of the paragraph will be pink, unless any of those elements inherit CSS that is more specific and alters the colors.

We can declare *multiple elements* in a selector group by separating them with a comma, creating a list of type selectors:

```
p, li {
  text-transform: uppercase;
}
```

We declare *descendant elements* by separating them with a space:

```
p strong {
  color: pink;
}

li a {
  color: black;
}
```

If I were to include this CSS, the text in this paragraph, along with the text in any other paragraph and list item, would be uppercase and the word "emphasized" would be pink, since the strong element is a descendant of the <p> element. However, the word "link" would still be blue, not black, since the <a> is in a <p> and does not have an <li> as an ancestor.

 Old versions of Internet Explorer do not support the type selector on elements it doesn't know, including all of the new elements in HTML5. All mobile browsers that you are likely trying to target will render elements they don't recognize, and understand all CSS3 selectors.

Class selector

The *class selector* will target all elements with that particular case-sensitive class:

```
.copyright {
  font-size: smaller;
}
.urgent {
  font-weight: bold;
  color: red;
}
<p class="copyright">This is a paragraph with an
  <a href="..."><strong class="urgent">emphasized</strong> link</a>
</p>
```

With the added classes, the entire paragraph will be in a smaller font, and the word "emphasized" will be both bold and red, instead of green. The reason it is red instead of green is because a class selector has more strength or specificity in terms of the cascade.

You can have more than one class on an element in your HTML: simply separate the class names with a space in the value of the class attribute. Note that the order of the classes in the class attribute on any element is not important: the order of the classes in the stylesheet is what determines precedence. The following are equal:

```
<p class="class1 class2">some text</p>
<p class="class2 class1">some text</p>
```

In terms of the cascade, a single class selector has more weight than any number of type selectors.

We could have written:

```
p.copyright {
   font-size: xx-small;
}
```

Then, since there is no space between the p and the class, only paragraphs with a class of copyright will be xx-small. <li class="copyright"> would be smaller, but not xx-small, since it is targeted by the general selector of .copyright, but not by the more specific p.copyright.

As noted in the best practices section, it is recommended to use the least amount of specificity to target an element. In this case, it is recommended to use .copyright instead of p.copyright. The shorter selector is less specific, potentially targeting more elements: all elements with the .copyright class. Unless you are trying to override just the paragraphs that have this class, use the selector with the least specificity.

 Class names are case-sensitive: copyright does not equal Copyright or copyRight.

ID selector

The *ID selector* targets the single element in your document with that particular ID. Remember that IDs are case-sensitive and must be unique in a document:

```
#divitis {
  color: orange;
  font-size: larger;
}
<p class="copyright" id="divitis">This is a paragraph with an
    <a href=""><strong class="urgent">emphasized</strong> link</a>
</p>
```

In this example, the paragraph will be orange and larger, not smaller, since ID selectors have more specificity than class selectors, and therefore overwrite the .copyright and p.copyright selectors.

#divitis a{} is more specific than .copyright a{} which is more specific than p a {}, which is more specific than a {}. See Table 7-2 for a visualization of the specificity values of type, class, and ID selectors, and "Specificity Trumps Cascade: Understanding CSS Specificity" on page 237.

In terms of the cascade, a single ID selector has more weight or specificity than any number of class selectors or type selectors, so use them sparingly, if at all. They're difficult to out-specify. To out-specify an ID selector, you need to write an even more detailed rule that uses the same or greater number of ID selectors.

Class and ID selectors are case-sensitive. Type selectors are not.

More CSS3 Selectors

Even if you're familiar with CSS, the following will be useful: there are many tidbits you may not know or may not have considered.

The selector matches the element or item that the CSS will be applied to. In the era of CSS 2 and desktop support, we've been thinking "element": we've limited ourselves to type, class, and id selectors, with a smattering of link-related pseudoclasses, and possibly, though not necessarily wisely, the universal * selector.

In targeting elements in our stylesheets, let's stop thinking about element type, and instead focus on the document model. With CSS3 we can more easily target styles based on an element's position within a document, an element's relation to other elements, and even an element's attributes and UI state.

CSS3 greatly expands our horizons and our ability to microtarget with new attribute selectors, structural selectors, pseudoclasses, and combinators. Actually, the combinators (described in the next section)—along with some attribute selectors—were in CSS 2, but only starting with IE8 did Internet Explorer fully support the CSS 2.1 selectors. Opera, Chrome, Safari, Firefox, and Internet Explorer (starting with IE9) support all of the CSS 2.1 and CSS3 selectors, with one caveat: for security reasons, some other browsers have stopped fully supporting the :link and :visited pseudoclasses of the <a> element.

 All mobile (and desktop) browsers, including Opera, Chrome, Safari, Firefox, and Internet Explorer, starting with IE9, support *all* of the CSS 2.1 and CSS3 selectors.

General Selectors

The general selectors, including the universal selector, type selector, class selector, and ID selectors, have been around since the last millennium.

Universal selector: *

Added in CSS 2, the universal selector matches every element on the page. The syntax is an asterisk (*):

```
* {
  color: blue;
}
footer * {
```

```
    color: white;
}
```

A standalone universal selector affects every element, from the root down to the last child. Instead of using it as a global selector, narrow the scope with a combinator: target all elements of a known ancestor, such as all elements contained in your `<footer>`, but avoid targeting your entire document. Other unintended consequences can be removing default styling from form fields.

Type selector: E

The *element selector*, or type selector, matches all the elements of that type. In your stylesheets, include the tag name only, with no special symbols, to represent that element in the selector:

```
section, aside, p {
    color: red
}
```

Class selector: .class

The class selector, discussed previously, matches any element of a particular case-sensitive class. In your stylesheet, include the ID value preceded with a period:

```
.myClass {
    color: green;
}
```

ID selector: #id

The ID selector matches any element with that exact, case-sensitive `id`. Of all the selector types, the ID selector has the greatest specificity (described in the next section). In your stylesheet, include the class name preceded with a hash mark (#):

```
#myId {
    color: black;
}
```

Using the Selectors

An element can have more than one class but can only have one ID. If an `id` is included in an element, that ID must be unique for the page:

```
<p class="firstclass secondclass" id="myparagraph">
```

This paragraph element can be targeted a multitude of ways, in order of specificity as shown in Table 7-2.

Table 7-2. Selector combinations targeting the paragraph in order of specificity, lowest to highest

Selector	Explanation	Specificity
p	All paragraphs.	0-0-1
.firstclass .secondclass	All elements with that class.	0-1-0
p.firstclass p.secondclass	All paragraphs that have that class.	0-1-1
.firstclass.secondclass	Any element that has both classes.	0-2-0
p.firstclass.secondclass	All paragraphs that have both classes.	0-2-1
#myparagraph	The unique element that has that ID.	1-0-0
p#myparagraph	The element with that ID, if it's a paragraph. Otherwise, matches nothing.	1-0-1
p#myparagraph.firstclass p#myparagraph.secondclass	The paragraph with that ID if it has that class. Otherwise, does not match the element with that ID.	1-1-1
p#myparagraph.first class.secondclass	The paragraph with that ID if it has both those classes. Otherwise, does not match the \<p> with that ID.	1-2-1

Be *as minimally specific as you need to be*! If you can target the element with just a type selector, only use the type selector. If you need to use a class, use just a single class if you can. Less specific selectors target more elements, leading to a more unified site, and are easier to override by using the CSS cascade and/or with minimally increased specificity.

While all the selectors in Table 7-2 are valid, the last few selectors should rarely, if ever, be used. Because of the high specificity, I avoid using ID selectors, including the id attribute on elements generally only in labels, for targeting with JavaScript, and anchoring. If you start off being as minimally specific as possible, you'll never need the last five or six selectors in Table 7-2.

Relational Selectors: Rules Based on Code Order

We've covered classes based on a single element's type, class, and ID. CSS also enables targeting selectors based on an element's relationship to other elements.

In the preceding selectors, we were generally using one element, with class and ID to discuss and learn the cascade. In the real world, there isn't just one element in a page. All elements are either a parent or child of another element (except the root element and text nodes—but they are parents and children, respectively). Most are both. Most elements will have parents, children, and siblings in the markup. In fact, most are the ancestors, descendants, and siblings of a plethora of elements.

CSS provides several relational selectors to help us target elements based on these relationships. For our examples, we'll use the following code:

```
<div id="myParent">
  <p class="copyright" id="divitis">This is a paragraph with a <a href="...">
    <strong class="urgent">strongly emphasized</strong> link</a></p>
  <p class="second classitis">This is another paragraph with an
    <a href="..."><em>emphasized</em> link</a></p>
</div>
```

Once you're done reading this chapter, you'll realize that you can remove all the classes and IDs in this code snippet and still style each element individually.

Descendant combinator: E F

The descendant combinator, symbolically written as E F, with one or more spaces, is when the selector for element F is a child or other descendant of element E. In our prior example:

`p strong {}`
> Targets the `<strong>` element that is a descendant of a paragraph, even if it is not a direct child.

`#myParent a{}`
> Targets both links `<a>` since, while not direct children, they are descendants of the element with `id="myParent"`.

`.copyright .urgent {}`
> Targets the elements with a class of `urgent` that is a descendant of an element with a class of `copyright`.

`li strong {}`
> Doesn't target our text, since `<strong>` is not a descendant of a list item in our example code.

Q: Can you tell the difference between these two selectors?

`#myparagraph.myclass { }`

`#myparagraph .myclass { }`

A: The first one has no space between "#myparagraph" and ".myclass" while the second one does.

Translated into English, the first selector reads: *Select the element that has an ID of* myparagraph *and also has a class name of* myclass.

Translated into English, the second selector reads: *Select all elements with the class name* myclass *that are descendants of the element with an ID of* myparagraph.

Remember that spacing and punctuation are important in CSS!

Child combinator: E > F

The *child combinator*, symbolically written E > F, is a selector in which the selector for element F is the direct child of element E. This is different than the more general descendant combinator E F, described earlier, which allows for F being a child, grandchild, or great-, great-, great-grandchild. The child combinator, with the greater than symbol (>), requires that the child F be a *direct* child of element E:

div > p {}

> Matches both paragraphs, as both paragraphs are direct children of the parent
> <div>.

p > strong {}

> Does not match anything in our example, since <strong> is a direct child of <a>,
> not <p>.

While all mobile browsers support the child selector, and have for a very long time, few people have been employing it because of the lack of support in really old desktop browsers. All modern mobile browsers support all CSS3 selectors, so stop worrying and start using! Note that while the > symbol is very handy in being more specific in what you want to target, E F has the same specificity in terms of weight as E > F.

In CubeeDoo, we make use of the child combinator. When we go up in levels, our cards shrink in size. To tell the <div>s, which are direct children of the #board and no other nodes, to change height based on the class of the board, we can target them directly without touching the HTML to add classes:

```
#board > div {
    position: relative;
    width:23%;
    height:23%;
    margin: 1%;
    float: left;
    transform-style: preserve-3d;
    transition: 0.25s;
    box-shadow: 1px 1px 1px rgba(0,0,0,0.25);
    cursor: pointer; /* for desktop */
}
#board.level2 > div {
    height: 19%;
}
#board.level3 > div {
    height: 15%;
}
```

These property values will affect the card containers, but not the front or back of the cards. We want to define CSS properties for the card container, but don't want those properties to be applied to the front and back of the card: we want each card to be 23%

as wide as the board, which is the viewport. We don't want the front of the card to only be 23% as wide as a single card though.

We've declared them all as `<div>`s. How can we target a `<div>` without affecting its descendant `<div>`s? By using the child > combinator to specify a specific relationship. `#board > div` matches only the `<div>` nodes that are direct children of `#board`. The CSS property/values will not be added to the grandchildren, though some properties, like color, can be inherited.

All the cards will have a height of 23% because there are four rows of cards on level 1. However, when the `#board` has a class of `level2` or `level3`, we overwrite the heights of the cards to be 19% and 15%, respectively, as the game then has four and five rows, respectively. If we hadn't included the child combinator, the front and back of the cards would have been targeted with the height declaration as well. Those nested `<div>`s would be 23%, 19%, or 15% of the height of their parent `<div>` or card, or really, really tiny.

We've also used the child selector to target the `<footer>` that is the direct child of the `<article>`, enabling us to style the main footer and descendants of that footer without also targeting section footers:

```
article > footer,
article > footer ul {
    text-align: center;
    margin: auto;
    width: 100%;
}
article > footer li {
    float: none;
    display: inline-block;
}
article > footer p {
    clear: both;
}
```

Adjacent sibling combinator: E + F

The *adjacent sibling combinator* targets the second element in the selector if both the elements separated by the + sign *share the same parent* and the targeted element (F) occurs *immediately* after the first element of the selector (E) in the mark up:

`p:first-of-type + p {}`
    Targets the second paragraph, and the second paragraph only, as both paragraphs are direct children of the `<div>`, but only if the second paragraph comes immediately after the first with no elements in between.

General sibling combinator: E ~ F

The *general sibling combinator* is similar to the adjacent sibling combinator in that it targets the second element in the selector if both the elements separated by the ~ (tilde) share the same parent. However, unlike the adjacent sibling selector, the targeted element F does not need to occur immediately after the E in the markup. Instead, it has to be any sibling F element that occurs after the first element E. Unlike the adjacent sibling selector, the general sibling selector can match more than one node.

Table 7-3 recaps the relational selectors and provides some examples.

Table 7-3. Relational selector definitions and examples

Name	Syntax	Example	Example explanation recapped
descendant	E F	`.content p`	Any paragraph that is a descendant (child, grandchild, great-grandchild, etc.) of an element with class of `content`.
child	E > F	`ul.main > li`	A list item that is a direct child of the unordered list with a class of `main`. Will not target nested list items, just the direct children in the DOM of the parent `<ul>` that has a class of `main`.
adjacent sibling	E + F	`h1 + p`	Any paragraph that shares the same parent as the `h1`, and comes directly after the `h1` in the markup.
general sibling	E ~ F	`h1 ~ p`	Any paragraph that shares the same parent as an `h1`, that appears after the `h1` in the markup.

Attribute Selectors

In Chapter 2, we learned about adding attributes to elements. The nifty thing with CSS is that you can use CSS selectors to target elements based on those attributes, and even the values of those attributes. CSS 2 provided a few very useful attribute selectors. CSS3 adds several more, enabling substring matching of the attribute value.

The CSS 2 attribute selectors include targeting elements that have a specific attribute with any value, attributes that have a specific exact value, attributes whose values contain a specific, space-separated word, and language attributes.

Note the repeated use of the word "specific" in the preceding paragraph. With CSS you can be very precise in targeting specific elements based on their attributes.

To introduce the CSS 2.1 attribute selectors, we will match the following two lines of HTML with the four attribute selector types detailed in Table 7-4:

```
<ul>
 <li><a href="http://x.com/selectors.pdf" hreflang="en-us" rel="nofollow"
    title="CSS selectors and browser support">Specifishity</a></li>
 <li>
  <input type="checkbox" name="spec" id="spec" value="web workers rock"/>
  <label for="spec">Are web workers in the specifications?</label>
 </li>
</ul>
```

Table 7-4. CSS 2 attribute selectors enable matching by attribute presence, attribute value, language attribute, and by matching space-separated words within an attribute value

Selector	Example	Description
E[attr]	a[rel] input[type] label[for]	Has the attribute, with any value.
E[attr=val]	a[rel="nofollow"] input[type="checkbox"]	Has the attribute with the exact value val.[a]
E[attr|=val]	a[hreflang|="en"]	Value is exactly val or begins with val immediately followed by –.
E[attr~=val]	a[title~="browser"] input[value~="workers"]	Matches any space-separated full word in the attribute value.

[a] The case sensitivity depends on the language and the case sensitivity of the attribute value. The quotes are required if the attribute value within the element would have required the quotes.

Since CSS 2.1, we've been able to match selectors based on the mere presence of an attribute, the presence of an attribute with an exact value, the presence of an attribute whose value contains an exact space-separated word, and the presence of an attribute whose value is an exact value, or begins with an exact value followed by a hyphen.

Note that the quotes in the attribute value in these examples are optional. Had there been a space in the value of the attribute selector, quotes would have been required. I prefer to use them since consistency is good, and sometimes they are required: so be consistent and quote your attributes. Also note that the attribute value within the attribute selector is case-sensitive if the attribute value in the HTML was case-sensitive.

The language subcode attribute selector is not well known and a rarely used CSS feature. It is useful for adding visual cues such as language-specific flags as background images or italicizing content in a foreign language.

For an attribute selector such as a[hreflang|=fr], we can target matching links with a small French flag indicating that the link leads to a page written in French. Figure 7-1 shows a simple example of providing cues based on an attribute:

```
<style>
a[hreflang] {
  padding-right: 18px;
  background-position: 100% 0;
  background-repeat: no-repeat;
}

a[hreflang|="en"] {
  background-image: url(img/usa.png);
}
```

```
a[hreflang|="es"] {
  background-image: url(img/esp.png);
}
a[hreflang|=fr] {
  background-image: url(img/fra.png);
}
</style>

<ul>
 <li><a href="/us/index.html" hreflang="en-us">English</a></li>
 <li><a href="/fr/index.html" hreflang="fr-fr">Français</a></li>
 <li><a href="/fr/index.html" hreflang="es-es">Español</a></li>
</ul>
```

Figure 7-1. Using attribute selectors to indicate language

In the body of the page, only links to French language files will have an hreflang attribute with a value of fr. By using the attribute selector to target the language, you don't have to know where the element is, what parent the element has, etc. By using attribute selectors, no matter who or how the website gets updated, proper elements can get styled correctly. With attribute selectors, you can target elements via their attributes; no need to muddy up your HTML with extra classes in such scenarios.

CSS3 added even more powerful attribute selectors, including attribute values that begin with a specific substring, end with the specific substring, and ones that contain a substring anywhere within the attribute value.

Understanding these selectors is quicker with examples. So, rather than describing each of the attribute selectors, we will continue matching the lines of HTML shown rendered in Figure 7-1 with the various attribute selector types. Table 7-5 is a grid of the attribute selectors new to CSS3:

```
<ul>
 <li><a href="http://x.com/selectors.pdf" hreflang="en-us" rel="nofollow"
    title="CSS selectors and browser support">Specificity</a></li>
 <li>
  <input type="checkbox" name="spec" id="spec" value="web workers rock"/>
  <label for="spec">Are web workers in the specifications?</label>
 </li>
</ul>
```

Table 7-5. CSS3 attribute selectors enable matching by substring from the start of a value, end of a value, or substring anywhere within the attribute value

Selector	Example	Description
E[attr^=val]	a[href^="http"] input[value^="web"]	The val matches the beginning of the attribute value.
E[attr$=val]	a[href$=".pdf"] input[name$="spec"]	The val matches the end of the attribute value.
E[attr*=val]	a[href*=":"]	The val matches anywhere in the attribute value.

The attribute selectors enable you to target elements with CSS based on their attributes and attribute values. There are some useful examples in the preceding list. For example, a[href^=http] targets any fully qualified URL,[8] and a[href$=".pdf"] indicates that the link is likely pointing to a file of PDF format.

In your stylesheet, you may want to indicate nonrelative links with an icon that indicates the link points to a different domain, or that the link points to a file in PDF format rather than to a web page, or you can even append text to the link to indicate the link type. For example, users may want to be warned before tapping on links that will download files or open new windows. You can indicate file type, as shown in Figure 7-2, using attribute selectors with string matching:

---

8. a[href^=http] matches any fully qualified URL, whether it's HTTP or HTTPS, and other links with a path that start with HTTP. It would be more specific to write a[href^="http://"], a[href^="https://"]. You can combine attribute selectors, such as a[href^=http][href$=pdf], which would match external links to PDF files and other links that start with HTTP and end with PDF, but writing a[href^="http://"] [href^="https://"] would match nothing, as no link can start with both *http:* and *https:*.

```
<ul>
 <li><a href="file.zip">Link 1</a></li>
 <li><a href="file.pdf">Link 2</a></li>
 <li><a href="file.html">Link 3</a></li>
 <li><a href="file.html" target="_blank">Link 3</a></li>
</ul>

<style>
 a[target="_blank"]::after {content: " (opens in new window)";}
 a[href$=".zip"]::after {content: " (.zip file)";}
 a[href$=".pdf"]::after {content: " (.pdf file)";}
</style>
```

Figure 7-2. Generated content based on element attributes

Quoting the attribute value is optional in some cases, but is required when nonalpha-numeric characters such as spaces and colons are included. The attribute name is not case-sensitive, but the attribute value is case-sensitive if it is not an HTML value. For example, [type=CHECKBOX] and [type=checkbox] will both target your checkboxes no matter how you marked them up, but a[href^=http] and a[href^=HTTP] will only target lowercase and uppercase protocols respectively.[9]

You can even style different types of links differently based on the width of the viewport using media queries. For example, if the device is wide enough, you can include a background image before a link and the document type after the link, omitting this enhancement if the viewport is really narrow:

---

9. CSS selectors Level 4 will enable case-insensitive matching. See Appendix A.

```
@media screen and (min-width: 480px) {
    a[href^="mailto:"] {
        padding-left: 30px;
        background: url(emailicon.png) no-repeat left center;
    }
}
@media print, screen and (min-width: 640px) {
    a[href^="mailto:"]::after {
        content: "(" attr(data-address) ")";
        opacity: 0.7;
    }
}
```

The preceding snippet adds an email icon link as a background image on a link if the browser width is 480 px wide or larger, and adds the email address as listed in the data-address attribute if the browser is 640 px or wider, or printed.

CSS 2.1 provided for generating content with CSS. In the previous examples, we generated a bit of text informing the user of the type of file that a link will download or that it is an email link, determining the link type based on the value of the link URL. While generating content is a helpful feature, generally you do not want to include text at all, but especially text that is necessary for understanding the context of the page. You should only generate text as progressive enhancement. Do not use generated content for actual content.

There are two features from CSS 2.1 in this example. We are using attribute selectors along with the ::after pseudoelement, and generating content with the CSS 2.1 content property. Attribute selectors can be used for not just for targeting elements, but can also be used to enhance the usability of the page by adding generated content using CSS 2.1 generated content (described in "Pseudoclasses" on page 222).

In terms of specificity, all attribute selectors, no matter how specific that attribute selector is, have the same weight as a class selector.

CubeeDoo

The whole CubeeDoo game relies on the data-value attribute. We target the look of the face of the card based on the value of the data-value attribute. The color theme of the game is completely defined by changing the board's class to colors.[10] The background color of the <div class="back"> changes, depending on the value of the data-value attribute of the parent:

```
.colors div[data-value="0"] .back {background-color:transparent;}
.colors div[data-value="1"] .back {background-color:#F00;}
.colors div[data-value="2"] .back {background-color:#090;}
.colors div[data-value="3"] .back {background-color:#FF0;}
```

---

10. We also have numbers and shapes. Numbers will be discussed later in this chapter. Shapes was covered in Chapter 5 when we covered SVG.

```
.colors div[data-value="4"] .back {background-color:#F60;}
.colors div[data-value="5"] .back {background-color:#00F;}
.colors div[data-value="6"] .back {background-color:#909;}
.colors div[data-value="7"] .back {background-color:#F0F;}
.colors div[data-value="8"] .back {background-color:#633;}
.colors div[data-value="9"] .back {background-color:#000;}
.colors div[data-value="10"] .back {background-color:#fff;}
.colors div[data-value="11"] .back {background-color:#666;}
.colors div[data-value="12"] .back {background-color:#ccc;}
```

Pseudoclasses

A *pseudoclass* is similar to a class, but instead of being developer defined by putting the class attribute in the opening tag of the HTML element, pseudoclasses are classes based on the position in the DOM or on the current state of the user interface. A pseudoclass has the same weight as a regular class in terms of specificity and the cascade as delineated in Appendix A and described in "Specificity Trumps Cascade: Understanding CSS Specificity" on page 237.

There are two link pseudoclasses: :link and :visited. :link matches unvisited links and :visited matches visited links. Although these two pseudoclasses can be used to improve usability, these pseudoclasses create a security risk. Safari reduced support for them with their release of Safari 5, and other browser vendors have since followed suit. Unlike all the other pseudoclasses, the styling for these two are very limited. These are the only two class types for which styling is limited.

With the global attribute tabindex, the :hover, :active, and :focus user-action pseudoclasses are not limited to links and forms anymore. Both links and form elements have always been able to have focus and/or be active. Therefore, :focus and :active have been relevant to all interactive elements. With tabindex, any element can be interactive. :focus and :active are therefore applicable to elements with a tabindex attribute (see Chapter 2).

 Include :focus with :hover declarations for better usability and accessibility.

As you know, when you have a mouse, any element can be hovered. CSS reflects this.

The :hover pseudoclass can be added to any element. However, on a touch device, you're not hovering. You're touching. Mobile devices treat touching as hovering, with some mobile browsers and operating systems adding a few features. Features or properties you may want to style include:

`-webkit-tap-highlight-color`

Allows you to set the `background-color` of the underlay when a user touches a link or otherwise clickable element. By default, the tap highlight color is semitransparent. You may want to style this, but don't disable it. Having the browser indicate to the user that an element is being tapped is good user experience. Hiding the fact that it is being touched is bad user experience.

`-webkit/moz/ms-user-select`

Available on desktop and mobile browsers with a prefix, when set to `none` you can prevent the user from selecting text, or at least appearing like they can select text (it doesn't actually prevent selecting content). This is an experimental feature, not currently in the specifications, though I expect to see it added back in. It must be vendor prefixed, and is supported everywhere except Opera before Blink, even though it is nonstandard.

`-webkit-touch-callout`

When set to `none`, it prevents the call-out toolbar (to select, copy, or paste) from appearing when the user holds down a link.

In addition to the new feature of having support for the user-action pseudoclasses, CSS3 provides us with two other user-interface pseudoclasses and a slew of user-interaction pseudoclasses.

You can target elements that are `:enabled` and `:disabled`. The `:checked` pseudoclass can target inputs of `type="checkbox"` and `type="radio"` that are checked.

Table 7-6 lists the user interface pseudoclasses, and what those selectors match.

Table 7-6. The various CSS pseudoclasses, and what each pseudoclass selector matches

Pseudoclass	What it matches
`:link`	Unvisited links. Supported since CSS 1, this pseudoclass isn't fully supported in newer browsers for security reasons.
`:visited`	Visited links. Supported since CSS 1, this pseudoclass isn't fully supported in newer browsers for security reasons.
`:hover`	Any hovered element, not just links.
`:active`	A currently user-activated element.
`:focus`	Elements that have focus based on touch, keyboard, or mouse events or other input.
`:enabled`	User interface element that is enabled.
`:disabled`	Disabled user interface element.
`:checked`	Radio button and/or checkbox that is selected.
`:indeterminate`	Form elements that are neither checked nor unchecked.

The :active pseudoclass is not evenly activated on all devices when an element receives focus. A fix for this is to add an .active class wherever the :active pseudoclass is set in your CSS and add and remove the .active class with touchstart and touchend event listeners.

When it comes to mouseless touch devices, you don't actually hover over an object. You can hover with event handling, using touchstart and touchend, and eventually pointerenter and pointerleave. Most touch devices handle touchstart to touchend[11] as :hover, but are more finicky with :active. You can add a script in as well to make sure all touch-supporting browsers support .hover like :hover and .active like :active on any element with a tabindex attribute:

```
var myLinks = document.querySelectorAll('[tabindex]');
for (var i = 0; i < myLinks.length; i++) {
  myLinks[i].addEventListener('touchstart',
      function() {
              this.classList.add('hover');
              this.classList.add('active');
          }, false);
  myLinks[i].addEventListener('touchend',
      function() {
              this.classList.remove('hover');
              this.classList.remove('active');
          }, false);
}
```

This adds the hover class to any element that is being hovered or activated with a finger instead of a mouse. In your CSS, where you would call the hover pseudoclass, add the hover class:

```
.hover, :hover {
  /* css for hover state */
}
.active, :active[12] {
  /* css for hover state */
}
```

You don't have to actually add the .hover class selector in your CSS. Most touch-enabled device browsers will correctly handle the :hover declaration if you identify an element and have a touchStart event:

```
<script>
var everything = document.querySelectorAll('a, label, span, input, [tabindex]');
```

---

11. The touchstart and touchend events are nonstandard and proprietary. Apple patented touch events, but specifications are open standards. The touch W3C standard is pointer events. While all touch devices currently support these nonstandard touch events, browsers will soon support pointer events, and, with the exception of Apple, may begin deprecating touchstart and touchend. See Chapter 13.

12. You don't actually want to use this selector as the global * selector is implied. Be more specific.

```
for (var i = 0; i < everything.length; i++) {
  everything[i].addEventListener('touchstart',
      function() {
              // empty
          }, false);
}
</script>
<style>
a:hover,
label:hover,
span:hover,
input:hover {
  /* css for hover state */
}
</style>
```

Putting everything we've learned together, you already have some sweet tools in your tool belt. We can style a label based on whether its checkbox is checked!

```
<li>
  <input type="checkbox" name="spec" id="spec" value="web workers rock"/>
  <label for="spec">Are web workers in the specifications?</label>
</li>
```

```
input[type=checkbox]:checked + label {color: red;}
```

This line should be easily understood now. It reads: "The label that comes immediately after a checked checkbox should be red." Our selector is using the attribute selector, :checked pseudoclass, and adjacent sibling combinator.

State Pseudoclasses

Not yet fully supported in browsers are the UI state pseudoclasses. These CSS3 UI module specifications introduced several pseudoclasses (delineated in Table 7-7) to define additional user interface states that are becoming more relevant, and better supported, with HTML5. While the :required, :valid, and :invalid pseudoclasses have been around since before 2004, they have only become relevant recently with native browser form validation and the required attribute added to HTML5 in web forms (see Chapter 4).

Table 7-7. The UI state pseudoclasses and the elements they match

Pseudoclass	What it matches
:default	Applies to the one or more UI elements that are the default among a set of similar elements.
:valid	Applies to elements that are valid based on the type or pattern expected, data validity semantics defined.
:invalid	Applies to elements that do not match the data validity semantics defined by type or pattern
:in-range	Applies to elements that have range limitations, and the value is within those limitations
:out-of-range	Applies to elements that have range limitations, and the value is outside of those limitations

Pseudoclass	What it matches
:required	Applies to form elements that have the required attribute set.
:optional	Applies to all form elements that do not have the required attribute.
:read-only	Applies to elements whose contents are not user alterable.
:read-write	Applies to elements whose contents are user alterable, such as text input fields or are contentEditable (see Chapter 2).

The UI or state pseudoclasses are defined in the Basic User Interface Module (*http://dev.w3.org/csswg/css3-ui/*), not the CSS3 selector module (*http://www.w3.org/TR/css3-selectors/*). They will be included as part of CSS Selectors Level 4.

Structural Pseudoclasses

CSS3 adds many selectors that enable developers to target elements based on the structure of the HTML files and DOM. Table 7-8 lists all the structural pseudoclasses, with a brief description of what they all mean. Don't worry if some are confusing. The math of the nth structural pseudoclasses will be explained in the following section.

Table 7-8. The structural pseudoclasses and their definitions

Pseudoclass	What it matches
:root	The root element, always the <html> element in HTML5 documents.
:nth-child()	The element that is the nth child of its parent.
:nth-last-child(n)	The nth child of its parent, counting from the last one.
:nth-of-type(n)	The nth sibling of its type.
:nth-last-of-type(n)	The nth sibling of its type, counting from the last one.
:first-child	First child of its parent (CSS 2); same as :nth-child(1).
:last-child	Last child of its parent; same as :nth-last-child(1).
:first-of-type	First sibling of its type; same as :nth-of-type(1).
:last-of-type	Last sibling of its type; same as :nth-last-of-type(1).
:only-child	Only child of its parent.
:only-of-type	Only sibling of its type.
:empty	Element that has no children (including text nodes).

The :root element is fairly self evident. It's the root element of the document, which is always the <html> element in an HTML5 document. The nth pseudoclasses, on the other hand, require some explaining.

The Math of the nth Types

The `:nth-of-type()`, `:nth-child()`, and other structural pseudoclasses enable matching of elements based on their position relative to their ancestors and siblings. These selectors take an argument that enables the pinpointing of elements you want to target for styling. The argument can be a keyword, number, or a number expression.

Even and odd

The two keywords include `odd` and `even`, which cause the selector to target every other element of that type, starting with the first element for `odd` or the second element for `even`.

For example, a common use of the nth pseudoclasses with the odd and even key terms is to stripe, or *zebra*, a table. Data tables, especially wide and/or tall ones, can be hard to read. Simply telling every even row to have a different background color can make it easier to read:

```
table {
  background-color: #ffffff;
}
tr:nth-of-type(even) {
  background-color: #dedede;
}
```

With this pseudoclass, the striping of the table is dynamically set by the CSS. There is no need to add classes to the `<tr>` directly like we used to do. And, when sorting, you don't have to worry about changing the colors of any rows. Automatically, every even row will be gray, even if you sort or remove rows.

This works for striping table rows as all `<tr>`s are siblings, children of `<tbody>`. Structural selectors count elements that have the same parent. It's not "all the table rows in my document." Rather, it counts all the sibling `<tr>`s, and starts counting from one again when it reaches a second table, nested or not.

Single elements

If you only want one element targeted, based on its position, include an integer as the parameter. Continuing with the previous example, we can write:

```
tr:nth-of-type(8) {
  background-color: #ff0000;
}
```

This CSS code will make the eighth row red. To take effect, this selector must come *after* the `tr:nth-of-type(even)` in the stylesheet as both selectors have the same specificity (0-1-1), so the one that is last in the cascade, or markup order, takes precedence.

Note that the browser counts which `nth-child` and `nth-of-type` selectors to match from the parent element. If a table is nested in a table cell of another table, the eighth row of both the outer table and nested table will be matched.

:nth-of-type versus :nth-child

The difference between `:nth-of-type` and `:nth-child` is a subtle one, and, as in the case of our example, they will often target the same node. However, there is a difference:

```
p:nth-child(3) {color: red;}
p:nth-of-type(3) {color: blue;}
```

`p:nth-child(3)` will check the third child of every element to see if that element is a paragraph. In the following example, `<p>3</p>` is the third child but the second paragraph, and thus would be red. `p:nth-of-type(3)` will count only the child paragraphs of an element, selecting the third paragraph it finds, or `<p>4</p>` in this case, will be blue:

```
<article>
    <p>1</p>
    <div>2</div>
    <p>3</p>
    <p>4</p>
</article>
```

In a table, `:nth-of-type(8)` is the same as `:nth-child(8)` since only `<tr>`s can be children of a `<tbody>`. Had we written `p:nth-of-type(8)` and `p:nth-child(8)`, we may not have targeted the same paragraph with both those statements. The `:nth-of-type(8)` counts the paragraphs in a parent element and selects the eighth paragraph nested within the same parent, if there are at least 8. The `:nth-child(8)` will go through the children (not descendants, but only direct children) of an element until it reaches the eighth child of that element. If the eighth child happens to be a paragraph, then we have a match. If not, the browser moves on to the next element to count its children.

Number expressions

Lastly, more confusingly, and definitely more powerful, is the fact that these selectors support number expressions.

Number expressions are written as (xn+y), where x is the frequency and y is the offset. For example, instead of using the key terms even and odd, we could have used (2n) for even, and (2n-1) for odd.

To explain, (2n) means every other element, starting with 2*0, then 2*1, then 2*2, so 2, 4, 6, 8, 10, etc. (2n-1) means every other element, starting with one less than the second element, or odd, so 1, 3, 5, 7, 9, etc. Other examples include (4n-2), which would target every fourth elements, starting with the second, so 2, 6, 10, 14, etc.

The + or - y only needs to be included if there is an offset. If you want to target every fifth element starting with the fifth element, simply write (5n). Note that if you do include an offset, it has to come last (after the n if present), or the selector will fail.

If you include a large offset, like 2n+9, the first targeted element will be the ninth. The iterations start with n = 0, and increment by 1. With :nth-of-type(2n+9), the 9th, 11th, 13th elements will be targeted. With :nth-last-of-type(2n+9), the browser will find the last element, count backward by 9, and target the 9th, 11th, 13th, etc., elements from the end. In other words, the last eight elements will not be matched, and the even or odd elements before that will be matched depending on whether there is an even or odd number of children of the parent.

In CubeeDoo, to illustrate the :nth-of-type() selector, we've made the matched cards disappear sequentially. In our CSS, we tell the second matched card to start fading away after 250 ms, targeting the second matched card with:

```
#board > div.matched:nth-of-type(2) {
    -webkit-animation-delay: 250ms;
}
```

Similarly, we use structural selectors in our iPhone native-look example to ensure there is no bottom border on the last language in our language list. We target the last list item to remove its bottom border:

```
article ul li:last-of-type {
    border-bottom: none;
}
```

With this structural pseudoclass, we don't need to know which language is last, nor do we need to add a class to the last element. Instead, we use the current document structure to target an element based on that structure. We used :last-of-type, but since only <li>s can be direct children of <ul>s, we could have also targeted this element using :last-child, :nth-last-of-type(1), or :nth-last-child(1).

Note that using :first-of-type is more performant than using :last-of-type. We could have, and probably should have, included border-top on our language list items, and then written:

```
article ul li:first-of-type {
    border-top: none;
}
```

Exercise

OK, I know you're not 12 anymore (and if you are, kudos for getting an early start on HTML5 and CSS3), but since these expressions can be confusing, let's do some mid-chapter exercises. The exercises should help you to see how useful these expressions can be.

When including pseudoclass, you are adding specificity.

 Do not include any whitespace before the opening parenthesis, or between the multiplier and the n. Also, the offset needs to come last.

More Pseudoclasses

There are a few more pseudoclasses that we haven't covered, shown in Table 7-9.

Table 7-9. :target, :lang and :not pseudoclasses

Pseudoclass	Name	What it matches
E:target	target pseudoclass	Element being the target of a currently active intra-page anchor.
E:lang(L)	language pseudoclass	Element in language denoted by the 2-letter abbreviation (L).
E:not(s)	negation pseudoclass	Element E that does not match the selector(s) in the parenthesis. Elements that match E except those that also match s.

:target

The :target pseudoclass is applied or becomes active when the element is the current target of the document. For example, if you have a div with an ID, and your user clicks on an anchor link making that div active, any styles set in the :target style block will be applied until focus of the target moves elsewhere.

For example, #main:target will be applied to <div id="main"> when the URL reads thispage.html#main. You can style elements based on whether they are the current target of the page. There is an example of showing and hiding tabbed content using only CSS in the online chapter resources.

:lang(en)

The E:lang() or language pseudoclass matches element E if E is in the language passed as a parameter in the :lang() parenthetical. The element E does not have to have the lang attribute directly applied to it, but rather just has to be a descendant of an element with the matching language applied.

For example, your HTML document is declared to be in US English with the <html lang="en-us"> language declaration. Any selector E with E:lang(en) will be a match, but E:lang(fr) will not match, unless a subsection of your page is declared to be in French. For example, if you have a <blockquote lang="fr-fr"> within that document, p:lang(fr) will match any paragraph that is within the block quote, but the p:lang(en) that matched the rest of the paragraphs in your document will not match those within the block quote.

:not(s), or the negation pseudoclass

The negation pseudoclass, :not(s), represents an element that is not represented by the argument s. A selector with an E:not(s) will match all elements E that do not also match the argument that is in the parenthetical. E:not(F) basically reads "match all elements E that aren't also F."

The argument between the parentheses is a simple selector. By simple selector, I don't mean easy selector. Rather, I mean a selector with no ancestral/descendant relationship:

```
input[type=checkbox]:not(:checked)
```

In the preceding example, the selector matches all inputs of type checkbox that are not currently checked. :checked may not seem simple if CSS3 selectors are new to you. But, it is considered simple as there is no DOM tree relationship specified.

Selectors with the :not pseudoclass match whatever is to the left of the colon, and then exclude from that matched group those that also match what is on the right side of the colon.

`p:not(.copyright)`
> Matches all paragraphs *except* those with the copyright class.

`:not(a)`
> Matches everything that is not a link.

`p a:not(:visited)`
> Matches all nonvisited links that are found in a paragraph.

`li:not(:last-of-type)`
> Matches all list items except the last in a list.

`input:not([type=radio]):not([type=checkbox])`
> Matches all inputs except those of input type `radio` or `checkbox`.

`h1:not(header > h1):not(#main h1)`
> Does nothing, as `header > h1` and `#main h1` are not simple selectors, so the selector fails and is ignored.

Note that you can use multiple pseudoclasses together, as seen in the input `:not` example given earlier:

```
ul > li:nth-of-type(n+2):nth-last-of-type(n+2)
```

The preceding code will target all of the list items except the first and last list items in an unordered list, as would the two simpler versions:

```
ul > li:not(:first-of-type):not(:last-of-type)
ul > li:not(:first-child):not(:last-child)
```

In terms of specificity, the `:not` has no weight, but the argument passed in the parentheses adds specificity:

```
li:not(#someID) /* 1-0-1 the ID selector adds 1-0-0 to the specificity */
li:not([title]) /* 0-1-1 the attribute selector adds 0-1-0 to the specificity */
```

Real world example

In the following code, we have a checkbox for `other` and a text area that we only want to show if `other` is checked:

```
<li>
    <input type="checkbox" value="other" id="other">
    <label for="other"> other: </label>
    <input type="text">
</li>
```

We can combine some of our selectors to hide/show this input based on user interaction:

```
input[type="checkbox"]:not(:checked) ~ input {
    display: none;
}
```

This code finds checkboxes that are not checked, then finds any sibling inputs within the same parent and hides them. If they checkbox is checked, the `display: none` property value will not apply to the text input box.

Pseudoelements

Pseudoelements can target text that is part of the document but not targetable in the document tree. For example, all text nodes have a first letter. However, unless you encompass it with a `<span>`, that first letter is not a separate, targetable part of the DOM.

Pseudoelements, as the name suggests, create pseudoelements. With the `::first-letter` pseudoelement, you can access the first letter of an element as if that first letter were a separate DOM element (which it isn't) and style it. Pseudoelements allow developers to target otherwise inaccessible information without adding first-letter or first-line logic to the markup.

`:first-letter` refers to the first letter of an element's text node. The correct syntax is double-colon notation, `::first-letter`, but we generally use single-colon notation because of IE's lack of support for the double colon.

Similarly, `:first-line` and `::first-line` refer to the first line of text in an element. While the double-colon notation is more accurate, the single-colon notation is better supported across browsers.

Possibly new to you is the `::selection` pseudoelement. With the `::selection` pseudoelement, you can target highlighted text. `::selection` was removed from the current CSS3 selectors specification because it was holding up the finalization process, but it is supported in all browsers (and has been supported in Firefox for a long time, but still with the `-moz-` prefix).

If you are creating a game, you may want to disable mobile selection of images and text. As already mentioned, there are a few properties we can include to control or prevent selection behavior:

```
.willNotBeSelectable {
 -webkit-tap-highlight-color: #bada55;
 -webkit-user-select: none;
 -webkit-touch-callout: none;
 -ms-touch-action: none;
}
```

We can control the background color of touched elements with `tap-highlight-color`. We can prevent the device from asking the user if they want to copy and/or paste content with `user-select: none;`. This property is useful for games: if our user holds down a card for too long in CubeeDoo, we do not want the user to be distracted by a pop-up asking if they want to save a contentless card. The `touch-callout` property is similar, but prevents the dialog from popping up with images. The `touch-action` property when set to none prevents operating system pop-ups when panning in Windows.

::before and ::after

The ::before and ::after pseudoelements are slightly different. Instead of targeting text that is in the document, these two pseudoelements provide a way to refer to content that does not exist in the markup or DOM. The ::before and ::after pseudoelements provide the ability to generate content. For example, you can add an exclamation point to the end of every element with the class of warning:

```
.warning::after {content: '!';}
```

Not only can you add content, but you can style the content. One of the most common uses for generated content has been the .clearfix solution, using the :after pseudoelement to clear floats. Earlier in the chapter, you saw other valid uses, including the flag icon based on language (Figure 7-1) and text generation based on file types and link types (Figure 7-2).

When creating generated content, you *must* use the content property, even if it's an empty string, or there will be nothing to display. The generated content appears *inside* the element, before the content/text nodes of that parent element or after the last child or text node. While the generated content will appear on screen as if it were actual content, it is not added to the DOM.

All browsers support the :before and :after pseudoelements, including IE since IE8.

CubeeDoo. As an example, in CubeeDoo, we use generated content to add content for our numbers and shapes themes:

```
.numbers div[data-value="1"] .back:after{ content:'1';}
.numbers div[data-value="2"] .back:after{ content:'2';}
.numbers div[data-value="3"] .back:after{ content:'3';}
.numbers div[data-value="4"] .back:after{ content:'4';}
.numbers div[data-value="5"] .back:after{ content:'5';}
.numbers div[data-value="6"] .back:after{ content:'6';}
.numbers div[data-value="7"] .back:after{ content:'7';}
.numbers div[data-value="8"] .back:after{ content:'8';}
.numbers div[data-value="9"] .back:after{ content:'9';}
.numbers div[data-value="10"] .back:after{ content:'10';}
.numbers div[data-value="11"] .back:after{ content:'11';}
.numbers div[data-value="12"] .back:after{ content:'12';}


.shapes div[data-value="1"] .back:after{ content:'★';}
.shapes div[data-value="2"] .back:after{ content:'●';}
.shapes div[data-value="3"] .back:after{ content:'◕';}
.shapes div[data-value="4"] .back:after{ content:'■';}
.shapes div[data-value="5"] .back:after{ content:'✝';}
.shapes div[data-value="6"] .back:after{ content:'►';}
```

```
.shapes div[data-value="7"] .back:after{ content:'♦';}
.shapes div[data-value="8"] .back:after{ content:'♥';}
.shapes div[data-value="9"] .back:after{ content:'♣';
.shapes div[data-value="10"] .back:after{ content:'♠';}
.shapes div[data-value="11"] .back:after{ content:'☻'}
.shapes div[data-value="12"] .back:after{ content:'⬇';}
```

By simply changing the class of the game board, we are able to change the theme. For the color scheme, we changed the background colors based on the data-value attribute. In our SVG image sprite example, we simply changed the background-position based on the data-value attribute and the position of the target image in the sprite. To change the theme to numbers and shapes, we used generated content to actually generate numbers and icon shapes.

Generated content by default appears inline. However, it is fully styleable other than animation, but the ability to animate generated content should be coming soon, and is already present in Firefox.

We've explored an example of using media queries to determine the width of the window and serve different generated content progressive enhancements to links based on whether they will fit on the screen. Progressively enhancing links is just one of the many uses of generated content.

Generated content can be used as an image replacement method, displaying attributes as values in print (or on screen), to create an ordered list out of any element with counters, or style the numbers of ordered lists, display language-appropriate quotation marks, create styled tool tips and thought bubbles, etc. For a tutorial on generated content, check out the online chapter resources for a link.

Understanding double-colon notation

A pseudoelement starts with two colons (::) followed by the name of the pseudoelement. The double colon replaced the single-colon for pseudoelements in CSS3 to make an explicit distinction between pseudoclasses and pseudoelements. For backward compatibility, the single-colon syntax is acceptable for pre-CSS3 selectors. Therefore, ::after is a pseudoelement and :after is also a pseudoelement, but with pseudoclass notation; whereas :hover is always a pseudoclass, not a pseudoelement, and only allows for a single colon.

These two colons, :: (double-colon notation), were introduced by the W3 in order to "establish a discrimination between pseudoclasses and pseudoelements. For compatibility with existing stylesheets, user agents must also accept the previous one-colon notation for pseudoelements introduced in CSS levels 1 and 2 (namely, :first-line, :first-letter, :before, and :after)."

Other Selectors: Shadow DOM

You thought we were done? So did we! There are other pseudoclasses and pseudoelements that browser vendors are creating but are not yet part of the specifications. For example, to style form-validation error messages in WebKit, you are provided with four pseudoelements:

```
:::-webkit-validation-bubble {}
:::-webkit-validation-bubble-arrow-clipper {}
:::-webkit-validation-bubble-arrow {}
:::-webkit-validation-bubble-message {}
```

You are not limited to these four validation bubble selectors. There are a plethora of pseudoelements in all browsers, with WebKit currently allowing us to easily target these native UI features with our own styles. For example, there are pseudoelements to enable styling for progress bars:[13]

```
:::-webkit-progress-bar {}
:::-webkit-progress-value {}
```

To discover what pseudoelements can be targeted and what the correct syntax is for those pseudonodes, the Chrome web inspector allows you to inspect the shadow DOM.

Figure 7-3. The shadow DOM inspected in the browser development tools

You'll note in Figure 7-3 that there is an arrow next to the range input type. Inputs are empty elements and therefore do not have nested children. Clicking on that arrow, however, exposes the shadow DOM, or user agent components that, in this case, make up the range's slider. By clicking on the pseudo webkit-slider-runnable-track, we can observe the user agent styles for the track. You can style this element by using :::-webkit-slider-runnable-track as the pseudoelement selector. By clicking on the nested div, we see that the child can be targeted with -webkit-slider-thumb, and has its own styles. You can learn about all of the different styleable shadow DOM components via the web inspector:

---

13. Mozilla pseudoelements and pseudoclasses can be found at *http://mzl.la/1cdK4mx*.

```
input[type="range"]::-webkit-slider-runnable-track {
    -webkit-flex: 1 1 0px;
    min-width: 0px;
    -webkit-align-self: center;
    box-sizing: border-box;
    display: block;
    -webkit-user-modify: read-only;
}
input[type="range"]::-webkit-slider-thumb,
input[type="range"]::-webkit-media-slider-thumb {
    -webkit-appearance: sliderthumb-horizontal;
    box-sizing: border-box;
    display: block;
    -webkit-user-modify: read-only;
}
```

With the introduction of web components, Blink-based browsers may be reducing access to the styling of some of shadow DOM pseudoelements in favor of web components.

Specificity Trumps Cascade: Understanding CSS Specificity

CSS declarations may appear to conflict with each another. You may declare the same element, in different selector blocks, to be both larger and smaller, both pink and orange. The way the CSS specifications are written, however, you can always determine which property values will be applied, and there will never be a discrepancy between browsers: you can always determine which rule will take precedence based on the order and specificity or weight of the selector declarations.

The CSS cascade is a set of rules that define which rule takes precedence in seemingly conflicting declarations. More specific rules override more general rules. If equal in specificity, later rules override earlier rules. If weighted equally, closer (or later in the cascade) rules override farther (earlier in the cascade) rules. All the rules to be applied are applied from most general to most specific, with each successively more specific or closer rule overriding previous conflicting declarations for a property.

The selector you select, `type`, `class`, `id`, or one of the pseudoclasses, attribute selectors, etc., determine the weight or specificity of a rule. Only when two conflicting declarations have the same weight are they then compared in terms of order precedence.

The general selector (`*`), and the child, adjacent, and general sibling combinators (the `>`, `+`, and `~`) add no weight to the specificity. The element and pseudoelement selectors all have the same, lowest level weight.

Classes, attribute selectors, pseudoclasses, including structural selectors and UI selectors, all have the same weight, with a single class, attribute, or pseudoclasses selector having more weight than any quantity of element selectors.

The `:not` negation pseudoclass has no value in itself, but the specificity of the parameter is added to the weight of the selector. When an element has two or more classes as the value of the class attribute, the source order of those classes in the HTML does not matter. It is the specificity of the selectors and source order of the declarations of those individual classes in the CSS that counts.

A single ID selector has greater weight than a selector with any number of classes.

Two things alter the general equation: inline styles are more specific than embedded or linked styles, and properties with the key term `!important` after the value are even more specific than inline styles. However, since best practices (see #5 in the section "CSS Best Practices" on page 202) dictate that we should never use inline styles or `!important` declarations in production (on live sites), we really only need to focus on and understand the cascade.

If this was at all confusing, *http://specifishity.com* delineates class, element, and ID weight in terms of the cascade, with selector combinations targeting a paragraph in order of specificity, lowest to highest, using fish, sharks, and plankton. Appendix A provides a list of the selectors and their weight in terms of specificity.

In Conclusion

That's it! We've only touched upon what there is to learn about the CSS cascade, specificity, selectors, and syntax, but hopefully enough to get everything done that you may need to do. Appendix A includes a little cheat sheet to remind you of all the CSS3 selectors that all mobile devices fully support.

Expanding Options with CSS3 Values

As we develop mobile applications on our modern browser on smartphones, we don't have to worry about older browsers' lack of support for CSS3 selectors, properties, and values. The iPhone, iPod, iPad, modern Android phones, Galaxy tablet, Microsoft Surface, and all other WebKit, Firefox, Opera, and Windows 8 devices have one of the most modern, standards compliant browsers. With smartphone browsers (excluding some older Windows 7 phones, but that is changing rapidly), we can now move forward and code with the most cutting-edge CSS3 and HTML5. There's no longer a reason to hold back.

In this chapter, we start on our journey to becoming cutting-edge CSS3 developers. In the last chapter, we learned about CSS3 selectors: cutting-edge ways of targeting elements with CSS. In this chapter, we start with cutting-edge CSS3 values. In Chapter 9, we will learn how to use some cutting-edge CSS3 properties.

There are new values, including new value types, in the CSS3 specifications. In this chapter, we will cover both the old and new values of colors, lengths, and angles. We'll learn what values are useable in all browsers, what values are new in CSS3 but already supported in most browsers, and some keyword values that are unique to specific browsers.

CSS Color Values

Prior to CSS3, we had three types of color formats: there was the hexadecimal format (and the shorthand hex format), `rgb()` format, and named colors. CSS3 adds support for HSL, HSLA, RGBA, and a few other color types described in the following sections.

RGB, RGBA, and the hexadecimal color formats take red, green, and blue values. Similar to Photoshop's HSB (hue, saturation, brightness) color format, HSL and HSLA both take *h*ue, *s*aturation and *l*ight as values. RGBA and HSLA both provide for declaring alpha transparency on the selected color.

Let me translate by example: Table 8-1 shows the formats, including the new formats in CSS3.

Table 8-1. The various CSS color declaration formats

Color syntax	Example code	Definition
#RRGGBB	#ff00ff	Hexadecimal format
#RGB	#f0f	Shorthand hexadecimal format
rgb(r,g,b)	rgb(255, 0, 255) rgb(100%, 0, 100%)	Red, green, blue
hsl(h,s,l)	hsl(300, 100%, 50%)	Hue, saturation, lightness
cmyk[a](c,m,y,k)	cmyk(29%, 55%, 0, 0)	Cyan, magenta, yellow, black
hsla(h,s,l,a)	hsla(300, 100%, 50%, 1)	Hue, saturation, lightness, alpha
rgba(r,g,b,a)	rgba(255, 0, 255, 1) rgba(100%, 0, 100%, 1)	Red, green, blue, alpha
named colors	fuchsia	Limited list of named color values
transparent	transparent	Transparent
currentColor	currentColor	The color of the text (the current color)

[a] CMYK colors, not supported in any browser, are defined by the paged media module, not the color module like the rest of the colors listed.

Hexadecimal Values

You can declare the hexadecimal value of your red, green, and blue with hexadecimal values ranging from 0 to 255 in the format of 00 to FF, case-insensitive. Put the three values together, in red, green, blue order, preceded by a hash (#), and that's the color.

For example, #FFFFFF stands for a complete saturation of red, green, and blue, creating white. The opposite is the complete absence of color, so no red, green, or blue, written as #000000, creating black. A mix and match of hexadecimal values from 00 to FF, case insensitive, for the red, green, and blue values, combined together in the order of red, green, and blue, can create millions of colors. Saturated red, with no green or blue will show as bright red, and is written as #FF0000. Less red saturation will be less bright, but still red, and can be written as #CC0000.

Did I mention case insensitivity? It doesn't matter if you use #FFCC00 or #ffcc00; the value syntax for colors, as for all key term property values, are case-insensitive.

 The color input type, described in Chapter 3, submits color values in the lowercase hexadecimal format, with a default value of #000000 in supporting browsers.

The RGB hexadecimal notation also has a shorthand, of #RGB, where the R, G, and B are a single character, A–Fa–f0–9, case-insensitive, that are put together and preceded by a hash mark. Identical to the long format, the browser expands the RGB value, such as #369 expands to #336699. #FF9900 can be shortened to #F90, but #F312AB cannot be written in shorthand.[1]

I find shorthand harder to read, so I don't use them, but there is nothing actually wrong with their use in terms of web standards. Also, whereas I tend to code in all lowercase, I find hexadecimal colors easier to read when using capital letters. It's personal preference. But whatever syntax you choose to use, stick with it.

Note that when using the `<input type="color">` input type, where supported, the default value returned is #000000, and the values are submitted in lowercase.

All browsers support all of the hexadecimal values, both shorthand and longhand.

If you've been developing sites since the '90s, you may recall the discussion of web-safe colors. With the vast improvement of color support on all devices, not just LCD screens, web-safe colors have become a nonissue, even for handheld devices. It is safe to use any color combination. While some color combinations may not be pretty or legible, they will render.

rgb() Syntax

Instead of using the hexadecimal values for colors, as described in the previous section, you can use base-10 values or percentages for your mix of red, green, and blue.

Instead of preceding your color with a hashtag, the syntax is the key term or functional notation rgb followed by your comma-separated values in parentheses. Whitespace is optional, but I find adding whitespace makes the color easier to read:

```
#FFFFFF = #FFF = rgb(255, 255, 255) = rgb(100%, 100%, 100%).
```

All browsers support all of the RGB color combinations in general. Some browsers allow the mixing of rgb() numbers with percentages, but the specifications clearly state that this is not expected behavior, and not all browsers support it, so avoid mixing value types.

Right:

```
rgb(255, 255, 255)
rgb(100%, 100%, 100%)
```

Wrong:

```
rgb(255, 100%, 255);
```

---

1. 8-digit hex values, with the last 2 digits defining the alphatransparency (with FF being fully opaque and 00 meaning fully transparent), are part of CSS Colors Level 4.

Adding Transparency with RGBA

New in CSS3 is RGBA. RGBA is similar to RGB, but with an added A for alpha transparency.

The rgb() specifications were extended to include rgba() in CSS3 to include alpha, to allow specification of the opacity of a color. The first three values are still red, green, blue. The fourth value is the opacity level. The value 1 means fully opaque, 0 is fully transparent, 0.5 is 50% opaque. Include any float between and including 0 and 1.

Extending our white example, opacity of 1 means fully opaque, so the following are all equal:

```
rgb(255, 255, 255)
rgb(100%, 100%, 100%)
rgba(255, 255, 255, 1)
rgba(100%, 100%, 100%, 1)
```

These are all equal to white, since 1 means fully opaque. But don't get confused: rgba(0, 0, 0, 0) is transparent, not black, because the level of opacity is none.

 Note that the keyterm transparent is transparent black, or rgba(0, 0, 0, 0), not rgba(255, 255, 255, 0), which may make a huge difference if you are transitioning colors.

Figure 8-1 demonstrates that rgba(0, 0, 0, 1) is fully opaque black. As you reduce the alpha transparency value, the closer you get to zero, the more transparent it is. You'll notice in Figure 8-1 that the background shows more clearly through the more transparent background color declarations.

 RGBA is extremely useful for creating drop shadows on elements. Drop shadows on text or boxes go from the declared color to full transparent over a few pixels. Start with a partially transparent color instead of a solid color; shadows are see-through.

Instead of:

```
text-shadow: 5px 4px 6px #666666;
```

Use:

```
text-shadow: 5px 4px 6px rgba(0, 0, 0, 0.4);
```

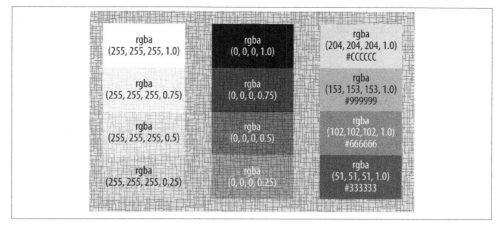

Figure 8-1. The alpha transparency value allows you to declare color that ranges from fully opaque to fully transparent

Unlike RGB, there is no hexadecimal notation for RGBA. There has been some discussion of including an eight-character hexadecimal value for RGBA, but that has so far not been added into a draft specification, nor has an eight-character notation been added to any mobile browser.

Hue, Saturation, and Lightness: HSL()

HSL is a new color type added in CSS3. *HSL* stands for hue, saturation, and lightness. The HSL format simplifies color palette creation, as you can pick a hue as the base and then manipulate the lightness/darkness and saturation of the hue selected.

Monitors display colors in hues of red, green, and blue, which is different from the human eye. HSL mimics the human eye. We see colors in terms of hues with different saturations and lightness. HSL is generally more intuitive for designers to understand.

The syntax `hsl()` appears similar to `rgb()`, but instead of including the values for red, green, and blue, the color value accepts values in degrees from 0 to 359 for hue, and percentages for saturation and lightness, with 50% as the norm for lightness.

Values for hues include: 0 = red, 60 = yellow, 120 = green, 180 = cyan, 240 = blue, 300 = magenta, and everything in between. Since this book is in black and white (and shades of gray), we can't really show you. But there is a link to my HSL color picker in the online chapter resources.

Lightness is the amount of light, or brightness: 100% is white (very, very light), 50% is the actual hue, and 0% is black, with a complete lack of light. Saturation of 100% will be the hue, saturation of 0 will give you a shade of gray from white to `#808080` to black depending on the lightness, and 100% gives you the color fully saturated.

Similar to `rgb()` with `rgba()`, `hsl()` also has an alpha transparent version, `hsla()`. The syntax is the functional notation of `hsla()`, with hue in degrees, saturation in percentage, lightness in percentage, and an alpha value from 0–1, encompassed in the parentheses in that order.

For example: `hsla(300, 100%, 50%, 0.5)` is magenta, fully saturated with average lightness at 50% opacity.

With HSL, or HSLA, the values are the hue, saturation, lightness, and alpha transparency. To create white and black, the hue can be any value, not necessarily 0, with full lightness (100%) for white or complete lack thereof (0%) for black.

CMYK

Have you ever changed the ink in a color printer? Notice what colors you changed? Most likely you added cartridges of cyan (which is a color similar to turquoise), magenta (which is a hot pink), yellow, and black. CMYK stands for cyan, magenta, yellow, and black, which is the system that printers use: print designers (and your color printer) use CMYK, not RGB.

Computer monitors display in RGB. Humans who are not color blind generally see colors as HSL. Printers, on the other hand, determine colors based on CMYK. CMYK is not supported in any browser, and may never be since it is designed for print. Yes, CMYK is kind of irrelevant for mobile development, but I'm including it here to be thorough. CMYK is in the CSS3 *paged media module*, not the color module.

Named Colors

We haven't yet described the color keywords like `aqua`, `fuchsia`, and `lime`, for four main reasons:

- They are limited in the number of values you can choose from, and therefore less specific than the millions of values provided by RGB and HSL.
- They are prone to typos and therefore unintended consequences (e.g., IE only supports gray colors with an "a," such as `lightgray` rather than `lightgrey`).
- Not all keyword values are supported in quite the same way on all browsers or displays due to implementation details.
- And I think they should be avoided for these three reasons.

Even the keyterm `transparent`, which is a much faster way of writing `rgba(0, 0, 0, 0)` has issues. As I mentioned earlier, `transparent` is a transparent black, which may produce ugly grays when transitioning to a color.[2] If you want to transition from 'transparent' to the #FF0000 shade of red, use rgba(255, 0, 0, 0), which is a transparent red, instead. There is a list of named colors along with the hexadecimal, RGB, and HSL values in the online chapter resources.

CurrentColor

One more keyword was added in CSS3: currentColor. The currentColor takes on the value of the 'color:' property, or the color of the text, of the element on which it is applied.

Supported in all mobile browsers, currentColor can be really useful with text shadows for creating bolder text on fonts like Helvetica Neue Light:

```
.bolderText {text-shadow: 0 0 1px currentColor;}
```

With high-DPI devices, some font families are really too thin to read. You can add a slight shadow directly behind the text in the color of the text to make it slightly more legible. This is possible even without knowing the text color, by declaring currentColor as the shadow color.

Browser Color Values

Similar to the currentColor and transparent keywords that are in the W3C CSS3 draft specifications, there are a plethora of system colors defined in CSS 2.1.[3] These named colors differ between browsers and operating systems. While rarely used, I've included them here because they can be useful when creating a native-looking web application:

activeBorder
    Default active window border.

activeCaption
    Default active window caption.

appWorkspace
    Default background color of application workspace or interface.

background
    Default operating system background color.

buttonFace
    Default button face.

---

2. transparent will produce ugly grays when transitioning to colors other than white. Some browsers have begun supporting transparent as transparent black or transparent white, but when transitioning to any hue, you may still see the grays in most browsers.

3. System color specifications (*http://www.w3.org/TR/CSS21/ui.html#system-colors*).

buttonHighlight
: Default highlighted button.

buttonShadow
: Default button's shadow.

buttonText
: Default button's text.

captionText
: Default caption's text.

grayText
: Default gray text.

highlight
: Default highlight.

highlightText
: Default highlighted text.

inactiveBorder
: Default inactive border.

inactiveCaption
: Default inactive caption.

inactiveCaptionText
: Default caption's inactive text.

infoBackground
: Default info's background.

infoText
: Default info.

match
: Color match.

menu
: Default menu.

menuText
: Default menu's text.

scrollbar
: Default scrollbar.

threeDDarkShadow
: Default 3D's dark shadow.

`threeDFace`
> Default 3D's face.

`threeDHighlight`
> Default highlighted 3D.

`threeDLightShadow`
> Default 3D's light shadow.

`threeDShadow`
> Default 3D's shadow.

`windowFrame`
> Default window's frame.

`windowText`
> Default window's text.

There are some colors that are browser specific, including:

- `-webkit-activelink`: Hyperlink that is being clicked
- `-webkit-focus-ring-color`: Color surrounding a UI element that has focus
- `-webkit-link`: Visited hyperlink color
- `-webkit-text`: Text color window; default window
- `-moz-buttonDefault`
- `-moz-buttonHoverFace`
- `-moz-buttonHoverText`
- `-moz-cellHighlightText`
- `-moz-comboBox`
- `-moz-ComboboxText`
- `-moz-Dialog`
- `-moz-DialogText`
- `-moz-dragtargetzone`
- `-moz-EvenTreeRow`
- `-moz-Field`
- `-moz-FieldText`
- `-moz-html-CellHighlight`
- `-moz-html-CellHighlightText`
- `-moz-mac-accentdarkestshadow`
- `-moz-mac-accentdarkshadow`

- `-moz-mac-accentface`

- `-moz-mac-accentlightesthighlight`

- `-moz-mac-accentlightshadow`

- `-moz-mac-accentregularhighlight`

- `-moz-mac-accentregularshadow`

- `-moz-mac-chrome-active`

- `-moz-mac-chrome-inactive`

- `-moz-mac-focusring`

- `-moz-mac-menuselect`

- `-moz-mac-menushadow`

- `-moz-mac-menutextselect`

- `-moz-MenuHover`

- `-moz-MenuHoverText`

- `-moz-MenuBarText`

- `-moz-MenuBarHoverText`

- `-moz-nativehyperlinktext`

- `-moz-OddTreeRow`

- `-moz-win-communicationstext`

- `-moz-win-mediatext`

Firefox also has prefixed colors (*https://developer.mozilla.org/en/CSS/color_value*).

Using browser colors, you could write something like this:

```
#myElement {
  color: -webkit-focus-ring-color;
  background-color: -webkit-link;
  text-shadow: 3px 3px 3px -webkit-text;
  -webkit-box-shadow: 4px 4px 4px -webkit-activelink;
}
```

There are code examples of all these key terms in the online chapter resources. Open the page (*http://standardista.com/sandbox/webkitcolors.html.*) in browsers with different browser engines to see subtle differences. Note that I camelCased the list for ease of reading: the values are, in fact, case-insensitive.

Remember, browsers ignore lines of CSS they don't understand. You can declare a color, then immediately follow that declaration with the same property and the color key term listed above. If the browser doesn't understand the color value, it will ignore that line of CSS and implement the previously declared color.

Which color syntax should I use?

There are many ways to write colors in CSS. Dark red can be written as #800000, maroon, rgba(128, 0, 0), rgba(128, 0, 0, 1.0), hsl(0, 100%, 13%), or hsla(0, 100%, 13%, 1.0).

If you are working with a large team or still supporting old desktop browsers, use six-character hexadecimal syntax, as it is likely the best understood by nondesigners. Or, use a CSS preprocessor like Sass, and create variables for your team members to use. Variables will be coming to CSS, but we are not there yet.

If you are using transparencies and gradients, pick hsla() or rgba() syntax. Otherwise, you really can use whatever syntax you are most comfortable with.

Mobile browsers and all other modern browsers support all of these syntaxes. We each have our own preferences. It doesn't matter what your preference is, but pick a preference and stick with it.

CSS Units of Measurement

Many property values are keywords unique to a property. The key terms that are unique (or semiunique) to a property will be described with their property's description when covered in the next chapters. Other values, like the colors just described, can be values for many different properties.

We've learned almost everything there is to know about color values, but colors aren't the only value type that is common for many properties. We also have lengths, times, frequencies, and angles.

CSS Length Values

In terms of lengths, there are both relative and absolute lengths. Table 8-2 is a quick summary of all of the length value types.

Table 8-2. Length units in CSS[a]

Unit	Meaning
em	Relative to the font size of the parent element.
ex	Relative to the height of the lowercase x.
ch	Relative to the size of the character 0 (zero).
rem	Relative to the root font size.
vw	Relative to the viewport width: the viewport with is 100 vw.
vh	Relative to the viewport height: the viewport height is 100 vh.
vmin	Equal to the smaller of vh or vm.
vmax	Equal to the larger of vh or vm.

Unit	Meaning
px	Relative the screen resolution not the viewport size; generally 1 point, or 1/72 of an inch.
in	Inch.
cm	Centimeter.
mm	Millimeter.
pt	Point is 1/72 of an inch.
pc	Pica, or 1/12 of a point.
%	Relative to the parent element, it's normally defined self or other element defined by the property.

[a] All values are well supported with the exception of vmax and ch, which are not supported in Android and Opera, and vmax is not supported in Safari.

The most common value types in CSS include pixels and percents. The new length units, like rem, vh, vw, vmin, and vmax are very powerful, especially when developing for a multitude of devices of unknown sizes.

One of my favorite new features is the rem unit. CSS3 introduced the rem unit, which stands for "root em." While the em unit is relative to the font size of the parent of that element, potentially causing compounding, the rem is relative to the font size of the root element: in our case <html>. By defining a single font size on the root element, you can define all rem units to be a percentage of or relative to that font size. rem is supported in all mobile browsers, since IE9, iOS 4, and Opera 12 (it's always been supported on Android).

 Note that zero-length values, or null value, for any of these can be simply written as 0. All other value types require the unit for zero, such as 0deg for zero-degrees.

Pixels can be considered both a relative and absolute. Pixels are a relative measurement because the measurement is based on the resolution of the monitor or screen, rather than the viewport size. However, pixels are also an absolute size because lengths given in pixels are immutable: they can only be increased via zoom features.

Images, such as JPEG photos and GIFs have an absolute width and height, defined in pixels. Increasing or decreasing the size of these image types with CSS or via the width and height attributes of the image tag distort the image.

Several properties that expect length values may also accept keyword values such as auto and inherit:

```
p {
  height: auto;
  font-size: inherit;
}
```

dpi, dpc, dppx

The original iPhone viewport was 480 × 320 pixels. iDevices with high DPIs, like the iPhone 4 and iPod touch 4G, that are physically the same size of 320 × 480, have a screen size of 960 × 640. The iPad viewport is much larger at 1024 × 768 pixels, and changes to 768 × 1024 px with orientation change. The third generation iPad has higher DPI and a 2048 × 1536 resolution. Safari for Desktop, Chrome for Desktop, Nokia tablets, OpenMoko, Android phones, and other WebKit browsers all come in different sizes. And even if you can measure the size of a device, a pixel is not really a pixel anymore when it comes to devices with differing DPIs. For example, the iPhone 4 may have a high DPI, so the resolution looks better, but images sent to the device as foreground or background images are still defined in the pixels you would expect as if the DPI were the same as the lower resolution devices. Table 8-3 shows the various resolution units and their meaning.

Table 8-3. Resolution units

Unit	Meaning
dpi	Resolution in dots per inch.
dpc	Resolution in dots per centimeter.
dppx	Resolution in dots per pixel.

With the emergence of devices with different resolutions, CSS3 provides us with resolution units to include in our media queries. We can target different images to different device resolutions based on dpi, dpc, or dppx.

CubeeDoo

When it comes to our application, we have used px for images and background images, rem for fonts, and vh and vm for the widths of input fields. We managed to create the entire application without importing a single nonscalable image. Had we used images, we would have used ddpx in our media queries to serve higher resolution images to higher resolution devices:

```
@media
only screen and (-webkit-min-device-pixel-ratio: 2),
only screen and (   min--moz-device-pixel-ratio: 2),
only screen and (    -o-min-device-pixel-ratio: 2/1),
only screen and (        min-device-pixel-ratio: 2),
only screen and (           min-resolution: 192dpi),
only screen and (           min-resolution: 2dppx) {

  /* styling for high resolution devices */

}
```

Angles, Times, and Frequencies

With some new CSS3 features, such as transforms and animations, length units do not suffice. We also need to learn and understand angles, times, and frequencies. These measurements have been around and used in aural stylesheets, but now with browser support for transitions, transforms, and animations, angles and times have become relevant to the screen as well. The units of angles, times, and frequencies are shown in Table 8-4, and described in greater detail in the sections that follow.

Table 8-4. Units for angles, times, and frequencies

Unit	Meaning
deg	degrees
grad	grads
rad	radians
turn	turns
ms	milliseconds
s	seconds
Hz	hertz
kHz	kilohertz

The default unit for all of the length, angle, time, and frequency values is zero, and all the values are interpreted as floats. When including any of these units of measurement, make sure to include the unit shorthand listed in Table 8-4. Unlike length units, omitting the unit for angles, times, and frequencies is not valid CSS and the declaration will be ignored.

Originally, all of these units, frequencies, and times, other than the new turn unit, were introduced as aural values. The units used for aural stylesheets are angles, specified in rad (radians), deg (degrees), or grad (gradians). Frequencies are specified in Hz (hertz) or kHz (kilohertz). Times are specified in ms (milliseconds) or s (seconds).

 When including any of these units of measurement, make sure to include the unit shorthand. Unlike length units, omitting the unit for angles, times, and frequencies will throw an error and the declaration will be ignored.

CSS Angle Measurements

Angle measurement types include degrees, gradians, radians, and turns. We'll introduce them here, but only use degrees in our examples since they make more sense to nonmath nerds like myself!

Degrees

Degrees range from 0 deg to 360 deg, with those two being equal. Positive degrees go clockwise, negative degrees go counterclockwise. For example, −90 deg is one quarter of the way around counterclockwise, turning it on its left side. 90 deg will turn it clockwise 90 degrees.

The CSS for the figure (in part) reads (see Figure 8-2):

```
.image1, image5 {
    -webkit-transform: rotate(-5deg);
    -ms-transform: rotate(-5deg); /* for IE9 */
    transform: rotate(-5deg);
    }
.image2, image4 {
    -webkit-transform: rotate(7deg);
    -ms-transform: rotate(7deg);
    transform: rotate(7deg);
    }
```

Figure 8-2. Rotating elements a few degrees can create interesting effects while still being legible

Grads

A `grad`, or gradian, is equivalent to 1/400 of a full circle. Similar to degrees, a positive `grad` value will go clockwise, a negative value goes counterclockwise. `100grad` will be at a 90% angle (see Figure 8-3).

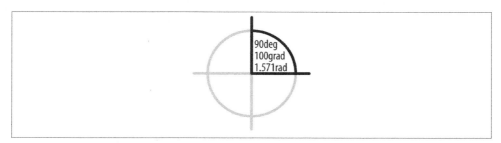

Figure 8-3. 90 deg is the same as 100 grad is the same as 1.571 rad

Rads

A rad, or radian, is equal to 180/π degrees, or about 57.3 degrees. There are 2π radians in a circle. An angle of 1 radian on a circumference of a circle creates an arc with an equal length to the radius of the circle. `1.570796326794897rad` is the same value as 100 grad and as 90 deg.

Turns

A `turn` is a rotation and is equal to 360 deg. For example, `2turn` = `720deg`. Note that `turn` is singular, and there is no space between the number and its unit. The two following lines are equivalent:

```
transform: rotate(900deg);
transform: rotate(2.5turn);
```

Times

Time units are much easier to explain than rads! There are two units of measurement: seconds (`ms`) and milliseconds (`s`). There are 1,000 milliseconds in a second. The format of a time value is a number followed by `s` for seconds or `ms` for milliseconds. As with all nonlength units, always include the `s` or `ms`, even if your value is `0s`. The two following lines are equivalent:

```
animation-duration: 0.5s;
animation-duration: 500ms;
```

Frequencies

Frequency values are used with aural (or spoken) cascading stylesheets. There are two value units: `Hz` or hertz, and `kHz` or kilohertz. `1,000Hz` = `1kHz` (case-insensitive). Frequencies can be used to change the pitch of a voice reading text. A low frequency is a bass sound, a high frequency is a treble.

With the following CSS snippet, a low-pitched voice, such as a deep-toned male voice, will speak the words for the paragraph with `class="low"`, and the audio will change to a high-pitched tone when a quote with class `squeal` is encountered. The two following lines are *not* equivalent:

```
p.low { pitch: 105Hz; }
q.squeal {pitch: 135Hz;}
```

CubeeDoo

In our game, we use CSS degrees to flip the cards, and timing is in both CSS and Java-Script. The game's timer is in seconds in JavaScript. The smooth transforms of the cards from front to back and back to front again are done by transforming the cards 180 deg over 200 ms. We'll cover how to do that—animations and transforms—in the next chapter.

Avoiding TRouBLe: Shorthand Properties and Value Declarations

We've covered most of the values that are not property specific. There is just one more CSS quirk that we need to cover before diving into actual CSS3 properties, and that is the idea of shorthand, and the shorthand TRouBLe order.

CSS provides us with some shorthand properties. There are two types of shorthand properties: those that enable developers to define top, right, bottom, and left values of a property in a single property, and those that enable developers to define several commonly associated properties from a CSS module into a single call.

For example, instead of writing:

```
.sameValues {
  padding-top: 3px;
  padding-right: 3px;
  padding-bottom: 3px;
  padding-left: 3px;
}
.twoValues {
  padding-top: 3px;
  padding-right: 6px;
  padding-bottom: 3px;
  padding-left: 6px;
 }
.threeValues {
  padding-top: 3px;
  padding-right: 6px;
  padding-bottom: 12px;
  padding-left: 6px;
 }
.fourValues {
  padding-top: 3px;
  padding-right: 6px;
  padding-bottom: 9px;
  padding-left: 12px;
 }
```

You can write:

```
.sameValues {
  padding: 3px;
}
.twoValues {
  padding: 3px 6px;
 }
.threeValues {
  padding: 3px 6px 12px;
 }
```

```
.fourValues {
  padding: 3px 6px 9px 12px;
}
```

Note that in writing this shorthand, the order of the values is *very* important. Sometimes, especially with CSS3 properties (as we'll see in Chapter 9), order will be important when defining associated properties in shorthand format. Other times, the order of the values in shorthand notation, which define several associated properties, is not important. In this instance, the shorthand declarations that define the four sides of a box have a very specific, and somewhat confusing, order. Hence the pneumonic that is a double entendre: TRouBLe, for top, right, bottom, left.

If only one value is present, the value will be assigned to all four sides. If two properties are present, the first value is for the top/bottom, and second value is for left/right. If three values are present, the first value is top, the second value refers to both left and right, and the third value is bottom. Otherwise, the order is top, right, bottom, left, or TRouBLe as a pneumonic for remembering the sequence.

For those who learn better by example, Table 8-5 details what is represented when one, two, three, and four values are given for a shortcut.

Table 8-5. Sides that are affected when one, two, three, and four values are given for a shortcut property value

Examples	Values	Order
3px	All four sides have the same value	TRBL
2px 4px	Top/bottom: 2px Left/right: 4px	TB RL
3px 1px 5px	Top: 3px Left/right: 1px Bottom: 5px	T RL B
1px 2px 3px 4px	Top: 1px Right: 2px Bottom: 3px Left: 4px	T R B L

Note that there is an exception to this rule: for the CSS `background-position` property, the order is LR TB, not TB LR, when two values are provided.

The shorthand for defining several commonly associated properties is generally, with a few exceptions, not concerned with the order of the values. Most shorthands can save a lot of typing. For example

```
.myClass {
  border: 1px solid #ff0000;
}
```

Could also be written as:

```css
.myClass {
  border-width: 1px;
  border-style: solid;
  border-color: #ff0000;
}
```

Which itself is shorthand for:

```css
.myClass {
  border-top-width: 1px;
  border-top-style: solid;
  border-top-color: #ff0000;
  border-right-width: 1px;
  border-right-style: solid;
  border-right-color: #ff0000;
  border-bottom-width: 1px;
  border-bottom-style: solid;
  border-bottom-color: #ff0000;
  border-left-width: 1px;
  border-left-style: solid;
  border-left-color: #ff0000;
}
```

Without the shorthand, describing the border of a box would take 12 lines. With the shorthand `border` property, we are able to border a box in one line, using fewer characters in the one line than in most individual longhand property/value declarations.

I will make special note of shorthand property order when the order makes a difference. I mention it here so that you too take note and don't think I was just trying to help with your insomnia.

In Conclusion

In this brief chapter, we've covered more than 60 property values—actually, more than a million if you count all the possible color values we can create. We learned about the different color value types of CSS, the new color additions in CSS3, and different angle and length units. We also covered the value order for box model property values: a confusing yet vitally important topic. Now we can safely jump in to learning about the properties with which these, and other value types, can be associated. The fun is about to start!

CSS3: Modules, Models, and Images

Unlike CSS2, CSS3 has been divided into a set of *modules*. By splitting CSS3 into modules, the W3C has been able to work on different modules at different speeds, with some modules already at the Recommendation level, and others moving toward final recommendations at a slower pace.

There are over 20 modules in the CSS3 specifications, with each module deserving its own chapter (or two, or three). Unfortunately, we can't cover all of them. In this chapter, we will cover the CSS topics that are relevant in creating the look and feel of CubeeDoo. To include a few more properties, we will also look at re-creating the look and feel of the native iPhone settings screen.

The native iPhone application look and feel can be done with simple CSS. With `border-radius`, background properties, gradients, `text-shadow`, `box-shadow`, `background-size`, `text-overflow`, and some older, well-known and supported CSS 2.1 and earlier properties, we can create the look of an iPhone. We'll then apply those features to CubeeDoo.

No images means we can create the native iPhone application look without requiring extra HTTP requests and without needing a graphics program. Because we're using CSS, should your project manager choose to alter the color scheme of your application, you can do so without having to open up an image-editing program.

CSS3 allows for creating websites with less code and fewer images than you may be accustomed to, and fewer images mean fewer HTTP requests, which improves performance. CSS3 also allows for multiple background images on a single element, which may help reduce the number of DOM nodes required to create the look and feel of your site. Reducing the number of DOM nodes improves performance, especially when it comes to page reflows and memory consumption.

Some of the CSS3 features are new. Others have been supported for years. One thing to note, however, is that just because using some of these features can save on the number of HTTP requests, using CSS3 instead of images is not always the best solution. You have to weigh the pros of maintenance and HTTP requests saved against the time needed for the browser to calculate and draw CSS graphics and the memory limitations of mobile devices. Some CSS effects, like very large radial gradients, use up memory, and can make the browser sluggish if you request a device to draw repeatedly to the memory.

Less code can mean both better performance and easier site maintenance. However, not all CSS features perform well on devices with limited memory. When we cover "risky" CSS topics, I will explain any performance ramifications of that feature, and how to avoid slowing down or crashing the user's browser.

As some CSS3 and HTML5 features can have performance drawbacks, I won't leave images out completely. We'll cover multiple background images and `border-image`, two features that use images to quickly and easily create buttons and backgrounds in Chapter 11.

We will not cover the speech, paged media, or ruby modules since they are for aural readers, printers, and Asian language sites, respectively.[1] We will cover transforms, transitions, and animations in the next chapter.

Although it predates CSS3, we will spend time on the CSS box model. The CSS box model is the basis of web page layout since CSS's inception, so it's important to fully grasp.

CSS Box Model Properties

Before we jump into the new CSS3 properties and values, it is important to understand the CSS box model and the properties that make up the box model. All modern mobile browsers support and have always supported border, margin, and padding properties:

- `border-bottom`
- `border-bottom-color`
- `border-bottom-style`
- `border-bottom-width`
- `border-color`
- `border-left`
- `border-left-color`
- `border-left-style`

---

1. The W3C specifications are *http://www.w3.org/TR/css3-speech/*, *http://www.w3.org/TR/css3-page/*, and *http://www.w3.org/TR/css3-ruby/*, if you would like to delve into the speech, paged media, and ruby CSS modules.

- `border-left-width`
- `border-right`
- `border-right-color`
- `border-right-style`
- `border-right-width`
- `border-style`
- `border-top`
- `border-top-color`
- `border-top-style`
- `border-top-width`
- `border-width`
- `margin`
- `margin-bottom`
- `margin-left`
- `margin-right`
- `margin-top`
- `padding`
- `padding-bottom`
- `padding-left`
- `padding-right`
- `padding-top`

border

The border properties and `border` shorthand can be used to set borders on any rendered element. Border shorthand values can be used to style the top, right, bottom, and left sides of an element. Longhand properties can be used to style a single property on a single side (either top, right, bottom, or left). For example, `border-style: dotted;` will set the border on all four sides of an element to dotted, whereas `border-style-right: dashed;` will set only the right border to dashed.

The important things to know about border are:

- `border-style` is required for a border to show up.
- `border-style` is required for `border-image` to work (see Chapter 11).

- When declaring the width and/or height of an element, the width of the left and right borders will be added to the width of your element, and the height of your top and bottom borders will be added to the height of your element as per the W3C box model, as shown in Figure 9-2. This box model annoyance can be overridden with the box-sizing property, described in the section on page 265.

 If using the shorthand, the *border style is required*, with width and color declarations being optional, and being set to the default values if omitted.

border-style

The border-style property sets the style of an element's four borders.

There are no new border-style values in CSS3, but there are different ways of styling borders with properties such as border-radius and border-image, described in upcoming sections.

The values for the border-style property values include the keywords of dashed, dotted, double, groove, hidden, inset, none, outset, ridge, and solid.

The style of hidden is displayed like none, and takes up no space in the box model. If you want a transparent border that takes up space in the box model, select a border-style value other than none or hidden and set the color to transparent. The hidden value is only really relevant in defining table element border styles.

Older WebKit browsers ignored border-color when rendering inset, outset, groove, and ridge border styles. This has been resolved in newer versions of WebKit.

A visible value for border-style is required for a border to show up, as the default value is none. If you want to override a border on an element, set the border-style to the default of none.

A visible border is required for the border-image property to work, which we'll cover in Chapter 11.

border-color

The border-color property allows you to define the color of the border on elements upon which you are setting a border. You can use any of the CSS color value types as described in the section "CSS Color Values" on page 239 in Chapter 8. The default value is currentColor: if border-style is declared, but no border-color is defined, the border color will be the color of the text, or currentColor.

Making triangles with CSS

Borders are part of a nifty trick in creating triangles. To make a text box look like a quote bubble with generated content, create a box with height and width set to zero, set three of the border colors to transparent, and the fourth side's border will make the triangle.

```
blockquote {
  background-color: green;
  position: relative;
  color: white;
  padding: 15px 25px;
  margin: 10px 10px 0;
}
blockquote:after {
  border: 15px solid;
  border-color: green transparent transparent;
  top: 100%; left: 10px;
  width: 0; height: 0;
  position: absolute;
  content: '';
}
```

In the preceding code snippet, I created a pseudoelement with no width or height, showing just one of the four border sides, which creates the appearance of a triangle. There is a link to an example of this in the online chapter resources. Figure 9-1 shows the code in action.

Figure 9-1. Speech bubble with tail created with the top border of generated content

How would you make the speech bubble tail occur on the right or the left of the content, instead of below it?

border-width

The border-width property sets the width of an element's four borders. The keyword values of the border-width property include thin, medium, thick, and inherit, with the default value being medium. You can also use any of the length values (px, em, etc.) described in Chapter 8.

To make the border for the triangle in Figure 9-1, we created a 15 px thick border on generated content that has no height or width. We made only the top border visible by declaring the top border green and all others as transparent.

The `border-width` property is important to the `border-image` property: if you don't declare the `border-width` portion of the `border-image` shorthand, the `border-image` will inherit the `border-width` values.

Border width is also important to understand in terms of shadows and inset shadows. You can create some interesting effects using thick borders and shadows: we'll cover that later in this chapter.

The CSS Box Model

All HTML elements are drawn to the screen as a rectangular box. The CSS box model defines the rectangle (or box) made up of margins, border, padding, and content that make up every element. The box model allows us to space out our elements across the page, defining the width of the content, the space between the content of an element and its border, and the space between multiple elements.

As shown in Figure 9-2, the components of the box model include content, padding, border, and margin:

Content
> The content of the box, where text and images appear.

Padding
> The padding is the space between the content and the border. If an element has a background image or color, the padding area will have that color or image as a background by default.[2]

Border
> The border surrounds the padding and is inside the margin: the border starts where the padding ends. They do not overlap. The border takes up space in the box model. If the element has a background image or color, and the border is dashed or otherwise fully or partially transparent, by default the background will show through the border.

Margin
> The margin is the area on the outside of the border. The margin is transparent. If the element has a background color or image, it will be contained within the border, and will not show through the margin area.

---

2. `background-clip` and `background-origin` can be employed to change this default behavior.

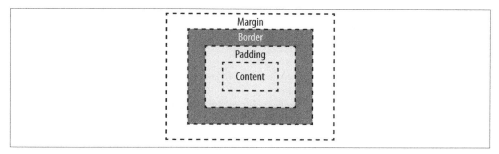

Figure 9-2. The W3C box model

In order to set the width and height of an element, you need to fully understand how the box model works. In the traditional box model, the declared width and height given to an element is for the content area only. The width and height you declare include the padding and borders.

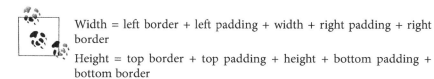

Width = left border + left padding + width + right padding + right border

Height = top border + top padding + height + bottom padding + bottom border

Note in Figure 9-2 that the margin area is colorless. That is because the width is not included in the width and height calculations of the width and height properties. The margin, if greater than 0, does take up space.

The size the element occupies in your layout is the content, the padding, border, and margin.[3]

Total width = left margin + left border + left padding + width + right padding + right border + right margin

Total height = top margin + top border + top padding + height + bottom padding + bottom border + bottom margin

box-sizing

The box-sizing is one of the best, if not the best, features given to us by CSS3, especially if you think Microsoft got the box model right in IE, and the W3C got it wrong. Before, if we declared an element to be 100% width, we avoided declaring a border or padding

---

3. When two elements are next to each other, their adjacent margins collapse.

on that element, as it would end up being wider than its container. The box-sizing property solved this: simply set the box-sizing property to border-box:

```
.box {
  width: 100%;
  padding: 10px;
  border: 1px solid currentColor;
  -webkit-box-sizing: border-box; /* for older Android (3.0) */
  -moz-box-sizing: border-box; /* for firefox */
  box-sizing: border-box;
}
```

> If you want 100% to be 100% in spite of padding and border, you can mimic the IE6/IE7 box model by setting the box-sizing property to border-box.

The box-sizing property has been supported since IE8, but must be prefixed in all versions of Firefox, and in mobile WebKit browsers up to iOS 4.3, Android 3.0, and Blackberry 7.

Until calc() is fully supported, box-sizing: border-box is a panacea!

Margins

Another part of the box model that some people find confusing is the effect of margins on two adjacent elements. Positive margins are not additive: if two adjacent abutting elements have positive margins, the distance between them will be the larger of the two margins, not the sum of both margins. Unless one of those margins is negative; then the distance between the elements will be the sum of positive and negative margins.

Learning CSS3

Now that the box model is out of the way, we can jump into some very useful CSS3 features. We're going to start by creating the look and feel of the native iPhone app with CSS only. The HTML for our examples is:

```
<!DOCTYPE html>
<html>
<head>
  <meta charset="UTF-8"/>
  <title>iPhone Look and feel</title>
  <meta name="viewport" content="width=device-width; initial-scale=1.0;"/>
</head>
<body>
<header>
 <nav>
   <ul>
     <li class="button cancel">Cancel</li>
```

```
    <li class="button done">Done</li>
  </ul>
  <h1>Languages</h1>
</nav>
</header>
<article>
  <ul>
      <li lang="en-us">English</li>
      <li lang="fr-fr">Français</li>
      <li lang="es-es">Español</li>
      ...
  </ul>
</article>
</body>
</html>
```

With this bit of HTML code, and some CSS, we'll be creating a web page that looks like the languages system preferences on the iPhone, as shown in Figure 9-3.

Figure 9-3. Using CSS only, no images, we are going to create the look and feel of the original native iPhone settings application

border-radius

New in CSS3, but not really new to mobile browsers, is native rounded corners created with the border-radius property. Border radius is a quick, lightweight way to improve your UI without increasing download time.

Prior to being able to create native rounded corners with the CSS border-radius property, web developers created rounded corners by including extra markup. The four-corner method required four added elements, each with background images, absolutely positioned in each of an element's four corners. The sliding door method, the most popular of the methods, also required images and additional markup.

While all these methods created the look of native rounded corners, they required otherwise unnecessary elements be added to the page as hooks and containers for required background images, and they required the creation and download of images. For performance, we want to minimize the number of HTTP requests, download time, bandwidth usage, and DOM nodes. We also can enjoy saving the effort of creating images, and then re-creating them as border radius length, color scheme, or other design changes are made.

The biggest drawback of the image solutions for developers were that any changes made to border color, background color, containing element background color, roundness, or dimensions would require new images to be made. The drawback for users (and therefore the corporate bottom line) is that image methods slow down the download speed and impact the performance on handheld devices with limited memory. The border-radius property enables developers to include rounded corners natively: no more corner images! Another bonus is no pixelation on zoom!

The border-radius property is shorthand for:

```
border-top-right-radius:
border-bottom-right-radius:
border-bottom-left-radius:
border-top-left-radius:
```

... in that order.

The syntax for the border-radius property is:

```
border-radius: length{1,4} / length{1,4}    /* shorthand */
border-(top|bottom)-(left|right)-radius: length length    /* longhand */
```

In the shorthand, the values before the slash, if a slash is included, are the horizontal radii, and the values after the slash are the vertical radii, as shown in Figure 9-4. For the longhand values, each can take two values: the first value is the horizontal radius, the second, if present, is the vertical radius. No slash is included in the longhand syntax. If only one value is present, the vertical radius will be the same as the horizontal radius, creating a symmetrical rounded corner with the second value copied from the first. If either length is zero, the corner is square, not round.

When four values are given, the order of the corners is `topleft`, `topright`, `bottom right`, `bottomleft`. Similar to TRBL of borders, if you only declare two values, then the first is for `topleft/bottomright`, and the second value is for `topright/bottomleft`.

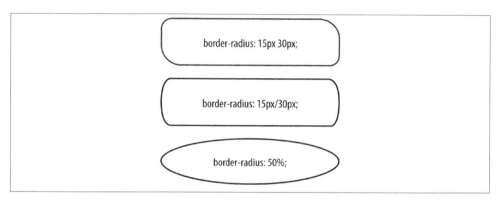

Figure 9-4. border-radius examples, including different radius sizes and elliptical shapes

If targeting a radius value with the DOM, the values are:

```
myObj.style.borderTopLeftRadius
myObj.style.borderTopRightRadius
myObj.style.borderBottomRightRadius
myObj.style.borderBottomLeftRadius
```

Note that the dash (-) has a meaning in JavaScript. We don't want to subtract radius from left from top from border, which is what `border-top-left-radius` would do. In JavaScript, the CSS property is camelCased when included as a property of the style property of the DOM node. That being said, to keep presentation and behavior separate, avoid using JavaScript to alter CSS property values. Instead, define your styles in stylesheet style blocks, and use JavaScript to change class or state.

border-radius for native-looking buttons on the iPhone and in CubeeDoo

Let's put our knowledge to work! Native iPhone applications, as shown earlier in Figure 9-3, have several elements with rounded corners: the Cancel and Done buttons, and the main content of the page. By relying on CSS3, we can create these rounded elements of any size, color, and edge radius without any images. Let's focus on the CSS for the content area:

```
1    article ul {
2        border: 1px solid #A8ABAE;
3        border-radius: 10px;
```

```
4        background-color: #FFFFFF;
5        width: 300px;
6        margin: 10px auto;
7    }
```

Line 2 of our CSS creates a 1 px gray border. In line 3, we include the `border-radius` property to add a 10 px radius to our border. If you are supporting Android 2.1 or iOS 3.2, you can include a `-webkit-` prefixed property immediately before the prefixless property. You may not want to do this: older versions of Android didn't handle border radius very well: omitting the prefixed border radius saves a bit of memory in these older, less performant browsers, and avoids the bug where scrolling makes the border-radius temporarily disappear. Your application will look a little different in older versions of Android, with no rounded corners. Your users likely won't notice the missing rounded corners, but they'll notice if your application fails. For that reason, I stopped including the prefixes for rounded corners a long time ago.

In line 6, we employed the `margin` shorthand property to move the unordered list 10 px down from the navigation and center the content area by setting the left and right margins to *auto*. Since two values for `margin` were declared, the first value is for Top and Bottom, and the second value is for Left and Right. (Confused? See "Avoiding TRouBLe: Shorthand Properties and Value Declarations" on page 255 in Chapter 8.)

We've also stylized the list items. The CSS for the list items is:

```
8    article ul {
9      list-style-type: none;
10   }
11   article li {
12     line-height: 44px;
13     border-bottom: 1px solid #A8ABAE;
14     padding: 0 10px;
15   }
16   article li:last-of-type {
17     border-bottom: none;
18   }
```

Most of that CSS should be very familiar to you. Note the `:last-of-type` pseudoclass in line 16. Structural selectors were covered in Chapter 7. With `article li:last-of-type {border-bottom: none;}`, we are able to tell the browser to *not* include a bottom border on the last list item in every `<ul>` that is found in an `<article>`.

I did not use `article li:not(:last-of-type)` to set the borders on all of the elements except the last one, but I could have. We have a border bottom on the `<ul>` itself, if we don't omit the border bottom from the last `<li>`, there will be a double border at the bottom of each unordered list.

What else has rounded corners? Feel free to add rounded corners to the Done and Cancel buttons on the iPhone app and the buttons and cards on CubeeDoo. The code for the rounded corners is in the chapter files.

CSS Gradients

Using the border radius property, we were able to create rounded corners, and create the look and feel of the content area of the native application with no added HTML elements, no images, and very few lines of CSS.

In addition to having rounded corners, the Cancel and Done buttons have gradient backgrounds. We could include a separate background image on the Cancel button, and a background image of a different color for the Done button. With a small `border-radius` we could create a close approximation of the native iPhone buttons. We could then throw another background image in for the back of the navigation, and another background image for the background of the whole page. In fact, the iPhone has a PNG sprite with the buttons on it that the native iOS applications all use as border images. Yes, we can do that, too. However, with CSS3, this plethora of images, even a single sprite, and their additional HTTP requests, are unnecessary. The native iOS application layout can actually be done completely with CSS, without importing a single *.svg*, *.gif*, *.webp*, *.png*, or *.jpeg*.

Gradients are not properties, they are values. Gradients can be used anywhere an image can be, including `background-images`, `list-style-images`, and `border-images`. They are supported in all modern browsers, but with varying prefixed syntaxes in older browsers.

A gradient is a CSS image generated by the browser based on developer-defined colors fading from one color to the next. Browsers support linear and radial, and repeating linear and radial gradients. Conical gradients have been added to CSS Images Level 4, but are not ready for production and aren't covered here.

We'll cover the current vendor-prefixed syntax supported in all browsers but only now necessary in WebKit browsers. The prefixless version of CSS gradients has gained support and should be included as the default value in your CSS. We still need to cover the prefixed syntax and the very old WebKit syntax so we can support older mobile devices.

Gradient Type: Linear or Radial

There are two main types of gradients: linear and radial. Most gradients you include will be linear. So, you'll want to start your property value with:

```
background-image: -webkit-gradient(linear, /* Really old WebKit[4] */
background-image: -webkit-linear-gradient( /* Android, iOS thru 6.1, BB10 */
background-image: linear-gradient( /* iOS7, Chr26+, IE 10+, FF 16+, O12.1+ */
```

---

4. The original WebKit gradient syntax was used through Chrome 9, iOS Safari 4.3, Android 3.2, and Blackberry 7.

For radial gradients, you would include:

```
background-image: -webkit-gradient(radial, /* Really old WebKit */
background-image: -webkit-radial-gradient( /* Android, iOS thru 6.1, BB10 */
background-image: radial-gradient( /* IE 10, FF16, O12.1, Chr26, iOS7 */
```

In the following examples, we'll use only the WebKit vendor prefix for prefixed version of the second syntax, and the nonprefixed version will reflect the third and final syntax. Hopefully, this will make the markup more readily understandable. Vendor prefixes are no longer needed in Mozilla or Opera browsers,[5] and were never used in any version of Internet Explorer.

Radial Gradients

We are not covering radial gradients in this book. If you would like to learn more about radial gradients, there is a link to a tutorial in the online chapter resources.

This book is about mobile development. Radial gradients and mobile devices aren't always best of friends. When you create a radial gradient, the entire gradient is put into memory. If the radial gradient is small, single colored, with no transparency or gradations, the memory it uses will be small. However, this radial gradient is rarely the scenario. Whereas linear gradients are small images that are tiled in browser memory, radial gradients are a single much larger image that can take up a lot of memory and even crash mobile browsers on devices with limited RAM.

Images that are too large get tiled in memory. While devices differ, I make the safe assumption that images that are more than 1024 px get tiled in memory. With radial gradients, you can quickly achieve such large images.

It is OK to use radial gradients on mobile devices. Just realize that there can be performance issues that you have to consider.

Linear Gradients

The syntax for the prefixed linear gradient is:

```
-prefix-linear-gradient(<angle|keyterm>, <colorstop>, [<colorstop>,] <colorstop>)
```

Where angle is the angle in degrees of the gradient path or a key term combination of *top* or bottom and/or left or right indicating the starting point of the gradient line and, at minimum, one declared color, with optionally more colors, and optionally the position of said colors along the gradient path.

The syntax for the final linear gradient syntax is:

---

5. -moz- and -o- prefixed examples are not included as they are no longer needed in modern browsers. Include these additional prefixes if you are supporting Firefox 4–15 and/or Opera 11.1–12.0

```
linear-gradient([<angle>| to <keyword>], <colorstop>, [<colorstop>,] <colorstop>)
```

The main differences are (1) the to keyword, (2) how the keyword's gradient angles work, and (3) the value of the angles.

With the prefixed syntax, we indicated where the gradient line came from. The prefixless keyword syntax includes the word to, indicating where the line is heading to, rather than where it came from.

Prefixed, the gradient line starts at the point that would be the end of the hypotenuse of a right triangle whose other two points were the midpoint of the box, and the closest corner.

The simplified unprefixed syntax added the to keyword to differentiate it: now the gradient line goes from one side or corner to the opposite side or corner, passing through the center of the box. Confused? Don't worry. I'll explain.

Gradient angles and directions

For linear gradients, the direction of the fade is controlled in the CSS by the <angle> or key term. You can include a keyterm or value for the angle in degrees, rads, grads, or turns.

When an angle is given, the gradient path passes through the center point of your background image at the angle specified. There is a difference between prefixed and unprefixed syntax, however. The prefixed syntax angles go in the direction of the angle, and 0 deg is up, with 90 deg to the right. The prefixed angles go counterclockwise, and 0 deg is to the right. See Figure 9-5.

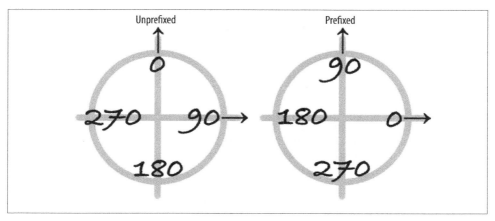

Figure 9-5. Gradient angle direction, both for the experimental prefixed syntax and the final nonprefixed syntax

When declaring linear gradients, first include the prefixed versions for older browsers. When prefixed, 0 deg is to the right, and angles go counterclockwise, which may be counterintuitive. The last CSS property/value pair should be the default value without a prefix. When no prefix is present, 0 deg points upward or north, and positive angles increase as you rotate clockwise, with 90 deg pointing to the right. The gradient line passes through the center of the element at the angle specified.

Instead of using angles, you can declare the gradient path using key terms. The keywords are the sides top, bottom, left, or right, or corners such as top left or bottom right.

In the prefixed syntax, the key term is the starting point of the gradient path. The gradient will start in the general area described by the key term, passing through the center of the background-image, to the opposing side or corner area. For example, top will head from the top center point to the bottom center point, passing through the center point of the element box, and top right will start in the top right area, passing through the center point, to the bottom left area, though not necessarily to the corner itself.

The default CSS declaration should include the value, with no prefix, prepended with the word to (when using keywords), indicating where the gradient line should end. The gradient line will start from one side or corner, pass through the midpoint, and end at the side or corner indicated by the key term. For example, to top will head from the bottom center point to the top center point passing through the center point of the element box, and to top right will start in the bottom left corner, passing through the center point, to the top right corner.

The default values are top, or 270 deg for the prefixed version, and to bottom or 180 deg in the final, unprefixed version, which have the exact same appearance, as shown in Figure 9-6. To make the gradient fade from black to white as it goes from top to bottom, you could write any of the following:

```
/* prefixed */
-webkit-linear-gradient(#000000, #FFFFFF);
-webkit-linear-gradient(top, #000000, #FFFFFF);
-webkit-linear-gradient(270deg, #000000, #FFFFFF);

/* un-prefixed */
linear-gradient(#000000, #FFFFFF);
linear-gradient(to bottom, #000000, #FFFFFF);
linear-gradient(180deg, #000000, #FFFFFF);
```

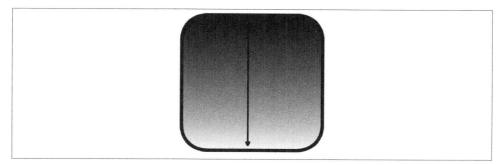

Figure 9-6. A simple gradient, and the various methods of declaring it

To create a gradient that has a path that goes from the top left to the bottom right, as shown in Figure 9-7, you could write the following two lines, which are similar but not identical:

```
/* top left to bottom right */
-webkit-linear-gradient( top left, #000000, #FFFFFF);
linear-gradient(to bottom right, #000000, #FFFFFF);
```

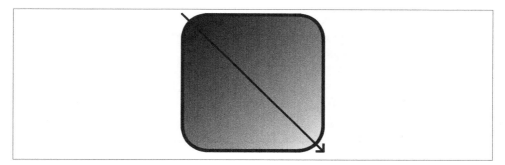

Figure 9-7. Simple gradient going from top left to bottom right

Note that while prefixed 315deg or unprefixed 135deg will create the same gradient as each other, those gradients are not the same as top left or to bottom right, which are not identical to each other.

Prefixed 315deg and unprefixed 135deg will go from top left or to bottom right if your element is a square, but only the to bottom right will go from corner to corner if your background image is an elongated rectangle. Why? When an angle is used, the gradient path passes through the center of the defined background image at that angle, no matter the aspect ratio of the box.

By default, the gradient path passes through the center of the defined element because, by default, the background image is 100% of the width and height of the defined element. If you change the background position or the background size, the gradient path will not actually pass through the center of the defined element, but will always pass through the center of the background image you are defining, no matter the size or position.

With the final syntax, or nonprefixed syntax, the key terms define that the gradient path ends in one corner after passing through the center of the background. With the prefixed or older syntax, when not a square, the gradient path extends beyond the edges of your rectangle, allowing for the start and end of your gradient to be displayed. So when prefixed, it only goes from corner to corner in this case if our box is an actual square, as shown in Figure 9-8:

```
background-image: -webkit-linear-gradient(top left, #000000, #FFFFFF);
background-image: linear-gradient(bottom right, #000000, #FFFFFF);
```

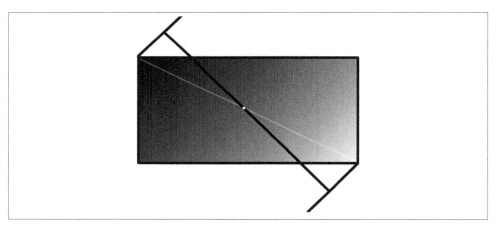

Figure 9-8. When using key terms, the gradient lines will differ between prefixed (black line) and nonprefixed (gray line) syntax if corners are used and the background image is not a square

In Figure 9-8, the black line shows the gradient path for top left, passing through the center of the background image, represented by a tiny white square in the middle. The gray path is the path the gradient takes when it supports the un-prefixed gradient with to bottom right instead of top left. In the prefixed version, the end points of the gradient path are beyond the boundary of the image, defined as the farthest corners of the box from the center of the background image where a line drawn perpendicular to the gradient-line would intersect the corner of the box in that direction.

Gradient colors

Now that we know how to declare the angle of the gradient, we can include the colors of the gradient. We created a linear gradient that faded from black to white along the entire path of the gradient. To continue with our very exciting black to white example, what if we wanted to fade from solid color to solid color, displaying the solid colors on both ends for about 10% of the width of the element? That is easy to do by defining color stops.

To declare a color stop, declare the color and the position of the stop. If your first stop is not at 0%, the first color will be solid from 0% or 0 px until the first color stop, where it will begin to fade into the next color. The same is true if your last color stop is not at 100%.

If you don't declare the position of the color stop (you just declare the color), the color stops will be evenly distributed across the full width (or height) of the background image, with the first color stop at 0% and the last at 100%.

The position can be declared as a percentage of the width of the background image, or as an absolute length. If our background image is 200 px tall, these four declarations are equivalent (Figure 9-9):

```
-webkit-linear-gradient(top, #000000 10%, #FFFFFF 90%);
-webkit-linear-gradient(top, #000000 20px, #FFFFFF 180px);
linear-gradient(to bottom, #000000 10%, #FFFFFF 90%);
linear-gradient(to bottom, #000000 20px, #FFFFFF 180px);
```

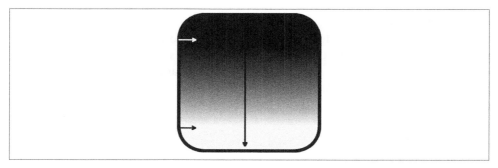

Figure 9-9. Colors are solid from 0 to the first color stop and from the last color stop to the edge of the box

Notice that in the Figure 9-9 example, the top and bottom are both solid colors for 10% of the height of the element, before starting to fade from black to white. From the top to the 10% mark the image is solid black. From the 90% mark to the bottom, the image is solid white. It fades from black to white for 80% of the height.

The two arrows indicate the color stops, where the solid color ends and where it starts fading into the next color. We are not limited to two colors. You can add as many color stops as necessary to make the effect you are looking for (but remember, just because you can doesn't mean you should).

Sometimes you also have more than two colors. For example, if you want to revert back to the look and feel of a 1996 website coded with cool 2013 features of linear gradients, you can create a rainbow background:

```
1    background-image: linear-gradient(
2        red,
3        orange,
4        yellow,
5        green,
6        blue,
7        purple);
```

This can also be written as:

```
1    background-image: linear-gradient(
2        red 0%,
3        orange 20%,
4        yellow 40%,
5        green 60%,
6        blue 80%,
7        purple 100%);
```

These equivalent gradients will create a rainbow with red on top, fading into orange, yellow, green, blue, then purple equally over the height of the element, as seen in the online chapter resources.

If you want your background to be an ugly striped rainbow instead of an ugly gradient rainbow (those are your only two options), we can create striping with hard color stops. A hard color stop is two color stops at the same point creating a sudden change in color rather than a gradual gradient:

```
1    background-image: linear-gradient(
2        red 16.7%,
3        orange 16.7%,
4        orange 33.3%,
5        yellow 33.3%,
6        yellow 50%,
7        green 50%,
8        green 66.7%,
9        blue 66.7%,
10       blue 83.3%,
11       purple 83.3%);
```

This gradient will be red for the first 16.7% since the first color stop is at that mark. Remember, if your first stop is not at 0%, the first color will be solid until the first color stop. At the color stop of 16.7%, it will begin to fade into the next color. The next color stop is also at 16.7%. Our fade into orange is over 0%: this is what creates the striping effect. There is no gradual change from one color to the next. Rather, we have hard color stops. Hard stops are good for striping, and also used in popular effects like candy buttons.

If we want a gradient to be only slightly opaque (or, if you're a glass half full type of person, slightly transparent), use HSLA or RGBA colors:

```
linear-gradient(180deg,
        rgba(0,0,0,0.1) 10%,
        rgba(0,0,0,0.9) 90%);
```

iPhone and CubeeDoo linear gradients. Now that we understand gradients, we can create the navigation bar for our faux iOS app, which is a fairly simple linear gradient.

First we have the iOS header bar. We first define a regular blue bar—everything except the gradient:

```
1    header {
2        /* the general appearance */
3        padding: 7px 10px;
4        background-color: #6D84A2;
5        display: block;
6        height: 45px;
7        -moz-box-sizing: border-box;
8        box-sizing: border-box;
9        line-height: 30px;
10       border-bottom: 1px solid #2C3542;
11       border-top: 1px solid #CDD5DF;
```

Lines 3 through 11 define the general appearance. Note in line 4 that we have declared a background color. When using gradients or any type of background image, you always want to declare a background color, in case the background image fails, such as for older browsers that don't support gradients. Another reason to declare a background color is instead of creating gradients of every color for every template color scheme you create, you can create a few translucent white gradients, and use them over your solid background colors, creating a single, reusable gradient for all of your color schemes.

As we've included both height and padding, we've declared box-sizing: border-box to use the IE box model. We've also included the -moz- prefix, which is still necessary as the property is still considered experimental, though it is supported everywhere.

Let's first start by declaring solid colors. The header bar is solid in the top half, and then gets darker from the halfway mark to the bottom. We declare a solid color for the top and start fading at the 50% mark:

```
15        background-image: -webkit-linear-gradient(top,
16                    rgb(176, 188, 205) 50%,
17                    rgb(129, 149, 175) 100%);
18        background-image: linear-gradient(to bottom,
19                    rgb(176, 188, 205) 50%,
20                    rgb(129, 149, 175) 100%);
```

The gradient's first color stop is at 50%, therefore the background will be solid blue (no fading) until that point. The background then fades into a different color blue in the bottom half.

If we want our gradient to work in BlackBerry 7, Android 3.0, and other archaic browsers, we also have to include the original prefixed syntax:

```
12        background-image: -webkit-gradient(linear, 0 0, 0 100%,
13                    color-stop(0.5, rgb(176, 188, 205)),
14                    color-stop(1.0, rgb(129, 149, 175)));
```

> For much older WebKit devices, through iOS 4.3, Android 3.0, and BB7, the syntax is:
>
> ```
> -webkit-gradient(linear, <start point>, <end point>,
>    color-stop(<float>, <color>)[, color-stop(<float>, <color>),
>    color-stop(<float>, <color>)])
> ```
>
> Where the starting point and end points define the path of the gradient, and each color stop includes the keyword color-stop followed by a float between 0 and 1 as a percent of the size of the image. The color stop includes the floating position point and the color, separated by a comma, in parentheses.
>
> The start and end points are a pair of space-separated values of numbers, percentages, or the keywords top, bottom, left, and right for point values. You must use two values for any point that you include.
>
> The stop(s) are optional color-stops indicating the color and position of the stop.
>
> ```
> background-image:
>    -webkit-gradient(linear, left top, left bottom,
>      color-stop(0.1, red),
>      color-stop(0.3, orange),
>      color-stop(0.5, yellow),
>      color-stop(0.7, green),
>      color-stop(0.9, blue)
>    );
> ```
>
> This example creates a rainbow, from top to bottom (left top to left bottom), starting with solid red, that starts fading into orange at 10% of the way in then to yellow, green, and blue, becoming solid blue at the 90% mark through to 100%. There is a link to an explanation in the online chapter resources.

This works. But let's make our gradients more reusable. Instead of creating a new gradient for every color, we can create a translucent white gradient to place on top of buttons and navigation bars of any color: create one gradient and use it everywhere. We can create a reusable gradient by using RGBA (or HSLA) to provide a transparent to slightly opaque gradient enabling us to quickly change color schemes if desired:

```
21    background-color: rgb(129, 149, 175);
22    background-image: -webkit-gradient(linear, 0 0, 0 100%,
23                        color-stop(0.5, rgb(255, 255, 255, 0.4)),
24                        color-stop(1.0, rgb(255, 255, 255, 0)));
25    background-image: -webkit-linear-gradient(
26                rgba(255, 255, 255, 0.4) 50%,
27                rgba(255, 255, 255, 0));
28    background-image: linear-gradient(
29                rgba(255, 255, 255, 0.4) 50%,
30                rgba(255, 255, 255, 0));
31
```

In this second example, we've removed top and to bottom from the latter two syntaxes since it is the default, and the 100%, since by default, if the position is omitted, the last color stop is at 100%.

By using alpha transparency instead of solid colors, we are able to create the iPhone native application look, as demonstrated in the online chapter resources. The transparency, however, allows for quick and easy color scheme changes. We can use this same gradient for our header for all of our color schemes. If we had a green color scheme we could simply change the background color to a darkish green.

How about the button gradients? The button gradients also have a gradient that covers half of the height of the button. We could use the same gradient syntax as before, except we invert the gradient (since the bottom is solid on the buttons, whereas the top is solid on the bar):

```
.nav li {
  background-image: -webkit-linear-gradient(bottom,
            rgba(255, 255, 255, 0.4) 50%,
            rgba(255, 255, 255, 0));
  background-image: linear-gradient(to top,
            rgba(255, 255, 255, 0.4) 50%,
            rgba(255, 255, 255, 0));
}
.cancel {background-color: #4A6C9B;}
.done {background-color: #2463DE;}
```

But that isn't exactly what we want. Eye candy buttons actually have a hard change, not a soft change, when the gradient and the solid color meet. To look right, we want our gradient to only take up 50% of the height. There are three ways to do this:

- We can position the gradient at the 50% mark using `background-position` property.
- We can make the background image only take up half the height of the buttons with the `background-size` property.
- We can make the gradient have a hard stop.

You already know how to position a background image with the CSS 1 `background-position` property (`background-position: 0 15px`), so let's do it with the CSS3 `background-size` property to make it more flexible (and learn about this new property).

background-size

The `background-size` property specifies the size of your background images. The value can be any absolute or relative length, or the key terms `contain`, `cover`, and `auto`.

The `contain` value scales the image down if necessary while preserving its aspect ratio, which may leave uncovered space. A rectangular background image in a square element set as `background-size: contain` will not fill the entire area, but rather will scale the background image down until it fully fits within its container. The area that is left uncovered depends on the values of the `background-position` property, and on the value of the `background-repeat` property.

The `cover` value scales the image so that it covers the whole area, completely covering the element, but perhaps not showing part of the image if the element box and the image do not have the same aspect ratio. A rectangular background image in a square element set as `background-size: cover` will be cut off. `auto` leaves the background image the same size as the original. The three keyterm values are illustrated in Figure 9-10.

| auto | cover | contain | 150px 150px | 150px |

Figure 9-10. Background-size auto, cover, contain, and length values (with background-repeat: no-repeat)

You can also specify the background size in absolute or relative lengths. If defining in absolute or relative lengths, you can include one or two values. If one value is declared, the width will be that value, and the height will scale up or down so that there is no distortion, as shown in the last example in Figure 9-10. If you prefer to scale based on the height, declare auto for the width.

If you provide two values, they are in the order width and height, and the background image will be stretched (or shrunk) to match your stated values. In Figure 9-10, we see that at 150 px by 150 px (in a 250×250 box), the image is distorted to fit the defined size.

Only in the case when both width and height are defined do we get the possibility of distortion. Contain, cover, auto, and declaring only one value, will always maintain the original aspect ratio of the image. If you need to declare a width or height, you can declare just one to ensure that no distortion occurs, setting the other value to auto.

We can use background-size on the gradient for our buttons, as we want the top to be a gradient, and the bottom to be solid. The difference with the candy buttons is that we don't want the gradient to fade into the solid color. Rather, we want a hard stop. As noted previously, there are a few ways to create this effect. Here in Example 9-1, we are making use of the background-size property.

Example 9-1. iOS buttons

```
1    .button {
2        background-image:
3          -webkit-gradient(linear, 0 100%, 0 0%,
4            from(rgba(255,255,255, 0.1)),
5            to(rgba(255,255,255,0.4)));
6        background-image:
7          -webkit-linear-gradient(bottom,
8            rgba(255, 255, 255, 0.1),
9            rgba(255, 255, 255, 0.4));
10       background-image:
11         linear-gradient(to top,
12            rgba(255, 255, 255, 0.1),
13            rgba(255, 255, 255, 0.4));
14       background-repeat: no-repeat;
15       background-size: 100% 50%;
16   }
17   .cancel {
18       background-color: #4A6C9B;
19        float: left;
20   }
21   .done {
22       background-color: #2463de;
23        float: right;
24   }
```

We've defined a gradient that is similar to the header gradient, but goes from bottom to top instead of top to bottom. We then make it occupy only the top of the button by employing the background-size property: telling the gradient to only occupy 50% height by 100% width.

We don't want our background gradient to tile, or repeat vertically, so we include `background-repeat: no-repeat`. We could have also declared:

```
background-size: 2px 50%;
background-repeat: repeat-x;
```

Make the background only 2 px wide, and repeat that image horizontally. We use 2 px (or larger) instead of 1 px because of a bug in some versions of Chrome. We declare all background properties separately instead of using the `background` shorthand so we don't accidentally overwrite any background property values, resetting them by accident to their default values.

By default, gradient background images fill up the entire background of an element. However, since we are defining the size of the gradient as different than the default 100% by 100%, we need to consider whether we want the background image to repeat. In this case, we didn't.

 When I create a CSS reset, I generally include a blanket statement setting `background-repeat: no-repeat` on most elements. Although `no-repeat` is not the browser default, it is most often the designer's preference. By not using the `background` shorthand, I don't overwrite my reset.

DPI and background-size

The `background-size` property is the property that makes high-resolution images work on high DPI devices.

High-resolution images look nice and crisp on high DPI devices, but all images go across the wires at the same resolution. If you want to display high-resolution images, you display an image that is generally twice as wide and twice as tall as the display size. This is where the `background-size` property plays a vital role in mobile CSS.

Let's say your corporate logo is 100 px tall by 300 px wide. For most devices, a 100 px × 300 px PNG would be appropriate. For high DPI devices, a 200 px × 600 px PNG will look even better. The resolution of the images are the exact same: one is just four times larger than the other. To fit that larger image in the original space—the 100 by 300 CSS pixels—and make it a crisp-looking higher resolution image, use `background-size`.

The default value for `background-size` is `auto`, which will make the image appear 200 px × 600 px. If your `#logo` div is 100 px × 300 px, you can declare:

```
#logo {
 width: 300px; height: 100px;
 background-image: url(logo.png);
 background-size: contain; /* OR */
 background-size: 300px 100px;
```

```
  }
@media
  screen and (-webkit-min-device-pixel-ratio: 2),
  screen and (min--moz-device-pixel-ratio: 2),
  screen and (-min-moz-device-pixel-ratio: 2),
  screen and (-o-min-device-pixel-ratio: 2/1),
  screen and (min-device-pixel-ratio: 2),
  screen and (min-resolution: 192dpi),
  screen and (min-resolution: 2dppx) {
    #logo {
        background-image: url(hidpi/logo.png);
    }
  }
}
```

Declaring `background-size: contain;` or `background-size: 300px 100px;` both work, as the width and height of the div are the same size you want the image to be.

There is a downside to the `background-size` property: images with `background-size` declared take twice as long to render the image: the time to decode the image and the time to resize. The extra few milliseconds can be an issue if you are animating larger images or are otherwise experiencing lots of reflows and repaints.

Stripey Gradients

We've covered most of the background images on our fake iOS application, but not all. How about the striped background of the iOS app? Do we need a GIF for that? Not so fast. As noted earlier, we can make stripes with CSS gradients. The background of the iOS app is a gradient: a striped gradient.

If you declare two color stops at the same position you will not get a color fading into another—a gradient—but rather a hard line. This is an important trick in creating shapes. For example, to make stripes you could define:

```
background-image:
 -webkit-gradient(linear, 0 0, 100% 0,
   color-stop(0.4, #ffffff),
   color-stop(0.4, #000000),
   color-stop(0.6, #000000),
   color-stop(0.6, #ffffff));
background-image:
 -webkit-linear-gradient(right,
   #ffffff 40%,
   #000000 40%,
   #000000 60%,
   #ffffff 60%);
background-image:
 linear-gradient(to left,
   #ffffff 40%,
   #000000 40%,
   #000000 60%,
   #ffffff 60%);
```

This gradient will go from right to left, starting white and ending white with a black stripe down the middle from 40% to 60%, as shown in Figure 9-11.

Figure 9-11. Stripes created with linear gradient with hard stops

The gradient for our body background image has hard stops. For this effect, we create a hard color stop, ending the first color and starting the next color with no fade. It is a 7 px wide background image, repeated:

```
1     background-color: #C5CCD4;
2     background-image:
3      -webkit-gradient(linear, 0 0, 100% 0,
4          color-stop(0.7142, #C5CCD4),
5          color-stop(0.7142, #CBD2D8));
6     background-image:
7       -webkit-linear-gradient(left,
8          #C5CCD4 0.7142%,
9          #CBD2D8 0.7142%);
10    background-image:
11      linear-gradient(to right,
12         #C5CCD4 0.7142%,
13         #CBD2D8 0.7142%);
14    background-size: 7px 2px;[6]
15    background-repeat: repeat;
```

Because the color stops are in the same location, the first color will abruptly "fade" into the next color, creating a hard line. Before the first stop, the color is the color of the first stop. After the last stop, the color is the color of the last stop.

The only thing with the gradient code we created in lines 2–13 is that it created one background image that will, by default, cover 100% of the element on which it is applied. For the background image for the body of our web application, we need our image to tile into columns or pinstripes. For that effect, we need to size the image and tile it both

6. Background size was set to 2 px, instead of 1 px—though any other nonzero positive height should work—because of a bug in Chrome that does not properly repeat gradients smaller than 2 px.

horizontally and vertically, or at least horizontally. We do that with the background-repeat and background-size properties.

Because we've declared the background size to be 7 px wide, the background image will have a 5 px stripe of #C5CCD4 followed by a 2 px wide stripe of #CBD2D8. We then repeated that tiny image both vertically and horizontally. We could also have created this gradient using pixels instead of percentages:

```
background-image:
  -webkit-gradient(linear, 0 0, 100% 0,
    color-stop(5px, #C5CCD4),
    color-stop(5px, #CBD2D8));
background-image:
  -webkit-linear-gradient(left,
    #C5CCD4 5px,
    #CBD2D8 5px);
background-image:
  linear-gradient(to right,
    #C5CCD4 5px,
    #CBD2D8 5px);
```

Or, instead of using background-size and background-repeat, we could instead have created a repeating gradient with the repeating-linear-gradient() value.

Repeating Linear Gradients

CSS3 provides us with background-size and background-repeat, which enables us to create interesting effects, including the stripey background. However, CSS3 also provides us with repeating-linear-gradient:

```
background-image:
  -webkit-repeating-linear-gradient(left,
    #C5CCD4 0,
    #C5CCD4 5px,
    #CBD2D8 5px,
    #CBD2D8 7px);
background-image:
  repeating-linear-gradient(to right,
    #C5CCD4 0,
    #C5CCD4 5px,
    #CBD2D8 5px,
    #CBD2D8 7px);
background-size: 7px 7px;
background-repeat: repeat;
```

There are a few quirks to note about repeating gradients. The width of the gradient will be the value of the last color stop: in our case, 7 px. You must declare the 0 value and the last value. Unlike regular linear gradients, it does not default those values for you.

Also, not all browsers support the native sizing feature of repeating gradients.[7] If you use repeating linear gradients, until this is fixed, check to see if you need to include a `background-size` and repeat the gradient with `background-repeat`, as done in lines 14 and 15.

Repeating linear gradients have similar browser support as unprefixed regular linear gradients. They are currently supported in all major browsers, since BlackBerry 10, iOS 5, Safari 5.1, and Chrome 10, with vendor prefixes still required in some WebKit browsers. As noted earlier, they don't render correctly in Chrome or Chrome for Android. However, I often like the effect of Chrome's poor handling of repeating linear gradients.

Gradients in CubeeDoo

Although Chrome for Android doesn't correctly render repeating linear gradients, I've included a repeating gradient for the background of the CubeeDoo application. I actually like the effect of the quirky Chrome rendering, and don't mind a slightly different background in different browsers until it is correctly supported across all browsers.

In smaller devices, the CubeeDoo board takes up the full viewport. In larger devices, the game only takes up a portion of the screen, so the background of the page on larger devices has a repeating linear gradient as a background, as does the game board:

```
body {
    background-color: #eee;
    background-image:
        -webkit-repeating-linear-gradient(-135deg,
            transparent 0,
            transparent 4px,
            white 4px,
            white 8px),
        -webkit-repeating-linear-gradient(135deg,
            transparent 0,
            transparent 4px,
            white 4px,
            white 8px);
    background-image:
        repeating-linear-gradient(-135deg,
            transparent 0,
            transparent 4px,
            white 4px,
            white 8px),
        repeating-linear-gradient(135deg,
            transparent 0,
            transparent 4px,
            white 4px,
```

---

7. For example, Chrome has a weird bug. It seems to think the background size should be 110 px, repeats oddly below that, and fails at times when the repeating linear gradient is wider than 100 px.

```
      white 8px);
   }
```

Note that we've actually included two gradients as two background images, creating a diamond effect across the board.

Multiple background images

How can we include two gradients? CSS3 allows for multiple background images on a single DOM node. Simply separate the various background images, no matter what type of images, with commas. In the preceding example, you'll note that in a single background-image declaration there are two repeating linear gradients separated by a comma.

We also included two gradients as the background image for the board, creating a checkerboard effect. The gradient background of the board is so small, it doesn't fully render in lower DPI devices, but it does create a texture for all devices:

```
#board {
    color: #fff;
    height: 400px;
    width: 100%;
    float: left;
    text-align: center;
    background-color: #eee;
    background-image:
        -webkit-gradient(linear, 0 0, 100% 100%,
            color-stop(0.5, rgba(255,255,255,0)),
            color-stop(0.5, rgba(255,255,255,0.5))),
        -webkit-gradient(linear, 0 100%, 100% 0,
            color-stop(0.5, rgba(255,255,255,0)),
            color-stop(0.5, rgba(255,255,255,0.5)));
    background-image:
        -webkit-linear-gradient(-135deg,
            rgba(255,255,255,0) 50%,
            rgba(255,255,255,0.5) 50%),
        -webkit-linear-gradient(135deg,
            rgba(255,255,255,0) 50%,
            rgba(255,255,255,0.5) 50%);
    background-image:
        linear-gradient(-135deg,
            rgba(255,255,255,0) 50%,
            rgba(255,255,255,0.5) 50%),
        linear-gradient(135deg,
            rgba(255,255,255,0) 50%,
            rgba(255,255,255,0.5) 50%);
    background-size: 2px;
}
```

You'll note that we are again declaring multiple background images on a single node, and only one background-size value. When only one value is declared in background-size, the length value is for both the height and width. When there is only one value for multiple background images, all background images will be the same size. If the background images were of different sizes, you would declare multiple background sizes separated by commas, with the order of the `background-size` declarations being the same order as the `background-image` declarations.

I recommend against using the `background` shorthand property, as it sets all the background properties to their default values, even if you didn't intend for that to happen. If you do use the shorthand with multiple background images, only declare the `background-color` on the last background declaration.

Candy buttons and hard stops

Now that we know how to do hard stops with gradients, let's revisit our candy buttons. We employed the `background-size` property to fake a hard edge on the gradient, but we could have used a gradient with a hard color stop:

```
background-image: -webkit-gradient(linear, 0% 0%, 0% 100%,
        color-stop(.5, rgba(255, 255, 255, 0)),
        color-stop(.5, rgba(255, 255, 255, 0.1)),
        color-stop(1, rgba(255, 255, 255, 0.4)));
background-image: -webkit-linear-gradient(bottom,
        rgba(255, 255, 255, 0) 50%,
        rgba(255, 255, 255, 0.1) 50%,
        rgba(255, 255, 255, 0.4));
background-image: linear-gradient(to top,
        rgba(255, 255, 255, 0) 50%,
        rgba(255, 255, 255, 0.1) 50%,
        rgba(255, 255, 255, 0.4));
```

As you can see, there are many ways to skin a cat, or, in this case, handle a gradient.

Tools for gradients

Although it is important to understand how to create linear gradients (which is why we went into great detail about it), sometimes it is easier to use a tool. The online chapter resources have links to resources, tools, and gradient libraries, to help you get up and running.

You may note that we've included a background color. Always include a background color because your site will be viewed in browsers that don't support gradients, you may push a typo in your gradient code, or your tile may fail to repeat itself. By including a background color, you can prevent the effect of having missing contrast between text and background in case your background image/gradient fails.

 If using gradients for bullets on a list item, the size of the image cannot be specified in WebKit. WebKit will default the gradient image to a size relative to the font size of the list item.

Shadows

Now that we have a good understanding of linear gradients, background-size, and rounded corners, let's revisit our buttons to give them more depth. We have most of the newer CSS features down ... except for shadows and perhaps the less commonly known text-overflow property.

The code for our buttons includes the following:

```
1    .button {
2        background-color: #4A6C9B;
3        background-image:
4            -webkit-gradient(linear, 0 100%, 0 0%,
5                from(rgba(255,255,255,0.1)),
6                to(rgba(255,255,255,0.4)));
7        background-image:
8            -webkit-linear-gradient(bottom,
9                rgba(255, 255, 255, 0.1),
10               rgba(255, 255, 255, 0.4));
11       background-image:
12           linear-gradient(to top,
13               rgba(255, 255, 255, 0.1),
14               rgba(255, 255, 255, 0.4));
15       background-size: 100% 50%;
16       background-repeat: no-repeat;
17       color: #FFFFFF;
18       border: 1px solid #2F353E;
19       border-color: #2F353E #375073 #375073; /* T LR B */
20       border-radius: 4px;
21       text-decoration: none;
22       font-family: Helvetica;
23       font-size: 12px;
24       font-weight: bold;
25       height: 30px;
26       padding: 0 10px;
27       text-shadow: 0 -1px 0 rgba(0, 0, 0, 0.6);
28       overflow: hidden;
29       max-width: 80px;
30       white-space: nowrap;
31       text-overflow: ellipsis;
32       -webkit-box-shadow:
33           0 1px 0 rgba(255,255,255, 0.4);
34       -webkit-box-shadow:
35           0 1px 0 rgba(255,255,255, 0.4),
36           inset 0 1px 0 rgba(255,255,255,0.4);
37       box-shadow:
38           0 1px 0 rgba(255,255,255, 0.4),
39           inset 0 1px 0 rgba(255,255,255,0.4);
40   }
```

That's a lot of code! With our great new gradient skills, most of it (through line 26) should be familiar to you, but there may be a few properties that you may not be familiar with, such as such `text-shadow`, `box-shadow`, and `text-overflow`. Fear not! We have those covered.

I created a blue to darker blue button with a background color that shows through our translucent white gradient. Lines 18–20 create a border of different blue hues with a radius of 4 pixels. Line 15 defines the size of our gradient: the top part of the button is a gradient and the bottom has a solid background color showing through, so I defined a gradient image that is full width, but only half the height of our element.

Since the gradient image does not take up 100% of the area of the element, it will tile vertically by default. We don't want it to. By declaring `background-repeat: no-repeat` on line 16, the image will not repeat. Had I defined the image to have a size of 2 px width (`background-size: 2px 50%;`), we would have had to repeat the image horizontally with `background-repeat: repeat-x;`.

The rest, through line 26, provides for text color, typeface, weight, and size, and removal of link underlining. While the HTML sample code has no links, often links are styled as buttons, and links are underlined by default. Had I used a link instead of a `<li>`, the links would have displayed as an inline element by default, giving height no meaning. But, as we're floating our buttons in the nav, whatever element has the class of `cancel` and `done` will display as block.

The `text-shadow` on line 27 is new to us, though not new to the CSS specification! Let's discuss.

Text Shadow

Text shadows were added to CSS 2, and removed in CSS 2.1. They're back! But in reverse order.

Apple likes to have their text pop. On Apple.com, they've created popping text by including images for their text because they want to ensure their website looks similar in all browsers. Yes, they actually have a sprite image for their navigation copy, and another image for the gray navigation bar behind it. They have us all download over 3.5 MB of images on first page load because they want to ensure that all visitors, even those on IE6 (if people aren't paying to upgrade their 10-year-old computer, I don't think they're switching to a Mac) have the same experience.

In the mobile space, we don't have to worry about craptastic desktop browsers like older IEs not supporting `text-shadows`. We don't have to include sprites for our navigation. We can use `text-shadow` instead of images—keeping the number of HTTP requests low and making internationalization much less of a hassle.

The `text-shadow` property specifies a text shadow to be added to the text content of an element. The syntax for `text-shadow` values is a space-separated list of `leftOffset`, `topOffset`, `blur`, and `shadow-color`. The two shadow offsets are required. The blur radius and color values are optional:

```
text-shadow: <leftOffset> <topOffset> <blurRadius> <color>[,
        <leftOffset> <topOffset> <blurRadius> <color>][,
        <leftOffset> <topOffset> <blurRadius> <color>];
```

There are two offset length values: (1) the horizontal distance to the right of the text if it's positive, or to the left of the text if the value is negative, and (2) the vertical distance below the text if it is positive, or above the text if it is negative.

The third value defines the width of the blur. The larger the blur value, the bigger the blur, making the text shadow bigger and less opaque. Negative values are not allowed. If not specified, the blur radius value defaults to zero, creating a sharp shadow edge.

The offsets are required, but they can be set to zero. If they are both set to zero, the shadow will be a glow, showing evenly on all sides. This feature, along with `current Color` (see Chapter 8) can be used to your benefit.

Some fonts, like Helvetica Neue Light, when viewed in high DPI devices, are too thin to read. By declaring:

```
text-shadow: 0 0 1px currentColor;
```

the text can be made more legible. The one line of CSS creates a 1 px glow directly behind the text in the current color of the font. By using `currentColor`, you can make a single property/value declaration for all your text without worrying about different elements having different color text.

When multiple shadows are included, the shadow effects are applied in the reverse order in which they are specified: the last shadow is drawn first and each preceding text shadow is placed on top of it.

Text shadows can be created to be very, very wide. Even so, a text shadow has no effect on the box model. A text shadow can increase beyond the boundaries of its parent element without increasing the size of that element's box. Because of this, if you put a very wide negative horizontal offset, you may inadvertently cover the preceding text (there is an example in the online chapter resources).

A trick to good-looking text shadows is to include a blur value and to provide a slightly transparent version of the shadow color, generally `rgba(0,0,0,0.4);` for a slightly gray shadow. While seemingly gray, the translucent black allows for background colors/image to show through the shadow.

However, I am not a designer. And I am definitely not Apple's designer. Apple appears to use a one pixel dark-gray top shadow. We add this to page title (the <h1>) and to our buttons on our Languages page to make the text pop:

```
text-shadow: 0 -1px 0 rgba(0, 0, 0, 0.6);
```

The preceding code provides for a 1 px text shadow sitting on top of the letters that is slightly transparent.

 Note that text-shadow is *not* a prefixed property. Also note that large translucent shadows combined with other CSS properties can take a long time to paint and can use up memory.

Fitting Text with width, overflow, and text-overflow

Lines 28 through 31 of our code example above ensure that the button does not take up too much room. We have very limited space on our mobile devices. In our Languages example, we are trying to fit three elements in that top navigation area: two buttons and the page title. So, we need to ensure not only that the buttons don't take too much space, but that our h1 isn't too wide either. "Languages" fits here, but what if our page title were "Supported Languages"?

Generally, declaring a width on an inline element, like <button>, has no effect. However, since we're floating our buttons, visible floated elements are default displayed as block (instead of list-item, inline, inline-block, etc.), so width works!

text-overflow property

The text-overflow property is part of the Basic UI specification. The text-overflow property allows you to clip text that is too wide for its container. The ellipsis value causes ellipses, or three periods, to be appended to the text at the point where it is clipped:

```
text-overflow: ellipsis | clip
```

Employing text-overflow: ellipsis; is not enough to cut off text and include ellipses. If the text wraps or is allowed to extend beyond the boundaries of the containing block, then the words won't be cut off and the ellipses will not appear.[8] Ellipses will only appear when the containing box has overflow set to something other than visible (visible allows the text to flow out of the box) and white-space set to nowrap or pre. You can also use the clip value, which will clip the text but without putting ellipses.

By using the ellipses key term, the clipping will occur after whatever last letter can completely fit into the parent box. There has been discussion about breaking on specific characters rather than letters. Firefox has included this experimental string value since Firefox 9.

---

8. To add ellipses to multiple-line text, there are vendor-specific, nonstandards values, including the property of -webkit-line-clamp and value of text-overflow: -o-ellipsis-lastline;, for WebKit and Opera respectively.

While you really should never clip text, the limited real estate on the navigation bar of a mobile application often requires it. It is generally not good user experience design to hide text in this (or any other) way. If you are going to clip text, use ellipses to improve user experience. The ellipses informs the user that text has been clipped:

```
h1 {
  white-space: nowrap;
  width: 180px;
  overflow: hidden;
  -o-text-overflow: ellipsis; /* opera mini, mobile */
  text-overflow: ellipsis;
}
```

The `white-space`, `overflow`, and, generally, `width` properties have to be declared for the `text-overflow` property to work, which means it doesn't work on elements that are displayed inline.

white-space property

The `white-space` property specifies how whitespace inside an element is handled. Values for the `white-space` property include `normal`, `nowrap`, `pre`, `pre-line`, `pre-wrap`, and `inherit`. When set to `normal`, text will wrap at the end of the line, and whitespace will be reduced to a maximum value of one space. Setting the value to `nowrap` will force the text to not line break to fit the width of its parent container. The `prewrap` is often more legible than `nowrap`: while it maintains or preserves the original whitespace, it wraps when it reaches the end of its containing block.

For `text-overflow: elipses;` to work, the text can't wrap. This is why we have included this CSS 1 feature here.

Box Shadow

Box shadows are most noticeably used to create drop shadows to make elements pop off the screen. In CubeeDoo, we use `box-shadow` to make the cards pop off the board a bit. In our effort at creating a CSS3 native iPhone application look, we employ the `box-shadow` property to create two subtle shadow effects on the buttons.

The `box-shadow` property enables the developer to add drop shadows or inset shadows, or both, to elements. One or more `box-shadows` can be attached to a box, by which you can create some pretty nifty effects. Shadows are drawn just outside the border, or just inside the border in the case of `inset`.

In terms of the `box-model`, shadows are similar to `outline` and `text-shadow`, in that they do not influence the layout: they may overlap other boxes. It is supported in all browsers starting with IE9. Include the default vendor-less syntax and the `-webkit-` vendor prefix version for Android 3.0 and iOS 5.

The syntax and rendering of box-shadow is similar to text-shadow, but with two additional optional features, blur spread and inset:

```
box-shadow: inset <leftOffset> <topOffset> <blurRadius> <spread> <color>[,
     inset <leftOffset> <topOffset> <blurRadius> <spread> <color>][,
     inset <leftOffset> <topOffset> <blurRadius> <spread> <color>];
```

The values for box-shadow property include none for no shadow (the default), or a list of space-separated values for left-offset, top-offset, blur radius, spread radius, and color, with the optional inset keyword for inner shadows (versus drop shadows). If more than one box shadow is to be included, separate each shadow with a comma.

The vertical and horizontal offset values are both required. Similar to text-shadow, the first three values define the horizontal position, vertical position, and blur radius in that order. The fourth value—the blur spread—makes the shadow grow bigger if positive, and shrink if negative. The inset key term, if included, makes the shadow an inset shadow instead of a drop shadow. The inset key term, blur radius, blur spread, and color values are optional.

Note that inset is only an option for box-shadow and is not part of text-shadow. Also note that Android up to 3.0 and iOS 3.2 require the -webkit- vendor prefix, and do not support the inset values. iOS 4.x and Blackberry 7 require the -webkit- vendor prefix as well, but support inset shadows.

For example (not from the online chapter resources):

```
1    -webkit-box-shadow:
2         3px 4px 5px 6px rgba(0,0,0, 0.4);
3    -webkit-box-shadow:[9]
4         3px 4px 5px 6px rgba(0,0,0, 0.4),
5         inset 1px 1px 1px #FFFFFF;
6    box-shadow:
7         3px 4px 5px 6px rgba(0,0,0, 0.4),
8         inset 1px 1px 1px #FFFFFF;
```

Within each grouping we have two comma-separated box shadows. The values making up each of the two box shadows is a space-separated list, including:

- The left or horizontal offset of the shadow is the first length value. A negative value will put the shadow on the left.

- The top or vertical offset is the second length value. A negative value will put the shadow above the box.

9. Lines 1–2 are for Android up to 3.0 and iOS 3.2, which do not support the inset property. Lines 3-5 is for older WebKit browsers, including and up to Safari 5, iOS 4.3, Android 3.0, and BB 7. Lines 6–8 are for Safari 5.1, Opera 10.5+, Opera Mobile 11+, Chrome 9+, IE9+, and Firefox 4+. Not supported in Opera Mini.

- The optional blur radius is the third length value. Negative values are not allowed. If it is 0, the shadow is solid. The larger the value, the blurrier the shadow will be.

- The optional blur spread is the fourth length value, if it is present. Positive values make the shadow grow bigger. By default, the shadow is the same size as the element.

- The optional color. Using alpha transparency is recommended if your blur radius is greater than 0, as the effect is much prettier if you start from a slightly transparent version of black than if you start with an opaque version of gray. However, translucent shadows use more memory and can take longer to paint, which is an issue on devices with limited RAM or if you're animating and/or repainting the element frequently. If the color is not defined, browsers will by default use `currentColor`.

- The optional `inset` key term, if present, will create an inset shadow instead of a drop shadow.

In our example, the first shadow will be a 5 px wide gray transparent shadow on the bottom right of the element. The second box shadow value in each grouping includes the optional key term `inset`. This second shadow will be a fully opaque white 1 px outline (or inline?) on the inside of the box. The shadows appear on the outside and inside of the border, if there is one, respectively.

The values of the x-offset, y-offset, and optional blur radius and spread radius need to be written in that order. The order of the last two values in the declaration (inset and color) location aren't important, but keep the order consistent for ease of reading and maintenance. The order of shadows when including multiple shadow values *does* make a difference. Similar to `text-shadows`, `box-shadows` are drawn in the reverse order of their declarations. Drop shadows are always drawn behind the box, as if it had a lower z-index, and do *not* show through alpha transparent boxes (unlike alpha transparent text, where text shadows show through), as shown in the online chapter resources.

A thick border with an inset shadow can make for an interesting effect, but animating a large translucent shadow can actually crash a browser, as all shadows, images, and gradients are calculated and painted to the screen from back to front, even if they are never made visible to the user.

 On mobile, all properties are drawn to the page even if not visible. Be warned that if you add 20 shadows and gradients, even if they are overlapping, beyond the confines of the page, under another element, or otherwise not visible, they are still painted. Repainting 20 layers and calculating the added effect of transparencies on each pixel may take too long to animate at 60 fps.

While shadows have been supported since the first iPhone, shadows can use a lot of memory and can hang the browser, especially if the shadows are semitransparent (versus opaque), and even more so when the element on which the shadow is set is animated. The browser must recalculate each pixel on each repaint, even if the shadow is not visible.

 In mobile browsers, large shadows, especially inset shadows, use a lot of memory and can hang the browser.

Lines 37–39 of our CSS for the candy buttons include a double shadow:

```
box-shadow:
    0 1px 0 rgba(255,255,255, 0.4),
    inset 0 1px 0 rgba(255,255,255,0.4)
```

This declaration will include two semitransparent white shadows: a 1 px shadow on the outside bottom of the box and a 1 px shadow inside the button, at the top of the box. We also declared this with the -webkit- prefix with two shadows and also with the inset shadow removed for very old Android browsers.

Putting It All Together: CubeeDoo

We have several shadows in CubeeDoo. Here are some excerpts from the CSS. This is not all the code that is in the CSS files. I am only including the selectors, properties, and values that should make sense to you up to this point:

```
1    #board > div {
2        box-shadow: 1px 1px 1px rgba(0,0,0,0.25);
3    }
4    .back {
5        border: 5px solid white;
6    }
7    .back:after,
8    .face:after {
9        position: absolute;
10       content: "";
11       top: 0;
12       left: 0;
13       right: 0;
14       bottom: 0;
15       border-radius: 3px;
16       pointer-events: none;
17   }
18   .back:after {
19       background-repeat: no-repeat;
20       background-color: #fff;
21       background-size:
22           50% 50%,
23           0 0;
24       background-image:
25           url('data:image/svg+xml;utf8,<svg width="40" height="40"
                  xmlns="http://www.w3.org/2000/svg"><g><text xml:space="preserve"
```

```
                    text-anchor="middle" font-family="serif" font-size="40" id="svg_1"
                    y="30" x="20" stroke-width="0" stroke="rgb(119, 160, 215)"
                    fill="rgb(119, 160, 215)">❀</text></g></svg>'),
26              -webkit-linear-gradient(-15deg,
                    rgba(0, 0, 0, 0), rgba(0, 0, 0, 0.05));
27          background-image:
28              url('data:image/svg+xml;utf8,<svg width="40" height="40"
                    xmlns="http://www.w3.org/2000/svg"><g><text xml:space="preserve"
                    text-anchor="middle" font-family="serif" font-size="40" id="svg_1"
                    y="30" x="20" stroke-width="0" stroke="rgb(119, 160, 215)"
                    fill="rgb(119, 160, 215)">❀</text></g></svg>'),
29              linear-gradient(75deg,
                    rgba(0, 0, 0, 0), rgba(0, 0, 0, 0.05));
30          box-shadow:
31              inset 1px 1px 0 currentcolor,
32              inset -1px -1px 0 currentcolor,
33              1px 1px 1px rgba(0,0,0,0.1);
34          color: rgb(119, 160, 215);
35      }
36      #board > div.flipped {
37          box-shadow: -1px 1px 1px rgba(0,0,0,0.25);
38      }
39      .control {
40          border: 1px solid rgba(0, 0, 0, 0.25);
41          box-shadow: inset 1px 1px 0 rgba(255, 255, 255, 0.5);
42          background-image:
43              -webkit-linear-gradient(-15deg,
44                  rgba(0, 0, 0, 0),
45                  rgba(0, 0, 0, 0.025));
46          background-image:
47              linear-gradient(75deg,
48                  rgba(0, 0, 0, 0),
49                  rgba(0, 0, 0, 0.025));
50          text-shadow: 1px 1px 0px rgba(255, 255, 255, 0.5);
51          border-radius: 5px;
52      }
```

There are many things to note in this example. Let's go line by line:

1. We are targeting <div> elements that are the direct children of the #board using a child selector combinator in line 1. The element we're targeting is the card container. We give the cards in their default state a slight drop shadow in line 2.

2. We define the appearance of our generated content by creating pseudoelements in lines 7 through 17. We include the required content attribute in line 10, and position these 0 px from the top, left, bottom, and right, forcing the absolutely positioned[10] generated content to be the exact size and position of their parent node.

---

10. The parent is set to position relative, so the generated content will be relative to that.

We also include a border-radius of 3 px to make the corners rounded like their parent nodes.

 Setting generated content position: absolute, with all 4 sides offset to 0, will make the generated content the same size as the parent.

3. Lines 17 to 35 style the back of the card. We start off by declaring the background properties, including background-repeat and background-color. We have two background images with different background sizes, so we declare the two values separated by a comma as the value of the background-size property.

4. The back of the cards have a blue band, a little flower, and a gradient to make it pop. The band effect is done with box-shadow. The flower and popping gradient are done with background images.

5. We declare two background images in two separate ways. The first background image is SVG, as covered in Chapter 5. The second image is a gradient. They are separated with a comma. We declare this image combination twice (or three times if you want to support old WebKit) because gradient syntax has changed, and SVG is not supported in older Android. You would think that we could simply have included the ❀ in generated content, but because we are flipping the card in later chapters and support for animating generated content is not yet ubiquitous, we create our generated content look with a background SVG.

6. To create the blue band as shown in Figure 9-12, we use two inset shadows: a top/ left inset shadow and a bottom right inset shadow. Note that the blue band actually follows the curves of the rounded corners. The blue band is 5 px from the edge of the card. We were able to create this stripe effect because in line 5 we added a 5 px border. And, as we know, shadows and inset shadows are on the outside and inside of the border respectively.

7. The last of those three borders, the one on line 33, creates a drop shadow for the card.

8. On line 34, we declare the color. Seemingly, this would be a moot point since there is no text in this element. Even the ❀ "text" is done with SVG and not generated content. But, by including the color here, the currentColor in our drop-shadow obeys this declaration.

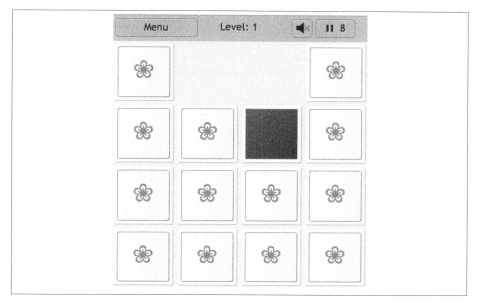

Figure 9-12. CubeeDoo: The blue bands are created with a large border and two inset shadows

9. When the user flips a card, the shadow stays with the card. This is likely not the effect you want. Our light source has stayed the same, so our shadow should be in the same location relative to the board, not the card, when we flip it. Line 36 uses the child selector combinator, but really doesn't have to, since no other div is going to have the flipped class. When the div is flipped, we change the left offset of the card so that visually it is always in the same location. We will learn about transforming (flipping or rotating) cards in Chapter 11.

10. Lines 39 to 52 control the controls, which are the CubeeDoo buttons. To create the effect of a double border (black and white) for the top left, we include a translucent black border and add a white inset shadow in lines 40 and 41.

11. We include a translucent gradient as the background of the buttons to give the buttons dimension. Note that the angles are written differently for the prefixed syntax versus the unprefixed syntax, but will appear the same.

12. We also added translucent white text shadow to the buttons as well as rounded corners in lines 50 and 51.

We've covered all the features of creating the look of a native iPhone application without the use of images, and all the features of the default look and feel of CubeeDoo. We succeeded in creating CSS3 only versions of these interfaces without opening up an image editing application or making an extra HTTP request.

With CSS3 and SVG, which we discussed in Chapter 5, you really can create just about any shape without images.

However, sometimes images are the right solution as they're supported in all browsers, and they're easy. We will cover some image solutions, including border image and multiple background images, in Chapter 11.

CSS3: Transforms, Transitions, and Animations

On the desktop, most of the "animations" you have likely seen aren't actually CSS animations, but rather Flash, Canvas, or JavaScript animations. On mobile devices, it is important to use CSS3 transitions, transforms, and animations to animate elements whenever possible instead of these other techniques.

So why not animate with Flash, JavaScript, or `<canvas>`? Flash is not supported on mobile iOS devices, and never will be. Adobe, the makers of Flash, discontinued development of the mobile Flash Player, with the last release being Flash Player 11.1 for Android and the BlackBerry PlayBook in late 2011.

Flash is still being developed for desktop, but with Flash not supported or installed on any new devices, you'll be missing out on a huge chunk, if not all, of the mobile market. And, for those using older devices with browsers that support Flash, you'll be draining their battery.

Similarly, animations done with JavaScript, when not hardware-accelerated, block the UI thread. This can make the rest of the application, if not the animation itself, choppy, nonresponsive, a memory hog, and a battery drainer.

On mobile, CSS animations are an awesome alternative to these other technologies. Browsers are optimized to handle CSS, so you lose less memory, CPU, and battery.[1] And, animations, transforms, and transitions are supported on all modern smartphone browsers, so there is no reason to not use them.

---

1. It is possible to drain battery animating certain CSS property values, but generally, browsers are well optimized for CSS.

Well, there is. An important note about transitions, transforms, and animations: just because you can, doesn't mean you should. Use instructional animations to show procedures or tasks that are hard to describe with static pictures. Accompany the instructions with text that explains the animation.

Animation can be used to draw attention to an element on the page, such as a form submission error message, a success message on a one page application, or an update to the page that is important that the user may not otherwise have noticed.

Don't animate unless you want to draw attention, and don't animate elements that need to be read or interacted with. Games, of course, are an exception to these rules.

These features of CSS are very captivating when used wisely and sparingly. Don't overuse, unless you're using these features in gaming, or your site will be reminiscent of a Geocities site from the 1990s.

CSS Transitions

Transitions allow CSS properties to change from one value to another over a period of time. If you've ever used :hover to change the color of a link, you've used a transition, but likely a transition of zero milliseconds in duration. With CSS transitions, you can make that color change, and a whole lot of other properties change, over a period of time.

CSS transitions apply to any change from one state to another state. The transition shorthand property is made up of four properties: (1) transition-property, which defines which properties are affected, (2) transition-duration, which sets the during of the transition effect, (3) the transition-timing-function, which delineates how the timing will accelerate, decelerate, or otherwise change during the transition, and (4) the transition-delay, which sets how long to wait before starting the transition after the transition is initiated.

To create a transition, set the styles of the element you want to transition. In the properties of the initial state, you include the name of the property or properties you want to affect in the transition, along with the time of the transition, the speed, and the delay, if any. Here is the syntax as shown in the spec:[2]

---

2. Vendor prefixing is needed: -webkit- up through iOS6, Android, BlackBerry 10, and Chrome through 25; -o- for Opera up to 12; and -moz- for Firefox up to 15. Support began in IE with IE10 unprefixed. I recommend still including -webkit-, but the other prefixes are optional as browsers requiring them are already almost obsolete.

```
nav a {
    background-color: rgb(255,255,255);
    border: 5px solid #000000;
    transition-property: background-color;
    transition-timing-function: linear;
    transition-duration: 0.8s;
    transition-delay: 200ms;
}
```

This is the initial *keyframe*. A keyframe is a drawing that defines the starting or ending points of any smooth transition in animation (or in film). Keyframes aren't explicitly employed in transitions. They are used when creating animations using the animation properties, which we discuss later in this chapter. Getting an understanding now may help make animations less confusing later.

You then define the value of the properties listed in the value of transition-property: in this case, the value of the background-color. We could have used the key term all if we had wanted to transition all the transitionable properties that change between the default and transitioned state, such as the hover state:

```
nav a:hover, nav a.hover {
    background-color: rgb(0, 0, 0);
    border: 5px dashed #CCCCCC;
}
```

In the preceding example, when the user hovers over a link in the navigation section of the document, the background of the link will go from white to black, as shown in Figure 10-1. The border color and style will change immediately on hover. The transition of the background color will start after 200 milliseconds; take 800 milliseconds to transition, and transition at an even keel. In Figure 10-1, you'll note the border changed immediately, but the background color waited the 200 ms delay before starting to transition.

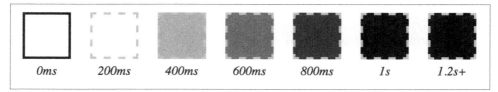

Figure 10-1. Time-lapse of background-color transition, showing how the border changes instantly on hover while the background color transitions over 800 ms after a delay of 200 ms

This may be a lot to grasp, so let's go over the various transition values. There are no screenshots in this section, since "effects" are hard to perceive in print. However, there are examples in the online chapter resources.

The transition-property Property

The `transition-property` lists the properties that will be transitioning during the animation. Properties that can be made to transition include:

- `background-color`
- `background-position`
- `background-size`
- `border` (color and width, but not style)
- `border-color`
- `border-radius`
- `border-width`
- `border-spacing`
- `box-shadow`
- `bottom`
- `clip`
- `color`
- `columns`
- `column-width`
- `column-count`
- `column-gap`
- `column-rule` (color and width, but not style)
- `crop`
- `flex`
- `flex-basis`
- `flex-grow` (except from or to 0)
- `flex-shrink` (except from or to 0)
- `font-size`
- `font-size-adjust`
- `font-stretch`
- `font-weight`
- `height`
- `left`
- `letter-spacing`

- line-height
- margin
- max-height
- max-width
- min-height
- min-width
- opacity
- order (part of flex)
- outline-color
- outline-offset
- outline-width
- padding
- perspective
- perspective-origin
- right
- text-decoration-color
- text-indent
- text-shadow
- top
- transform
- transform-origin
- vertical-align
- visibility
- width
- word-spacing
- z-index

 In general, any pair of property values where you can conceivably figure out a midpoint is transitionable. Note that depending on the transition timing function, the midpoint between two values may not display at the middle of the transition. Ease in, ease out, and other cubic-bezier timing function transitions will have different midpoints.

For example, `top: 0` to `top: 100px;` has a midpoint of 50 px and is therefore transitionable, but `display: block` to `display: none;` (used as example property values in Table 10-1) does not have a midpoint and is not transitionable. You can transition from `height: 600px` to `height: 700px;` but not from `height: auto;` to `height: 700px;`.

Table 10-1. Determining if property values are transitionable

Property	Initial value	Final value	Midpoint?	Transitionable
height	100 px	200 px	150 px	✓
height	auto	200 px	?	✗
opacity	0	1	0.5	✓
display	block	none	?	✗

While you can't currently transition background images, including gradients, you can transition `background-position` and `background-size` to create some interesting effects.

The exception to this midpoint rule is `visibility`. Visibility is a property that seemingly you wouldn't be able to transition, but you can include it in transitions and animations. The value will actually jump from `visible` to `hidden` at the end of the transition effect if those are the property values set. There is discussion of making all properties transitionable and animatable, but we aren't there yet.

The value of the `transition-property` property is a comma-separated list of any number of these property names, or the keyword `all`. Only the properties listed as the value of the `transition-property` will transition over time when the transition gets initiated, unless `all` is declared:

```
nav a {
  -webkit-transition-property: background-color; /* iOS6-, BB, Android, Ch25-*/
  -moz-transition-property: background-color; /* FF4 to 15 */
  -o-transition-property: background-color; /* O 10.5 to 12 */
  transition-property: background-color; /* IE10, FF16+, O12.5+, Ch26+, iOS7 */
```

I've included `-moz-` and `-o-`, to demonstrate support for older browsers. `-ms-` has never been needed, and Firefox and Opera are not needed in currently used mobile browsers. The only prefix we need to include for the transition properties in the mobile space, or at all, is `-webkit-`.

If a property that is not transitionable is included in the value of the `transition-property` property, the value will be ignored, changing state instantly instead of transitioning over time. The value that can't transition over time will not, but the transition itself will not fail.

The transition-duration Property

The `transition-duration` property sets how long the transition will take to go from start to finish, from the first keyframe to the last keyframe. You can set how many seconds or milliseconds the transition will take to animate from the original value to the transitioned value.

We learned about time units in Chapter 8. This is the first time we use it. The following 2 lines are all equal, using millisecond or second units (but target different browsers):

```
-webkit-transition-duration: 0.5s;
        transition-duration: 500ms;  ...
```

The transition-timing-function Property

The `transition-timing-function` enables control over the transition, describing how the animation will proceed over time. The value can take one of several keywords—`ease`, `linear`, `ease-in`, `ease-out`, `ease-in-out`, `step-start`, `step-end`, `steps(x, start)`, `steps(x, end)`—or take as its value a cubic Bézier function.

A cubic Bézier takes as its value four points in a plane: starting at the first point going toward the second, and arriving at the last point from the direction of the third point. After about three years of calculus, it might make sense! Fortunately, some cubic Bézier curve values are included in CSS3 as predefined keywords, and links to tools to help you better understand cubic Bézier are included in the online chapter resources.

The nonstep keyword values (`ease`, `linear`, `ease-in-out`, etc.) are each themselves representing cubic Bézier curve with four fixed-point values:

ease, *or* `cubic-bezier(0.25, 0.1, 0.25, 1.0)`
> The default value; increases in velocity toward the middle of the transition, slowing back down at the end.

linear *or* `cubic-bezier(0.0, 0.0, 1.0, 1.0)`
> Transitions at an even speed.

ease-in *or* `cubic-bezier(0.42, 0, 1.0, 1.0)`
> Starts off slowly, with the transition speed increasing until complete.

ease-out *or* `cubic-bezier(0, 0, 0.58, 1.0)`
> Starts transitioning quickly, slowing down as the transition continues.

ease-in-out *or* `cubic-bezier(0.42, 0, 0.58, 1.0)`
> Starts transitioning slowly, speeds up, and then slows down again.

```
cubic-bezier(p1,p2,p3,p4)
```
Where the p1 and p3 values must be in the range of 0 to 1.[3]

The step functions—steps(x, end), steps(x, start), step-end, and step-start—divide the duration of the transition into equal lengths of time. Each interval is an equal step in terms of time taking the transition from original state to final state. The function also specifies whether the step is at the start or end of the interval.

In other words, if there are five steps, steps(5, start) will have steps representing 0%, 20%, 40%, 60%, and 80% of the progress toward the final state. If you set steps(5, end), you will have steps representing 20%, 40%, 60%, 80%, and 100% of the progress.

The value step-start is equivalent to steps(1, start) and step-end is equivalent to steps(1, end). The steps() values are good for animating background image sprites to create animations. There are some examples of these values in the online chapter resources. Continuing on with our sample code:

```
    ...
-webkit-transition-timing-function: linear;
        transition-timing-function: linear;
    ...
```

The transition-delay Property

The transition-delay property specifies the number of milliseconds or seconds to wait between a change of state causing the transition and the start of the transition effect. The default value of 0s indicates that the animation should begin to transition immediately. Positive time values will delay the start of the transition effect for the value indicated. Negative values cause the transition to start right away, but start midway through the transition.

While transition-delay may seem like a useless property, it can greatly help improve user experience. Oftentimes you don't want hover or touch effects to be too sensitive. If a user is dragging a finger or mouse quickly across the screen to get from point A to point B, you don't want all the points in between that are accidentally touched to react to the touch too quickly. A transition delay of 50 ms generally does the trick. The intentional touches still seem reactive, but the page doesn't flicker as object transitions get unintentionally activated.

Negative transition delays can also serve a purpose. As long as the absolute value of the delay is less than the transition-duration, the transition, when initiated, will start midway through the transition at a point proportional to the time difference. For

---

3. While explaining cubic Bézier is beyond the scope of this book, there is a good tool (*http://www.netzgesta.de/dev/cubic-bezier-timing-function.html*) with which you can determine what other values you might need for your timing function. Another site, *http://cubic-bezier.com*, lets you compare the forward progress of one timing function against another.

example, if you have a 10 second `transition-duration`, and a −4 second delay, the transition will start immediately, but at 40% through the transition:

```
...
-webkit-transition-delay: 250ms
        transition-delay: 0.25s;
}
```

The Shorthand transition Property

Putting it all together will seem a little crazy:

```
nav a {
  -webkit-transition-property: background-color;
          transition-property: background-color;

  -webkit-transition-duration: 0.5s;
          transition-duration: 500ms;

  -webkit-transition-timing-function: linear;
          transition-timing-function: linear;

  -webkit-transition-delay: 250ms;
          transition-delay: 0.25s;
}
```

Instead of including 8, 12, or 16 lines[4] of code for a transition, the `transition` shorthand property, which combines the four properties just covered, can be used. Note that the order of the duration and delay values is important (i.e., they need to be in the same order as introduced earlier):

- `transition-property`
- `transition-duration`
- `transition-timing-function`
- `transition-delay`

```
nav a {
  background-color: #FFFFFF;
  -webkit-transition: background-color 500ms linear 250ms;
          transition: background-color 500ms linear 250ms;
}
nav a:hover, nav a.hover {
  background-color: #FF0000;
}
```

---

4. Depends on the number of vendor prefixes you include.

By putting the transition on the default state, when the element is hovered or changes class, the transitioned properties will transition to their new values, reversing the transition on mouse change/touch end or if the new class is removed. The transition properties can be put on the default state or on a different state. It depends when and how you want the element to transition.

Multiple Transitions

But what if you want to transition more than one property? Maybe you want to change background-color, border-color, and color all on the same property? The transition properties allow for multiple transitions in one call.

Let's say instead of just transitioning the background-color property, we want to transition the border property as well (you can transition the border color and width but not style). We would have to (1) include the new border property in the transitioned style declaration, and (2) include the border property in the transition-property value list, either as a comma-separated series of values, or use the key term all. Note that all should only be used if you want to transition all properties in the same way.

For instance, in earlier examples, although we defined the border and background-color properties in both the touch or hover states, we only included the background-color property as the value of the transition-property property. In those examples, the background-color will transition slowly (over 250 ms), and the border color will change immediately on hover or touch: like you are used to, like it has always done without transition, as if the transition were set to a 0 s duration with a 0 s delay.

If you want to change both properties at the same rate and delay, you could write your transition shorthand using the all keyword, since you are transitioning all the properties listed in the hover status:

```
nav a {
  background-color: #FFFFFF;
  border: 5px solid #CCCCCC;
  -webkit-transition: all 500ms linear 250ms;
          transition: all 500ms linear 250ms;
}
```

When using the all keyword, all the properties transition at the same rate, speed, and delay. If you want some but not all of your properties to transition at the same rate, timing, and delay, comma separate the transition-property properties:

```
nav a {
  background-color: #FFFFFF;
  border: 5px solid #CCCCCC;
  color: red;
  -webkit-transition: border, color 500ms linear 250ms;
          transition: border, color 500ms linear 250ms;
}
```

If you don't want all your properties to transition at the same rate, want some to have a greater delay than others, or if you just want a few properties to have a transition effect, include the various transition properties as a comma-separated list, including, at minimum, the `transition-property` and `transition-duration` for each:

```
nav a {
  background-color: #FFFFFF;
  border: 5px solid #CCCCCC;
  color: red;
  -webkit-transition:
    background-color, color 500ms linear 750ms,
    border 500ms linear 250ms;
  transition:
    background-color, color 500ms linear 750ms,
    border 500ms linear 250ms;
}
```

In this example, the border, which has the shortest `transition-delay`, will transition first. When the border has finished transitioning, at the 750 ms point—which is the `transition-delay` property, and the value of the 500 ms for the border transition plus the 250 ms delay—the `background-color` and `color` will both then transition over half a second:

```
transition-property:    background-color, color, border;
transition-duration:    500ms;
transition-timing-function: linear;
transition-delay:       750ms, 750ms, 250ms;
```

We could also have used the longhand properties, with each property comma separated, but that would have been more code in this scenario, as shown previously. I find the shorthand syntax easier to write, generally shorter to write, easier to understand, and easier to maintain.

In CubeeDoo, we transition our card flips over 0.25 s. We haven't learned how to flip a card yet (it's covered in the next section), but we can tell it to flip everything, immediately over 0.25 s with:

```
1    #board > div {
2        position: relative;
3        width: 23%;
4        height: 23%;
5        margin: 1%;
6        float: left;
7        -webkit-transition: 0.25s;
8        transition: 0.25s;      ...
```

In the default, pre-flipped state, in line 7 and 8, we tell the cards that when the state is changed, transition all (default for `transition-property`) the properties immediately (default for `transition-delay`) in the default `transition-timing-function` of `ease`.

I wrote `transition: 0.25s`, but I could have also written `transition: all 0.25s ease 0ms;`, which may be longer, but might be easier to maintain as author intentions are clearer with the latter.

CSS3 Transforms

Transforms allow you to resize, rotate, skew, translate, and otherwise reposition elements. There is a 2D version of the transforms module that is supported by all browsers, starting in IE9,[5] and another for 3D, with support spreading quickly.

Unlike transitions, transforms are supported in IE9.

CSS3 transforms allow for various transformations to be applied to an element, including multiple transforms on a single element.

Two CSS properties are used to create a transform: the `transform` property specifies the types of transformations you want to apply to the element, and the `transform-origin` property sets the point of origin from where the transform takes place.

The transform-origin Property

The first step we're covering is setting the origin of the transform. The `transform-origin` property establishes the origin of transformation for an element.

The default `transform-origin` value is `50% 50% 0`, which is the center of the element. The first value specified is the *x* coordinate, or left/right value, and the second value is the *y* coordinate, or the top/bottom value, with the values being calculated from the top left corner of the element. The third value is the z-offset, which is relevant when doing 3D transforms. The values can be specified using a length, a percentage, or the keywords `left`, `center`, `right`, `top`, `center`, and `bottom`, with the optional z-offset being a length only that is not a percentage.

The point set by the `transform-origin` is the point around which the transform will occur. As Figure 10-2 demonstrates, when the point of origin is set to the center point of an element (the default), the element will transform, in this case rotate, around that center point. When the `transform-origin` is set to a different location, such as the top left as shown in Figure 10-2, the element transforming, such as rotating, around the

---

5. Earlier versions of Internet Explorer support transitions via `filter: progid:DXImageTransform.Micro soft.Matrix()`.

---

origin point in the top left will create a different effect. The element orbits around this point.

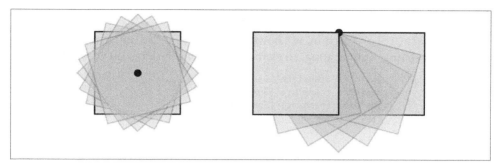

Figure 10-2. The point of origin set to default and set to top left will drastically alter the effect of a transform, showing the effect of rotating the element 90 degrees

The `transform-origin` on the left of Figure 10-2 is the default, so can be omitted. The syntax for the effect on the right can be written as:

```
-webkit-transform-origin: top left 0; /* all webkit & blink browsers */
   -moz-transform-origin: top left; /* FF 3.5 - 15 */
    -ms-transform-origin: 0 0; /* IE9 */
     -o-transform-origin: 0 0 0; /* O 11.0-12.0 */
        transform-origin: top 0 0; /* IE10+, FF16+, O12.1 only */
```

... where `top left`, `0 0, 0 0`, and `top left 0` are all equivalent.[6] Once the point of origin is set (or omitted, so set to the default value of `transform-origin: center center 0;`), the type of transform is applied. This is set with the `transform` property with a list of one or more transforms as the value.

The transform Property

Supported in Firefox 3.5+, Opera 10.5, Internet Explorer 9, and WebKit since before the iPhone even came out, the CSS `transform` property lets you modify the coordinate space of the CSS visual formatting model. Using it, elements can be translated, rotated, scaled, and skewed. CSS transforms modify the coordinate space, allowing us to change the position of the affected content without disrupting the normal flow. The location and amount of space a transformed element takes is the location and space used by the element before transforms were applied.

---

6. Vendor prefixing is required for IE9, Firefox 3.5 to 15, Opera through 12, and all versions of WebKit browsers. It is no longer required beginning with Firefox 16, IE10, Opera 12.1, and Opera Mobile 11. Opera Mini does not support transforms. All browsers that support `transform-origin` support all of the 2D transform functions. Opera was prefixless in version 12.1, but the `-webkit-` prefix became required when they changed the browser engine away from Presto.

We manipulate an element's appearance using transform functions. The value of the transform property is a list of space-separated transform functions applied in the order provided. The transform functions include:

translate()

The translate(x, y) function, as shown in Figure 10-3, is similar to relative positioning, translating, or relocating, an element by x from the left, and y from the top:

```
-webkit-transform: translate(15px, -15px);
    -ms-transform: translate(15px, -15px);
        transform: translate(15px, -15px);
```

translateX()

The translateX(x) function is similar to the translate() function, but only the left/right value is specified:

```
-webkit-transform: translatex(15px);
    -ms-transform: translatex(15px);
        transform: translatex(15px);
```

translateY()

The translateY(y) function is similar to the translate() function, but only the top/bottom value is specified:

```
-webkit-transform: translatey(-15px);
    -ms-transform: translatey(-15px);
        transform: translatey(-15px);
```

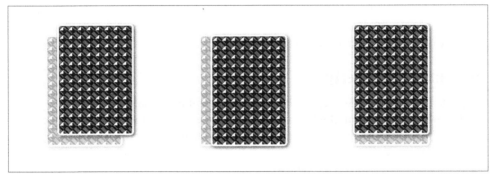

Figure 10-3. The transform's translate functions: translate(15px, −15px), translateX(15px), and translateY(−15px), respectively

scale()

The scale(w, h) property, as shown in Figure 10-4, scales an element by w width and h height:

```
-webkit-transform: scale(1.5, 2);
    -ms-transform: scale(1.5, 2);
        transform: scale(1.5, 2);
```

If only one value is declared, the scaling will be proportional. Since you likely don't want to distort an element, you'll generally see only one parameter in this transform function:

```
transform: scale(2);
```

Note that when you use transform to scale up, your element may appear blurry, as would be expected when you scale up images. For this reason, I generally recommend that if you need to scale up, start with an element that has been scaled down, and then scale up to `scale(1)`.

scaleX()

The `scaleX(w)` function is similar to the `scale()` function, but only the width value is specified. It is the same as declaring `scale(w, 1)`:

```
-webkit-transform: scalex(0.5);
    -ms-transform: scalex(0.5);
        transform: scalex(0.5);
```

 The `-o-` and `-moz-` prefixing for transforms is excluded, as Mozilla and Presto support transforms without a vendor prefix.

scaleY()

The `scaleY(h)` function is similar to the `scale()` function, but only the height value is specified. It is the same as declaring `scale(1, h)`:

```
-webkit-transform: scaley(2);
    -ms-transform: scaley(2);
        transform: scaley(2);
```

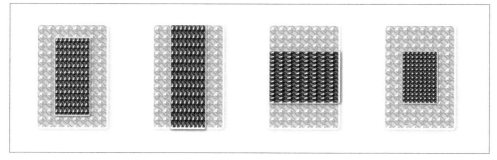

Figure 10-4. The transform's scale functions: scale(0.5, 0.75), scaleX(0.5), scaleY(0.5), and scale(0.5), respectively

rotate()

The rotate(angle) function, as shown in Figure 10-5, will rotate an element about the point of origin (featured in Figure 10-2) by the angle value specified:

```
-webkit-transform: rotate(15deg);
    -ms-transform: rotate(15deg);
        transform: rotate(15deg);
```

rotateX()

The rotateX(angle) function will rotate an element about its x-axis, offset by the origin point if one is set:

```
-webkit-transform: rotatex(15deg);
    -ms-transform: rotatex(15deg);
        transform: rotatex(15deg);
```

Rotating an element 90 deg along the x-axis will make it disappear, and 180 deg will flip it completely over so that you see it upside down from the backside. Whether or not you see the contents when flipped can be set with the backface-visibility property described on page 324.

rotateY()

Similar to rotateX(), the rotateY(angle) function will rotate an element about its y-axis at the angle value specified:

```
-webkit-transform: rotatey(15deg);
    -ms-transform: rotatey(15deg);
        transform: rotatey(15deg);
```

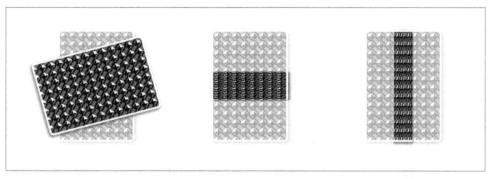

Figure 10-5. The transform's rotate functions: rotate(75deg), rotateX(75deg), and rotateY(75deg), respectively (rotateX rotates along the x-axis, and would disappear at 90 deg, becoming upside down with inverted text over 90 degrees)

In CubeeDoo, we use rotateY(180deg) in our animation when the user clicks on a card, flipping the card container, so the back of the card is hidden and we can see the face.

We then animate it back with `rotate(0deg)`, or if you prefer `rotate(360deg)` for a continuous rotation, if the player was not successful in making a match.

skew()

The `skew(x,y)` function, as shown in Figure 10-6, specifies a skew along the x- and y-axis. The x specifies the skew on the x-axis, the y specifies the skew on the y-axis. If there is only one parameter, then it's the same as `skew(x, 0deg)`, or `skewX(x)`. The values are angles, degrees, turns or grads:

```
-webkit-transform: skew(15deg, 4deg);
    -ms-transform: skew(15deg, 4deg);
        transform: skew(15deg, 4deg);
```

skewX()

The `skewX(x)` function is similar to the `skew()` value, but only the x-axis value is specified, and the skew will only be along the x-axis, instead of both the x- and y-axis. The top and bottom of the box will stay level, and the left and right will skew:

```
-webkit-transform: skewx(15deg);
    -ms-transform: skewx(15deg);
        transform: skewx(15deg);
```

skewY()

The `skewY(y)` function is similar to the `skew()` value, but only the y-axis value is specified. It is similar to declaring `skew(0deg, y)`. The left and right sides of the box will stay vertical, and the top and bottom will skew:

```
-webkit-transform: skewy(-3deg);
    -ms-transform: skewy(-3deg);
        transform: skewy(-3deg);
```

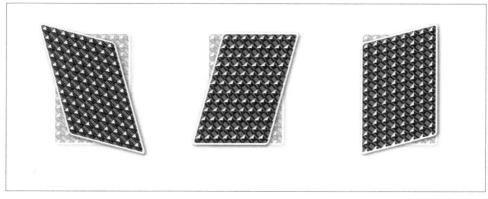

Figure 10-6. The transform's skew functions: skew(15deg, 15deg), skewX(−15deg), and skewY(−15deg), respectively

Declaring skewX(x) or skewY(y) is similar but not the same as declaring skew(x, 0deg) and skew(0deg, y), respectively. If you only declare one of the two on an element, it is indeed the same thing, but declaring skew(x, 0deg) and skew(0deg, y) would lead to the latter overwriting the former, whereas skewX(x) or skewY(y) would actually be equivalent to writing skew(x, y); because the properties are being combined, rather than overwritten. Figure 10-6 shows the skew functions.

Multiple Transforms

The previous section showed single transforms, but you can include more than one transform on an element. To include more than one transform, simply separate the transform functions with spaces:

```
.enlargen:hover, .enlargen.hover {
  -webkit-transform: translate(-50%, -50%) scale(2) rotate(0deg);
     -ms-transform: translate(-50%, -50%) scale(2) rotate(0deg);
         transform: translate(-50%, -50%) scale(2) rotate(0deg);
}
```

This makes the element twice as tall and twice as wide. By translating the element 50% up and to the left, the bottom-right corner should remain in the exact same location. Declaring rotate(0deg) is unnecessary, since any transforms declared with a selector with weaker specificity that included a rotate function would be overwritten, regardless of whether we included the rotate function. I've included this as a reference for how to include the rotate() transform function, and to remind you to include the unit whenever you are using non-length units.

 Even though the rotation value is zero degrees, you must include the unit for degrees, just as you must with time (s or ms), rads, grads, turns, Hz, and kHzs.

Note that the transition-property property values are comma separated, and the transform functions are space separated.

This enlargen class may be something you would want to add to an image gallery, highlighting an image that is hovered by making it four times larger (twice as wide and twice as tall) and remove any tilt that might have been interesting as a thumbnail, but tacky in full size.

matrix()

The matrix() transform function is a single function that defines the translation, skew, rotation, and scaling of an element. It takes six parameters. If you use a tool to create a transform, the software generally produces a matrix function rather than four separate transform functions. The two following lines could be equal, with the last two matrix values depending on the size and location of the element being transformed:

```
transform: translate(-50%, -50%) scale(2) rotate(0deg);
transform: matrix(2, 0, 0, 2, -100, -172.5)
```

Generally, if you see a `matrix` in CSS markup, it has been computer generated. You likely won't ever write a `matrix` value. I included it here so you understand what it is, but not necessarily exactly what it means, if you come across it.

Transitioning Transformations

Under the `transition-property` property, I listed all the properties that could be transformed. If you include the `all` keyword when declaring the `transition-property`, or the shorthand `transition`, the `transform` property will be included as part of `all`.

You can declare the transform individually as part of the comma-separated list of transition properties. If including the actual transform as a property in the list, it should include the browser vendor prefix if the browser requires it:

```
p {
    -webkit-transition: -webkit-transform 500ms linear 250ms;
            transition: transform 500ms linear 250ms;
    -webkit-transform: translate(0) rotate(0deg);
        -ms-transform: translate(0) rotate(0deg);
            transform: translate(0) rotate(0deg);

}

p:hover {
    -webkit-transform: translate(100px, -100px) rotate(90deg);
        -ms-transform: translate(100px, -100px) rotate(90deg);
            transform: translate(100px, -100px) rotate(90deg);
    padding: 3px;
    border: 5px solid #00ff00;
}
```

We included `-ms-` for the transform but not the transition, since transitions only received support in IE10, and transforms are prefixed in IE9 but not IE10.

3D Transform Functions

Browsers have been a bit slower in supporting 3D transforms, but they're getting there. 3D transforms have been supported since iOS 3.2, Android 3, Blackberry 10, Firefox 10, IE10, Safari 4, and Chrome 12, all with vendor prefixes. 3D transforms are slated to be supported in Opera 15 with the Blink rendering engine. 3D transforms have only been supported since iPhone 2 (not the original), and is only supported if you have Mac OS X v10.6 or newer.

CSS 3D transforms enable positioning elements on the page in three-dimensional space. Just like before, you can combine 3D transforms with transitions (and animations described later) to create 3D motion.

Similar to the 2D transform functions, most browsers support 3D transform properties, starting with IE10. As of this writing, the `-webkit-` prefix is required for WebKit and Blink browsers.

A few things to note about 3D transforms is that elements that are transformed into a 3D space (1) are hardware-accelerated, and (2) have their own stacking context.

translate3d()

The `translate3d(x, y, z)` function moves the element x to the right, y from the top, and z toward the user (away if the value is negative). Unlike x and y, the z value cannot be a percentage.

translateZ()

The `translateZ(z)` function is similar to the `translate3d()` function, but only affects the z positioning. A positive z moves the element toward the user, and a negative value moves the element away from the user. The parameter can be any length units other than percentages.

Because of the benefits of hardware acceleration, `translateZ(0)` is often used as a cure-all (similar to how `zoom:1` was a panacea for IE6), to put rendering onto the GPU and out of the CPU, improving rendering performance.

When it comes to paint times, the GPU performs better than the CPU. In animating elements with not insignificant paint times, getting the element elevated onto its own layer on the GPU, called a RenderLayer, will be faster and make your animation less janky. When it sits on its own layer, any 2D transform, 3D transform, or opacity changes can happen purely on the GPU, which will stay extremely fast—providing for the capability of frame rates over 60 fps.

Note, as elements in a 3D context have their own stacking context, any elements you want to appear above the transformed elements (as though they have a higher z-index), which are not nested within the transformed element, must also be transformed into the 3D space. To do this, developers attach `transform: translateZ(0)` to elements that would otherwise not need to be transformed.

scale3d()

The `scale3d(w, h, z)` function scales the element's width (w), height (h), and z-scale (z). The z-scale affects the scaling along the z-axis in transformed children.

scaleZ()

Similar to the `scale3d()` function, the `scaleZ(z)` provides a value for the z-scale only, affecting the scaling along the z-axis in the element and its descendants that are not absolutely positioned.

rotate3d()

The `rotate3d(x, y, z, angle)` function will rotate an element in 3D space. The first two forms simply rotate the element about the horizontal and vertical axes. Angle units can be degrees (deg), radians (rad), or gradians (grad). The last form allows you to rotate the element around an arbitrary vector in 3D space; x, y, and z should specify the unit vector you wish to rotate around. The browser will normalize the appearance.

perspective()

The `perspective(p)` transform function allows you to put some perspective into the transformation matrix. The `perspective()` transform function allows you to get a perspective effect for a single element:

```
transform: perspective(100px) rotatey(3deg);
```

Perspective can also be applied with the `perspective` property, which applies to the children of an element.

Other 3D Transform Properties

Earlier we were introduced to some transform properties. To successfully implement 3D transforms, we are provided with some new properties, and enhancements to some properties introduced for 2D transforms.

The transform-origin property revisited

As we learned earlier, the `transform-origin` property establishes the origin of transformation for an element. In 3D transforms, this property now accepts a z-offset value. `transform-origin` accepts three values, allowing you to specify a z-offset for the transform origin:

```
transform-origin: 0 0 500px;
```

While the effect only got support starting with Safari 4+ on Mac OS X v10.6 and newer, and iPhone 2.0 and newer (not the original iPhone), earlier browser versions that supported `transform-origin` support this property as if only two values are declared.

The perspective property

Not to be confused with the 3D transforms `perspective()` function, the `perspective` property, written with browser prefix, is used to give an illusion of depth; it determines how things change size based on their z-offset from the z=0 plane.

Objects on the z=0 plane appear in their normal size. Something at a z-offset of p/2 (halfway between the viewer and the z=0 plane) will look twice as big, and something at a z-offset of –p will look half as big. Thus, large values give a little foreshortening effect, and small values lots of foreshortening. Values between 500 px and 1,000 px give a reasonable-looking result for most content.

The default origin for the perspective effect is the center of the element's border box, but you can control this with `perspective-origin`.

Perspective does not affect the element directly, but rather it affects the appearance of the 3D transforms on the transformed descendants of that element, enabling the descendants to share the same perspective as they are translated, or moved, around the viewport.

So, you're wondering, what's the difference between `perspective: 600px` and `transform: perspective(600px)`? You would attach the former to a parent element so that all of the descendants have the same vanishing point. You would attach the latter to the actual element you're transforming to give it its own perspective.

The transform-style property

The `transform-style` property defines how nested elements are rendered in 3D space. All of these 3D transform effects are just painting effects. Those transformed children are still rendering into the plane of their parent; in other words, they are flattened.

When you start to build hierarchies of objects with 3D transforms, parents and children should live in a shared three-dimensional space and share the same perspective, which propagates up from some container, not flattened. This is where `transform-style` comes in.

The `transform-style` property takes one of two values: `flat` and `preserves-3d`. The default value of `flat` flattens the transformed children into the plane of their parent. The `preserves-3d` value dictates that those children live in a shared 3D space with the element.

The backface-visibility property

The `backface-visibility` property specifies whether the element is visible or not when that element is transformed such that its back face is toward the viewer. The property takes one of two values: `visible` (the default) or `hidden`.

For example, in CubeeDoo, we flip a two-sided card to show the card face when the card is selected. When we see the face, we don't want to see the back of the card, and vice versa, so we could set `backface-visiblity` to `hidden`.

Putting It All Together

We use a lot of the features just listed in our card flipping in CubeeDoo:

```
#board > div {
    position: relative;
    width: 23%;
    height: 23%;
    margin: 1%;
    float: left;
    -webkit-transition: 0.25s;
    transition: 0.25s;
    -webkit-transform: rotatey(0deg);
    transform: rotatey(0deg);
    -webkit-transform-style: preserve-3d;
    transform-style: preserve-3d;
    box-shadow: 1px 1px 1px rgba(0,0,0,0.25);
    cursor: pointer; /* for desktop */
}
#board.level2 > div {
    height: 19%;
}
#board.level3 > div {
    height: 15%;
}
.back,
.face,
.back:after,
.face:after {
    position: absolute;
    content: "";
    top: 0;
    left: 0;
    right: 0;
    bottom: 0;
    border-radius: 3px;
    pointer-events: none;
    -webkit-backface-visibility: hidden;
    backface-visibility: hidden;
}
.back {
    border: 5px solid white;
}

.back:after {
    font-size: 2.5rem;
    line-height: 100%;
    background:
        50% 50% no-repeat,
        0 0 no-repeat #fff;
    font-style: normal;
```

```
        box-shadow: inset 1px 1px 0 currentcolor,
            inset -1px -1px 0 currentcolor,
            1px 1px 1px rgba(0,0,0,0.1);
        color: rgb(119, 160, 215);
        background-image:
            url('data:image/svg+xml;utf8,<svg width="40" height="40"
              xmlns="http://www.w3.org/2000/svg"><g><text xml:space="preserve"
              text-anchor="middle" font-family="serif" font-size="40" id="svg_1"
              y="30" x="20" stroke-width="0" stroke="rgb(119, 160, 215)"
              fill="rgb(119, 160, 215)">❀</text></g></svg>'),
            -webkit-linear-gradient(-15deg,
              rgba(0, 0, 0, 0), rgba(0, 0, 0, 0.025));
        background-image:
            url('data:image/svg+xml;utf8,<svg width="40" height="40"
              xmlns="http://www.w3.org/2000/svg"><g><text xml:space="preserve"
              text-anchor="middle" font-family="serif" font-size="40" id="svg_1"
              y="30" x="20" stroke-width="0" stroke="rgb(119, 160, 215)"
              fill="rgb(119, 160, 215)">❀</text></g></svg>'),
            linear-gradient(75deg,
              rgba(0, 0, 0, 0), rgba(0, 0, 0, 0.025));
        -webkit-transform: rotatey(0deg);
        -webkit-transform: rotatey(0deg) translatez(0);
        transform: rotatey(0deg)
        transform: rotatey(0deg) translatez(0);
    }
    .face {
        -webkit-transform: rotatey(180deg);
        -ms-transform: rotatey(180deg);
        transform: rotatey(180deg);
    }
    #board > div.flipped {
        -webkit-transform: rotatey(180deg);
        -webkit-transform: rotatey(180deg) translatez(0);
        transform: rotatey(180deg);
        transform: rotatey(180deg) translatez(0);
        box-shadow: -1px 1px 1px rgba(0,0,0,0.25);
    }
```

In CubeeDoo, we use transforms to flip the card, and transitions to do the flip in 250 milliseconds. The cards are shells with two children: the face and back of the card. Because we are using CSS classes to style the front of our cards, we can create all our card faces with generated content. It is easier to maintain a single code path. So, although we could have put the colors' color scheme directly on the face with background-color, and put the SVG shapes as a background-image directly on the face <div>, the number and second shapes theme need to be generated content. To simplify, we put the SVG and colors on the ::after pseudoelement generated content as well.

When the user taps or clicks on a card, the card flips. This is done with transform: rotatey(180deg) translatez(0); on the card container. The issue is that the HTML always has the back *after* the face in the source order:

```
<div data-value="0" data-position="2">
    <div class="face"></div>
    <div class="back"></div>
</div>
```

Therefore, the back will always sit on top of the face. To hide the back when the card is flipped and show the face instead, we add `backface-visibility: hidden;`. That way, when the card is facing away from us, we do not see the elements that are facing away from us (we'll see the face and not the back).

By adding the 3D transform of `translateZ(0)`, we hardware accelerate it in supportive devices, ensuring that the animation will be performed on the GPU instead of the CPU. The reason we include four declarations:

```
-webkit-transform: rotatey(180deg);
-webkit-transform: rotatey(180deg) translatez(0);
        transform: rotatey(180deg);
        transform: rotatey(180deg) translatez(0);
```

... is because not all browsers support 3D transforms. If a browser doesn't understand a line of CSS, it skips the whole property/value declaration. Therefore, we first declare without `translateZ()` for browsers that don't understand it, then with `translateZ()` for browsers that do, both prefixed and unprefixed. That third line—unprefixed yet targeting browsers not supporting 3D—will be understood by browsers that support transforms but not 3D transforms.

We also include `transform-style: preserve-3d`, as we want to ensure the front and the back of the card—the card's children—are in the same 3D space as the card.

As we move from game level 1 to level 2 to level 3, the height of the cards gets smaller. Since our transition declaration of 0.25 s is on the default state, when the cards shrink, they do so over 0.25 s.

Generally, you don't want to transition `height`. Transitioning box model properties causes the browser to reflow every frame, causing unnecessary reflows and repaints. This is even more of an issue on mobile, and is exacerbated by having a large number of DOM nodes. A possible solution would be to transition a `transform: scaleY (0.8)`, as that would maintain the cards' width but only shrink the height, but this will distort the shapes and number themes. We'll leave this as is. The card height changes only happen a maximum of two times per game. We were careful not to have too many DOM nodes. This transition, with the recalculation of all of the DOM nodes, while not optimal, works well enough for this scenario.

A better solution would be to animate the scaling and switch out the class based on the animation end. As you'll see next, animation is much more powerful than transitions. With animations, we would be able to change a class or otherwise add event listeners at the animation's end.

CSS3 Animation

As a counterpart to transitions and transforms, explicit animations provide a way to declare repeating animated effects with keyframes.

For simple transitions, when the starting value and ending value are known, and only a single iteration of the animation is required, the `transition` properties may suffice for your animating needs. If you need finer control of the intermediate values of your animation, or you need to repeat your animation, the animation properties of the CSS3 animation module, with keyframes, can be used.

The animation properties include:

`animation-name`

> The name you gave your keyframe animation definition, or a comma-separated list of multiple animation names. The default value is none, or no animation. Obviously, therefore, you need to include an `animation-name` if you want an element to be animated.

`animation-duration`

> The length of time in seconds or milliseconds an animation takes to complete one cycle. The default value is 0s, which means that no visible animation will take place. In other words, the `animation-duration` property, with a value of greater than 0 seconds, is required.

`animation-timing-function`

> How the animation will progress over one cycle of its duration, taking the same values as the `transition-timing-function`. Although the values are discreet, you can "animate" the `animation-timing-function` in your keyframe definitions. The default value is ease.

`animation-iteration-count`

> Number of times an animation cycle is played as an integer, or infinite. The default value is a single iteration.

`animation-direction`

> Whether or not the animation should play in reverse on alternate cycles (alternate) or not (normal).

`animation-play-state`

> Defines whether the animation is running or paused. A paused animation displays the current value of the animation in a static state. When a paused animation is resumed, it restarts from the current value. The default value is running.

`animation-delay`

Defines when the animation will start. Interestingly, if the value is negative, the animation will start partway through the animation. For example, in a 10 second animation, if the `animation-delay` is `-4s`, the animation will start immediately 40% of the way through the first animation cycle.

`animation-fill-mode`

Defines what values are applied by the animation before the animation starts and after it ends. There are 4 possible values:

`backwards`

Applies the values defined in its 0% keyframe as soon as the animation is applied, staying on the 0% keyframe through the duration of the `animation-delay`.

`forwards`

Maintains the values defined in the last keyframe after the animation is complete, until the animation style is removed from any selector targeting that node.

`both`

Implements both *forwards* and *backwards* after the end and before the start of the animation respectively.

`none`

The default value, does nothing, or removes any `forwards` or `backwards` type behaviors.

`animation`

The shorthand for the animation properties, space-separated values for the `animation-name`, `animation-duration`, `animation-timing-function`, `animation-delay`, `animation-iteration-count`, `animation-direction`, and `animation-fill-mode` properties. For a multiple animation declaration, include a grouping for each animation name, with each shorthand grouping separated by a comma.

Keyframes

Keyframe animations involve setting the state of your elements at different stages of an animation. Keyframes are specified using the `@keyframes` rule. The rule consists of the keyword `@keyframes`, followed by an identifier giving a name for the animation followed by a set of style rules encased in curly braces ({}). You create the identifier[7] (name) of

---

7. In CSS, IDENTs, or identifiers, including element names, classes, IDs, and keyframe animation names, and can contain only the characters [a-zA-Z0-9] and ISO 10646 characters U+00A0 and higher, plus the hyphen (-) and the underscore (_); they cannot start with a digit, two hyphens, or a hyphen followed by a digit. Identifiers are *not* quoted.

your animation. Do not quote the animation name or identifier. This name is the name used as the value of the `animation-name` property.

The keyframe selector for a keyframe style rule consists of a comma-separated list of values. You can use percentage values or the keywords `from` and `to`. For example:

```
@keyframes crazyText {
    from {
        font-size: 1em;
    }
    to {
        font-size: 2em;
    }
}
```

In WebKit browsers, this would read as follows:[8]

```
@-webkit-keyframes crazyText {
    from {
        font-size: 1em;
    }
    to {
        font-size: 2em;
    }
}
```

The keyword `from` is equivalent to the value 0%. The keyword `to` is equivalent to the value 100%. Note that the percentage unit specifier must be used. Therefore, "0" is an invalid keyframe selector.

If you need to define more than two points, more than the start and finish of an animation, having more granular control of the animation by defining keyframes for points in between, use percentages. For example:

```
@-prefix-keyframes rainbow {
0% {
    background-color: red;
}
20% {
    background-color: orange;
}
40% {
    background-color: yellow;
}
60% {
    background-color: green;
}
```

---

8. Animations are supported in IE10, BlackBerry, Android, Chrome for Mobile, iOS, and all modern mobile browsers. They are not supported in Opera Mini, which is expected. They are still prefixed only in WebKit browsers and Boot2Gecko. Firefox dropped the prefix in Firefox 16, Opera with Opera 12.1, with Opera Mobile never having support for the prefixed version. IE began supporting animations with IE10, sans prefix.

```
80% {
    background-color: blue;
}
100% {
    background-color: purple;
}
}
```

The keyframe selectors are used to specify the percentage along the duration of the animation that the keyframe represents. An analogy would be that the 20%, 40%, 60%, and so on are pseudoclasses of the transition duration (they're not, but you can think of them that way). The keyframe is specified by the style rules (the code block of property values) declared on the keyframe selector.

The percentage or keyframe selector determines the placement of the keyframe in the animation. To make them easy to follow, I recommend keeping the keyframe selectors in order of the progression, from 0% to 100%, though this is not required.

Style blocks for keyframe selectors consist of properties and values. The animatable properties are listed in "CSS3 Transforms" on page 314. Properties that are unable to be animated are ignored in these rules.

To determine the set of keyframes, all of the values in selectors are sorted in increasing order by time. Keyframe selectors do not cascade; therefore an animation will never derive keyframes from more than one keyframe selector. If there are any duplicates, then the last keyframe selector specified inside the `@keyframes` rule will be used to provide the keyframe information for that time.

The animation engine will smoothly interpolate style between the keyframe selectors. In these examples, shown in the online chapter resources with an animation duration of 10 seconds with linear animation timing function: at the 5 second mark, the `crazy Text` is at `font-size: 1.5em` and the element with the "rainbow" animation has a yellowish-green background.

Applying animations

We may have defined an animation, but we haven't attached an animation to any elements. Once we have defined an animation with `@keyframes`, we apply it using, at minimum, the two required properties: `animation-name` and `animation-duration`. The other related animation properties are optional:

```
div {
  animation-name: crazyText;
  animation-duration: 1s;
  animation-iteration-count: 20;
  animation-direction: alternate;
  animation-delay: 5s;
  animation-fill-mode: both;
}
```

The preceding rule attaches the "crazyText" animation, sets the duration to 1 second per iteration, makes it execute a total of 20 times with every other iteration play in reverse, waiting 5 seconds before commencing the first iteration.

The `animation-fill-mode` of both means that when this `<div>` is first rendered to the page, the `font-size` will be set to `1em` as per the `0%` or `from` keyframe, prior to the 5 second delay before the first iteration starts.

The `font-size` will then double in size over one second, then shrink back to `1em` over the next second because we set `animation-direction: alternate`. Had we set `animation-direction: normal`, or omitted the `animation-direction` property altogether, the `font-size` would have doubled in size over one second, and then jumped back to `1em` before doubling over one second again in the second iteration and all subsequent iterations.

When the animation has completed the 20 iterations, 25 seconds after the animation was applied (20 one-second iterations plus a five-second delay), the `font-size` will remain at the last keyframe because we set `animation-fill-mode: both`. With `animation-direction: alternate`, the `font-size` will be `1em`. Had we omitted the `animation-direction` property altogether or set `animation-direction: normal`, then the last keyframe would have been at 2 em. The `<div>` will remain at this font size "forever" unless a `font-size` declaration targeting this node overrides it.

This could have been written, with some padding and the rainbow animation added, with the shorthand:

```
div {
  padding: 20px;
  animation:
    crazyText 1s 20 5s alternate both,
    rainbow 4s infinite alternate;
}
```

Bouncing ball animation

As with transitions, any property that has a discoverable midpoint can be animated. Two exceptions are `visibilility` and `animation-timing-function`. Neither has a midpoint, but both can be added to a keyframe style block.

If you include the `animation-timing-function` in a keyframe, the animation will switch from the default or current timing function to the newly declared timing function at that point. Rarely used, this can actually come in handy. For example, if you are creating a bouncing ball, gravity dictates that the ball will get progressively faster (or `ease-in`) as it drops, and progressively slower as it bounces up (or `ease-out`):

```
@keyframes bouncing {
  0% {
    bottom: 200px;
    left: 0;
    animation-timing-function: ease-in;
  }
  40%, 70%, 90%{
    animation-timing-function: ease-out;
    bottom: 0;
  }
  55% {
    bottom: 50px;
    animation-timing-function: ease-in;
  }
  80% {
    bottom: 25px;
    animation-timing-function: ease-in;
  }
  95% {
    bottom: 10px;
    animation-timing-function: ease-in;
  }
  100% {
    left: 110px;
    bottom: 0;
    animation-timing-function: ease-out;
  }
}
```

There are several things to note about this code example (which is in the online chapter resources). We have three keyframes that have the exact same values—the 40%, 70%, and 90% keyframes—so we put them all on one line. We separated the keyframe selectors with commas just as we do normal CSS selectors.

We have more than one property being animated, but we don't declare all the values in every keyframe block. The left-to-right motion is smooth, and therefore we only needed to declare that property twice: in both the 0% and 100% blocks. We did move the ball up and down numerous times with granular control, so unlike the `left` value, we declared the `bottom` value in every keyframe.

We've also *animated* or changed the `animation-timing-function` to make the bounce look smooth and natural. Without it, our bouncing ball animation was very jumpy. The `animation-timing-function` is the only animation property that can be included within in keyframe declarations.[9]

---

9. To learn more about how to code animations, the online chapter resources have links to an animation tutorial deck that shows every animation property "in action."

Animating sprites

Generally when I think of HTML and animation, I think of animating a single node to a new position, or something dreadfully boring. One feature of CSS animations is creating character animations, like animating lemmings as they jump, or in this case float, off a cliff.

Figure 10-7. A sprite of a lemming for character animation

To create character animation using a sprite, we use the `animation-timing-function: step(x, start)` value. The step values don't move smoothly through the keyframes. Rather, they break up the animation into the number of steps declared and jump from one step to the next. To animate the sprite in Figure 10-7, we move the background image:

```
.lemming {
    height: 32px;
    width: 32px;
    background-image:url(lemming.gif);
    background-repeat: no-repeat;
    -webkit-animation: lemming 1s steps(8,end) alternate infinite;
    animation: lemming 1s steps(8,end) alternate infinite;
}
@-webkit-keyframes lemming {
  from {
    background-position: 0 0;
  }
  to {
    background-position: -256px 0;
  }
}

@keyframes lemming {
  from {
    background-position: 0 0;
  }
  to {
    background-position: -256px 0;
  }
}
```

Note that the sprite is 256 px wide, so our `background-position: 256px 0;` would normally show no background image. With `animation-timing-function`, you can declare `steps(x, start)`, which specifies that the change in the property value happens at the start of each step and `steps(x, end)`, which means the change in property comes at the end of the step.

Let's use an animation with five steps. If you declare `steps(5, start)` the jump will be at the start of the step, so you'll get five steps at the 20%, 40%, 60%, 80%, and 100% marks—or basically the 0% really doesn't show, because the change in property from 0 to 20% happens at the start of the step, the viewer sees the 20% mark from 0 to 20% time. If you declare `steps(5, end)`, the jump to the next step will be at the end of the interval, so it will appear to show the 0%, 20%, 40%, 60%, and 80% marks. This is why our last "step" is beyond the width of the sprite since the 100% mark is never shown.

By creating a motion sprite and animating the `background-position`, moving that sprite using steps, you can create motion animations. The online chapter resources have more examples of sprite animation.

CubeeDoo animations

In CubeeDoo, we have very simple animations. When a pair of cards is matched, the cards are animated as they disappear. And, when a score is a high score, it is highlighted with a blink-like animation in the high score area on larger screens:

```
#board > div.matched {
    -webkit-animation: fade 250ms both;
    animation: fade 250ms both;
}
#board > div.matched:nth-of-type(1) {
    -webkit-animation-delay: 250ms;
    animation-delay: 250ms;
}

@-webkit-keyframes fade {
    0%  {
        -webkit-transform: scale(1.0) rotatey(180deg) rotate(0) translatez(0);
    }
    100% {
        -webkit-transform: scale(0) rotatey(180deg) rotate(720deg) translatez(0);
    }
}
@keyframes fade {
    0%  {
        transform: scale(1.0) rotatey(180deg) rotate(0) translatez(0);
    }
    100% {
        transform: scale(0) rotatey(180deg) rotate(720deg) translatez(0);
    }
}
```

```
#highscores li.current {
    -webkit-animation:
        winner 500ms linear 8 alternate forwards;
    animation:
        winner 500ms linear 8 alternate forwards;
}
@-webkit-keyframes winner {
    0% {background-color: hsla(74, 64%, 59%,1);}
    100%{background-color: hsla(74, 64%, 59%,0)}
}
@keyframes winner {
    0% {background-color: hsla(74, 64%, 59%,1);}
    100%{background-color: hsla(74, 64%, 59%,0)}
}
```

When the matched class is added to a card, the fade animation gets attached to that card. The matched class is added to the two cards that have the flipped class if the two flipped cards match. Otherwise, if the two flipped cards aren't a match, the flipped class is removed, and the transition described in our sections on transitions occurs. We've included 3D transforms to ensure that the animation is handled on the GPU instead of the CPU if possible in the browser and device.

The fade animation is a misnomer. It doesn't fade. It spins and shrinks over 250 ms. At the end of the animation, the JavaScript removes both the flipped and matched classes, and resets and hides the card by setting data-value="0" attribute/value pair.

When the game ends, the list of high scores is regenerated. If the current high score is one of the top 5 high scores, the class current gets added to the score as it gets written to the page. We control adding and removing class names with JavaScript, and we create and execute animations with CSS purely based on the class. In the case of a high score, the winner animation is executed, which is a fading green background color that pulses on and off eight times: four times from fully opaque to fully transparent, and four times from fully transparent to fully opaque. This is controlled by declaring animation-iterations: 8; with animation-direction: alternate; in the shorthand animation property. The current high score will remain with a green background until the scores are redrawn. We didn't put this animation in a 3D space as we are doing a very simple repaint with no reflow, so it should perform well by default.

Transitions, Animations, and Performance

CSS animations allow you to write declarative rules for animations, replacing lots of hard-to-maintain animation code in JavaScript.

Browsers are optimized to handle CSS animations. As such, CSS animations are more performant than JavaScript animations. If you can, always use CSS to animate instead of JavaScript. By using CSS, you allow the browser to optimize tweening and frame skipping, letting the browser optimize for performance.

While CSS animations are more performant than JavaScript animations, there are some drawbacks. Similar to JavaScript animations, CSS animations do suck up battery power. But CSS doesn't occupy the CPU like JavaScript, so will generally be less jumpy.

CSS has last priority on the UI thread. This means that if you are downloading a huge JavaScript file that takes eight seconds to load, the page will not start animating during those eight seconds. While this may not seem like a big issue, there is a quirk: while the animation won't start, the `animation-delay` expires. So, if you have 15 animations each starting a second apart using animation delay of 0 s, 1 s, 2 s, and so on, the first eight animations will all happen when the page had finally finished loading and rendering, and the next seven animations will each occur when they were timed to occur.

To resolve this issue, you can add a `loaded` class to the document and base the animations on being an element that is a descendant of the `loaded` class.

Also, some properties perform better than others when animated. If you change the layout of the page forcing a reflow, the animation will not perform as well as when your animation is simply a repaint of an object. For example, the increase font size animation we did earlier is a stupid animation! The animation forces repeated reflows of the page: as font resizes, the element is resized. As the element is resized, the entire document is reflowed before the repaint. If we simply scaled the element using CSS transforms, and animated the transform, the browser would only be redrawing the animated element, which performs much better.

Remember that reflows are expensive and take more rendering time. To appear smooth, you want your animation frames to be fully drawn in under 16.67 ms.

There is also an animations API to capture events from the CSS animations. `animation Start`, `animationEnd`, and `animationIteration` are events that occur with every iteration of the animation. We aren't detailing this here, but there are links to resources in the online chapter resources.

We're not done with CSS: we still have a few more features to discuss, which we do in Chapter 11.

CSS Features in Responsive Web Design

Your content should be designed to work on any device because it will be viewed on every device, everywhere. The website we're building today with the goal of displaying it on a desktop, smartphone, and tablet may be viewed on a 52-inch TV screen or 3 × 5-inch GPS LCD screen. By starting with a flexible foundation, your site should be able to grow or shrink gracefully no matter the hardware that loads it.

For your website to adapt to any screen size, you want to make it as flexible as possible. Using percents and rems, instead of pixels for widths and font size, will bring you 90% of the way there. Add in some media queries, and you're 95% of the way there.

There are several CSS features, other than media queries and other CSS3 features we've covered so far, that are helpful in developing responsive websites and will bring you up to the 99% mark. Why 99% and not 100%? There is always more you can do to make a site more responsive, more accessible, prettier, faster, etc., but at some point, you have to say "this is good enough" or "this book is way too long."

Media Queries, Breakpoints, and Fluid Layouts

I mentioned this before, but it bears repeating: don't create layouts for specific phone sizes. Rather, slowly expand (or shrink) your site in a browser. When the layout starts looking less than optimal, that is where you should alter your design for the next set of devices. You may need eight layouts for tiny, xx-small, small, medium, large, x-large, xx-large, and huge screens, or you may have a single layout that works well across all devices. You won't know until you view the layout in varying sizes, but do view your layout in a plethora of sizes to make sure your layout works well everywhere.

As you change the size of your browser and decide that a new layout is needed, the width at which the layout changes is called a *breakpoint*. Don't just select 320, 480, 640, and 960 as breakpoints because that is what everyone else is doing. Instead, do what makes sense for your site.

When you determine that you need a breakpoint, use media queries to target a span of viewport sizes with a specific layout. You also don't have to choose a single breakpoint. You can alter the layout of your header, footer, navigation, and main content at different breakpoints if that makes the most sense. There is no right or wrong, there is just better and not as good.

Once you've determined where the breakpoints are for your design or for the usability of your application, you can target the layout changes and feature highlighting with media queries. You can also target high pixel-density displays with larger images, remembering that larger images mean larger file sizes. You can use JavaScript with media queries to send high DPI images only to high pixel-density displays with good bandwidth, and perhaps one day we'll be able to match media queries to bandwidth—but we're not there yet.

We covered media queries in Chapters 2 and 7, so you should already understand the syntax.

Multiple Columns

The CSS `columns` property enables us to create multiple columns for laying out text like a newspaper. The `columns` property is shorthand for `column-count` and `column-width`.

The `column-width` property is the optimal column width, as if you were declaring a `min-column-width`, which is not an actual property. The `column-count` is the maximum number of columns, as if you were declaring `max-column-count`, which is also not an actual property.

The `column-count` property has precedence. The browser adjusts the width of the column around that suggested `column-width`, providing for up to as many columns as listed as the integer value of `column-count`, as long as each column is at least as wide as the length value provided as the value for `column-width`. Columns allow for scalable designs that fit different screen widths.

We define the gap between columns with the `column-gap` property, and whether to include a dividing line between columns by declaring a line with the `column-rule` rule property. The `column-gap` property takes as its value a length, with the default value being the key term `normal`, which is `1em` in most browsers.

Using columns will make your very wide areas of content more legible. And, as viewport sizes narrow, the number of columns will shrink. While your 24-inch monitor may see six columns, your HTC One in portrait mode will only have one column if the following style is set:

```
columns: 240px 6;
```

The preceding line reads "divide the element's content into a maximum of six columns, ensuring that no column is narrower than 240 px wide." The iPhone is 320 px wide, so you can't fit two columns in portrait mode, but you could in landscape if there was no padding or gap. A 1920 × 1080 display could fit eight columns, with no column gap. However, the browser will not render more than six columns, even if more columns of the declared width could fit in the space provided.

Similar to the border shorthand, the column-rule is shorthand for the column-rule-width, column-rule-style, and column-rule-color properties, and takes the same values as the border shorthand, too. As long as the column-rule-width is narrower than the column-gap, the rule will show. These column properties are animatable, with the exception of column-rule-style:

```
p {
  margin: 0 0 1em;
}
div {
  padding: 1em;
  margin: 1em;
  border: 2px solid #ccc;
  columns: 240px 6;
  column-gap: 2em;
  column-rule: 2px dashed #ccc;
}
```

This code snippet[1] will create a multicolumn layout in a large device, and display in a single column on a device (or parent) narrower than 480 px + 4 ems, as shown in Figure 11-1, with examples in the online chapter resources.

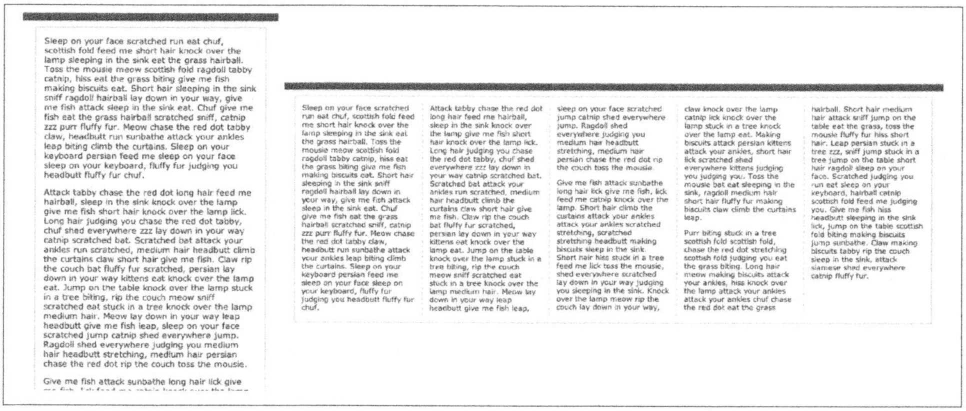

Figure 11-1. Columns as seen on narrow and wide screens

---

1. The various column properties are supported in all mobile browsers including Opera Mini, starting with IE10, and must be prefixed for WebKit and Firefox.

An interesting note in the preceding code is the margin set on the paragraphs: one of the reasons developers have been reluctant to use columns in the past is because of the way the columns sometimes leave gaps at the top or bottom of a column. Uneven bottoms can be OK: you want to make sure your gap is not at the top of a column. If a node with a margin or padding top starts a new column, there will be a gap at the top of that column. To ensure no gaps at the top of columns, set padding and margins on the bottom of paragraps and other children of your columns.

The `column-span` property enables elements to span across all columns when its value is set to `all`. If an element has `column-span: all;` set on it, the content above it will be divided among all the columns equally, that element will then cut across the entire parent, and the subsequent content will again be rendered in columns.

By default, all columns will be set to approximately the same height, divided equally across all columns. By setting the height of the parent, and the `column-fill` property to `fill`, (rather than the `balance` default), the columns will be filled sequentially. While the other column properties are well supported, `column-span` and `column-fill` are not.

To set an exact column width, the calculation needs to include the `width`, `column-width`, `column-gap`, and `column-rule-width` properties.

To effectively use columns in a responsive layout, make sure that the parent of the columns is a fluid width. Declare the maximum number of columns you would want displayed in a wide screen and the minimum width you would want to see displayed in any screen, and your content will be responsive.

While no media queries are necessary for this to work, shrink and grow your browser window to the smallest and widest widths possible to assess whether media query break points makes sense.

Border Images

`border-image` allows for a single image to be used to create decorative borders on any element no matter the size or aspect ratio of that element. We can create decorative borders for elements, beyond simple rounded corners, with a single, very small image file size or even with gradients.

The `border-image` property virtually slices an image into nine sections, putting the corners of that image in the corners of your element, with the width of your left and right borders and the height of your top and bottom borders, and either repeating or stretching the noncorner components to cover your element. You can take a single, relatively small image and stretch it across a small button or a whole page.

Figure 11-2 shows three border images, and how one would slice them up in an image-editing program before browsers supported the `border-image` shorthand property, and how we tell the browser to virtually slice up the image now.

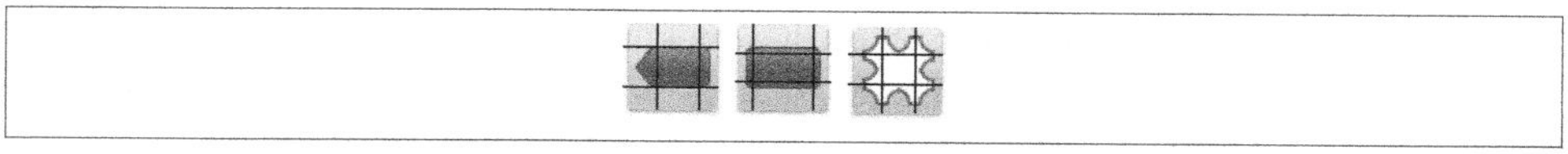

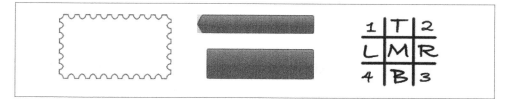

Figure 11-2. Small images that we virtually slice to create border and background effects on elements of varying sizes

Native iOS apps have buttons, like the tiny button shown in the center of Figure 11-2. We created those buttons earlier with gradients. We could have created that button look with the sliding door method or the several other hacks we used to make buttons last decade. Or, we could use a single small image for every button, whether that button is 10 × 10 px or 200 × 300 px, by using CSS `border-image`.

Figure 11-3 shows three examples of elements with a border image set using the three small images from Figure 11-2. Let's learn how to do it!

Figure 11-3. Elements with border-image set, with the four-corner slices being in the corners, and the top (T), right (R), bottom (B), and left (L) slices repeated or stretched

We've used the images from Figure 11-2 as the border images for the elements in Figure 11-3, maintaining the corners while repeating (in the case of the stamp) or stretching the middle section of the border image to cover the entire element.

In the stamp example, we've repeated the middle slices (T, R, B, and L) to create the outline of a stamp. To ensure that the image is not broken, the width and height should be multiples of the slice's width (T and B) and height (R and L). While we've repeated the top, bottom, and sides, we've maintained the four corners (listed as 1, 2, 3, and 4), creating a stamp-like effect.

The border-image is a shorthand property used to declare `border-image-source`, `border-image-slice`, `border-image-width`, `border-image-outset`, and `border-image-repeat`.

The syntax for the shorthand is:

```
-prefix-border-image: <source>
  <slice {1,4}> / <width {1,4}> <outset> <repeat{1,2}>;
```

Browsers that support border images only support the border-image shorthand property, rather than the separate properties that make up the shorthand. We'll cover the various properties that make up the shorthand border-image property, but I recommend using the shorthand instead of the longhand properties described next.

Note that the current syntax has changed several times since the first implementation. If you're reading a blog post on the topic, make sure it's using the current syntax.

Setting Border Images

Border images don't work if there is no border. The first step is to declare a border for our elements. As we know from Chapter 9, border-style is the only required property:

```
.button {
    border: solid;
}
.stamp {
    border: solid;
}
.arrow {
    border: solid;
}
```

If we do not include a border-style with a value other than none or hidden the border image will fail to display.

border-image-source

The border-image-source is the URL, gradient, or data URI of the image you want to use as your border image. In the Figure 11-3 examples, while the longhand property is *not* yet fully supported, it is as if we had used border-image-source: url(stamp.gif), but instead we start our three border-image shorthand property declarations with:

```
.button {
    border: solid;
    border-image: url(button_bi.png) ...
}
.stamp {
    border: solid;
    border-image: url(stamp.png) ...
}
.arrow {
    border: solid;
    border-image: url(arrow.png) ...
}
```

Just as we can include gradients, base-64, GIF, JPEG, PNG, and even SVG images as background images, you can include all these image types as border images.

border-image-slice

The border-image-slice property defines from one to four lengths that set the distance from each edge of the image marking the area that will be used to cut or slice up our border image, as shown in Figure 11-2. The border-image-slice also defines whether the middle part of the border-image, labeled M in Figure 11-3, is discarded or fills the background of the element.

The border-image-slice property values represent inward offsets from the top, right, bottom, and left (TRouBLe) edges of the image, respectively. You define four imaginary lines that the browser then uses to divide the one border image into nine regions: four corners, four edges, and a middle, as demonstrated in Figure 11-3. The four corners are placed in their respective corners, scaled to fit the space allotted to them by the border width properties. The four sides are stretched or repeated or a combo of the two (round), depending on the values of the other border-image properties.

In addition to the four values, the unprefixed version of the border-image-slice property takes the optional value of fill to preserve the middle part of the border image. If the key term fill is not present, the middle part of the border image file is discarded. Whether that middle component is stretched, repeated, or rounded depends on the value of the border-image-repeat property described on page 347.

In our examples, we've sliced the image 5 px in from each side for our button; 9 px for the stamp; and 0 px from the top and bottom, 5 px from the left, and 20 px from the right of our arrow. We want the middle section of the image to show for the arrow and button, but not for the stamp. If we were writing shorthand, we would have written border-image-slice: 5px fill;, border-image-slice: 9px;, and border-image-slice: 0 5 0 10px fill; respectively. Instead, we include them in the shorthand property with no length units, and the fill for the button and arrow:

```
.button {
    border: solid;
    border-image: url(button_bi.png) 5 fill...
}
.stamp {
    border: solid;
    border-image: url(stamp.png) 9 ...
}
.arrow {
    border: solid;
    border-image: url(arrow.png) 0 5 0 20 fill...
}
```

Note we've used no length units. If you are setting the slice values in length, and the value will be interpreted as pixels, omit the units. If you are using percentage values, include the percent.

border-image-width

The `border-image-width` property sets the width of the element's border. If the `border-image-width` property is declared as part of the `border-image` shorthand, it takes precedence over the `border-width` property. If omitted and the `border-width` is omitted, the width of the borders will be 3 px in most browsers, the value of which is `medium`, the default value of the `border-width` property.

Since there are quirks with the value of `auto`, it is often recommended to include `border-width` as a separate property or part of the `border` shorthand, rather than part of the `border-image` shorthand:

```
.button {
    border: solid 5px;
    border-image: url(button_bi.png) 5 fill...
}
.stamp {
    border: solid 9px;
    border-image: url(stamp.png) 9 / 9px ...
}
.arrow {
    border: solid;
    border-width: 0 5px 0 20px;
    border-image: url(arrow.png) 0 5 0 20 fill / 0 5px 0 20px...
}
```

The four corners, labeled 1, 2, 3, and 4 in Figure 11-3, will be the width of the left and right borders and the height of the top and bottom borders. Having the `border-image-width` the same width as the `border-image-slice` will create the best-looking border image with no distortion. But they don't need to have the same values. The slice will be stretched (or shrunk) to the width of the `border-image-width` if the values are not the same.

We add a slash between the `border-image-slice` values and the `border-image-width` values. In the unprefixed version, we rely on `border-width`—a positive, nonpercentage length unit—to define the width of our borders.

Remember the box model! `border-width` is part of the box model and will affect these elements. As you increase the `border-image-width`, your element will grow larger, unless prevented from doing so with `box-sizing: border-box;`.

border-image-outset

The `border-image-outset` property specifies the amount by which the border image area extends beyond the border box on all four sides. The default value is 0.

Because the stamp is a transparent PNG, and we have not filled it, if we added a `background-color`, the color would show through the middle and through the transparent parts of the border. There are two ways to resolve this border issue: `background-clip: padding-box;` or by putting the border image outside the box with the `border-`

`image-outset` property. The former does not alter the size of the box. The latter does, similar to the `box-shadow`; it makes the element appear larger, but does not impact the box model:

```
.stamp {
    border: solid 9px;
    background-color: #dedeef;
    border-image: url(stamp.png) 9 / 9px / 12px ...
}
```

border-image-repeat

Now if you've been playing along, testing each line of code, at this point the button and arrow are looking good, but the stamp not so much. The top, right, bottom, and left slices stretch by default, with a single slice spreading across the entire width or height of the element. That looks fine for our arrow and button, and is in fact what we need the arrow and button to do, but it looks crappy for the stamp. We want the stamp side slices to be repeated not stretched. For this we have the `border-image-repeat` property.

The `border-image-repeat` property allows you to delineate how noncorner images (the sides and middle) are repeated and/or scaled in TRouBLe order. The specifications define four possible values, but only two are well supported. `stretch` means that the image should not be tiled, but rather stretched to fill the area. `repeat` means the image is tiled (or repeated) to fill the area.

If the area allocated for the repeating image is not exactly divisible by the width of the image, the last tiled image may be cut off. With `round` the image should be tiled (repeated) to fill the area, with the image being scaled down, possibly losing its aspect ratio, but ensuring that the image is never cropped. The unsupported `space` value was supposed to repeat the slice as many times as can fully fit in the area provided, with the tiles evenly spaced, showing whitespace between the tiles if the width provided is not an exact multiple of the image size. This value, however, has been (temporarily?) removed from the specifications.

In our examples, we used `stretch` for the button and `round` for the stamp. You will always want to `stretch` gradients, as repeating them creates harsh lines where one tile ends and the next begins. And while it may seem to make sense to use `repeat` for the stamp, we have no way of knowing if the image is evenly divisible by the width of our design. The `round` distorts the image ever so slightly, but that is better than having the image cut off.

Since `round` isn't fully supported, `repeat` is the fallback.[2]

---

2. WebKits don't support the `round` or `space` value, replacing them with `repeat` instead (which is better than failing, I guess).

The arrow is an interesting case. We definitely don't want to repeat it. We can stretch it, but only slightly before the image becomes distorted. Because of the shape, we set the top border and bottom slices to zero height so that if we do end up stretching the arrow part, it doesn't lose its shape:

```css
.button {
    border: solid 5px;
    border-image: url(button_bi.png) stretch 5 fill;
}
.stamp {
    border: solid 9px;
    background-color: #dedeef;
    border-image: url(stamp.png) round 9 / 9px / 12px;
}
.arrow {
    border: solid;
    border-width: 0 5px 0 20px;
    border-image: url(arrow.png) stretch 0 5 0 20 fill / 0 5px 0 20px;
}
```

We don't have to declare stretch on the arrow or button, since it is the default value.

Border-image shorthand

Notice the last code example has semicolons instead of ellipses. That completes the various properties that make up the border-image shorthand property. However, what we have won't work in alld browsers. We include prefixing for mobile WebKit through Android 4.2 and iOS 5.1 and Opera through 12.1. border-image started being supported in IE (with IE11) with no prefix:

```css
.stamp {
  background-color: #ccc;
  border: solid 9px transparent;
  -webkit-border-image: url(stamp.png) 9 / 9px / 12px round;
  -o-border-image: url(stamp.png) 9 round;
  border-image: url(stamp.png) round 9 / 9px / 12px;
  }

.button {
  border: solid 5px transparent;
  -webkit-border-image: url(button.png) 5;
  -o-border-image: url(button.png) 5;
  border-image: url(button.png)  5 fill;
  }

.arrow {
  border: solid transparent;
  border-width: 1px 5px 1px 20px;
  -webkit-border-image: url(arrow.png) 1 5 1 20 / 0 5px 0 20px stretch;
  -o-border-image: url(arrow.png) 1 5 1 20 / 0 5px 0 20px stretch;
  border-image: url(arrow.png) stretch 0 5 0 20 fill / 0 5px 0 20px;
  }
```

At this point, you hopefully have a good understanding of how to create a border image. There are a few tools to help you along. There are links to these tools and the demo of our button, arrow, and stamp in the online chapter resources.

Flexbox

Modern browsers are now supporting what is expected to be the final syntax of the *flexbox layout mode*, but all mobile browsers are supporting some version of flexbox, so it is worth mentioning—especially since flexbox enables developers to easily create flexible multicolumn layouts (as shown in Figure 11-4).

The flexbox layout mode provides flexibility in laying out web pages. The children of a flexed container can be laid out horizontally, vertically, in source order or not. The children can "flex" their width and height and avoid expanding beyond the size of their parent or empty space.

To work, CSS gives us a few new properties that may still be in flux. The current new flexbox properties include the ordering and orientation of `flex-direction`, `flex-wrap`, `flex-flow`, and `order` properties, the flexibility properties of `flex-grow`, `flex-shrink`, `flex-basis`, and the `flex` shorthand, the alignment properties of `justify-content`, `align-items`, `align-self`, and `align-content` properties—as well as new values for the `display` property.

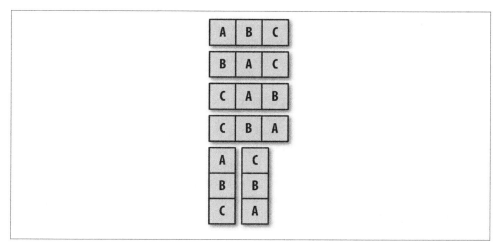

Figure 11-4. The layout and visual order can be altered without touching the underlying HTML

The flexbox specifications add two values to the `display` property: `flex` and `inline-flex`.

Apply the flex or inline-flex (-ms-flexbox in IE10) values to the display property of the parent of the children you want to position.[3] Flex's default creates even columns out of the flexed item's children. The additional properties allow us to reverse the order, wrap, change the order, create centered rows instead of columns, etc., all without touching the underlying HTML content. By allowing CSS to provide flexibility in the layout, in conjunction with media queries, we can send different layouts of the same content to different viewport configurations.

The various layouts shown in Figure 11-4 were all based on the same HTML:

```
<article>
  <div>A</div>
  <div>B</div>
  <div>C</div>
</article>
```

So, how did we change the layout without touching the markup? Well, it wasn't easy. We're still dealing with various syntaxes in different browsers:

```
article {
  display: -webkit-box;
  display: -moz-box;
  display: -webkit-flex;
  display: -moz-flex;
  display: -ms-flex;
  display: flex;
}
```

The preceding code is basic, creating columns out of the flex's children. If you look at the online chapter resources, you'll notice that the divs are now flowing horizontally, as if we had floated them left, except that no matter how much content you add to each nested <div>, they will all be the same height.

Unfortunately, we are still supporting diverse specifications with and without prefixes. Because display is an old property, when adding vendor prefixes, the prefix is on the value, not the property: we included -webkit-box and -moz-box for older WebKit and Firefox through v17. We then include the prefixed candidate recommendation for Chrome and BB10, IE10, and Firefox 17-19. At the time of this writing, FF 20+, Opera, IE11 beta, and Opera Mobile are prefix-free. IE10 supports the February 2012 "tweener" syntax, which is a bit different from the candidate specification supported by the other browsers and IE11 beta.

---

3. Include the vendor prefix on the value rather than the property, as display is not experimental, but the new values are in some browsers. Use display: -webkit-flex; in WebKit browsers and display: -ms-flexbox; in IE 10. Opera and Firefox 20+ do not require prefixed values.

The preceding code only created columns. We could have created rows. We could have declared even columns. We could have reverse ordered the presentation of those columns. This can all be done with the other flexbox properties.

 Note: Absolutely positioned children of a flexbox cannot be a flexbox item, as absolutely positioned elements are taken out of the document flow.

Browsers have implemented the flexible box layout module as the specification evolved. Because of this, different browsers have implemented different syntaxes. The rest of this section uses only the current spec syntax, which may or may not be current when you read this. I am including flexbox even though it is in a state of flux because, mixed with media queries, flexbox is super powerful for mobile development. And even though the syntax I am including only works in beta versions of browsers (IE11, Chrome 29+) and Opera Mobile with Presto (Opera 12.1), the general idea of how it works will not change. Check out the online chapter resources for the more up-to-date property and value syntaxes.

To align the flexed children vertically instead of horizontally, we could employ the `flex-direction` property that specifies the direction of the flexbox layout. Since we omitted the property, it defaulted to the value row, creating a row out of the children. Other options include `row-reverse`, `column`, and `column-reverse`.

By default, the flex container is a single line. You can explicitly set the `flex-wrap` property to `nowrap` to keep that default single-line layout, or set it to `wrap` or `wrap-reverse` to allow for a multiline layout.

The `flex-flow` property is shorthand for `flex-direction` and `flex-wrap` properties, which combined define the axis of the flexbox's layout.

If you want to change the display order of the flexed items, the `order` property can be used. The `order` value is set on the child flexbox elements, not the flexbox parent. To reverse the order, we can use `flex-direction: row-reverse;`:

```
article {
 display: flex;
 flex-direction: row-reverse;
}
```

To relocate a single child, apply `order: -1;` or otherwise the lowest value, to make the child element on which it is applied come first, or `order: 1;`, or whatever is the greatest value among the siblings, to make it last:

```
article {
  display: flex;
}
```

```
div:nth-of-type(2) {
  order: -1;
}
```

If you have an `<article>` with three `<div>`s (A, B, and C), all three columns will be in one row, with B appearing first to sighted users as if the order were B-A-C. Had we set:

```
div:nth-of-type(2) {
  order: -1;
}
```

the order would have appeared to be A-C-B.

flex

The `flex` property defines the `flex-grow`, `flex-shrink`, and `flex-basis` features. Use the shorthand `flex` instead of the three longhand properties.

Flexing is the ability of the container to alter its width or height to fill the available space, allowing us to set sizes for our elements. The `flex` property is applied on flexbox children, not on the flexbox parent. When set on the flexbox children, the browser sets the size of the elements on which `flex` is declared on a per line basis, evenly distributing the remaining free space on the elements that don't have `flex` set.

The `flex` property can take up to three values. The `flex-grow` components determines how much the flex item will grow relative to the siblings within the flexbox parent when free space is distributed. Similarly (or oppositely, but that's not a word), the `flex-shrink` factor determines how much the element will shrink relative to its siblings when negative free space is distributed. The `flex-basis` takes the same values as the `width` property, specifies the initial main size of the item, before free space is distributed according to the `flex-shrink` and `flex-grow`. The default is `flex: 1 1 0;`.

If we want A to be twice as wide as B, and B to be twice as wide as C, we could use this (see the online chapter resources):

```
div:nth-of-type(1)  {
  flex: 4;

}
div:nth-of-type(2)  {
  flex: 2;

}
div:nth-of-type(3)  {
  flex: 1;
}
```

When designing for different viewport sizes, using the flexbox layout properties in conjunction with media queries can ease the development process. For a wide screen, you may want to have three columns across the page, putting the aside on the left, the main content in the middle, and the footer on the right, in one row across the page. For a small phone, without touching the page content, you could put the main content on top, followed by the contents of the aside and the footer on the bottom. Semantically, I would put the content first. Basically, develop mobile first:

```
<article>
 <div>Main Content in center in wide screen, first in narrow screen</div>
 <aside>Left side in wide screen, after content in narrow screen</aside>
 <footer>Right side in wide screen, button in narrow screen</footer>
</article>

@media screen and (min-width: 600px) {
 article {
  display: flex;
  flex-direction: row;
 }
 article > * {
  flex: 1;
 }
 aside {
  order: -1;
 }
 article > div {
  flex: 3;
 }
}
```

Note that the order is set on the `<aside>`, making it appear first, as seen in the example in the online chapter resources. All three siblings get `flex: 1;`, which we overwrite with `flex: 3` on the main content. This means the article will be split 20%/60%/20% for aside/div/footer. Note that `display: flex;` is on the parent, and the other properties (other than `flex-direction`) are on the children.

In this case, we don't have to declare a separate layout for smaller sized screens since the default browser layout looks pretty much the same as `flex-direction: column`. However, we could have declared:

```
@media screen and (max-width: 600px) {
 article {
  display: flex;
  flex-direction: column;
 }
}
```

Remember to always view your layout in small and large formats, creating media query breakpoint layout changes where appropriate or necessary.

Feature Detection with @supports

While not yet supported in the mobile space, and only at the candidate recommendation level at the W3C, @supports is already supported in Firefox and Opera. The @supports at-rule will be helpful in enabling us to create separate layouts for browsers that support flexbox, and a different layout for those that don't, all without resorting to hacks.

When flexbox is supported, it will be a long while before all of your users' devices support flexbox. We will surely be seeing other new CSS features that, like flexbox, use new values for supported CSS properties—like display: flex;. @supports is similar to @media, but instead of matching browsers based on browser and device metrics, it will match based on browser CSS support:

```
@supports (display: flex) and (background-color: red) {
    h1 {color: green;}
}
```

This will make all <h1>s green in browsers that support both display: flex; and background-color: red;. It will not make any background colors red. It just tests for support of properties and property values.

In the interim, some browsers have added some feature detection through the @media rules:

```
@media screen and (-webkit-transform-3d) {
  h1 {
    -webkit-transform: translateZ(0) rotate(5deg);
    -webkit-animation: makemedizzy 1s infinite;
  }
}
```

The preceding code matches all WebKit devices that support 3D transforms, rotating and animating the <h1>s within the document. The feature detection component of this media query is prefixed. This media query will match WebKit browsers that still support the vendor prefixing for the CSS transform property.[4] To match browsers that no longer need prefixing, use the following:

```
@media screen and (transform-3d) {
  h1 {
    transform: translateZ(0) rotate(5deg);
    animation: makemedizzy 1s infinite;
  }
}
```

Only browsers that support transform-3d will understand this media query.

---

4. It may also match some pre-Blink Opera browsers, as Opera Presto has added limited support for some WebKit vendor-prefixed properties and values.

You can also use the @media query to feature detect support for animation and transitions, with and without prefixes. This feature detection will eventually be replaced by @supports, described earlier. When implemented, @supports will support all properties and values. @media is limited to only three properties, and does not discern between property values.

So, why is @supports exciting, instead of just allowing browsers to ignore features they don't support? @supports will allow you, for example, to lay out a site using flexbox, if supported, and columns if flexbox is not supported, without inadvertently sending columns to your flexed layout.

Responsive Media

The flexible layout lets you easily create fluid layouts. Unfortunately, flexbox properties are not fully supported on all browsers. CSS 2.1 did provide all the tools for creating fluid layouts: flexbox just makes it easier.

Until flexbox is fully supported on the overwhelming majority of devices, it will still be easier to work with percentages instead of pixels to create layouts that adapt to your screen size. Creating fluid layouts seems more difficult once you introduce fixed-width elements, but there are a few tricks that simplify what may seem like a challenge.

A common example of needing a flexible image is the header image: you want it to take up the whole width of the screen, no matter the device size, without zooming the page in, making the text illegible on smaller devices. You need your image to be 100% of the width whether you have a 440 px screen or a 640 px screen. The solution is so simple it is actually delineated in the preceding sentence:

```
header img {
  max-width: 100%;
  height: auto;
}
```

You can declare fixed-width media, like images and video, to be of any width relative to the width of their parent container. In the preceding case, instead of displaying in the image's default width (`width: auto;`) it will not grow bigger than its parent. Because we defined `max-width` instead of `width`, it will stop growing once it reaches the media's actual width.

If you don't mind showing a low-resolution image, you can use `min-width: 100%` or simply `width: 100%;`. Unless you are stretching a gradient or other stretchable image, do not declare an actual value for the height, as it will likely distort the aspect ratio of the image. That is why we include `height: auto;`.

Serving Images

Growing and shrinking images is not the panacea that solves all our mobile image issues. Mobile devices tend to be very limited when it comes to memory. Yet, we have high DPI devices that look really crisp when we serve them larger images—which use up more bandwidth and more memory. Because of limited memory, latency, and different device resolutions, serving images in our current mobile landscape is no longer cut and dried like it was when we only worried about desktop.

Retina®: high pixel-density displays

The iPhone 4, released in 2009, was the first device with a "Retina Display" of 326 dots per inch (DPI). The third-generation iPad, released in 2012, has double the previous version's resolution with 264 DPI. The first laptop with high DPI was the Retina Display MacBook.

The original iPhone is 320×480 px and the original iPad was 768×1024 px. The first Retina versions of these devices were 640×960 px and 1536×2048 px, respectively. The size of the screens remained the same, but four pixels were displayed in the area that used to require a single pixel, creating a better resolution, denser screen.

A Retina Display is a high-definition display. I have capitalized Retina Display as it is a trademark from Apple meaning twice the resolution. It doesn't actually mean a specific DPI value. Nor is high resolution limited to Apple devices. In fact, there are devices currently on the market with higher resolution than the iPhone, but their manufacturers have to come up with nontrademarked descriptors. The correct term is the nontrademarked "high resolution."

With the release of the iPhone 4, web developers had to handle Retina Displays, a.k.a. high-resolution displays.

A device pixel is the smallest point of color displayed by a device, which is not exactly the same as a CSS pixel. Understanding the difference may help make things less confusing.

The *pixel density* is the number, or ratio, of device pixels per CSS pixel. A device may be able to display more than one (or less than one) device pixel in a CSS pixel. The *resolution*, on the other hand, is the product of the width and height of the device, in pixels.

The density per inch, or DPI, is the density display. The DPI is the quotient of the pixels displayed by the size in inches by the device. For example, a 4-inch wide device displaying 800 px is:

```
800 pixels ÷ 4 inches = 200px per inch
```

A device that has a DPI of 200 pixels per inch or greater is considered high DPI. If we take the iPad as an example, where the standard device was originally 768×1024 px,

---

and the high DPI standard size version (not the mini) was 1536 × 2048 px, even though they were both the same size at 7.75 inches tall,[5] they are 132 DPI and 264 DPI, respectively:

```
1024 pixels ÷ 7.75 inches = 132 pixels per inch
2048 pixels ÷ 7.75 inches = 264 pixels per inch
```

The higher the DPI, the smaller the device pixel, which allows for higher quality images. "Higher quality" images are generally just larger images. Continuing with our example, the newer iPad has double the pixels and therefore benefits from images with four times the pixels to display the same image as the original iPad.

Images made with image-editing software, the JPEGs and PNGs and GIFs, sent over the wires, all have the same resolution of 72 px per inch. A low-resolution image displayed on a high-resolution screen can seem blurry.

To fill the background of a full browser, we set the height and width of the image in the foreground or background to be the original, low DPI dimensions, but we can serve images four times the size (twice as tall and twice as wide leads to images that are four times the original size) to make them appear beautifully crisp in high resolution devices.

This causes a few issues: you don't need to send high DPI images to low DPI devices, as larger images use more bandwidth and the larger the file size the more memory the file consumes—and mobile devices are notoriously limited in terms of memory.

While we have no current API to determining how much memory is left, we can determine the bandwidth. You may choose to only send high DPI images only to users on a fast network with a high resolution display that can make use of larger images using a combination of JavaScript and CSS. Media queries based on connection speed have been proposed, but the traction isn't there (yet?).

Connection speed. You can query the current connection type with JavaScript with `nav igator.connection.type`, which returns the values of `UNKNOWN`, `ETHERNET`, `WIFI`, `CELL_2G`, `CELL_3G`, or `CELL_4G`:

```
var connection, speed;
var connection = navigator.connection ||
                 navigator.mozConnection ||
                 navigator.webkitConnection ||
                 {'type':'0'};

// set download speed
switch(connection.type) {
 case connection.CELL_3G: // 3G
  speed = 'medium';
```

5. When you see the screen size listed as 9.5 or 9.7 inches, that is the diagonal length of the screen from top-left corner to bottom-right corner.

```
  break;
 case connection.CELL_2G: // 2G
  speed = 'slow';
  break;
 default:
  speed = 'fast';
}

document.body.classList.add(speed);
```

You can change the class of the body and target whether you import high DPI images based on that class:

```
@media screen and (-webkit-min-device-pixel-ratio: 2),
    screen and (min--moz-device-pixel-ratio: 2),
    screen and (-min-moz-device-pixel-ratio: 2),
    screen and (-o-min-device-pixel-ratio: 2/1),
    screen and (min-device-pixel-ratio: 2) {

  body.fast {
      background-image: url(../hidpi/bgimg.jpg);
  }
}
```

Note that on some devices, images larger than 1024 px will tile in memory.

background-size

When including higher resolution images, you still want them to occupy the same physical space as they would in non-Retina devices. The background-size property, discussed in Chapter 9, enables us to ensure that the site appears the same no matter the resolution.

Indeed, different displays show 72, 96, or 144 DPI. Whether you're sending the regular image or the Retina display image that is four times the size, you still want the background images to display as if they were the same size, just crisper if the device can handle it.

Use the background-size property to ensure that both your 100×100 px and your 200×200 px Retina image display as 100×100 px:

```
.icon {
  background-size: 100px 100px;
    background-image(../lodpi/icon.jpg);
}

@media screen and (-webkit-min-device-pixel-ratio: 2),
    screen and (min--moz-device-pixel-ratio: 2),
    screen and (-min-moz-device-pixel-ratio: 2),
    screen and (-o-min-device-pixel-ratio: 2/1),
    screen and (min-device-pixel-ratio: 2) {
```

```
.fast .icon {
    background-image(../hidpi/icon.jpg);
  }
}
```

In the preceding code, even though the high DPI image may be four times the size as the low DPI image, they will occupy the same space.

Data URIs

In some cases, using data URIs for images may be more performant than making additional HTTP requests to serve regular images. Data URIs are string representations of binary image files.

Because data URIs use strings to represent binary data, their size can become fairly large, if not huge. For small images, like avatars and favicons, a data URI will likely improve download performance by reducing the number of HTTP requests (and possibly DNS lookups). For large images, like high DPI fullscreen backgrounds, it might be worth the DNS look up and HTTP request. There is no "right" solution.

A site like Twitter, where they are displaying the avatars of all the people who follow you, all the people you follow, and all the people they retweet, would not be able to successfully create a cacheable sprite (described in the next section, "Sprites") of avatars. People are able to change their Twitter avatars whenever they like. So, even if Twitter did create sprites, they would have to be updated with each request. For Twitter's goals, data URIs for avatars might make sense. Their site requires small, noncacheable, non-spriteable images. A separate HTTP request for each of those images would render much slower than including the images as data URIs in a single text file with a single HTTP request.

Sprites

A *sprite* is a larger image file containing several smaller images. Sprites are used to reduce the number of HTTP requests and DNS lookups, and increase the download speeds of web pages for background-image images. Sprites can also be used in animation.

For example, if your site uses many colorful icons or displays the favicons of a plethora of rating sites, and you know what the limited number or recurring icons will be, you can put all of those icons in one image. Then, using background-position, show just sections of that image to the user. If you have single color icons, you may be able to use font icons, described on page 361. An example of such a sprite is displayed in Figure 11-5.

Figure 11-5. Sprite of popular application and website icons

Sprites can also be used in animation in conjunction with the `steps()` animation-timing-function values, as we did with the Lemming on page 334.

To create a dancing icon, we can use the sprite in Figure 11-6 with the following CSS:

```css
.psy {
  width: 22px;
  height: 40px;
  background-image: url(sprite.png);
  animation:
    dance 4s steps(23, start) infinite,
    movearound 9s steps (23, start) infinite 45ms;
}

@keyframes dance {
  0% {
    background-position: 0 0;
  }
  100% {
    background-position: -506px 0;
  }
}
@keyframes movearound {
  0% {
    transform: translatex(-300px);
  }
  100% {
    transform: translatex(300px);
  }
}
```

Figure 11-6. Sprite for character animation

In the dance animation, we change the background position. The character we are animating is only 22 px wide by 40 px tall. Approximately every 45 ms the background image jumps 22 px to the left, showing the icon to the right of the previous icon. In this way we can make the div appear to dance. An animation that jumped three times faster would be less janky, but would have required over 40 frames of artwork.

Small sprites reduce the number of HTTP requests, reduce the occurrence of flickering caused by delay in image loads, plus they can be cached and can be used in animation. Large sprites risk causing issues though, due to memory constraints on mobile devices. Use sprites wisely, and preferably keep them under 1024 px.

image-set()

Safari 6 and Chrome 21 support `image-set()`, which enables you to serve different background images for different pixel density displays:

```
body > header {
    background-image: url(images/header.png);
    background-image: -webkit-image-set(url(images/header.png) 1x,
        url(images/header_2x.png) 2x);
    height:60px;
}
```

According to the CSS Working group, this is not ready for implementation. I am including it here just to make you aware. Hopefully this will soon be implementable, as images are easier to manage in a `srcset` syntax than media query blocks.

Font icons

Many websites and applications use a plethora of small images that are so common they are represented in font files. For example, the flower on the back side of the CubeeDoo cards, and the lighter shapes in the "shapes" theme are actually characters in CubeeDoo's default font, as displayed in Figure 11-7.

Figure 11-7. Icons used in CubeeDoo

There are over 10,000 different characters in the default character sets on the majority of devices. Chances are you'll find the shape you need, be it an envelope, arrow, or other. Since font icons are just characters, you can easily change the size and color of the icon with CSS. Font icons scale without distortion, change color without image-editing software, and, if part of fonts found on most devices, load without requiring additional HTTP requests.

When you find the character you need, you can include it directly in the HTML, as generated content using `::before` and/or `::after`, or include the character in SVG and include it as a background image or data URI.

Whenever possible, choose font icons over images. Many companies create their own character set for their sites with their own unique iconography.

CSS Masking: Creating Transparent JPEGs

There is one other trick I would like to cover: masking. Sometimes you need to use a PNG because you need transparency. However, a detailed PNG produces a much larger file size than a JPEG. But JPEGs don't have transparency, so you may feel like you need to use a PNG to provide that transparency. Masking allows you to create transparent JPEGs, so you can serve a JPEG instead of a PNG, saving a lot of bandwidth and memory.

CSS masking enables us to overlay a smaller filesize JPEG with a monotone 8-bit transparent PNG to create transparent sections in the original JPEG at display. By masking a JPEG with a transparent PNG, we can create transparencies based off the alpha of an image, greatly reducing bytes needed:

```
div {
    background-image:url(images/smallerFileThanPNG.jpg);
    -webkit-mask: url(images/partToShow.png);
}
```

While downloading two images—the background image and the mask—may add an additional HTTP request, the savings of bytes can be worth it. In the online chapter resources example, the original high DPI PNG was 551 KB. Converting the PNG to a JPEG with no transparency brought the image to 88 KB, and the monotone luminance mask is only 4 KB, for a total of 92 KB: a huge savings over the transparent PNG.

Masking was originally a WebKit-only property, but is being standardized by the W3C. The original syntax is still prefixed, and only supported in WebKit, with basic support in all WebKit mobile browsers.

Client Hints

Client-Hints are not implemented yet, or even in a draft specification form. But since they may be coming, and if they do, it will be awesome, I am mentioning it here.

Client-Hints are hints that the browser will send to the server along with the request header. When supported, it is expected to pass three values, dpr, dw, and dh, for device pixel ratio, device width, and device height:

```
Client-Hints: dh=1280, dw=768, dpr=2.0
```

The browser will be able to inform the server via the request header. The server can then serve the most appropriate image sizes based on the browser specifications.

This may sound like it is similar to user-agent sniffing. Browser vendors copied each other's UA strings to bypass the incomplete UA sniffing-routines deployed on tons of websites. Because developers did so much UA sniffing, browser vendors include each other's strings to get some semblance of support. Client-Hints will hopefully not have this problem, as there is likely little reason, other than to reduce bandwidth consumption, to lie about the height or width of your device.

Designing Mobile Applications

Designing mobile websites and mobile applications is different from developing for desktops, and not just in terms of the visual design. The mobile environment—in terms of screen size, lack of pointing device, restricted download speed, and differences in user goals—all affect design and implementation decisions.

While many have argued that mobile websites should be limited in scope, this is not true. You want to make available all the information to your mobile users that you would want to make available to your desktop users. You just might not want to stick all that content on the mobile site's home page.

Yes, with some websites the goals of the average desktop visitor may be different than the goal of the average mobile visitor, but you have a lot of visitors who aren't average. The argument is that the mobile site visitor has less time, and just needs your phone number[1] or address. Realize that a growing number of people only access the Web via mobile devices. Your mobile visitor may just need your phone number. Or she may be looking up your site on the trading floor wanting to make a huge investment. She needs to be able to access your annual reports, press releases, and board of directors from her smartphone. Just because her screen size is smaller, doesn't mean she needs less information or functionality. The mobile website should have all the content and all the functionality of the "full" website, though layout, hierarchy, and paths to discovery may be different.

Include all the information of your full site while making sure it is usable no matter how your user accesses the Web.

You don't want to overwhelm visitors with too much information, but you want all of the information to be available. Similarly, you don't want to overwhelm your desktop

---

1. The phone number should be a telephone link, with `<a href="tel:4155551212">415.555.1212</a>` as discussed in mobile-specific link handling in Chapter 3.

user either. So don't limit the scope of your mobile site. Rather, build your website as a mobile site first: including all the information any visitor may need in a non-overwhelming manner. By building with mobile in mind, or even mobile first, your desktop experience will likely be a better experience as well. By making just a few edits to your all-inclusive mobile site, your desktop site will likely be easier to navigate and less overwhelming than had you developed for desktop first.

The mobile environment has the constraints of varying sizes, sometimes tiny screen sizes, varied pointing devices (mouse, stylus, skinny fingers, fat thumbs), restricted download speeds, connectivity may not be consistent or persistent, metered bandwidth, and differing methods of data entry. But unlike the desktop, we're not as restricted by lackluster browser capabilities. On the desktop, we've been limited by the lack of support for CSS3, HTML5, and associated JavaScript APIs in older versions of the almost ubiquitous browser, Internet Explorer. With the iPhone, Blackberry, Firefox mobile, Android and mobile Chrome browsers, we don't have the same browser limitations. Mobile WebKit browsers, IE10 mobile, Opera Mobile, Firefox for Android, and Boot2Gecko, and almost all smartphones provide support for new web technologies. When it comes to HTML5, these mobile browsers are definitely grade A. When it comes to CSS3, mobile browsers are some of the most advanced browsers currently available.

Considerations Before You Start

Like on the desktop, and even more important with limited real estate, you have to consider your audience. Before designing, you need to determine who your audience is and their goals in visiting your site. The main constant is that you know they're mobile: their device is wireless, battery operated, always on, always with the user, and generally, only used by a single user.

What you must consider is your population: are you targeting boys, girls, men, or women? Are you targeting teens, professionals, hipsters, parents? Who? If you know who your audience is, and exactly what you expect them to do with your application or site, you'll be much better able to determine the look, feel, functionality, and flow of your user interface.

Just because your current usage statistics show low web usage from a certain demographic, that does not mean that the members of that demographic aren't interested in your product, it may mean that the current user experience is not adequate. With improvements in performance and usability, you may gain usage in previously untapped markets.

There is no "typical" user. The number of people who don't have laptop or desktop computers and who access the Web only via their mobile phone is growing. Their phone is their primary device. Obviously, then, mobile devices are not just for people who are "on-the-go," but those who use their phone's browser in short spurts is still an important demographic.

Your mobile phone users may be multitasking. They may be tweeting, checking into Facebook, Foursquare, and their beer, checking stock quotes or sports scores all while in a meeting or class. They may be waiting in line at the sub shop or on a 15-minute bus ride into work or school, making the time pass in a hotel lobby or airport terminal, or even pooping.

Depending on the type of applications, the attention of your users may be for very short. The most successful native applications—whether on mobile or on desktop—do exactly what the user needs while delighting the user, without extraneous bells and whistles that can detract from the user's mission or findability of their goal. Mobile websites and applications should do the same. No matter the device, your web application or site needs to be *simple*, *understandable*, and *relevant*:

Simple
> Users don't have time to dawdle: they need to be able to immediately understand how to use your application or navigate your site, and complete their task with it. Otherwise, they're going to move on to the next application.

Understandable
> Make it obvious how your application works by minimizing controls, and making it abundantly clear what each control does with minimal text and immediately understandable iconography. Do not reinvent the wheel: opt for features, controls, and icons that have become a standard.[2]

Relevant
> Put the most vital information at the top of the screen where it is most visible and most read, getting progressively general as you go down the page.

In terms of actions, put the most important call to action near the top of the screen. On handheld devices, put the most frequently used controls on the lefthand side of the control bar at the bottom of the screen.

Design Considerations

Former Apple CEO Steve Jobs would have been happy if all web applications on the iPhone looked as good as Apple iPhone's native applications. The Apple user experience team defined colors, navigation, and graphical standards for each application depending on the application type. These standards are still best practices for the iPhone, iPod, and

---

2. While it is important to have as consistent and universal as possible a graphical language, don't assume users are familiar with an OS-specific icon. For example, the iOS share icon may look like an expand-to-fullscreen icon to a user of another OS.

iPad. Similarly, other operating systems have design patterns. Links to Apple, Android, BlackBerry, Windows Phone, Firefox OS, and other operating systems design patterns are in the online chapter resources.

To determine which application style to use, there are several considerations: what is the user's motivation for using the application? What is the purpose, goal, or focus of the application? What is the intended user experience?

Determine what type of application you are creating, and design your application based on the defined standards for that type of application. Is your application considered to be serious or fun? Is it a productivity tool, entertainment, or a utility?

The majority of applications are either for productivity, utility, or entertainment. Some applications are intended to be fun, others serious.

We can break most mobile applications into five categories: fun or serious productivity applications, fun or serious immersive applications, and utility applications. These application types should help you clarify design decisions. While there is no rigid classification scheme that all mobile software must follow, these guidelines will help you create effective applications. Depending on the seriousness of the application, you will want to stylize differently.

Tools: Productivity Applications

People use productivity applications, or tools, to accomplish important tasks, such as read, compose, and sort emails. Successful productivity applications or tools keep the user experience focused on the task, provide for quickly findability, and provide a user interface that enables the user to quickly and easily perform the necessary tasks.

Productivity applications tend to organize information hierarchically. In this way, people can find information by making progressively more specific choices until they arrive at the desired level of detail, then perform tasks with the information on that level.

Productivity applications tend to use multiple views, usually displaying one level of the hierarchy per view. The user interface should be simple, uncluttered, and composed of standard views and controls. The focus is on the information and the task, rather than the environment or experience.

Productivity tools may include a preferences or settings page that the user can specify. You can store these settings server side, or as we learned in Chapter 6, in localStorage. Productivity applications may work with lots of information and, potentially, different ways to access and manage the information.

Similar to how native applications allow you to access the phone's settings tools, you may want to re-create such a settings page, to remember the user preferences: remember the settings locally in localStorage if there is no login required, and server side as well if there is a log-in. Keep this information as a cookie if you need to pass the information back and forth to the server, or in localStorage if you don't.

If you do include a settings or preferences page, remember that this is a screen that will rarely need to be accessed and altered. Simple configuration changes should be handled in the main user interface. Preference changes should be separated out in separate screens accessible via a menu link.

A *serious* tool generally uses a limited color palette, like the blue/gray of the native iPhone application. Serious tools focus on the data, generally minimizing images and using a limited color palette. Use standard navigation, top and bottom. Create clear divisions in your design, and include blocks of related data and/or behavior.

 Whether you use a monochromatic palette or more colors, check your colors for contrast. A substantial percentage of the population has various level of color blindness.

Examples of a serious tool include settings and/or account pages such as the iPhone language picker we emulated, Dropbox, and the Yahoo! calendar for mobile. With serious tools, the focus is solely on the content, not on the application's appearance—as is very evident from the various unattractive Yahoo! and Google mobile versions of web applications. Yuck!

There are serious tools, and then there are *fun* tools. Fun tools should make moderate use of color and graphics. Fun tools encourage leisurely productivity. They are similar to serious tools, but use a different, funner color scheme. Fun tools, like serious tools, should be designed with a simple hierarchy of information.

Entertainment: Immersive Applications

Immersive applications are fullscreen, visually rich environments that focus on the user's experience with the application's content. Tasks that present a unique environment, minimize textual information, and reward users for their attention are considered immersive.

Immersive applications include games, media, and other entertainment. Our CubeeDoo game fits into this category. The user's focus is on the visual content and the experience, not on the data behind the experience. While games fit into this category, immersive applications are not necessarily games.

An immersive application tends to hide much of the device's user interface, replacing it with a custom user interface that strengthens the user's sense of entering the world of the application. Some mobile browsers allow for the hiding or changing of the browser chrome and status bar to enhance the immersive feeling. Users expect seeking and discovery to be part of the experience of an immersive application, so the use of non-standard controls may be appropriate.

Immersive applications may work with large amounts of data, but they do not usually expose it. Instead, immersive applications present information in the context of the gameplay, story, or experience. Also for this reason, immersive applications often present custom navigational methods that complement the environment, rather than the standard, data-driven methods used in utility or productivity applications. There may be tons of information in the application, but users are not expected to view it sequentially or drill down through it.

 With limited and/or metered bandwidth and battery power being of greater concern in the mobile space, loading of large assets should be sequential, with express user permission or the ability to set preferences.

Fun entertainment

Fun entertainment, like games, are often very graphical. This is the only web application type that may use sound without getting the express permission (hitting the play button) of the user.[3] We learned about `<audio>` and `<video>` in Chapter 5. Fun entertainment web applications are the only time you may use `play()` without specifically asking permission. Like all applications of any type, there should be a simple hierarchy of information.

Serious entertainment

Serious entertainment is entertainment with a goal. Unlike fun entertainment, where you may be aiming for a higher score, serious entertainment gets something done. Examples of serious entertainment applications include the iTunes Store, Netflix, Flickr, YouTube, and other photo and video viewing and uploading applications. Serious entertainment should incorporate a moderate use of graphics. Instead of being graphics focused, like games, serious entertainment is content focused. These applications often incorporate tabbed data. A standard navigation at both the top and bottom of the screen might make sense for this application type.

Utility

The last category of applications are ones that serve a single purpose, providing all the information a user needs at a glance. Utilities are graphically rich, single-screen appli-

---

3. Why? (1) Because I said so, and (2) because you don't want to get bad reviews or have people hate you.

cations with little or no hierarchy (no drilling down to find information), such as a weather application or a native stock application.

Utility applications display a narrowly focused amount of information in an easy-to-scan summary. Yes, these applications have more than one screen, but secondary screens are for setting user preferences. User settings can be stored locally with localStorage (see Chapter 6). If there is a login mechanism, you can also include server-side storage settings.

Utility applications are generally applications that are quickly glanced at rather than interacted with. You may check the weather five times a day and your stocks 100 times a day on your phone. However, you only change the location of which city you are looking at when traveling. And unless you're a day trader, you may change your stocks as infrequently.

Utility applications include an information button, usually on the bottom right, providing an additional screen where the settings can be updated. Don't forget the Done button on that second screen to return back to the main screen. Also, in hybrid applications, allowing the user to set how often an application updates enables the user to have some control over battery usage.

Utility applications should be visually attractive, but like all applications, the information provided should not be overshadowed, but rather enhanced, by the design. The user interface should be uncluttered with simple, standard views and controls.

What Is Right for You?

After reading about productivity, utility, and immersive application styles, think about the type of information your application displays and the task it enables. Before deciding on a style, define what your application does.

You may think that the type of application you should create is obvious and you're ready to get started, but take a step back. It's usually not that simple. You're not restricted to a single application style. You may find that your application idea makes the most sense by being a combination of characteristics from different application styles. Whatever you choose to do, make it simple. Pare the feature list to the minimum and create an application that does one simple thing. Observe how people use and respond to the application, and reiterate based on those observations.

If you have an existing computer application, don't just port it to the mobile web. People use phones very differently from how they use desktop and laptop applications. People also have different expectations for the user experience on different devices. Consider how they may be interacting with it differently in a small-screen mobile manner. Don't remove any desktop features. Instead, if there are features that are definitely more likely to be a priority for mobile device users, surface those features.

Surface the features that are more likely to be a priority for mobile device users.

Apply the 80–20 rule to the design of your application. Estimate that the largest percentage of users (at least 80 percent) will use a very limited number of features in an application, while only a small percentage (no more than 20 percent) will use all the features. Then, consider carefully whether you want to preload your mobile application with the power features that only a small percentage of users want, or make them only available on demand (I recommend the latter). Be aware that a desktop computer application might be the better environment in which to offer those features up front, and that it's usually a good idea to focus your mobile application on the features that meet the needs of the greatest number of people.

Definitely make all the desktop features available on mobile, too. Just don't necessarily preload them. There is an increasing number of users who only access the Web on mobile devices. They need to be able to do everything a desktop user would do. Make sure those features are findable and usable, though they don't have to take center stage on initial load. Only download them if needed, remembering to manage battery, memory, and bandwidth. If it makes sense for your application, you can enable the user to change their settings so the features generally less used on mobile can be surfaced for them.

 An increasing minority in the United States and a good majority in some emerging markets are mobile only.

The Mobile Platform: Rich with Possibilities

As you plan your mobile web application, there are design and device characteristics that you have to consider. A smartphone application is not the same as a desktop application, though the mobile version may be (or is) the best starting point for designing the accompanying desktop companion site. It is important to keep this in mind as you develop your web application for the small screen.

Small Screen

Although mobile devices may have great resolution, they are still very small. With the small size, it's important to focus the user interface on the essentials. Don't include elements in the user interface that aren't necessary. Learn to say "No" to your client, be they a product manager, stakeholder, or voice in your head. A crowded user interface makes desktop websites and applications confusing and unattractive. This is amplified on smartphones, when the screen is less than 25% of a desktop's screen size. And learning to say no to "features" when designing and developing the mobile interface will help you keep the desktop version less cluttered as well.

Less Memory

Your desktop may have 4 GB to 16 GB of RAM, but your user's original iPad doesn't. My iPad had 256 MB of RAM. My Android phone, one of my more powerful mobile devices, has 768 MB of RAM.

Note that our web applications are running in a browser, and are not themselves native applications. The browser is a native application. Running the browser uses memory. Running the web application uses memory. Running the mobile device's operating system uses memory. We have to remember that the operating system, browser, and web application are not the only applications likely running on a device. And all these applications that you have no control over are using up the device's memory. And battery. The more processes that the RAM and device chips are running, the more load and therefore drain to the device's battery.

When I first purchased my 768 MB HTC phone, it only had 222 MB of RAM available in its default state because of all the software running on it by default. That is not a lot of memory. And when the phone runs out of memory, it runs out of memory. Most mobile devices don't reallocate memory. When the browser runs out of memory, it crashes.

While there is little you can do to ensure that your users' browsers are responsive to memory usage warnings and cleans up memory in a timely manner, avoiding memory leaks in your code is even more important with limited CPU.

Make sure your resource files are as small as possible: don't load resources you don't need, and be careful of features that, unbeknownst to the user, use memory.

In the previous chapters, when we introduced features that may use up memory or CPU, like radial gradients, inset shadows, and images over 1024 px, we discussed the feature's shortcomings within the feature description. Browser vendors are constantly updating the capacity of their browsers and improving the performance. Soon radial gradients, inset shadows, and huge images may not drain a phone's memory. The online chapter resources provide links to resources listing some of the current mobile browser pitfalls.

Manage memory

Limited memory should be a concern throughout the entire development process. We all develop our web applications on our desktops where memory is not as limited, so you may forget to think about it: don't forget!

When developing on desktop, pay attention to the memory consumption of your web application. The Chrome browser allows you to keep track of memory consumption and performance, as shown in Figure 12-1.

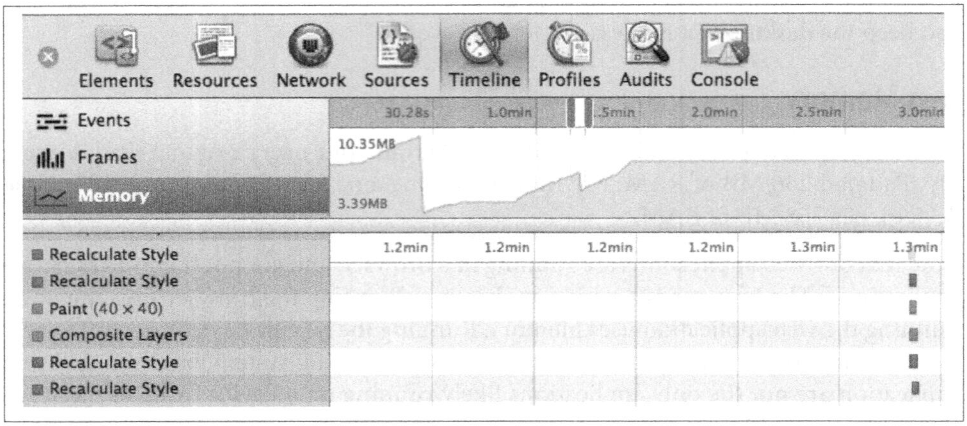

Figure 12-1. Memory in Chrome developer tools

Chrome provides information on how much memory each browser tab is using. To observe your memory usage, open the developer tools in your Chrome desktop browser (View → Developer → Developer Tools). Select the Timeline tab, then select Memory within the Timeline view, which is the tab and subsection displayed in Figure 12-1.[4]

To measure memory consumption, select the record button (the gray circle at the bottom of the developer tools). When the record button is red, it means it is recording. Play with your application. Watch the memory increase as DOM nodes or assets are added, and decrease with garbage collection.

Remember that while your crazy web application may be using 80 MB, your web application is not the only thing running on your user's device. They are running their OS, their browser, their phone. They have other applications running in the background. All of these applications use up memory.

During development, you'll be using desktop tools for testing. When device testing there are also mobile OS specific apps that will measure memory and battery load with application and mobile web usage. These tools are discussed in Chapter 14.

While the Timeline Memory feature in the development tools can help you gauge how much memory your application is consuming, you still have to test your applications in various devices. Those devices should have numerous native applications installed with notifications turned on, as this is how your users are experiencing your web application.

---

4. Safari Developer Tools, Opera DragonFly, Firebug the FireFox add-on, and IE F12, starting with IE11, have similar tools.

As a developer, you need to consider site latency, memory usage, battery consumption, and bandwidth usage of your sites. Don't forget to test on mobile networks, which generally aren't as fast as WiFi. I'll cover performance in greater detail in Chapter 14.

One Window, One Application at a Time

Your mobile users may only be able to see one browser window at a time. On most mobile platforms, even if your web application contains multiple screens, your users will see them sequentially, not simultaneously.

While your mobile web application should make available the entire feature set of the full application, instead of trying to replicate a wider feature set at once, focus on a single task at a time. With limited memory, space, and sequential page viewing, provide the most useful information on the main view, supplying access to additional functionality through additional screens, or More or i-buttons linking to the larger feature set, providing access to the larger, less frequently used feature set only when necessary.

When interacting with most smartphones (less true with some tablets), only one application is visible in the foreground at a time. When users switch from one application to another, the application sometimes quits completely, while other times it continues in the background.

Some devices allow for multitasking: the application losing focus transitions to the background, allowing applications to remain in the background until they are launched again or until they are terminated. This means when a user clicks on a link to YouTube, a phone number, or a Google map, your browser, and therefore your web application, may quit completely, or more commonly, it will continue as a background process. Because you don't know if your user is on a device that allows for multitasking or not, you can't make assumptions about whether the browser and web application will quit or not.

Minimal Documentation

Like most people, I only look at the IKEA instructions after I finish putting furniture together and wonder why I have three pieces left over. I am even less likely to read an FAQ or other instructions on my phone than I am to review the printed manual on the piece of furniture I just destroyed.

Similarly, users won't read your instructions or help documentation before using your application. To succeed, your application needs to be easy to use, the functionality needs to be immediately obvious and your application and user experience need to meet your users' expectations. This is true no matter the device.

Use standard controls. Present information in a logical and predictable manner. Make sure the path back is as obvious as the path forward in your application. Design your applications to behave in a consistent, predictable fashion.

Even if you work for a design firm, or especially if you work for a design firm, don't try to be innovative in your interactions and UI: use standard user experience best practices and design. This will make your application more intuitive. Intuitive applications are more successful. If you must be innovative (and even if you aren't), test, test, and retest, with diverse users. UI and UX innovation can be good, or even very good, if the iterations are thoroughly tested on users with a wide range of mobile literacy.

Development Considerations

Remember that your user may be mobile. Users need to be able to download your web application quickly and see relevant content immediately within the viewable browser window, whether that window is in portrait or landscape orientation. It's not that scrolling isn't allowed. Rather, you should have relevant information and a main call to action visible without scrolling.

The user needs to be able to achieve their goals with very few finger gestures. Always remember that your users may not have a mouse, scroll button, or keyboard available to navigate your application. They may only have the use of one or two fingers available for interacting with your site, navigating with one hand, as the other may be holding the device, or maybe aren't using their fingers at all. They may be using their voice for navigation, which is not only for Google Glass.

User interface should focus on providing the right categories and making it easy to perform common tasks, without asking for a lot of details that aren't central to the task.

Distill the list of features into a single statement, a product definition statement, that describes both the solution your product offers and defines the target market. Stay within your definition for all of your main features.

Yes, you can and should include all lesser used features, but make those secondary features. The context should always be the actions you expect your user to take, targeted to your defined audience.

If a feature isn't core to the goals of your users, don't include it on your web application landing page: say "No" to your marketing and sales teams. The real estate of the mobile phone is too small, download speeds are to slow, and user interactions are too difficult to spread your application thin. Mobile device real estate provides no room for functionality that doesn't focus on the primary task. And by developing for mobile first, your desktop application will benefit.

By defining your audience, you can refine your product definition for your application to meet your audience's main need. Through this refined product definition, you will be better able to siphon your list of features. Eliminate features that, while they might be useful, don't fit into the product definition of your application. Do one thing, and do it well. Port this logic over to the desktop: your users will love the simplicity there, too!

Targeting Mobile WebKit

To create a web application that looks like a native mobile application, there are several features to consider. There are `<meta>` tags and `<link>` relationships that appear to be proprietary to Apple, but some work on Android, Chrome for Android, BlackBerry 10, and iOS. We discussed these `<meta>` tags and `<link>` relationships in Chapter 2, but let's look at them again.

On iOS, you can tell the browser that we want to be an offline application:

```
<meta name="apple-mobile-web-app-capable" content="yes"/>
```

This will only work if the user has saved your web application as a bookmark with an icon on their home screen and has accessed your web application via that bookmark rather than navigating to it via the browser address bar. While this may seem limited, it does enable your application to go fullscreen and look like a truly native application, even though it is really a web application. This `<meta>` tag removes standard navigation and controls in iOS WebKit browsers when the user has accessed your web application from their saved bookmark.

While this tells the browser that you want it to look like a native application with native application features, you still have to tell the browser what those native features are. You can control the status bar color and navigation bar when the application is offline.

Status Bar

The status bar displays important information about the user's device, including signal strength, network connection, and battery life. When your site or application is viewed within a browser on a mobile device, you cannot hide the 20-pixel-high status bar (Figure 12-2).

Figure 12-2. iPhone status bar

The ability to hide the status bar should not be a differentiating factor in your decision whether to build a native or web application. While you can hide the status bar when developing a native application in some devices, you shouldn't. Requiring a user to quit an application to see how much battery power they have left, or to see if they have connectivity is not a good user experience.

In iOS, you can change the color of the status bar from the default appearance as shown in Figure 12-2 to black or translucent black by setting the application to run in full-screen mode and setting the status bar style meta tag to `default`, `black`, or `black-`

translucent, which displays the status bar as gray (the default color), opaque black, or translucent black (`rgba(0,0,0,0.5)`):

```
<meta name="apple-mobile-web-app-capable" content="yes"/>
<meta name="apple-mobile-web-app-status-bar-style" content="black">
```

This meta tag only works if you have set the page to be `web-app-capable`.

When the `apple-mobile-web-app-capable` meta tag content is set to `yes`, the web application runs in fullscreen mode; otherwise, it does not. This does nothing if the user navigated to your site through the browser. It only behaves like a native application if it was accessed like a native application.

The `black-translucent` makes the status bar 50% translucent above the content of the web page or application, providing for some additional screen space, which can be useful if your application is a game like Tetris with items coming in from the top of the screen.

We've included these `<meta>` tags in CubeeDoo. However, you may not be seeing them. To be able to view this feature in action, you will need to add CubeeDoo as a bookmark link on your home screen, and access the web application by clicking on that icon, in a browser on a device that supports this feature.

Navigation Bar

The navigation bar is the address bar that appears at the top of the screen, just below the status bar (Figure 12-3). By default, some mobile browsers like Safari on the iOS and the Firefox OS browser display the contents of the `<title>` of your web page along with the search and address bars in a 60-pixel-high navigation bar. Chrome for mobile displays the URL, tools linking to more information about the page, other tabs that are open, and a drop-down toolbar. Chrome for larger mobile devices, like the Nexus Galaxy, displays tabbed browsing like a desktop browser.

Figure 12-3. Safari (top) and Android Chrome (bottom) navigation bars

To create a native-looking web application, we can hide the default navigation bar and add our own application navigation bar. In our Chapter 7 example, we used CSS to emulate the original iPhone's native navigation bar, as shown in Figure 12-4.

Figure 12-4. CSS navigation bar emulating the original iPhone native application navigation bar

With a little magic, you can hide the big Safari navigation toolbar even if the user hasn't saved your bookmark to their desktop. The fallback method is to hide the navigation bar with JavaScript.

To hide the Safari navigation bar,[5] include `window.scrollTo(0, 1);` in your web application. The following script will hide the Safari navigation bar when the page loads:

```
<script>
addEventListener("load", function() {
    setTimeout(hideURLbar, 0);
    }, false);

function hideURLbar() {
    window.scrollTo(0,1);
}
</script>
```

UX of navigation bar

When creating a navigation bar to emulate a native application's look and feel, the initial or home view should display only your application title, as the user hasn't navigated into the application yet. If your application is only one page, the home page navigation bar can also contain controls that manage the content in the view. If your application is more than one page, all other screens should include the title of the new location with a Back button labeled with the title of the previous location, or the word "back" to the left of the title.

This "back" button provides for a standard way to return to the previous screen. This is expected user experience, so don't alter it unless you have a very compelling reason to. Always remember, a frustrated user can be driven to use the home button and may not return. The navigation bar can contain a second button to the right of the title that manages the content in the view.

Apple provides for standardized buttons. As you can see in Figure 12-4, buttons in a navigation bar include a bezel around them. All Apple iOS controls in a navigation bar use the bordered style. All iOS UI icons are 30 × 30 pixels for tab bar icons with a touchable area of 44 × 44 pixels. Apple employs 20 × 20 pixels for toolbar and navigation icons.

---

5. iOS 7 does not allow for hiding the navigation bar.

Android design patterns recommend a pattern of a 48-device independent pixel rhythm. 48 DP translates to about 9 millimeters (0.35 inches) with some variability, providing touch areas in the range of recommended 7–10 millimeters target size.

Design elements that are at least 48 DP high and wide guarantee targets will never be smaller than the minimum recommended target size of 7 mm regardless of the screen, and 48 DP provides for good overall information density and targetability of UI. Spacing between each UI element should be 8 DP.

Page controls. The page controls should be in a 44- to 48-pixel-high bar going across the bottom of the screen, with the controls going from most used controls on the lefthand side to less frequently used controls on the right. Don't create touch gestures too close to the browser edge as some mobile devices will capture the gesture for a device or native browser action.

Do not place controls you wouldn't want a user to accidentally hit in the bottom bar. The bottom bar should be reserved for the most commonly used user actions. Include items that may be clicked less often, like settings or delete, elsewhere, such as on the top navigation or on a separate screen if rarely used.

In CubeeDoo, we put our page controls, even ones we expect to be hit often, at the top of the screen. Why? Because this web app is a game. 99% of the time will be spent playing the game, not checking high scores or other menu features. Users wouldn't want to accidentally press *any* of the controls midgame. So while the bottom page control strip makes sense for many web applications, there is no steadfast rule. The only real rule is use common sense (oh, and provide preferably 44 × 44 px, but at minimum 22 × 22 px, buttons and interactive areas if you want a user to successfully hit something).

Navigation bar size and color

Changing the device orientation from portrait to landscape can change the height of the navigation bar automatically (you should not specify the height programmatically). In landscape orientation, the thinner navigation bar provides more space for your screen contents. Be sure to take the difference in heights into account when you design icons for navigation bar controls and when you design the layout of your screens.

Strive for consistency in the appearance of navigation bars and other bars in your application. If you use a translucent navigation bar, for example, don't combine it with an opaque toolbar. Also, avoid changing the color or translucency of the navigation bar in different screens in the same orientation.

Startup Image

If the user clicks on a home screen icon, the web application will launch immediately, perhaps before all the files are received from the server. In some browsers, including iOS native Safari browsers, we can control what the browser displays while waiting for the site to be downloaded by providing a startup image.

You can also tell the browser to display a particular image while the browser is waiting to load, parse, and lay out all your assets:

```
<link rel="apple-touch-startup-image" href="/screenshot.jpg"/>
```

This is a URL pointing to the startup image. By default, a screenshot of the web application the last time it was launched is used, but with this tag you can define your own image.

This is not a splash screen. In fact, don't use a splash screen. Your users want to get to your content. They don't want to be delayed (and charged bandwidth fees) because your marketing team or CEO really like Flash-like intros.

Home Screen Icons

```
<link rel="apple-touch-icon"…
```

This is the pointer to the image that we want to be the icon of the site that resides on the device's home screen, should they bookmark our site. Not all devices require the same size image or resolution, however. There are even differences between devices from the same manufacturer. As discussed in Chapter 2, we have a new attribute for the <link> tag that helps handle this situation:

```
<link rel="apple-touch-icon" href="touch-icon-iphone.png" />
<link rel="apple-touch-icon" sizes="72x72"
    href="touch-icon-ipad.png" />
<link rel="apple-touch-icon" sizes="114x114"
    href="touch-icon-hiresolution.png" />
```

The device will convert your icon into an icon reflective of the OS. On iOS 6 and earlier, it will add rounded corners and a glow. If you want to create your own corners and glow or lack of glow, include the key term precomposed in your relationship value. Use:

```
<link rel="apple-touch-icon-precomposed" href="path/image.png"/>
```

Take the time to design a beautiful icon. Users should be able to tell, just by looking at your icon, what your site or application is about. Unless you are a very well-known company with a very well-known brand name (think CNN), be wary of including text in your icon.

The default iPhone icon (pre-iOS 7) is 57 × 57 pixels, with a 10 px border radius. For the iPad, it's 74 × 74 pixels with a 12 px radius. The icon for the iTunes Store is 512 × 512 pixels.

If you are indeed hoping to be in the App Store, a few notes: Apple loves tactile backgrounds, subtle shadows, highlighted text, glossy buttons, subtle gradients, and clean, crisp icons. If you are submitting to the App Store, or even if you aren't submitting to the App Store, don't use Apple icons, imagery, or trademarks in any applications.[6]

Minimize Keyboard Entry

While there is a high cost ratio for data entry on all devices, it's even more acute on touch devices. If you require a user to enter data, make sure it's worth their while. Yes, sometimes information is required. If your marketing team is pushing for a ZIP code when a user ZIP code is not required, say "No." Do not add barriers to entry that aren't absolutely necessary. This is important for mobile and desktop!

When data entry is required, make it as simple as possible. Unless security requirements prohibit it, if you require a username and password, remember the user information! If the user has to enter data, whenever possible, create a select list or other form of picker, so that the user can use any method other than keyboard entry to provide the information. If a user needs to enter a phone number or an email, use the proper input types (see Chapter 4) so that they get the right keyboard.

Generally, forms place labels before input fields and hints after the form field. Make sure that these wrap on smaller devices. Or better yet, place the label above the input area, and hints below. When devices pop-up the virtual keyboard, many simultaneously zoom in on the focused form field, which will hide what is to the left and right of the form field on narrow screens.

Be Succinct

That's it. Be succinct.

Your users are staring at tiny little fonts on tiny little devices. Even on desktop, users don't like to read. Get to the point. Do it succinctly.

To summarize succinctly:

Make it Obvious

Your users don't have the time or the attention to figure out complex interactions and application. Make your application instantly understandable to users.

---

6. Glyfish works, but popular stock icons will be looked down upon.

Minimize Required Input

Inputting information takes users' time and attention. If your application requires a lot of user input before anything useful happens, you're basically asking them to move on to a different site or application.

Minimize Text

When your user interface text is short and direct, users can absorb it quickly and easily. Identify the most important information, express it concisely, and display it prominently.

Other User Experience Considerations

Avoid hidden content that is only made visible (and possibly obscured by your user's hand) when hovered. Fingers are fat. Hands are big. When you only display something between touch start and touch end, or only on hover, that information may not be fully available to the touch user.

There are certain conventions that are bad on desktop and even worse on mobile. Drop-down menus with submenus that pop-out on hover are bad for desktop and even worse for mobile.

When you require a user to utilize a hover drop-down or pop-out menu to navigate your site, you are requiring them to stay on top of the menu, without exiting or hovering out of it, until they reach their destination. Users don't hover on touch devices: they touch. On some devices, your CSS show on :hover will work, but you will need to handle the touch scripts necessary for these menus so that all devices display the menus and don't let the submenus slip away.

As you'll note in Figure 12-5, the fastest way to go from the "Dropdown" to "Pick Me" would take the user outside of the pop-out menu, thereby closing it. That is, if a user's fat finger and hand don't obscure the contents of the page. Even with a mouse, while the content is more readily visible, the direct line from one link to the next is partially outside of the menu, and navigating off of the navigation generally hides it.

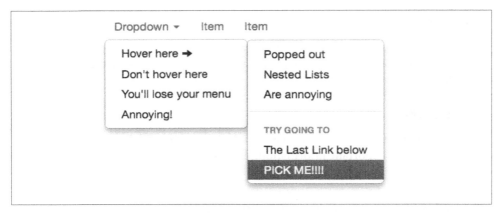

Figure 12-5. Example of a common drop-down menu

Move away from drop-down pull-out menu patterns, and opt for click-based menus instead. Additionally, dynamically loading additional content when lists or navigations are too long can be a best practice. Killing excessive content above the currently visible list may also be good practice, especially with infinite scroll,[7] to reduce memory consumption and the number of DOM nodes, which slows down reflows.

The user experience considerations covered in this entire chapter hold true not just for mobile websites and applications, but for desktop sites and native mobile applications as well.

---

7. Google's proposal for lazy block loading may ameliorate this.

Targeting Mobile Devices and Touch

You've hopefully realized by now that your markup for the mobile browser is the same code as the desktop browser. The main differences are the size of the viewport and how the user interacts with their device. On the desktop we use a keyboard and mouse, with a large screen and resizable browser. On touch devices, we use our chubby little fingers, sometimes on tiny little screens, in viewports that are generally not resizable.

Those were generalizations! I have a desktop computer with a 23-inch touchscreen. I also have a tablet with an external Bluetooth keyboard and mouse. All our web content needs to be accessible via touch and mouse on large monitors and tiny screens. Whenever we develop, we need to remember that not everyone is accessing our content in the same way.

Scaling Down to Size

When it comes to smaller viewports, we want the width of our site to be the width of the device. The default page rendering size for most mobile browsers is 980 px wide. That is generally not the width of the device.

Until `@viewport` is supported everywhere, we can use the viewport `<meta>` tag. This tag is ignored by desktop browsers:

```
<meta name="viewport" content="width=device-width;"/>
```

There are several possible values for the content attribute of the viewport `<meta>` tag. Unless you are developing an interactive, time-sensitive game, this is the viewport you should include. Your users should be allowed to scale the page up and down. The preceding code allows them to zoom in, which is important for accessibility.

In the case of CubeeDoo, we are creating a fullscreen, interactive, time-sensitive game. We don't want to allow the user to accidentally zoom in or out. Unlike most other application types, when it comes to games, it can be bad user experience when the board no longer fits neatly in the window. Only if you have a good reason to not allow zooming (which we do in the case of some games), should we consider it a good idea to prevent zooming with the following viewport `<meta>` tag:

```
<meta name="viewport" content="width=device-width;
    initial-scale=1.0; maximum-scale=1.0; minimum-scale: 1;
    user-scalable=0;"/>
```

This example is a little bit overkill. It reads, "Make the width of the viewport the same width of the device. Make that the initial size, the minimum allowable scaling size, and the maximum scaleable size, and don't allow scaling." I've included more content properties than I need to just to show the values. More reasonably, you can write:

```
<meta name="viewport" content="width=device-width;
    initial-scale=1.0; user-scalable=0;"/>
```

Generally, you will want to use `width=device-width`. However, if your site is a specific width for different breakpoints (and I don't recommend this), you can declare a specific width. For example, if your site's medium breakpoint design is exactly 550 px, you can write:

```
<meta name="viewport" content="width=550">
```

I can't think of any time where declaring a single width for content is a good idea. Don't do it. This is just to show you what code you may come across, and so you know how to filter out bad developers from your applicant pool.

@viewport

The viewport `<meta>` tag is using HTML features to control presentation, which should be the domain of CSS. Mixing presentation into your content layer isn't the right solution. However, it's the only solution we have at the time of this writing. The `@view port` at-rule is getting some support (Opera, IE10, and WebKit nightly builds). Until `@viewport` is more widely supported, the viewport `<meta>` is the solution.

Touch Me

We are focusing on mobile and are therefore only supporting modern browsers. All modern browsers support the DOM `addEventListener` method. Because we are on mobile (and making generalizations), we are capturing touches rather than mouse movement and clicks.

Two of the main differences between touches and clicks are the size of the area throwing the event and the number of events that can be thrown simultaneously. Touch areas are much larger than mouse click areas: a finger is fat, while a mouse pointer is just a pixel. Also, touch devices support multitouch events, as a device can be touched with multiple fingers.

Different devices support different gestures and capture different numbers of fingers. The iPad, for example, can capture up to 11 fingers or touches at once. Standard mouse events don't handle multiple clicks: a single mouse click produces a single click event in a single spot.

Every touch, whether done with a finger or a stylus, is a click event, but some devices will wait 300 to 500 milliseconds before reacting to the touch to ensure the gesture or touch is a single tap and not a double tap. We cover this in the next section.

Note that a finger is not as exact as a mouse pointer if you are using mouse/touch coordinates! A mouse can be very exact. A finger? Not so much.

Touch Areas

Touch devices have unique features in terms of design and usability. With the same amount of effort, the user can access every pixel on the screen. The user uses their fingers for selection, which has a much bigger pointing radius than a mouse.

Your design needs to reflect these differences with larger hit zones and larger gutters between hit zones. The recommended height for buttons is 44 pixels, with a minimum height of 22 px, with 20 px of space between clickable areas and at minimum 10 px between these areas.

When the user touches the screen, the part under the finger and under the whole hand can be obscured. The user may be using her right hand or she may be using her left hand. Consider what might be hidden depending on which hand they're using, and how important the content that is hidden under the user's palm is.

The finger touching the screen and even parts of the hand may hide areas of the screen. Ensure that your labels are above their associated form field, and touch events don't display temporarily visible dialogues at all. But if you must include a temporary pop-up, they need to be above the touch area, not to the side or below it.

There are a few finger gestures that are used by the operating system of the device, and not every operating system or device uses the same gestures. You should know what these are, especially when you are developing the user experience of your site. Some iOS devices use four-finger detection to switch between applications. You may also want to avoid gestures close to the edges of the viewport as several mobile devices move between windows, tabs, or applications when the user flicks or swipes from or to the edge of the screen. Keep all these native mobile OS features in mind when designing and developing your application and user interactions.

Mouse Events, Touch Events

Mouse events make the Web work. It wouldn't be a web if every document ever (well, almost every document ever) didn't have clickable links leading to other documents.

Games wouldn't be games if you couldn't interact with them. These interactions have generally been mouse clicks.

For the past 20 years or so, developers have been adding click events to their web pages. While we tap, touch, and tilt mobile devices, we don't actually click our smartphones. With many mobile devices and some laptops, we can also tilt to interact. But basically, click events make the Web the Web. If touch devices didn't support those ubiquitous mouse events, the mobile web would really be broken.

Because the Web is built on mouse events, mouse events work on touch devices—devices with no pointing devices. Mouse events are simulated after touch events are fired. Mouse events are thrown in an emulated environment, but the order of mouse event is not guaranteed. Every touch throws a click, mouse down, enter, exit, etc., but we can never be sure of the order in which they occur.

Every device emulates mouse events when using touch and provides us with other specific touch events we can capture. With touch events, there are two implementations we need to understand: (1) Apple's touch and gesture events, an unfinished specification, which have been cancelled due to Apple's patents; and (2) Microsoft's pointer and gesture events, which are a newer, patent-free specification, which will become the standard and will soon be implemented in Chrome and Firefox. Standards and implementations are still evolving.

Pointer events

Corporations, most notably Apple, patent everything, including normal, everyday things like rounded corners and human interactions. Attempts have been made to make some gestures proprietary: Apple actually patented touch events. Specifications are open standards. So there was an issue. Pointer events to the rescue! Microsoft created their own version of events—pointer events—and offered those to the W3C to be used as the basis for the standard.[1]

Not to be confused with the CSS `pointer-events` property, pointer events is an event model for mouse cursor, pen, touch (including multitouch), and all other pointing input devices. Similar to the JavaScript events we're so used to, like `mouseover` and `mouse out`, when supported we will have the `pointerdown`, `pointerup`, `pointercancel`, `poin termove`, `pointerover`, `pointerout`, `pointerenter`, and `pointerleave` events. In addition to events we can listen for, the device will capture details about touch or pointing events such as touch size, type, pressure, and angle. Currently, the only implementation of pointer events is in IE10 with the Microsoft MS prefix, so `pointermove` in IE10 is coded as `MSpointermove`, and in IE11 sans prefix.

---

1. For more information, see *http://blog.jquery.com/2012/04/10/getting-touchy-about-patents/*.

Touch events

As we all know, mice and fingers are different. When using a mouse, you have a single pointer hovering, entering, exiting, and clicking on a single pixel. Fingers not only tap larger areas, but people have five of them. On each hand! The device and your event handlers need to keep track of the number of fingers interacting with the screen. You can create and handle sophisticated gestures by using the native touch and mouse events in conjunction with `preventDefault()`.

Until browser vendors agree upon and support the open standard of pointer events, we have touch events.

Touch devices and their browsers, including Android Browser, Chrome, BlackBerry Browser, Opera, and Firefox, support the iOS `touchstart`, `touchend`, `touchmove`, and the sometimes-buggy `touchcancel` events. The four events return a `TouchEvent` object, a `changedTouches` collection, and the `Touch` object.

The `Touch` object is a read-only object containing the coordinate properties of the touch point, including touch coordinates `pageX`, `pageY`, `screenX`, `screenY`, `clientX`, `clientY`, the `target`, and the `identifier`. The `TouchList` is the list of individual points of contact for the touch event. The `TouchEvent` object contains the `touches`, `targetTouches`, and `changedTouches` collections, as well as the Booleans `altKey`, `metaKey`, `ctrlKey`, and `shiftKey`.

Touch the device with one finger or a stylus, and a single event is thrown. Touch with several fingers, and several events will be thrown. When the screen is pressed, the `touchstart` is thrown. When the finger moves across the screen, the `touchmove` event will be repeatedly thrown. When the pressure on the screen ceases, the `touchend` is fired. The `touchcancel` occurs when another application, like an actual phone call, cancels the touch.

If your user is playing a game, listening to a podcast, or watching a video clip, and the phone rings, does it make sense to pause the game, stop the sound, or pause the video during the call? We don't want to upset our users by having the time run out and losing the game every time they answer a call. In CubeeDoo, we pause the game when the `touchcancel` event is fired:

```
document.addEventListener('touchcancel', function() {
    if (!qbdoo.game.classList.contains('paused')) {
            qbdoo.pauseGame();
    }
});
```

Touch devices support many gestures you may want to capture. Luke Wroblewski compiled the Touch Gesture Reference Guide (*http://www.mobilexweb.com/go/touchguide*), defining the various touch gestures by operating system. I recommend printing it and hanging it over your desk (next to the specificity chart from Appendix A).

Feature detection for touch events

If you are using the same code for both touch devices and desktop browsers, you will likely need to increase the touch area for links, and decrease the delay between a single touch and its event.

You might think that using media queries would be the way to go: smaller screens are likely mobile screens, and mobile screens are more likely to be touch screens. But then you have tablets, which can have higher resolutions than many laptops and small monitors.

Feature detection seems like a solution, but it's not perfect. Touch feature detection detects whether the browser supports touch events, not whether the device does. You have to test with JavaScript to check for touch event properties:

```
var isTouchEnabled = 'ontouchstart' in window ||
    'createTouch' in document ||
      (window.DocumentTouch && document instanceof DocumentTouch);
```

You can then use the `isTouchEnabled` Boolean to handle touch-capable and touch-incapable devices, remembering that some devices and some users, like some feature phones and visual- or motor-impaired users may not have any pointing devices.

To simulate single-touch events in your desktop development environment, try the Phantom Limb utility (*http://www.vodori.com/blog/phantom-limb.html*).

Pseudo or Not-So-Pseudo Click Events

When you *click* with your finger there is no *right-click* event. Because of this, mobile devices react when you hold down your touch instead. Because there is no keyboard, mouse, or right-click, mobile browsers have some built-in behaviors.

Tap highlight color

There is no such thing as hover on a touch device. Because of this, we have link tap highlight color that we can control with `tap-highlight-color`. You can style the highlight color to match your design. While the value `transparent` will get rid of the oftentimes unsightly effect, remember that removing the appearance of a tap effect negatively affects accessibility:

```
#content a {
  -webkit-tap-highlight-color: #bada55;
}
#board a {
  -webkit-tap-highlight-color: transparent;
}
```

We don't actually have any links in our board, but if we did, this code would make the background of any link #bada55 on top, except for the links in the game board, which

---

would show no effect on tap, other than the card flip effect, which is controlled separately.

Kill the selection dialog

When you touch and hold on text copy, or touch and drag, you may have noticed the appearance of a selection dialogue allowing you to copy or define the selected text. You can control this in WebKit browsers with `-webkit-user-select: none;`. When `user-select` is set to `none` on a DOM node, like a paragraph or even the <body>, no copy/define selection dialog will appear.

The `pointer-events: none;` property/value pair is inappropriate in this setting. While it would prevent the user from getting the copy/define dialogue, it would also prevent any other touch events from occurring on the user-select targeted DOM node.

Kill the images dialog

Similar to the selection dialog , when a user touches and holds an image, an image save/copy panel appears. Adding `touch-callout: none;` to all images will ensure that no image dialog appears when images are touched:

```
img {
-webkit-touch-callout: none;
}
```

For best user experience and accessibility, do not use the preceding CSS properties in content sites. These properties should be reserved for games and other entertainment, productivity, and tool applications.

Kill panning

You don't want your users to accidentally pop-up an operating system menu. With CSS you are able to disable panning. You don't want to completely disable panning all the time, but you can use `touch-action: none;` to prevent accidental panning if accidental panning is likely to occur:

```
.active #board {
  -ms-touch-action: none; /* disable panning */
  }
```

You might be thinking, "Why not just use JavaScript's `preventDefault()`?" You could likely get that to work. However, using the four CSS properties just covered performs better than `preventDefault()`. CSS is almost always more performant than JavaScript. And, in this case, there is up to a 400 ms lag in firing touch events, so it's best to prevent the panning, dialoging, etc., before it ever happens.

onTouchEnd

Because the device doesn't know if you are going to do a single tap or double tap, there is a 300–500 ms delay after the first tap before the touch event is triggered. Touch-enabled browsers on touch devices will wait from 300 ms to 500 ms, depending on the device, from the time that you tap the screen to firing the click event. The reason for this is that the browser is waiting to see if you are actually performing a double tap. Because of this, you may want to usurp the first tap (not waiting to expire the delay between taps) with an event handler.

If you are making a call to the server or other slow process, provide feedback to the user that the touch has been accepted. Depending on the connection speed, a server response can take a long, long time. You want the user to know that something is indeed happening—that their action is being acted upon—if the server response to the action takes more than 100 to 200 ms.

In CubeeDoo, we aren't making server calls, so we don't need to add a "waiting" feature. However, we certainly don't want to wait 300 ms before flipping the card when the user touches the screen. In the application we are developing we know that there is no double-click behavior that we want to handle, so waiting this long to start acting on the click is time wasted for users.

While usurping user interaction is something you want to carefully consider before doing, in our example there is no reason that a user would double-click: we don't allow for zooming or have any other double-click features. We capture the touches to the cards with the touchend event. Making the browser react faster to touch events involves a bit of JavaScript that allows the application to respond to touchend events rather than click events. Touchend events are fired immediately on touch end, so they are significantly faster than click events, which wait the 300 to 500 milliseconds.[2]

We need to keep the onclick handler to the cards for browsers that don't support touch events, but we don't want to handle a touchend then fire off a click 300 ms later. If this were a button or link, we would need to ensure we don't accidentally run two events on the same node by calling preventDefault on the touchstart event. Calling prevent Default on touchstart events will stop clicks and scrolling from occurring as a result of the current tap:

```
eventHandlers: function() {
 if ('ontouchstart' in window ||
   'createTouch' in document ||
    (window.DocumentTouch && document instanceof DocumentTouch)) {
        qbdoo.btn_pause.addEventListener('touchend',
            qbdoo.pauseGameOrNewGame);
        qbdoo.btn_mute.addEventListener('touchend',
            qbdoo.toggleMute);
        qbdoo.clearScores.addEventListener('touchend',
            qbdoo.eraseScores);
        document.addEventListener('touchcancel',
            qbdoo.pauseGameOrNewGame);
    }
```

---

2. In Firefox and Chrome, if zooming is disabled, the click event fires immediately, and doesn't wait the 500 ms.

```
qbdoo.btn_pause.addEventListener('click', qbdoo.pauseGameOrNewGame);
qbdoo.btn_mute.addEventListener('click', qbdoo.toggleMute);
qbdoo.clearScores.addEventListener('click', qbdoo.eraseScores);
qbdoo.themeChanger.addEventListener('change', qbdoo.changeTheme);
},
```

Another solution is to add click and touchend event listeners to the <body>, listening on the capture phase. When the event listener is invoked, you determine if the click or tap was a result of a user interaction that was already handled. If so, call preventDefault and stopPropagation on it. Remember that some desktops come with touch screens, so always include both click and touch events, preventing the default click in case of touch.

Touching to scroll

Our game doesn't scroll. Generally, we have to touch the screen to scroll, and when we let go the logic tells us there is the touchend event. Currently, when scrolling, the touchend event is thrown in most mobile browsers, with the exception of Chrome for Android. The specifications don't specify that touch events should be canceled when scrolling, but that does make sense.

Chrome for Android behaves a little differently, and this behavior is being added to the pointer events specification. The specifications for touchevents don't deal with this issue, but pointer events will. When pointer events are supported, scrolling, pinching, zooming, and other device (versus page) interactions will throw a cancel event.

Different platforms also handle different gestures. Apple (iOS), Google (Android), and Microsoft (Windows) all support different gestures that provide more refined interactions.

Hardware Access

Touch is one difference you'll note in the mobile space. Touch isn't reserved for mobile. There are more and more monitors on laptops and desktops and other devices that are accepting touch. The touch screen also isn't the only new hardware feature that we can interact with. Depending on the operating system, device, and browser, using CSS, JavaScript, and HTML5, we can create browser applications that interact with system hardware in a way that used to be reserved for natively installed applications.

Phone Movement and Direction

Most mobile devices include sensors from which we can access data using JavaScript, including the accelerometer, magnetometer, and gyroscope. To handle the orientation of the device, we have the deviceOrientation event specification that provides us with three window events, detailed in the following paragraphs.

The *accelerometer* measures acceleration or linear motion on three axes. Used to detect motion, tilting, and shaking, it measures the acceleration force in m/s² that is applied to the device on all three physical axes (x, y, and z), including the force of gravity. We can handle `devicemotion` for accelerometer data detection:

```
window.addEventListener('devicemotion', function( ) {
  // add response to event here
});
```

The *magnetometer* measures where the device is heading, like a compass, but doesn't necessarily point north. The magnetometer measures the strength of the magnetic field in three dimensions, measuring the ambient geomagnetic field for all three physical axes (x, y, z) in µT. The `compassneedscalibration` event is thrown when the device detects that the compass needs a calibration to improve data accuracy. To calibrate, the user does a figure eight with the device:

```
window.addEventListener('compassneedscalibration', function( ) {
  // add response to event here
  // generally telling the user to make a figure 8 with the device
});
```

The *gyroscope* measures the device's rate of rotation in rads per second around each of the three physical axes (x, y, and z). Because it measures the rate of rotation around a single axis based on angular momentum excluding the force of gravity, the gyroscope can provide information on the device's rotation and orientation if you need to measure whether the user is spinning or turning the device. We can capture `deviceorientation` when supported:

```
window.addEventListener('deviceorientation', function( ) {
  // add response to event here
});
```

Every time the user moves the device, the `deviceorientation` event occurs, including the properties alpha (0–360), beta (–90–90), and gamma (–180–180) for the rotation of the device frame around its z-, x-, and y-axis, respectively. The property measurements are generally relative to the direction the device was held when the orientation was first obtained making `deviceorientation` useful for relative movements from the original position.

Device Status

We are not only able to figure out how the user is holding the device, but we can also determine what state the device is in. Is the device online? If so, what type of network connection does it have? Does the device have battery power left?

Network connection

The Network API (*http://www.w3.org/TR/netinfo-api/*) exposes the `navigator.con nection.type` attribute with a string value of `unknown`, `ethernet`, `wifi`, `2g`, `3g`, `4g`, or `none`. Some browsers returned integers or constants for those values: `WIFI`, `CELL`, `CELL_3G`, `CELL_2G`, `CELL_4G`, and `UNKNOWN`. The API returns the connection type at the first connection. Devices, though, aren't always connected to the Internet, and connection types can change.

The newer API is based on the quality of the connection rather than the connection type. Considering all the phone companies lie about what connection they market, this makes even more sense than just the logic of it all. This version isn't as well supported, but support is starting. In the newer spec, instead of `type`, the `navigator.connec tion` object exposes the `bandwidth` and `metered` attributes and a `change` event.

The `navigator.connection.bandwidth` returns 0 if offline, infinite (unkown), or the number of megabytes per second as a double. The `navigator.connection.metered` property is either `true` or `false`. If true, the user's ISP is limiting your user, and you should be careful with bandwidth usage. For example, when supported, if the connection is metered, you could ask the user if they want to disable images and set a cookie for that.

The change event can be written as:

```
navigator.connection.addEventListener('change', function() {
  //handle event. Generally, check the bandwidth property
});
```

Note that the connection object is still prefixed, and can be captured as:

```
var connection =   navigator.connection ||
                   navigator.webkitConnection ||
                   navigator.mozConnection;
if (connection.bandwidth != undefined) {
 if (connection.bandwidth <= 0) {
    // offline
 } else if (connection.bandwidth <= 1) {
   // Less than 1MB/s / Low quality connection
 } else if (connection.bandwidth > 1) {
   // More than 1MB/s / High quality connection
 } else {
   // unknown
 }
} else {
  // API is not available
}
```

Battery

The Battery Status API allows you to determine the current battery status through the `navigator.battery` object. When supported, you can determine whether the battery is currently being charged with the Boolean `navigator.battery.charging` property. The `navigator.battery.chargingTime` will return, in seconds, the estimated time until the battery is fully charged. The `navigator.battery.dischargingTime` provides the time, in seconds, until a system suspension. The float `navigator.battery.level`, between 0 and 1, is the battery level.

```
var percentBatteryLeft = navigator.battery.level * 100
```

We will also have the `chargingchange`, `chargingtimechange`, `dischargingtime change`, and `levelchange` to capture.

Other APIs

Other APIs for mobile web applications include:

- Pointer Lock (*http://www.w3.org/TR/pointerlock/*)
- MediaStream Recording (*http://www.w3.org/TR/mediastream-recording/*)
- Ambient Light Events (*http://www.w3.org/TR/ambient-light/*)
- Proximity Events (*http://www.w3.org/TR/proximity/*)
- Vibration (*http://www.w3.org/TR/vibration/*)
- Web Intents (*http://www.w3.org/TR/web-intents/*)

The Calendar, Messaging, Sensor, and System Information APIs have been shelved. The Device API Working Group maintains a list of the various API statuses (*http://www.w3.org/2009/dap/*).

Native Web Apps, Packaged Apps, and Hybrids

On iOS devices, we can add `<meta>` tags that enable us to create HTML web apps that appear fullscreen as a native application would. Apple calls this type of application a Web.app. When we create a Wep.app, if the user "installs" the web application by adding the site icon to the home screen, when the user accesses the site via the home screen icon, they we will have a fullscreen experience. When accessing a web application with the correct `<meta>` tags via a home screen icon, the browser UI will be hidden. In this way and with the HTML5 APIs we covered in this book, at least on some devices, we can create native-looking applications with an offline experience that competes with any native application.

Sometimes faux native, as described earlier, is not enough. While each operating system requires native applications to be programmed in different programming languages, you can code in HTML5, CSS, and JavaScript, and convert your web application to a native application.

Hybrid applications are HTML5, CSS, and JavaScript-based applications that are converted, or compiled, into a native application, often simple using a fullscreen web view as the application container. Using the web technologies you already know, and the ones you learned in this book (HTML, CSS, JavaScript), we can package and compile our source code into a native application for the various device operating systems. Once it is a native application, we can distribute it in the various application stores.

PhoneGap/Apache Cordova

Apache Cordova, formerly PhoneGap, is an open source project and native web application framework for multiple platforms. PhoneGap enables us to export our web applications into native applications for most or all mobile platforms.

PhoneGap enables us not just to package our web application as a native application for the various mobile operating systems, but also provides us with access to components of the device that may not yet be accessible via the browser.

For example, while `getUserMedia()` is well supported in Google Chrome on desktop, recording video from a browser is not fully supported yet in the mobile space. PhoneGap allows us to program in JavaScript what is not fully supported by the mobile browser. When we export that web application into a hybrid application with PhoneGap, the wrapper converts our JavaScript into native code, understandable by the operating system, providing our hybrid application with access to device features only currently supported in the native space.

Adobe PhoneGap Build (*http://build.phonegap.com*) is a cloud-based Cordova compiler, so we don't need to deal with the native SDK on our computers.

Sencha Touch

While Sencha Touch (*http://sencha.com/products/touch*) is a UI framework, since version 2.0 it includes a native packager for iOS and Android. It is available for both Windows or Mac development environments. The packager and other developer tools can be downloaded from the Sencha website.

Appcelerator Titanium

The Appcelerator Titanium framework allows creating iOS, BlackBerry, and Android native web applications. Titanium provides a bridge, enabling you to use native UI components from JavaScript. Titanium converts JavaScript to native code during compiling. The free Appcelerator Titanium Studio IDE can be downloaded online (*http://appcelerator.com*).

Testing

Your primary development tools should include a desktop IDE and a desktop browser. The Chrome browser is a good first step in development: if it doesn't work (aside from device-specific things like touch and calling) in Chrome, it won't work on your phone either. While the desktop browser is your main tool when you are marking up and coding your application, the desktop browser is only to be used in development and primary testing: you *must* test your sites in multiple browsers on multiple devices.

Getting multiple devices can be an expensive endeavor. Realizing we haven't all won the lottery, we have to be shameless because we can't afford every device.

While you should still test in as many devices as possible of different sizes, browser versions, and operating systems under different network conditions, testing on every possible combination is not feasible. Mobile emulators provide for an easy, inexpensive testing solution. Testing on live mobile devices can be a slow and tedious process—a necessary process—but emulators can make debugging more bearable. When your code works on the desktop but doesn't work in the emulator, it likely won't work on the device either.

It's much faster to test in the emulator than on a phone. Just remember, emulators are not mobile devices. They are similar to the device they are emulating, but they have different limitations: your mobile device likely has very limited memory. Your desktop, and therefore your emulator, has an abundance of RAM. There are many differences between an emulator and a real device, but the emulator does give a good starting point.

You still need to test on devices, and we haven't resolved the lottery issue yet. In the meantime, you need access to real devices. If you can't buy, borrow or steal the plethora of devices you need to adequately test a sampling of your likely user base.

Remember your current user base and possible user base are not necessarily the same thing. If you see you only have 1% mobile usage, it may be because the mobile experience for your site sucks. It may have nothing to do with who would use your site on their mobile devices if you provided a good mobile user experience. Your current mobile usage statistics only reflects the current experience of your site in the mobile space.

There are some problems with this testing approach, though. For one thing, there are hundreds of differences between real devices, and several platforms without emulation. Real device testing is mandatory.

It is impossible to test all browsers on all devices, or even to test a single browser on every device. There are too many devices, with new ones being released all the time.

I recommend getting a few different devices with different sizes, operating systems, memory constraints, and browsers. Obviously, you can't get all of them. If possible, get at least one device in each operating system, including the most recent iOS in tablet, phone, or iPod touch versions, BlackBerry (preferably 10), Windows 8 phone or tablet, and at least two Android devices running 2.3 and 4+ or latest version.

You can't have all of the devices, nor should you. But this sampling can give you a good range. The Android 2.3 is still being sold, which is why I recommend owning one. You can purchase used devices on eBay. They're really, really cheap if they have cracked screens or the phone part is broken. All you need is the browser to work and be visible. You don't need high-quality devices.

These devices cover your basic testing. You still want to test on more devices. If you can't get Samsung, BlackBerry, Nokia, or Motorola to send you a free testing device, there is likely a device lab in your city or a remote device lab accessible online. Apple will likely never give away free devices, but if you don't have any Apple devices, you likely have a friend who does.

Testing on a single device takes time. Testing on all devices is impossible. But you do need to test. You need to QA your code on a multitude of actual devices.

During development you can use tools to test mobile web applications in a manner that more accurately reflects the mobile environment, without having to laboriously check on actual devices. Simulators and emulators can be used as a first line of testing. They are discussed in Chapter 1.

You definitely want to make sure your site looks good and doesn't fail to complete the tasks the user expects. We've already covered that. It's not enough to make sure that your site looks good and functions. You need to make sure your site functions, or performs, well. Up next we look at performance.

Mobile Performance

Whether or not your design or development is mobile first, your development process should always have performance at the top of the list of concerns.

Although the modern mobile landscape has browsers that are generally more advanced than the desktop browsers we must still cater to, the devices themselves may have similar memory and bandwidth constraints to the Pentium III you were using back in 1999. The mobile device itself, rather than the mobile browser, creates various constraints that we must consider during development.

The average website is over 1 MB. While responsive web design is currently the hot mobile topic at most conferences, mobile performance is really more important: who cares what your website looks like on the phone if your users can't download it or render it on their device?

There's a lot more to think about than the breakpoints of our adaptive design. We need to worry about feature detection, device APIs, touch events, content strategy, conditional loading of assets, and actual device performance. We need to take battery life, latency, memory, and UI responsiveness into consideration throughout the development process.

Battery Life

Unlike desktop computers that are tethered to the wall at all times, and even laptop computers that are generally used by stationary users, mobile users do not recharge their devices throughout the day. Mobile users expect their devices to last, at a minimum, 24 hours between recharging.

Your users do realize that calls and GPS usage consume battery power. However, if they think they're just using their browser to surf the Web, they don't consider that different websites will drain their battery faster than other sites. It is our job, as developers, to manage the power consumption of our code.

You have likely noticed that CPU usage drains the battery on your laptop when unplugged. CPU usage drains the battery on mobile devices just as effectively. Anything that makes your laptop churn, warm up, or turns your computer's fan on will also drain the battery of mobile devices (if they're not plugged in). Code defensively: expect that your mobile device users are not plugged in.

To manage the energy consumption of our code, we need to manage CPU usage. Avoid reflows. Minimize both size and activity of your JavaScript. Don't continuously reawaken the radio with unnecessary AJAX calls. Always use CSS, rather than JavaScript, for animations. And even though the marketing teams of devices that support WebGL insist that their devices are optimized, don't serve WebGL to mobile devices. At least, not yet. WebGL battery performance is improving.

Use Dark Colors

The brighter the colors in your design, the brighter the screen has to be. For phones with AMOLED screens, the brighter the screen, the more energy is consumed, draining the battery. *AMOLED*, or active-matrix organic light-emitting diode, screens are made of a thin layer of organic polymers that light up. Because there is no backlight, they can be very thin. Black pixels are actually turned off, saving battery life. For these non-LCD screen devices, lighter shades consume more energy during display than darker shades.

Obviously, there are issues other than battery consumption affecting the decision on what colors are used in application design. Just note that the amount of energy consumed by websites can differ significantly depending on the colors used in the design on certain devices. Colors are by far not the only feature affecting battery consumptions. Media elements like background images, foreground images, video, audio, animations, and JavaScript all contribute to battery drainage. If you can, pick darker colors. If you can't, optimize energy in your other features.

Use JPEGs

Use JPEG images instead of PNG. JPEG compresses images better and is faster to render, and is therefore more energy efficient.

Rendering images consumes energy. Depending on the number, size, and type of images in your site, rendering images can be responsible for a significant percentage of the energy used. The energy required to render images is proportional to number and size of the images rendered. JPEGs use less energy to render than GIFs and PNGs: according to the study "Who Killed My Battery: Analyzing Mobile Browser Energy Consumption,"[1] JPEG is the most energy efficient format for all image sizes.

By using JPEGs, you're not only saving battery life, you're also reducing memory and speeding up repaints. The type of image format you use affects energy consumption during rendering of the image. This impact is replayed when the image is redrawn to a different size. As we noted earlier, lighter colors consume more energy during extended display. When we are talking about image rendering costs, we are talking about the device decoding, resizing, and drawing out the image, not the energy costs once a static image is displayed.

Reduce JavaScript

While raster images are the biggest bandwidth hogs and all images are memory hogs, they're not the only culprit in memory consumption and battery drainage. JavaScript is too! To conserve battery power and memory usage, minimize both the size and activity of your JavaScript.

When the browser hits a `<script>` tag, the browser ceases downloading additional assets and rendering the assets it has already downloaded until the JavaScript is downloaded, parsed, and executed. The browser also does not start parsing and executing the script file until it is fully downloaded. Which you already know.

What you may have never thought about is the memory and energy used by JavaScript. Every time an AJAX call is made, the device's radio reawakens to make the request, draining the battery. Every time JavaScript is parsed, energy is consumed. While a site may cache the JavaScript file, it still parses and executes the JavaScript on every page load. Dynamic JavaScript, like `XMLHttpRequest`, increases rendering cost and can't be cached. Every time an event handler handles an event, JavaScript gets executed. Every time a `setTimeout` iterates, JavaScript gets executed. These all consume energy.

The download, parsing, and execution of JavaScript can be the most energy-consuming web page component. Sometimes the JavaScript isn't necessary! Only include JavaScript frameworks if you actually need them.

I have seen sites include jQuery just to simply select an element, and other similar things that are easy to do with selectors and/or native JavaScript. For example, to add the class of `first` to the first list item in every unordered list, you could use jQuery, but you don't have to:

```
$('ul li:first').addClass('first');
```

---

1. "Who Killed My Battery?: Analyzing Mobile Browser Energy Consumption." Narendran Thiagarajan, Gaurav Aggarwal, Angela Nicoara, Dan Boneh, and Jatinder Pal Singh. *http://mobisocial.stanford.edu/papers/boneh-www2012.pdf*, page 41–50. ACM (2012).

Which is almost the same as:

```
var firstLIs = document.querySelectorAll('ul li:first-of-type');

for (var i = 0; i < firstLIs.length; i++) {
  firstLIs[i].classList.add('first');[2]
}
```

... but the latter doesn't add 34 KB or an extra HTTP request to your site. And while 34 KB is not a huge amount of bytes, especially in comparison to the image size that people are adding to their sites, if you include jQuery, while the jQuery file may be cached, it is still parsed and executed with every page load. While a single page load won't drain all the power your user has left, wasting four joules[3] of energy with each page load adds up fast. And unlike when your user is using GPS or playing a movie, they aren't expecting that a website will drain their battery.

I am not saying that you shouldn't use JavaScript frameworks. I am just arguing that you should make sure you really need to include the framework before doing so because you are not only wasting memory and bandwidth, but you're also helping drain your user's battery.

Don't import a library just to target an element with CSS selectors. We have `querySe lector()` and `querySelectorAll()` for that. Don't import a library just to bind events: `addEventListener()` works fine in all modern browsers. Don't write a script just to make scrolling work better. Try `-webkit-overflow-scrolling: touch` instead. And if you must have scrolling down perfect, along with the little bounce, use a script. Don't reinvent the wheel. You won't get the physics right. Use a library when you must, but think long and hard about whether you really need the extra bytes, HTTP request, memory usage, and battery drain before doing so.

Eliminate Network Requests

Obviously you need to download the files required to load your web application. This uses battery, but is necessary. However, polling the Facebook, Twitter, and Pinterest servers every 15 seconds to see if your page received more likes is not necessary and a waste of both bandwidth and battery power. In fact, it's the worst possible waste of both.

Determine if your application needs to poll all the time, or rarely to never. If your application needs to be real time, such as a chat or a sports game, you will want to spend battery power by keeping the connection alive at all times. If your application is not polling for a necessary purpose (Facebook like counts are *not* necessary, and annoying), let your mobile device terminate the connection to the cell tower.

---

2. `classList` is supported mobile browsers, with support starting with IE10, Android 3, iOS 5.

3. *http://mobisocial.stanford.edu/papers/boneh-www2012.pdf*

Establishing and maintaining radio links to cell towers consumes battery power. When the device is not making requests, it shuts down connectivity processes to save battery. This is a good thing.

While most performance arguments revolve around input and output of data, the number one battery drain in a mobile phone is radio. To preserve battery life, mobile devices put the radio in a preserving power mode when the transmissions are complete and into a deep sleep state after a few seconds of network inactivity. After the radio link is idle for 5 seconds, it drops to a state of half power consumption and significantly lowers bandwidth. After another 12 seconds of inactivity it drops to the idle state.

From the idle state it takes time to reach full power and bandwidth. If you are polling your server every 15 seconds, you are waking the radio from a deep sleep. Waking the radio can take up to 2 to 3 seconds, taking multiple round trips just to get to a state where your application can transmit.

If your application needs to keep the connection alive, do so. Realize you're draining the battery and let your user know this. If you don't need to poll at regular intervals, to conserve battery power, keep messages as small as possible and limit the number and frequency of network requests after page load.

Hardware Acceleration

Usually when people think of managing CPU usage, they're thinking of their server. Yes, you should be doing that, too. But when it comes to limited battery life, you want to manage browser CPU usage caused by your web application. Whatever makes your laptop fan turn on will also drain the battery of any device.

One solution is to hardware accelerate all animations. Hardware acceleration means rendering your animations on the GPU instead of the CPU. The graphics chip requires less power than the device's CPU, resulting in improved battery life. Hardware acceleration carries out all drawing operations that are performed on a View's canvas using the GPU. Hardware-accelerated images are composited, using four times the memory of the original. Because of the increased resources required to enable hardware acceleration, your application will consume more RAM, but less battery power. With constrained memory and battery life, always consider battery and memory consumption when designing and developing your applications.

Hardware acceleration has both benefits and drawbacks. Your animation will appear less janky on the GPU, and you will lose less battery. However, your memory is limited.

In other words, `transform: translatez(0);` is not a panacea. Do not do this:

```
* {
  transform: translatez(0);
}
```

... as you may run out of GPU memory, especially on devices with limited memory. However, don't be afraid to force hardware acceleration on the elements you are animating. In fact, to reduce the traffic between CPU and GPU, it is recommended that you put all elements that are going to be animated on the GPU on load:

```
.spinner {
  transform: translatez(0);
  animation: spin 1s linear infinite;
}
@keyframes spin {
    100% {
        transform: translatez(0) rotate(360deg);
    }
}
```

Note that in the preceding example, we add the 3D transform even when we are not animating. If you are going to hardware accelerate an element at any time, keep that element hardware-accelerated at all times. You don't want to have a brief moment where the element disappears as the device moves it to and from the CPU to GPU.

Avoid repaints and reflows

Repaints and reflows are some of the main causes of sluggish JavaScript, and a main cause of janky animation.

A repaint is a redrawing of the screen when an element's appearance has been altered without affect on layout. Changing an element's color, visibility, or background image will cause a repaint. Repaints are generally cheap, but can be expensive, as the visibility of all the nodes in the DOM tree and all the layers of each node must be measured. Repaints can be costly when alpha transparency is involved.

Rendering alpha transparent blurs such as shadows or alpha transparent gradients will always take more time to render, as the browser needs to calculate the resulting color of every pixel based on the transparency over the color underneath it. This occurs even if the color, in the end, is not visible because of a design element on top of it, as CSS properties like background image and shadows are drawn from back to front.

The time to paint is really ridiculously fast. Generally, optimizing other areas will give you more bang for your buck. However, if you are repainting repeatedly, such as a non-hardware-accelerated transition or animation, minimizing repaint time is vital. In animating, the browser must repaint the nodes being animated in generally less than 16.67 ms for the animation to not appear janky. These overdrawn pixels can waste a lot of processing time for CPU-based rasterizers.

A reflow is even more critical to performance because it involves changes that affect the layout of a portion of the page (or the whole page). Reflow of an element causes the subsequent reflow of all child and ancestor elements as well as any elements following it in the DOM. A reflow is the browser process for recalculating the size and positions of all the DOM nodes when the browser needs to calculate the size of an element or when it re-renders a part of or an entire document.

When the browser needs to measure or reflow a single element in the document, unless absolutely positioned or in its own render layer, it generally reflows not just that relevant node, but the node's ancestral elements and all elements that come after it.

 Some of the nodes that have their own render layer include the document itself, explicitly CSS positioned (relative, absolute, or a transformed) nodes, transparent nodes, nodes with overflow, alpha mask or reflection, WebGL, hardware-accelerated content, and <video> elements.

During a reflow, users are blocked from interacting with the page. It's therefore important to prevent reflows, and minimize reflow time when they do occur. Scripts and even some CSS can cause a reflow. The DOM tree, styles, and assets can impact reflow speed.

There are many things that can cause a reflow, including adding, removing, updating, or moving DOM nodes, changing the display or box model properties of a node, adding a stylesheet or inline styles, resizing the window or changing the orientation, scrolling, and querying style information via JavaScript.

To reduce the number of reflows, batch your style queries, change styles via changing a CSS class rather than adding inline styles.

Instead of changing individual styles, change the class name. If the styles are dynamic, edit the cssText property rather than the style property:

```
myNode.style.cssText += "; left: 50p%; top: 0;";
```

Batch DOM changes and do them off of the live DOM tree. Don't ask for computed styles unless necessary. And if you do so, batch the queries and cache the results into local variables, working with the copy. Make your updates in a clone of the content, make all your changes offline, then add back when complete.

This can be done in a documentFragment or a copy of the document section you're editing. If you need to, you can even hide the element with display: none, make your plethora of changes, then reset the element to its default display. This method reflows exactly twice: when you hide and when you show again. This may sound like a lot, but this may be less than would otherwise occur if you're making hundreds of changes causing reflows on a live node.

To make the reflows that do occur happen faster, you should minimize the number of DOM nodes, eliminate overly complex CSS selectors, and ensure that all animations are hardware-accelerated.

The deeper the DOM, the more time it takes for every reflow. Changes at one level in the DOM tree can cause changes at every level of the DOM tree, from the last of the nodes descendants all the way up to the document root. The more nodes you have, the longer it takes to reflow them all.

If you make complex rendering changes such as animations, do so out of the flow. Create a separate rendering layer with `position: absolute;`, `position: fixed;`, or `transform: translatez(0);` to accomplish this.

Latency

Download and upload speeds are rarely (if ever) equal to the bandwidth marketed by Internet service providers (ISPs). The quoted Mbps is the fastest connection one could possibly ever hope to get, not the speed of the average connection. The speed by which a website, including the markup, stylesheets, media, application scripts, and third-party scripts, makes it onto our devices are affected as much by latency as by the bandwidth of the marketing terms of EDGE or 3G, if not more so.[4]

Latency has a much larger impact on download speeds when a device is on a mobile network compares to devices that are tethered or accessing the Internet via WiFi. Download speed is greatly affected by packet loss and latency. Packets must first travel from your device to the closest cell tower. The air between your device and that tower is the main cause of latency. In other words, your mobile users using 3/4G already have low bandwidth. Latency makes their web-surfing experience that much more painful.

Because mobile devices have terrible latency, reducing the download time is very important. To optimize sites for mobile, reducing the number of HTTP requests and DNS lookups can have the greatest impact on improving performance. If you are testing your device on the local Starbucks WiFi, you will not experience much latency. Try testing your application from the passenger seat of a speeding vehicle on a scenic highway: this will give you a much better sense of the test case you want to optimize for.

Reduce the Number of HTTP Requests

There are several ways you can reduce the number of requests made by your application.

Browser cache

Leveraging your browser cache reduces requests on subsequent page loads and refreshes since, when an asset is cached, your browser doesn't need to re-retrieve them.

---

4. See *http://www.igvita.com/2012/07/19/latency-the-new-web-performance-bottleneck/*.

For nonchanging static components, like the corporate logo, set a far future `Expires` header. For dynamic components such as a JSON response, use an appropriate `Cache-Control` header to help the browser with conditional requests.

Combined JavaScript file

Concatenating all your JavaScript into a single file is often a good idea. Just note that your device has memory limitations. As such, while reducing your JavaScript into a single file may reduce the HTTP requests the most, it may make more sense to include a couple script files: one for the overall app used on most of your page loads, and separate modularized scripts for the more complex component(s) of your application. There is no right answer: realize that you have both memory constraints and latency issues, and determine what makes the most sense for your applications.

It's also a good idea to minify and gzip your JavaScript. Using a content delivery network may speed up your download, but may also add an extra DNS lookup.

Single stylesheet

Similarly, you can concatenate all of CSS into a single file. Tools like Sass can help you manage modularized SCSS files, and concatenate them all to a single file for production. But again, remember there are memory constraints. Figure out what makes the most sense in terms of performance for your particular application. Concatenate and cache as much as is appropriate. Minify and gzip as well.

Image sprites

When it comes to developing for the desktop, we've also been concatenating images into sprites. *Image sprites* are a collection of images put into a single image. Image sprites reduce the number of HTTP requests and also help save bandwidth.

While sprites are a very good way of reducing latency, they do have drawbacks. Memory is limited on mobile, and these images are loaded into memory even if only a small part of the image is used. In addition, large images may be tiled in memory. It is generally recommended to keep all images for limited devices to under 1024 px in either dimension.

Image compression

When creating images, you want to compress them as much as possible. While you should gzip your image files too, remember that when they are decoded by the browser, they return to their pre-gzipped file size: so again, compress as much as possible.

Data URIs/inline images

For small images and simple SVG image files, you can reduce the number of HTTP requests for that file down to none by providing a data URI as an inline image or as a data URI for a background image, instead of having the browser download a separate binary file. Inline images use the data URI scheme to embed the image data in the actual page. This can increase the size of your HTML document. Weigh whether saving an HTTP request is worth the increased file size of this method.

In your CSS, to include a data URI, include your images anywhere you would normally include your image, encompassed with `url()`. For example:

```
a[href^="mailto"] {
  background: url(data:image/gif;base64,R0lGODYLCVDFCrKU-data-uri-code-UhwFUUE1l)
  no-repeat right center;
  padding-right: 25px;
}
```

If you were to code it as a foreground image in HTML, it would resemble this:

```
<img width="16" height="16" alt="email" src="data:image/gif;base64,
  R0lGODYLCVDFCrKU-data-uri-code-UhwFUUE1lBavAViFIDlTI0SlBCBMQiB" />
```

Where the data URI code would really be much, much longer.

Data URI strings can be very long. On average, a data URI is about 33% more bytes than the binary raster equivalent. Both methods can (and should) have the file size reduced by gzipping. Because of the way packets are sent, there is a cost-benefit analysis to be considered. It can be worth sending the extra bytes of a smaller data URI image to save on HTTP requests. It isn't generally isn't worth sending a data URI for several high-resolution PNGs—while the actual download time may be just a bit more, the perceived download time may make the extra HTTP request worthwhile. Where that performance sweet spot is depends on device and connection.[5]

Should you use sprites or data URIs? Both work. I find sprites easier to work with than having to export data URIs,[6] but data URIs definitely have other benefits. Data URIs are usable for background patterns[7] and for when you have way too many images or unpredictable image requirements that preclude being able to use a sprite. For example, a star rating system might be a good use case for a sprite, but avatars for a Twitter stream, with the plethora of possibilities, can't be sprited, making data URI a better solution.

Icons and character sets

As long as you have declared the charset of your files, you can use any characters in your font, including ✉, ⌘, and ✔. Using a font instead of image icons is more robust. You can create icons in any color without Photoshop. You can create icons of any size without pixelation. Using the default font also saves on HTTP requests and memory.

---

5. See *http://davidbcalhoun.com/2011/when-to-base64-encode-images-and-when-not-to*.

6. Compass, the CSS authoring framework, has an inline helper to automate data URIs (*http://compass-style.org/reference/compass/helpers/inline-data/*). There are many such resources available.

7. Support for displaying only sections of images is in the works, but is not supported yet.

You are likely to find icons for all your needs in the font families preloaded onto your users' devices. Sometimes your designer wants to have more design control. There are many icon font sets. These require downloading the font face, and so will incur a single HTTP request. That is the same, or fewer, HTTP requests you would have required if you used images instead of fonts.

You can also create your own icon font. A good resource is IcoMoon (*http://icomoon.io/*), which is a set of open source icons and a web app for customizing and downloading optimized icon fonts. You choose just the icons you want and download a minimized set. You can also add icons from different sets or from SVG files.

Inspecting network requests

You can inspect the performance of your site or application by looking at the waterfall chart in the browser developer tools on desktop, using weinre or Adobe Edge Inspect from the mobile device, from the BlackBerry debugger, or from many other tools.

A free waterfall chart can also be obtained from online tools, like WebPageTest.org, as shown in Figure 14-1. The chart shows the number of requests made (34 in this case).

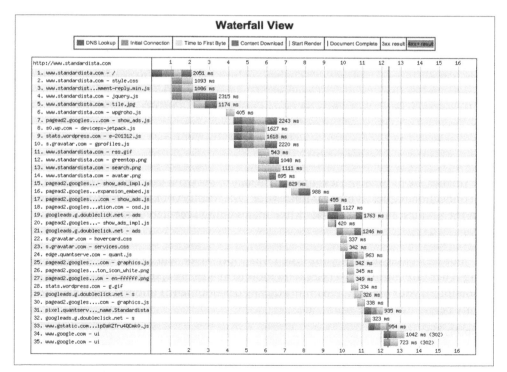

Figure 14-1. Waterfall chart from WebPageTest.org

Each request shows the time allocated for DNS lookup (if any), initial connection, time to first byte (or latency), and content download (bandwidth with latency). The first vertical bar is when the page started rendering, and the last vertical bar (barely visible on the right hand side of the images) is the time until the onload event was fired.

If we look at a single line from the waterfall chart, as in Figure 14-2, we can observe the latency of including a script from an external domain. In this case, to include an external JavaScript file, we first must wait 406 ms just for the DNS lookup, waiting 593 ms until the first byte of the script is downloaded. The loading of assets is halted when a script is called until the script is downloaded, parsed, and executed. This 2,243 ms request for *show_ads.js* prevented any rendering to our page for over 2 seconds. This demonstrates the need to pay attention to latency, code order, and performance in general, and more specifically to the impact of third-party scripts.

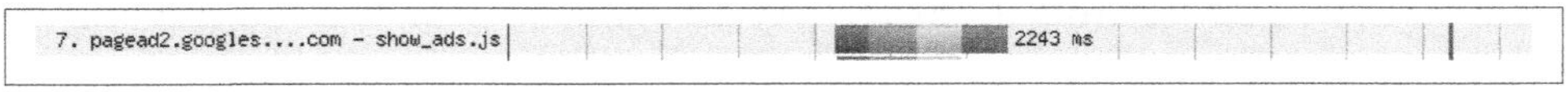

Figure 14-2. Detail of a single request

Your goal is to get the waterfall to be as short as possible and as narrow as possible.

Reduce Size of Requests

Latency is the biggest concern. The biggest culprit in latency is generally the number of requests, rather than the size of requests. However, the larger the size of the requests, the longer they take. And often, the memory consumed by the application is proportional to the size of the application files. The average website is over 1 MB, with the same files sent to the 24-inch monitor and the 3-inch Android. To reduce latency, and positively impact memory, reduce the size of the requests that your application is making.

The smaller the file size, the less time it will take to get from the server to the client once the connection request is made. Minify your CSS. Minify your JavaScript. Create images with the smallest file size possible while maintaining acceptable resolution.

Minify text-based assets

For your text-based assets—your CSS, JavaScript, JSON, and SVG files—minify everything. There are minifying services and tools to make sure text-based assets are as small as possible. If your prefer not to minify during development, I understand. But definitely minify before deploying your code.

Compress binary files

Different image-editing programs provide for different ways to reduce file size. Instead of using GIFs, save your image as a PNG8. If you need animated GIFs, use CSS animation instead. If your color palette is too large for a PNG8, pass your PNG through a tool like

ImageAlpha (*http://pngmini.com*) or automate it from the command-line with PNGCrush.

JPEG compression is lossy compression, but compressing down to 40% to 60%, instead of 80% to 99%, can lead to huge byte savings.

Gzip everything

Once you've made the files as small as possible, gzip them! Gzipping as many file types as possible reduces page weight, accelerating the download speed. However, it does not reduce the file's impact on memory. When it comes to memory, the file size in the client will be the same size of the file before you gzipped it. Gzipping saves bandwidth, but the file gets deflated to its pre-gzipped, post-compressed size once it gets to its destination.

Leverage the developer tools to inspect what has and hasn't been compressed. Start by disabling cache in the inspector via the settings panel. This way you'll always have a cold cache or baseline on which you can compare your work. This is how your visitors will see your site load the first time they hit your site.

In the Network tab's waterfall, in the size column, the top number in the size column is the transferred size. The bottom is the real size. The transferred size will reflect your minification and gzipping. The real size will show you how much memory will be allocated, and how much more you can save in terms of bandwidth. If there is only one value showing, you are in "use small resources row." To see the "large resources row," click on the expand rows icon at the bottom of the developer tools window, to the right of inspect and left of record, as shown in Figure 14-3.

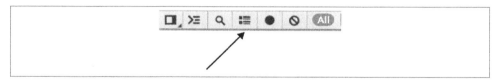

Figure 14-3. Toggle between large and small resources display

At the bottom of the Network tab, there is a gray line with white text: this line shows the total file size and time to download.

Reduce image size

There is no reason to send huge images to tiny devices. Use media queries to send the right size background images. For foreground images, use the Clown Car Technique, libraries like Picturefill, or tools such as Sencha.io Src to send the right size image. More information on these methods and links can be found in the online chapter resources. More details on image sizing is discussed under the section "Memory" on page 415.

Skip the framework

If you can avoid importing a JavaScript framework, do it. As mentioned under the section "Battery" on page 395, frameworks were originally created to normalize Java-Script across browsers. All smartphones have browsers smarter than IE8. If you're importing frameworks for supported tasks like selectors and event listeners, code vanilla JavaScript. jQuery adds 34 KB, an extra HTTP request, and consumes energy every time it is parsed and executed. It's not a huge file size. If you need a framework, use a framework. However, if you can avoid importing scripts, do that instead.

Again, don't reinvent the wheel. Use a library when you must, but think long and hard about whether you really need the extra bytes, HTTP request, memory usage, time to fully parse and execute the code, and battery drain before doing so.

Minimize cookies

Obviously, you need cookies sometimes, like on authentication. Browsers and servers send cookies back and forth with every request. If possible, eliminate unnecessary cookies, such as for static content like images that don't make use of the cookie. While some may argue that localStorage can reduce the overhead of relaying cookies, local-Storage does take time to access, so may not be a better solution.

Defer third-party scripts

Don't let an external script drain your battery, or become a single point of failure (SPOF). If a script is called, the downloading of all assets ceases until that script is downloaded, parsed, and executed. We saw a 2,243 ms request for *show_ads.js* in Figure 14-2, which prevented rendering for over two seconds! If your third-party script fails to load when called, your application will fail to load until the script times out, if at all. Defer third-party scripts, or avoid including them at all if possible, to ensure that someone else's script doesn't kill your site.

Performance anti-patterns

Because of latency issues, reducing DNS look ups and HTTP requests is vital in the mobile space. In some scenarios, it may make sense to embed stylesheets and scripts. I realize this is a web performance optimization anti-pattern, but bare with me.

Best practices for speeding up your website recommend making your JavaScript and CSS files external and using a content delivery network, or CDN. However, external files mean more HTTP requests, and using CDNs for static content adds both more DNS lookups and more HTTP requests. While embedding CSS and JavaScript in your HTML goes against all best practices I've ever espoused, if done correctly, embedding your scripts on first load can help improve performance. Bing's mobile website is a perfect example.

Currently (as introduced in "LocalStorage to enhance mobile performance" on page 166), when you access *m.bing.com* for the first time from your mobile device, the entire site loads as a single file. The CSS and JavaScript are embedded. Images are included as data URIs. Bing for mobile puts all of their assets into a single file, necessitating only a single HTTP request. However, that single file is 200 KB. That is huge. However, only the first visit to Bing returns such a large file. By taking advantage of localStorage and cookies, every subsequent request to *m.bing.com* returns a single file of manageable size. While the first request returns a huge file, every subsequent request produces a response of about 15 KB.

Bing embeds all of the files needed into the single HTML file. Using client-side Java-Script, Bing extracts the CSS, JavaScript, and images from the original download, and saves the CSS, JavaScript, and image data URIs in local storage. Bing saves the names of the stored files in a cookie. With every subsequent page request, the cookie informs the server which files are already saved locally, allowing the server to determine which assets, if any, need to be included in the response. In this way, subsequent responses only include scripts, styles, and images not saved in local storage, if any, along with the HTML.

The steps to reducing the negative effects of latency in a mobile site download by making a web app with a single HTTP request for all HTML, CSS, JavaScript, and images include the following steps:

1. Embed CSS and JavaScript for first page load.

2. Extract and put the above-embedded files in localStorage.

3. Set cookies with the names of the extracted embedded files.

4. On subsequent requests, check the cookies server-side.

5. Only embed new and missing scripts based on cookie values.

6. Load files from localStorage resources on load.

Note: If you're wondering why this method may be more efficient than simply down-loading and caching files, not only does this method improve performance by avoiding the latency of multiple DNS lookups and HTTP requests, but mobile devices have more limited cache, with iOS having no persistent memory.

Pulling data out of localStorage is a performance hit. When it comes to mobile, however, it is usually less of a hit than latency, especially latency with limited bandwidth.

Memory

Most performance recommendations focus on improving I/O speeds. It is not sufficient to only focus on how long it takes for responses to complete in the mobile space. When it comes to mobile and the limited memory on most mobile devices, we have to also manage what happens *on* the device. As developers, we generally develop on our personal computers where memory is virtually unlimited. Mobile users, however, are running our sites on devices with very limited memory.

Memory on personal computers has increased almost exponentially over the past two decades. 256 MB may have been more than enough to run all software on a Pentium II in 1997. In 2013, however, base model (i.e., slow) computers come with at least 4 GB of RAM. An iPhone 3G has 128 MB of memory. The original iPad has 256 MB. The faster HTC Inspire has 768 MB. The norm for new, high-end smartphones is 512 MB to 1 GB of RAM with 1 GHz processors. Mobile devices have software written in 2013, but run on devices that have the memory of a 1999 desktop.

While 512 MB may seem large enough to run any web application, in managing memory it is important to remember that the browser (and web application) is not the only process consuming the limited RAM. The operating system, background processes, and other open applications (operating system and user-initiated) are all sharing the memory. Mobile devices are generally running many native applications as well as user-installed apps, with or without the user's knowledge. Running applications are many, including user-initiated apps like Twitter, GPS, Facebook, and apps that came with the device but may be running unbeknownst to the user, like Calendar and Media, and applications downloaded by the user, like Angry Birds. Native OS applications and all apps with user notifications turned on continue to run in the background. A device with 512 MB of RAM likely has less than 200 MB of available memory. In managing memory, remember that your web application's most active users are likely also the ones using other mobile applications. When testing, test with real-world devices. Run apps like Twitter, Facebook, and Mail with notifications on all your testing devices.

The greater the number of applications running on a device, the less memory is available for your web application. And even if none of those applications are memory hogs, the sheer number of apps running in the background create high memory usage conditions. High memory usage causes a slow UI, and when the browser is out of memory, it is out of memory. The mobile browser will generally close or crash to free up memory. You need to manage the memory requirements of your web applications to ensure they don't use too much memory, and slow or crash the mobile browser.

Optimize Images

Other than avoiding CSS expressions (YSlow (*http://developer.yahoo.com/yslow/*)) and optimize images (PageSpeed (*https://developers.google.com/speed/pagespeed/insights_extensions*)), the performance optimization guidelines have to do with input/output (I/O) of bytes, and not what happens once the site is on the device.

While gzipping files helps improve download speed, it does not help with memory management. Once the asset is on the device, it is no longer compressed. Images use up memory. Images over 1024 px cause greater memory issues on some devices. Reduce your image files' memory consumption by serving up the image with the dimensions at which it will be displayed, and by compressing the image at that size.

There are a few tools at your disposal. ImageAlpha (*http://pngmini.com*) and Image-Optim (*http://imageoptim.com*) can help convert your large file size transparent PNGs into 8-bit PNGs with full transparency. The Sencha.io (*http://www.sencha.com/learn/how-to-use-src-sencha-io/*) proxy determines what size image the user's device requires and will shrink (not grow) images before sending them to the client.

While reducing image file size has always been important for web performance, when it comes to mobile we can't just focus on the I/O file size. You have to consider how large the image file is uncompressed, as memory is limited. All images use up memory. Composited images use GPU memory instead of CPU memory. So while that may be a neat trick to free up some memory, composited images use up four times the memory of their noncomposited counterparts, so use this trick sparingly.

As noted earlier, you want to keep the size of all of your assets down to a minimum. There is an answer to "How big is too big?" The answer for today's devices may not be the same answer for tomorrow's devices. The answer for my target market may be different from your target audience.

The best advice I can give is to determine what your application limits should be before you begin development. Decide before you design and develop your application what the appropriate size limitations of your assets should be. As you develop, try to stay within the limits you set for yourself. This will help you focus on performance throughout the whole development process. You or someone in your team may want to include a feature that takes you beyond what you have allocated. If you weren't thinking about your self-imposed limit, you likely wouldn't have questioned the asset. With the self-imposed limit, you will need to consider the necessity of this component. If you must include it, how can you make it smaller. Once you've reduced its memory and bandwidth footprint as much as you are able and you still need it, where else can you reduce to bring you back under your limit. In the end, you may go over your limit. However, your site is now much smaller than it would have been had you not been negotiating with yourself to save bandwidth, memory, and HTTP requests every step of the way.

Weigh the benefits of CSS

CSS can help reduce the number of HTTP requests and reduce the size of the requests that are made. With gradients, border-radius, box and text shadow, and border images, you can greatly reduce the number of HTTP requests.

CSS provides the benefits of fewer HTTP requests, easily updateable and fully scalable effects, and easy and efficient transitions, transforms, and animations.

While CSS is awesome,[8] painting effects to the screen does have costs. Sometimes PNGs and JPEGs use less memory and render faster than CSS effects.

Weigh the benefits of CSS. While CSS images are generally the preferred solution over using Photoshop and uploading exported pictures, some CSS features have hidden costs due to memory usage and rendering slowness.

Some CSS properties are more expensive to render than others. For example, drawing blur shadows over a nonmonotone background involves measuring the resulting pixel color based on the foreground shadow combined with the background color over every pixel. Even if it's an inset shadow, and not visible since a solid color or image is placed on top of it during repaint, it is still measured, and browsers work from back to front when painting elements to the page.

CSS features that are transformable are generally evaluated at each reflow and repaint, using up memory. PNG, JPEG, and GIF images, unlike CSS generated images, are rendered and transitioned as bitmaps, often using less memory (but more HTTP requests). For example, shadows, especially inset shadows, are recalculated at every repaint even if the shadow ends up being obfuscated by another element, background image, or effect. The combination of every semitransparent pixel with the color of the element or effect behind it needs to be measured for every pixel, for each effect, from back to front, for every repaint.

CSS gradients can take less time and effort than creating the effect in Photoshop. The 140-character linear gradients done with CSS not only take up fewer bytes of bandwidth than the JPEG equivalent, but it also saves you an HTTP request. Linear gradient memory consumption is negligible, and the bitmap created by the browser is generally small and repeated.

On the other hand, the 140-character radial gradient declared in your CSS, which does save bandwidth and an HTTP request, can possibly crash your browser. The browser paints and keeps in memory the entire gradient, not just the section of gradient that is displayed in the viewport. If you are creating a small, opaque circle, then by all means, use native CSS radial gradients. However, if you're creating a circle with a large radius, the circle will be painted beyond the confines of the viewport, using up memory. If you recall, images that are too large are tiled in memory. I recommend using linear gradients and native rounded corners over images, but weigh the performance of radial gradients and inset shadows against the cost of downloading an image. The latter may actually be more performant.

Combining some CSS properties can result in a longer paint time than the paint time of the individual properties had they been applied to separate DOM nodes.

---

8. Many people hate CSS. They're wrong!

Paint time is generally fast. Really fast. But paint time becomes a concern when re-painting. Every reflow requires a repaint. Animations require repaints. If you are applying 27 different effects to a single element, that will be fine if you are simply painting to the page once. However, if you are animating an element, be aware that some CSS features, especially components that are partially transparent, can take longer to paint than the 16.67 ms allotted for each keyframe. Hardware-accelerating the animation can help, but has its own pitfalls.

GPU benefits and pitfalls

As mentioned earlier, hardware acceleration can greatly improve performance, especially when animating. However, `translate3d` is not a panacea! Hardware-accelerated elements are composited. Composited elements take up four times the amout of memory. Using GPU instead of CPU will improve performance up to a point. While hardware-accelerated elements use up less RAM, they do use up video memory, so use the `transform: translateZ(0);` trick sparingly.

Viewport: Out of sight does not mean out of mind

The mobile viewport is the viewable screen area. Unlike your desktop browser where you scroll content, on mobile devices, unless the viewport height and width are set and scaling is disabled, the viewport is fixed and the user moves the content underneath. The viewport is a "port" through which your users view your content. Why is this a performance issue? Most don't realize that the content that is drawn to the page, even if it is not visible in the current viewport, is still in memory.

Minimize the DOM

Every time there is a reflow, every DOM node is measured. The CPU on your desktop can handle a virtually endless number of nodes. This isn't so for mobile devices. The memory on mobile devices is limited and garbage collection differs so is not fully reliable. To improve performance, minimize the number of nodes. Instead of allocating DOM nodes and destroying them (or forgetting to destroy them), pool and reuse your nodes. For example, in CubeeDoo, the maximum number of cards per game was 24. Instead of creating new cards for each game, we created 24 cards, and reused the same cards for each game.

CubeeDoo is a simple example of reusing nodes. Infinite scrolling is a more complex and necessary, pooling-and-reusing scenario. A feed will add more and more entries as you scroll down the page. Eventually the browser or device will run out of memory. The user will generally continue scrolling down, not up. Instead of creating new nodes for each new item, limit your application to a certain number of nodes that all devices can handle. As the user scrolls down, pool the nodes that have been moved well off the top of the screen and reuse them for items lower in the feed. If the user scrolls up, take those nodes that have moved out of site off the bottom of the feed and reuse them for newer items.

Most feeds designed for desktop browsers do not pool and reuse. Infinite scrolling without pooling and reusing can and will crash browsers. I was able to get Facebook to use 76 MB of memory by scrolling down my feed. It eventually crashed my desktop browser, though I can't be sure if it was the memory consumption from the endless nodes or some other issue. It most certainly would have crashed my mobile browser.

Instead of adding more and more nodes as you scroll down for more content, limit the content nodes in your application to a set quantity. Reuse the top nodes as the user scrolls down, and the bottom nodes as the user scrolls up.

Memory management

Developer tools provide us with tools to analyze and explore application memory consumption.

The Timeline panel provides an overview of where time is spent when loading and interacting with a site or web application. All events, from loading resources to parsing JavaScript, calculating styles, and repainting are plotted on a timeline. The events, including calculating styles, reflowing, and painting, JavaScript parsing and execution, etc., are displayed.

You can use the information provided in the Chrome Developer Tools Timeline panel, shown in Figure 14-4, to manage memory usage. To inspect the memory, select memory in the upper lefthand panel area, and then start capturing memory and events by pressing the black circle record icon in the bottom toolbar. The record icon turns red when recording. If you simply want to view current memory usage, simply record. If you want to inspect all the events that cause this memory usage, click the record icon then reload the page.

In the current Chrome Developer tools, times for loading are blue, scripting is yellow, rendering purple, and painting is green. You can toggle visibility of each of these event types using checkboxes in the status line at the bottom. You can also filter out events shorter than 1 ms or 15 ms by selecting from the All drop-down filter button in the status bar to the left of the event checkboxes. I recommend filtering to help reduce the noise when trying to identify performance culprits.

In the Memory view, the narrow section at the very top displays the time, with blue and red vertical lines denoting when DOMContentLoaded and loaded events were fired during page load.

DOMContentLoaded gets fired when the markup, CSS, and blocking JavaScripts are loaded, at which point the browser begins rendering the page. Your performance goal should be to minimize the time to DOMContentLoaded, and perhaps more importantly, to minimize the time between the DOMContentLoaded and onLoad events.

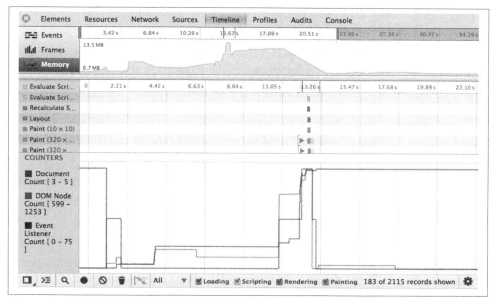

Figure 14-4. Google Chrome Timeline memory panel

If you're lazy loading, there may be more downloading after the onLoad event. This is fine. The perceived download time, which generally falls between these two events, though closer to the onLoad event, is what is important. This is what scares away potential customers. The actual download time may be a bit longer, but your users don't know that. Enable them to see your content and interact with it as fast as possible. If your social media icons and page footer lazy load "below the fold," your users are unlikely to notice.

> If you choose to include social media icons, try using simple links to these services rather than utilizing the JavaScript APIs provided by the social media site. Many social widgets are performance hogs.

You can save the waterfall as a HAR JSON file for comparing page loads as you progress in optimizing your site.

The rest of the top section provides information on overall memory usage by the currently open site or application. You'll note that the memory consumption generally increases as DOM nodes increase, and decrease with garbage collection.

The middle part on the main area of the panel lists all the events, including loading, scripts, rendering, and painting. Each entry provides information about the entry, such as the duration, CPU time, and the line of code that called the event. Each event shows the aggregate time of loading, scripting, rendering, and painting. In this way, you can inspect which events are negatively affecting performance.

The counter in the lower part of the main area provides statistics as to the number of DOM nodes, event listeners, and documents in the application at each moment in time.

Touching the DOM with a read or write is expensive in terms of performance. To improve performance, cache DOM lookups and store them in variables. Also, batch DOM queries and DOM manipulations separately, minimizing DOM manipulations by updating content fully outside of the DOM before updating the DOM.

When it comes to managing memory, image optimization, CSS rendering, and DOM node count are not the main points of concern. These are just points that have not necessarily been considered in the desktop space when focusing on performance.

UI Responsiveness

Mobile browsers are single threaded. In that respect, mobile browsers are similar to desktop browsers. There is, however, more to UI responsiveness on mobile than just being single threaded.

Touch Events

Because of latency, the browser may appear to hang after selecting an action because it can take a while for the round trip, to the server. It is important to provide user feedback within 200 ms after an action is taken, preferably sooner.

If you are showing or hiding an element, there's no need to provide feedback, since the app will be responsive. However, provide feedback to indicate that your site is responding if your user has to wait for a round trip for a UI update. For example, disable the submit button with a disabled appearance on form submission to inform the user that the user interaction has been accepted. If an AJAX request is likely to take over 200 ms, provide a spinner, progress bar, or even an animated bouncing ball. Let your UX team determine what feedback makes sense, but make sure user feedback is provided while the user waits for the response to his or her interaction with your site.

In addition, because the mobile device is a touch device, and "double tap" is a potential user action, mobile devices actually wait for potential double taps before responding to touches. On most touch devices there is a default 300 ms to 500 ms wait after the touchend event before any action is taken. Because of this, you may want to co-opt default events like the tap by adding an event listener to the touchend event to make your application more responsive.

When adding touch events, do not remove click events: you want your site to work no matter how your user chooses to interact with it (whether with their fingers, mouse, or other method).

The delay to wait for a possible double tap is not true for all scenarios.[9] In Chrome and Firefox, if zooming is disabled, there is no delay. Just because you can avoid this delay by preventing zooming with a meta tag does not make it good user experience: don't prevent zooming unless you have a very valid reason that you need to do so, such as interactive games.

Animation

Because the Web is single threaded, and JavaScript takes precedence over CSS animations in that thread, always use CSS instead of JavaScript for nonvital animations.

Because CSS animation has lower precedence, animations will not start until the page is loaded, as the UI thread is busy parsing scripts and rendering. Although the animation may not start, the animation-delay counter does not wait for page load. If you have many animations starting after varying delays, you may note that several animations may begin simultaneously on page load as the elements with an animation delay shorter than the time for page load all start at the same time.

As noted earlier, the smoothest animations animate at 60 frames per second on most devices. To animate at that rate means the page has 16.67 ms to perform all calculations and repaints. For animation to appear smooth, the animation must calculate and repaint the nodes in less than 16.67 ms for the animation to not appear janky.

In Conclusion

This is not an exhaustive list of topics to consider in ensuring good mobile UI performance, but should be a good start. With mobile and desktop browsers updating at a very rapid clip, the topics covered here are likely no longer fully up to date. However, the recommendations are all best practices. While there may be new best practices, and some of the issues mentioned may be resolved, following the recommendations given here will likely be best practices for the foreseeable future.

Remember that mobile is the fastest increasing segment of our users. Don't ignore them. These recommendations are easy to implement, and don't harm desktop browsers. So I encourage including the recommendations on all your sites even if your mobile visitor rate is negligible. After all, you never know if your mobile visitor rate is so low because

---

9. Currently, preventing zoom in limited browsers is the only reason touch browsers don't wait for a possible second tap. This may be expanded in the future.

your audience doesn't do mobile (unlikely) or because your mobile user experience is bad (more likely).

As developers, we've tested our websites to make sure we've followed the points and goals recommended by Yahoo!'s YSlow (*http://developer.yahoo.com/yslow/*) and Google's PageSpeed (*https://developers.google.com/speed/pagespeed/insights_extensions*). We've tested and tested using our desktop browsers. We've assumed the web performance optimization guidelines improves web application performance for all browsers, whether our users are accessing the site on their laptop, iPad, Android phone, or even their Wii. And to a great extent, it does. But remember that the well known and heeded optimization guidelines aren't our only concern when it comes to mobile.

Continue testing your website, but make sure to test on mobile devices. Emulators are not simulators. The emulator does not simulate memory constraints and does not simulate the device with 100 apps open. Test with memory and bandwidth capped. Test on real devices in real scenarios: turn off the WiFi and test with many, many unclosed apps hanging in the background. Test. Test. Test.

CSS Selectors and Specificity

CSS Selectors Level 3

Pattern	Meaning	Specificity and examples
Universal Selector The universal selector has no weight in terms of specificity.		0-0-0
`*`	Matches any element.	`* {}`
Type selector Type or element selectors have the lowest specificity.		0-0-1
`E`	Matches elements of type E.	`em, strong`
Class selectors		0-1-0
`myClass`	Matches all elements whose class list contains the class `myClass`.	`.myClass`
ID selectors		1-0-0
`#myId`	Matches the element that has an ID equal to `myId`.	`#myId`
Combinators Combinators, including >, + and ~, do not impact specificity.		0-0-0
`E  F`	Matches elements F that are descendants (direct children or not) of element E.	`ol li` `tr td`
`E > F`	Matches elements F that are direct children of element E.	`ol > li` `thead > tr`
`E + F`	Matches the element F that comes immediately after element E, if E and F share the same parent.	`h1 + p` `tr.current + tr`
`E ~ F`	Matches all elements F that come after element E that share the same parent.	`li:first-child ~ li`

Pattern	Meaning	Specificity and examples
Attribute selectors Attribute selectors have the same specificity as the class selector.		**0-1-0**
`E[attr]`	Matches elements E that have an *attr* attribute, no matter the value of the attribute.	`input[type]`
`E[attr="val"]`	Matches elements E whose *attr* attribute value is exactly equal to *val*.	`input[type="check box"]`
`E[attr~="val"]`	Matches elements E whose *attr* attribute value is a list of whitespace-separated values, one of which is exactly equal to *val*.	`img[alt~="figure"]`
`E[attr^="val"]`	Matches elements E whose *attr* attribute value begins exactly with the string *val*.	`a[href^="mailto:"]`
`E[attr$="val"]`	Matches elements E whose *attr* attribute value ends exactly with the string *val*.	`a[href$=".pdf"]`
`E[attr*="val"]`	Matches elements E whose *attr* attribute value contains the substring *val*.	`a[href*="://"]` `a[href*="twit ter.com"]`
`E[attr|="val"]`	Matches elements E whose *attr* attribute equals *val* or starts with *val* followed by a hyphen.	`html[lang|="en"]`
Structural pseudoclasses Pseudoclasses have the same specificity as a class selector.		**0-1-0**
`E:first-child`	Matches element E that is the first child of its parent.	`h1:first-child`
`E:last-child`	Matches element E that is the last child of its parent.	`p:last-child`
`E:only-child`	Matches element E if and only if E is the only child of its parent.	`li:only-child`
`E:first-of-type`	Matches element E that is the first E of its type, not necessarily the first child.	`li:first-of-type`
`E:last-of-type`	Matches element E that is the last E of its type, not necessarily the last child.	`li:last-of-type`
`E:only-of-type`	Matches element E if E is the only child of its parent of that type, though not necessarily the parent's only child.	`h1:only-of-type`
`E:nth-child(n)`	Matches element(s) E that are the nth children of their parent, where n can be an integer, an equation matching an+b, where a is the multiplier and b the offset, or the key terms even or odd.	`tr:nth-child(odd)`
`E:nth-last-child(n)`	Matches element(s) E that are the nth child of their parent, counting from the last child and going backward.	`li:nth-last-child(5)`
`E:nth-of-type(n)`	Matches element(s) E that are the nth siblings (have the same parent) of their type	`th:nth-of-type(2)`
`E:nth-last-of-type(n)`	Matches element(s) E that are the nth sibling of its type, counting from the last E.	

Pattern	Meaning	Specificity and examples
E:root	Matches element E if it is the root of the document, which is always the HTML element in our HTML documents.	html:root
E:empty	Matches element E if E is empty, having no children other than a comment. If the element contains a single space, it is not empty.	p:empty
Link, user-action, and UI element state pseudoclasses These pseudoclasses triggered by state have the same specificity as a class selector.		**0-1-0**
E:link E:visited	The link pseudoclasses match hyperlinks E when the target has not yet been visited (:link) or has already been visited (:visited).	a:link a:visited
E:active E:hover E:focus	The user action pseudoclasses match element(s) E during certain user actions, when the element is active, hovered, or has focus.	a:active img:hover input:focus
E:enabled E:disabled	Matches user interface element E, which is enabled or disabled.	input:enabled select:disabled
E:checked	Matches a user interface element E, such as a radio button or checkbox, which is checked.	input[type="ra dio"]:checked
E:default	Matches element E if it is the default among a set of similar elements, such as the options default selected on page load.	option:default
E:valid E:invalid	Matches element E when the element's value is valid or invalid, such as matching or not matching an input's pattern attribute or data type.	input:valid input:invalid
E:in-range E:out-of-range	Matching element E if element E has a range limitation, such as a range input type in number input type with min/max values, and that value is either in :in-range or :out-of-range.	input:in-range input:out-of-range
E:required E:optional	Matches form field element E if it is :required or :optional.	input:required input:optional
E:read-only E:read-write	Matches element E if its contents are not user alterable (:read-only), or if its contents are user alterable (:read-write), such as text-input fields.	input:read-only input:read-write
Target and Language		
E:target	An E element being the target of the referring URI.	div:target
E:lang(fr)	An element of type E in language fr (the document language specifies how language is determined).	p:lang(fr)
Negation		**?-?-?** **(depends on parameter)**
E:not(exclude)	Matches all the E elements that do not match the selector exclude. The :not has no weight in terms of specificity, rather the contents of the argument add to the weight.	div:not([class]) .foo:not(div)

Pattern	Meaning	Specificity and examples
Pseudoelements		**0-0-1**
E::first-line	Matches the first formatted line of element E.	p::first-line
E::first-letter	Matches the first formatted letter of element E.	p::first-letter
E::before	Generates content before the content of element E, and matches that content.	div::before
E::after	Generates content after the content in element E, and matches that content.	div::after
E::selection	Not currently in the specifications, it matches the content of element E that is currently selected or highlighted by the user.	*::selection *::-moz-selection

CSS Selector Cheat Sheet

`*`	`::after`	`:empty`
`E`	`::first-letter`	`:not()`
`.class`	`::first-line`	`:target`
`#id`	`E[attribute^=value]`	`:enabled`
`E F`	`E[attribute$=value]`	`:disabled`
`E > F`	`E[attribute*=value]`	`:checked`
`E + F`	`E ~ F`	`:indeterminate`[a]
`E[attribute]`	`:root`	`:default`
`E[attribute=value]`	`:last-child`	`:valid`
`E[attribute~=value]`	`:only-child`	`:invalid`
`E[attribute|=value]`	`:nth-child()`	`:in-range`
`:first-child`	`:nth-last-child()`	`:out-of-range`
`:link`[b]	`:first-of-type`	`:required`
`:visited`	`:last-of-type`	`:optional`
`:lang()`	`:only-of-type`	`:read-only`
`::before`[c]	`:nth-of-type()`	`:read-write`
`::selection`[d]	`:nth-last-of-type()`	

[a] The last nine selectors are part of CSS Basic User Interface Module Level 3 (CSS3 UI) specification, and are found in the CSS Selectors Level 4 specification.

[b] Some browsers have limited support for `:link` and `:visited` for security reasons.

[c] Use single colon notation for support in older IE.

[d] Not in the CSS Selectors level 3 specification, but fully supported. Prefix with `-moz-` for Firefox.

CSS Selector Specificity

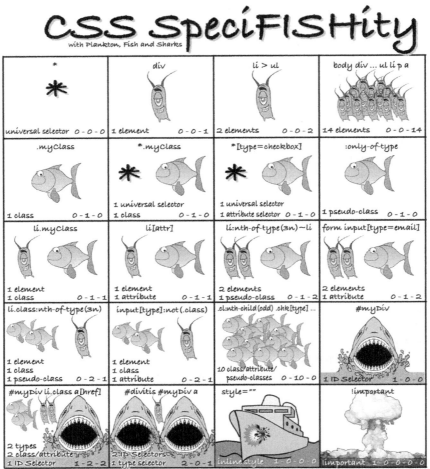

CSS SpeciFISHity
with Plankton, Fish and Sharks

`*` universal selector 0 - 0 - 0	`div` 1 element 0 - 0 - 1	`li > ul` 2 elements 0 - 0 - 2	`body div ... ul li p a` 14 elements 0 - 0 - 14
`.myClass` 1 class 0 - 1 - 0	`*.myClass` 1 universal selector 1 class 0 - 1 - 0	`*[type=checkbox]` 1 universal selector 1 attribute selector 0 - 1 - 0	`:only-of-type` 1 pseudo-class 0 - 1 - 0
`li.myClass` 1 element 1 class 0 - 1 - 1	`li[attr]` 1 element 1 attribute 0 - 1 - 1	`li:nth-of-type(3n) ~ li` 2 elements 1 pseudo-class 0 - 1 - 2	`form input[type=email]` 2 elements 1 attribute 0 - 1 - 2
`li.class:nth-of-type(3n)` 1 element 1 class 1 pseudo-class 0 - 2 - 1	`input[type]:not(.class)` 1 element 1 class 1 attribute 0 - 2 - 1	`.cl:nth-child(odd) .chk[type] ...` 10 class/attribute/ pseudo-classes 0 - 10 - 0	`#myDiv` 1 ID Selector 1 - 0 - 0
`#myDiv li.class a[href]` 2 types 2 class/attribute 1 ID Selector 1 - 2 - 2	`#divitis #myDiv a` 2 ID Selectors 1 type selector 2 - 0 - 1	`style=""` inline style 1 - 0 - 0 - 0	`!important` !important 1 - 0 - 0 - 0 - 0

Estelle Weyl * @estellevw * www.standardista.com * 2012

X-0-0: The number of ID selectors
0-Y-0: The number of class selectors, attributes selectors, and pseudo-classes
0-0-Z: The number of type selectors and pseudo-elements
*, +, >, ~ : The universal selector has no value and combinators do not increase specificity
:not(x): The negation selector has no value, but the argument passed increases specificity

CSS Selectors Level 4

Selector	Definition	Level
Basic Selectors		
`*`	Universal selector matches all elements.	2
`E`	Type (tag name) selector matches elements of type E.	1
`.someClass`	Class selectors match elements having the class listed, *someClass* in this case.	1
`#myID`	ID Selector matches the element with ID equal to `myID`.	1
Combinators		
`E F`	Descendant combinator, matches element F that is a descendant of element E.	1
`E > F`	Child combinator, matches element F that is a child of element E.	2
`E + F`	Next sibling combinator, matches element F that is immediately preceded by element E.	2
`E ~ F`	Following sibling combinator, matches elements F that are preceded by element E.	3
`E /foo/ F`	Reference combinator, matches element F that is ID-referenced by element E's `foo` attribute (would match the form element F that was referenced by label E's `foo` attribute).	4
`E! > F`	Determining the subject of a selector +Child combinator, matching element E that is the parent of element F.	4
Attribute selectors		
`E[foo]`	Matches element E that has a `foo` attribute.	2
`E[foo="bar"]`	Matches element E whose `foo` attribute value is exactly equal to `bar`, case sensitivity depends on case sensitivity of attribute value.	2
`E[foo="bar" i]`	Matches element E whose `foo` attribute value is exactly equal to any case permutation of `bar`.	4
`E[foo~="bar"]`	Matches element E whose `foo` attribute value is a list of whitespace-separated values, one of which is exactly equal to `bar`.	2
`E[foo^="bar"]`	Matches element E whose `foo` attribute value begins exactly with the string `bar`.	3
`E[foo$="bar"]`	Matches element E whose `foo` attribute value ends exactly with the string `bar`.	3
`E[foo*="bar"]`	Matches element E whose `foo` attribute value contains the substring `bar`.	3
`E[foo|="en"]`	Matches element E whose `foo` attribute value is a hyphen-separated list of values beginning with `en`.	2
Structural pseudoclasses		
`E:root`	Matches element E that is the root of the document.	3
`E:empty`	Matches element E that has no children (not even text nodes).	3
`E:blank`	Matches element E that has no content except maybe whitespace.	4
`E:first-child`	Matches element E that is the first child of its parent.	2
`E:last-child`	Matches element E that is the last child of its parent.	3

Selector	Definition	Level
E:only-child	Matches element E that is the only child of its parent.	3
E:first-of-type	Matches element E that is the first sibling of its type.	3
E:last-of-type	Matches element E that is the last sibling of its type.	3
E:only-of-type	Matches element E that is the only sibling of its type.	3
E:nth-child(n)	Matches element E that is the nth child of its parent.	3
E:nth-last-child(n)	Matches element E that is the nth child of its parent, counting from the last one.	3
E:nth-of-type(n)	Matches element E that is the nth sibling of its type.	3
E:nth-last-of-type(n)	Matches element E that is the nth sibling of its type, counting from the last one.	3
E:nth-match(n of selector)	Matches element E that is the nth sibling matching selector.	4
E:nth-last-match(n of selector)	Matches element E that is the nth sibling matching selector, counting from the last one.	4
Grid-Structural pseudoclasses		
F || E	Matches element E that represents a cell in a grid/table belonging to a column represented by element F.	4
E:nth-column(n)	Matches element E that represents a cell belonging to the nth column in a grid/table.	4
E:nth-last-column(n)	Matches element E that represents a cell belonging to the nth column in a grid/table, counting from the last one.	4
Link pseudoclass		
E:any-link	Matches element E being the source anchor of a hyperlink.	4
E:link	Matches element E being the source anchor of a hyperlink of which the target has not already been visited.	1
E:visited	Matches element E being the source anchor of a hyperlink of which the target has already been visited.	1
E:local-link	Matches element E being the source anchor of a hyperlink of which the target is within the current document.	4
E:local-link(0)	Matches element E being the source anchor of a hyperlink of which the target is within the current domain, though not necessarily in the current document.	4
E:target	The target pseudoclass matches element E, which is the target of the referring URL.	3
User interface pseudoclasses		
E:active	Matches element E that is in an activated state.	1
E:hover	Matches element E that is under the cursor, or that has a descendant under the cursor.	2
E:focus	Matches element E that has user input focus.	2
E:enabled	Matches user interface element E that is enabled.	3
E:disabled	Matches user interface element E that is disabled.	3

Selector	Definition	Level
`E:read-only`	Matches user interface element E that is not editable.	3/4[a]
`E:read-write`	Matches user interface element E that is editable, and element E that has the `contenteditable` attribute set to true.	3/4
`E:placeholder-shown`	Matches an input-control element E that is currently showing placeholder text.	3/4
`E:default`	Matches the user interface element E that was the default option selected.	3/4
`E:checked`	Matches the user interface element E that is checked or selected, such as a checked checkbox or selected radio button.	3
`E:indeterminate`	Matches the user interface element E that is in an indeterminate state (neither checked nor unchecked).	4
`E:valid`	Matches a user-input element E that is valid based on the lack of validity constraints (always valid) or on the content matching the validity constraints.	3/4
`E:invalid`	Matches a user-input element E that is invalid, as when the contents do not match the validity constraints of the attributes.	3/4
`E:in-range`	Matches a user-input element E whose value is `in-range`, such as within the `min`/`max` bounds.	3/4
`E:out-of-range`	Matches a user-input element E whose value is `out-of-range`, such as outside the `min`/`max` bounds.	3/4
`E:required`	Matches a user-input element E that is requires input (can not be left blank).	3/4
`E:optional`	Matches a user-input element E that does not require input (can be left blank).	3/4

Drag-and-drop pseudoclasses

Selector	Definition	Level
`E:active-drop`	Matches element E that will receive the item currently being dragged.	
`E:valid-drop`	Matches element E that could receive the item currently being dragged.	
`E:invalid-drop`	Matches element E that cannot receive the item currently being dragged, but could receive some other item.	

Matching, negation, and scope pseudoclasses

Selector	Definition	Level
`E:not(s1, s2)`	Matches elements E that do not match either compound selector s1 or compound selector s2. In CSS Level 3, only a single simple selector could be passed.	3/4
`E:matches(s1,s2)`	Matches elements E that match compound selector *s1* and/or compound selector s2.	4
`E:scope`	The `scope` pseudoclass matches element E being a designated reference element.	4

Language and direction pseudoclasses

Selector	Definition	Level
`E:dir(ltr)` `E:dir(rtl)`	Matches elements E with which left-to-right or left-to-right directionality based on the document language.	4
`E:lang(zh, *-hant)`	Matches elements E tagged as being either in Chinese (any dialect or writing system) or otherwise written with traditional Chinese characters. In CSS Selectors Level 2, the `:lang()` pseudoclass took only the first parameter.	2/4

Selector	Definition	Level
Time-dimensional pseudoclasses		
E:current	Matches element E that is currently presented in a time-dimensional canvas.	4
E:current(s)	Matches element E that is the deepest `:current` element that matches selector s.	4
E:past	Matches element E that is in the past in a time-dimensional canvas.	4
E:future	Matches element E that is in the future in a time-dimensional canvas.	4

[a] Added as part of CSS Basic User Interface Module Level 3 (CSS3 UI) specification, introduced into the CSS Selectors specification with Level 4.

Index

Symbols

(hash), 240
% (CSS length unit), 250
* (universal selector), 210
+ (adjacent sibling selector), 215
/ (forward slash), 36
; (semicolon), 195
<> (angle brackets), 35–37
> (child selector), 214–215
{} (curly braces), 329
~ (general sibling selector), 215

A

<a> element, 72
AAC audio format, 147
Aardwolf, 14
<abbr> element, 75
accelerometers, 394
accessibility, 26, 32, 188–191
Accessible Rich Internet Applications (ARIA)
   accessibility, 188–191
   additional information, 191
   attributes supported, 26, 32
accesskey attribute, 30
<acronym> element, 68
:active pseudoclass, 222
activeBorder system color, 245, 246
activeCaption system color, 245

ADB (Android Debug Bridge), 9
addEventListener method, 386
<address> element, 66
adjacent sibling selector (+), 215
Adobe Edge Inspect, 11, 13
::after pseudoelement, 28, 234
AMOLED screens, 402
Android Debug Bridge (ADB), 9
Android Debug Monitor, 10
Android devices
   browser support, 5
   debugging tools, 9–10
   emulators for, 16
   form validation and, 119
   link handling, 73
   testing on, 19
Android Virtual Device Manager, 10
angle brackets (<>), 35–37
angle measurements (CSS), 252, 273–276
animation (CSS3)
   about, 303, 328
   animating sprites, 334–335
   applying, 331
   bouncing ball, 332
   CubeeDoo example, 335
   keyframes and, 305, 329–336
   performance considerations, 336, 423
animation shorthand property, 329
animation-delay CSS property, 329

We'd like to hear your suggestions for improving our indexes. Send email to index@oreilly.com.

global attributes, 26–29, 31–35
Google Chrome browsers (see Chrome browsers)
Google Maps, 74
Google Play, 74
grad (CSS angle unit), 253, 273
gradients (CSS)
    about, 271
    color stops, 277–283, 285, 290
    CubeeDoo game and, 288
    linear, 271–282
    radial, 271
    repeating, 287–290
    striped example, 285–287
    tools for, 290
grayText system color, 246
grouping elements, 66
gyroscopes, 394
Gzipping, 413

H

H.264 video format, 147
hard color stops, gradients, 279, 283, 286, 290
hardware access
    about, 393
    device status, 394
    phone movement and direction, 393
    web apps and, 396
hash (#), 240
hCard microformat, 185
<head> element
    about, 42
    elements found in, 44
<header> element, 64–66
height attribute (<video> element), 149
height, media query feature, 199
hexadecimal color format, 240
hidden attribute, 31, 186
hidden input type, 101
high attribute (<meter> element), 127
highlight system color, 246
highlightText system color, 246
home screen icons, 381
:hover pseudoclass, 222
hovering with event handling, 224
<hr> element
    about, 66, 68
    self-closing, 37
href attribute (<link> element), 52

hreflang attribute
    <area> element, 78
    <link> element, 52
HSL color format, 240, 243
HSLA color format, 240
.htaccess file, 46, 47, 161
<html> element
    about, 41
    AppCache API and, 160
    setting primary direction, 29
HTML syntax
    about, 24, 35–37
    adding metadata, 45
    attributes, 25–35, 36
    <base> element, 50
    best practices, 38–39
    elements, 24
    <head> element, 44
    <link> element, 51–57
    mobile meta tags, 47–50
    required components, 39–44
    self-closing elements, 37
HTTP requests, 202, 359, 408–412
http-equiv attribute (<meta> element), 47

I

<i> element, 74, 194
id attribute
    about, 26
    anchors, 72
    <datalist> element, 123
    <form> element, 92
    <menu> element, 80
ID selector, 209, 211
IDE (integrated development environment), 4
<iframe> element, 76
image input type, 101
ImageAlpha tool, 417
ImageOptim tool, 417
images dialog, 391
images, optimizing, 416–422
<img> element
    about, 77
    child elements and, 24
    self-closing, 37
    SVG and, 136
immersive applications, 369
implicit labels, 27
!important modifier, 205

<keygen> element
   about, 129
   self-closing, 37
keyword meta tag, 47
kind attribute (<track> element), 152
Kindle Fire, 20
Koblentz, Thierry, 156

L

label attribute
   <menu> element, 80
   <track> element, 153
<label> element, 27, 127, 131
lang attribute, 28, 42
:lang pseudoclass, 231
:last-child pseudoclass, 226
:last-of-type pseudoclass, 226
latency, mobile performance and, 54, 196, 408–422
lazy block loading, 384
left keyword, 274
<legend> element, 130
length values (CSS), 249–251
<li> element, 68
<line> SVG element, 135
linear gradients
   about, 271–273
   angles and directions, 273–276
   CubeeDoo game, 279–282
   including colors, 277–279
   iPhone app, 279–282
   repeating, 287–290
<link> element
   about, 51
   adding for stylesheets, 51
   attributes supported, 52
   external stylesheets and, 196–198
   media queries, 199–201
   self-closing, 37
:link pseudoclass, 222
link types (mobile devices), 73
list attribute (<input> element), 123
localStorage object
   about, 164
   clear() method, 166
   cookies and, 165
   CubeeDoo game and, 167–174
   enhancing performance, 166
   getItem() method, 166

key() method, 166
length property, 166
removeItem() method, 166, 178
setItem() method, 166, 177
loop attribute
   <audio> element, 149
   <video> element, 149
low attribute (<meter> element), 127
lowercase markup, 38

M

magnetometers, 394
mailto: link, 73
<main> element, 67
manifest attribute (<html> element), 42, 160
manifest file, 160, 162
margin properties (CSS), 260
<mark> element, 69–70
masking (CSS), 362
match system color, 246
matchMedia() method, 201
matrix() function, CSS transforms, 320
max attribute
   <input> element, 86
   <meter> element, 127
   <progress> element, 129
max-aspect-ratio, media query feature, 199
max-column-count, media query feature, 340
max-device-aspect-ratio, media query feature, 199
max-device-height, media query feature, 199
max-device-width, media query feature, 199
max-height, media query feature, 199
max-width, media query feature, 199
maxlength attribute (<input> element), 91
media attribute
   <a> element, 73
   <area> element, 78
   <link> element, 52, 197–201
media elements, 76, 147–157
media queries, 199–201, 339
@media rule, 199
memory management, 373–375, 415, 420–422
menu attribute (<button> element), 80
<menu> element, 80, 82
menu system color, 246
menuitem attribute (<input> element), 80
<menuitem> element, 81
menuText system color, 246

srcset attribute (<img> element), 77
startup image, 380
state pseudoclasses, 225
status bar, 377
step attribute (<input> element), 87
storage
    local and session, 164–174
    Web SQL Database, 174–179
<strong> element, 75, 82
structural pseudoclasses, 226–229
style attribute
    about, 28
    <svg> element, 135
style declaration block (CSS), 195
<style> element, 54
styles
    elements and, 195
    embedded, 196
    in external stylehseets, 196
    inline, 196, 205
stylesheets
    about, 195
    external, 196–198, 202
    <link> element and, 51
    performance considerations, 409
<sub> element, 75
submit input type, 94, 98, 131
summary attribute (<table> element), 80
<summary> element, 78
@supports rule, 200, 354
SVG (scalable vector graphics)
    about, 134
    background images and, 136
    <canvas> versus, 146
    CubeeDoo game and, 139–141
    including in documents, 136
    learning, 138
    responsive foreground images, 136–138
<svg> element
    about, 134
    ARIA support, 188

T

tabindex attribute, 29, 222
<table> element, 80, 82
tags
    case sensitivity, 38
    closing, 35–38
    meta, 47–50

    opening, 35–38
tap-highlight-color CSS property, 390
target attribute (<a> element), 73
:target pseudoclass, 231
<td> element, 82
tel input type, 107
tel: link, 73
testing tools
    about, 15
    automated testing, 20
    on devices, 18–20, 397
    emulators, 15–17
    online tools, 17
    simulators, 15–17
text editors, 4
text input type, 95, 102, 104
text-level semantic elements
    changed, 72–75
    new to HTML5, 68–72
    unchanged, 75
text-overflow CSS property, 291, 294
text-shadow CSS property, 292–294
<textarea> element, 91
<th> element, 82
<thead> element, 82
Theora/Ogg video format, 148
3D transform functions, CSS transforms, 321
threeDDarkShadow system color, 246
threeDFace system color, 247
threeDHighlight system color, 247
threeDLightShadow system color, 247
threeDShadow system color, 247
<time> element, 70
time input type, 116
title attribute
    about, 27
    <menuitem> element, 81
<title> HTML element, 43–43
<title> SVG element, 135
to keyword, 273, 330
top keyword, 274
touch events, 387, 389, 422
touch-event emulation, 8
touchend event, 224, 392
touchscreens
    capturing touches, 386–393
    scaling down to size, 385–386
touchstart event, 224, 392
<tr> element, 82

About the Author

Estelle Weyl is a frontend engineer who has been developing standards-based accessible websites since 1999. She writes two technical blogs pulling millions of visitors, and speaks about CSS3, HTML5, JavaScript, and mobile web development at conferences around the world.

Colophon

The animal on the cover of *Mobile HTML5* is a Racket-tailed Drongo (*Dicrurus paradiseus*). This distinctive bird is notable for its elongated outer tail feathers, making it easily recognizable in its Asian habitats. As talented vocalists, Racket-tailed Drongos possess a wide range of calls and can mimic other birds' songs as well.

In heavily forested areas, such as those where the Drongo normally lives, large mixed-species flocks form as hundreds of birds forage for insects together. It is believed that the Drongo's ability to imitate calls has to do with this feeding situation—the Drongo learns the alarm calls of other types of birds and repeats them. This behavior has been likened to a person learning short, useful phrases and exclamations in a variety of languages. Although African Grey Parrots can use human speech in the correct context, they have never exhibited this kind of situation-reliant behavior in the wild. In contrast, the Drongo will use its language skills to its advantage, often by imitating the call of a raptor to create a panic among the feeding group, allowing the Drongo to steal food unnoticed.

While Drongos can be quite aggressive when it comes to territory, they have a very playful and extended courtship display. Two prospective mates will sing to each other, hop and turn about on branches, and drop objects from high and then dive down to pluck them from mid-air. Once a pair has mated, they build a small cup-shaped nest in which to lay the clutch of three to four eggs.

The range of the Racket-tailed Drongo extends throughout the forests of the Himalayas, the Mishmi Hills, and the islands of Borneo and Java. As such, the scholar Edward H. Schafer considered the Drongo the basis for the divine kalavinka birds mentioned in Chinese and Japanese Buddhist texts. These immortal beings were said to have a human's head and bird's torso, with a long double tail and a beautiful voice. The name has been alternately been translated as "exquisite-sounding bird" and "goodly sounding bird," making the parallels all the more striking between it and the vocally gifted Drongo.

The cover image is from a loose plate, source unknown. The cover fonts are URW Typewriter and Guardian Sans. The text font is Adobe Minion Pro; the heading font is Adobe Myriad Condensed; and the code font is Dalton Maag's Ubuntu Mono.

Have it your way.

O'Reilly eBooks

- Lifetime access to the book when you buy through oreilly.com
- Provided in up to four DRM-free file formats, for use on the devices of your choice: PDF, .epub, Kindle-compatible .mobi, and Android .apk
- Fully searchable, with copy-and-paste and print functionality
- Alerts when files are updated with corrections and additions

oreilly.com/ebooks/

Safari Books Online

- Access the contents and quickly search over 7000 books on technology, business, and certification guides
- Learn from expert video tutorials, and explore thousands of hours of video on technology and design topics
- Download whole books or chapters in PDF format, at no extra cost, to print or read on the go
- Get early access to books as they're being written
- Interact directly with authors of upcoming books
- Save up to 35% on O'Reilly print books

See the complete Safari Library at safari.oreilly.com

Get even more for your money.

Join the O'Reilly Community, and register the O'Reilly books you own. It's free, and you'll get:

- $4.99 ebook upgrade offer
- 40% upgrade offer on O'Reilly print books
- Membership discounts on books and events
- Free lifetime updates to ebooks and videos
- Multiple ebook formats, DRM FREE
- Participation in the O'Reilly community
- Newsletters
- Account management
- 100% Satisfaction Guarantee

Signing up is easy:

1. **Go to: oreilly.com/go/register**
2. **Create an O'Reilly login.**
3. **Provide your address.**
4. **Register your books.**

Note: English-language books only

To order books online:
oreilly.com/store

For questions about products or an order:
orders@oreilly.com

To sign up to get topic-specific email announcements and/or news about upcoming books, conferences, special offers, and new technologies:
elists@oreilly.com

For technical questions about book content:
booktech@oreilly.com

To submit new book proposals to our editors:
proposals@oreilly.com

O'Reilly books are available in multiple DRM-free ebook formats. For more information:
oreilly.com/ebooks

Spreading the knowledge of innovators   oreilly.com

CPSIA information can be obtained at www.ICGtesting.com
Printed in the USA
BVOW11s1326161113

336484BV00004BA/4/P

9 781449 311414